THE SECULAR MIND

ROBERT COLES

The Secular Mind

PRINCETON UNIVERSITY PRESS

Copyright © 1999 by Princeton University Press
Published by Princeton University Press, 41 William Street,
Princeton, New Jersey 08540
In the United Kingdom: Princeton University Press,
Chichester, West Sussex

Library of Congress Cataloging-in-Publication Data
Coles, Robert
The secular mind / Robert Coles.
p.   cm.
ISBN 0-691-05805-9 (alk. paper)
1. Secularism—United States.   I. Title.
BL2760.C65   1999
291.1'7—dc21   98-39388

This book has been composed in Adobe Garamond

The paper used in this publication meets
the minimum requirements of
ANSI/NISO Z39.48-1992 (R1997)
(*Permanence of Paper*)

http://pup.princeton.edu

Printed in the United States of America

1   3   5   7   9   10   8   6   4   2

*Remembering
Dorothy Day and
Paul Tillich*

CONTENTS

Introduction

WHAT follows began in my thinking some four decades ago when I was a resident in child psychiatry at the Children's Hospital in Boston. For various reasons of mind, heart, soul I found myself wanting to be a part of a seminar given by Paul Tillich, who had departed New York City's Union Theological Seminary in order to teach at Harvard University. I still remember the shift in my head as I left a hospital (where the emphasis, even in psychiatry, was on *doing*, on trying to accomplish a specific task) for quite another world, across the Charles River, where we were, as Tillich kept reminding us, "free to let our minds wander," take us where we wanted to go, with no set limits. Again and again our professor would make that distinction for us: the world of action, the world of reflection—and ask us, always, whether the latter qualified as the former. A lot of nit-picking, I sometimes felt. On the other hand, at other moments, I felt so lucky to be able to stop and ponder the meaning of this life—mine, of course, but also that of all of us who for a while exist, go through time, oc-cupy our own infinitesimally small places in the endless space of the universe.

Almost every week Tillich made mention of "the sec-ular mind." I wasn't quite sure what he had in his mind with respect to that kind of mind; nor did he seem in-terested in defining the phrase. He seemed to assume that we all knew what he meant. I remember wondering one October day, as I rode my bike along the Charles on my way to his seminar, whether "the secular mind" had to do with me then and there going through my motions on wheels, and before that in the hospital, and after that in a classroom: my head responding to necessary tasks, and my head directing my body's actions, and my head in search of—well, "heady stuff" (what a fellow hospital resident of mine chose to call the reading I was doing for that seminar).

Several weeks later, at the end of the class, I decided to approach Tillich, ask him about that phrase "secular mind," because yet again he'd used it. I can still see his broad smile as I put my question to him—and then a surprising response on his part: "I'm sorry, I use the expression too much; it's a theologian's reflex." He must have noticed my unsatisfied, still inquisitive face—and so he went into a disquisition of sorts, which at times I had trouble following, though the heart of it, I surmised, was the distinction he wanted to make between Man the thinking materialist and Man the anxiously aspiring creature who bows his head and prays, and who "looks outside himself to Another, to God," for explanations, understanding, guidance. The foregoing words are, of course, mine, except for the ones in quotation marks, which I remembered hard, wrote down inside the first volume of his *Systematic Theology*, a book we used in his course. For Tillich, I gathered, a secular person was one who looked within himself or herself, within our species, for whatever comprehension of the world is to be found, whereas the sacred mind (he often spoke of our "sacred self," its "search for meaning") looked toward the beyond, toward that "Another," that "God" so often mentioned in our daily lives, that "God" who ironically (Tillich kept reminding us, as had so many others before him, such as Kierkegaard, most powerfully) has become such a part of our secular life—the pietistic reflex (more neurological imagery) as a purveyor of calm, of reassurance, of self-satisfaction. Here is Tillich word-for-word on that score: "Church attendance for us can become a weekly social rite, a boost to our morale." Is that the secular mind in operation? I ventured to inquire. A smile from the professor: "Yes, you have it, there."

I can still visualize that moment—can hear his terse but original way of responding, of using colloquial English, of acknowledging an irony: religious practice as a motion of sorts in the course of ordinary living, as one more exercise of the secular mind. I can also remember myself sitting in a church a month or so afterwards—wondering, courtesy of Professor Tillich, what I was doing there. In fact, I was thinking of that class, of some of its moments, of the above-quoted words. Meanwhile, there was singing and praying and reading from Scripture, even as I had put all of that aside to call upon (if not dote on) my own mind's past experiences as they continued, in a church, to exert their forceful pull on me. It was then, strangely, amidst all the architectural and aesthetic (and, yes, substantive) expression of the sacred (the stained glass windows with their narrative message, the stately hymns, the words spoken from the Old Testament, the New Testament) that I had begun to understand Tillich's "secular mind" in all of its constant ambiguity.

Years later, in New York City, at 36 East First Street, in St. Joseph's House, where Dorothy Day lived, I would hear her use that same phrase, uttering it with a memorable mix of awe, no less, and wry humor. I was tape-recording her comments—an effort on my part to learn about the history of the Catholic Worker Movement. I had spent some time during medical school in a Catholic Worker "hospitality house" but had never really come to a full understanding of that tradition, its intellectual and spiritual underpinnings—so I began to realize in the early 1970s, when I started talking at some length with Dorothy Day, and pursuing the reading she suggested. During one of those meetings, she remarked upon her "secular life"—and continued this way in amplification: "I get so busy doing the things I want to do, love doing, that I forget to ask myself the why of it all; and I forget to ask myself what *might* be, what *ought* be, because I'm in the midst of doing, doing. Thank God for this wonderful secular life—but thank God for giving us a mind that can turn to Him, to ask 'why' and 'wherefore' as well as spend itself to exhaustion getting things done! Some people say to me, 'the secular mind is your enemy.' I say no, no; I say the secular mind is God's huge gift to us, for us to use for the sake of one another, and that way, for His glory. Then, those folks want me to explain myself—and I have to admit, I get cranky, impatient. I want to get on with things—my secular mind working away! But then I'll just be stopped in my tracks. I feel something inside me wanting to express itself: it's me wanting to be on my knees before God and His mystery. That's when your secular thinking stops and your spiritual being takes a front and center place in your life. You're silent and your mind has left you (the 'you' of this life) and it's gone elsewhere, to meet the Lord—somewhere out there, don't ask me where: the secular having a brief time with the sacred. The next minute it's all over; you're back here in full swing."

So she put it, the complexity of our mind's life, the alternations of thinking and doing, of being this and being that, of secular days, sacred moments; and it is in that spirit of hers (she placed herself on the front line of a lived but interrupted secularity) and of Tillich's (in the classroom, he struggled paradoxically to figure out the contemporary, secular manifestations of the sacred) that I try to explore this matter of two minds, our secular thinking and its constant search for moral, if not spiritual, sanction.

I

Secularism in the
Biblical Tradition

THROUGHOUT the history of Christianity the authority of the sacred has never been taken for granted as a compelling moral and spiritual given of unassailable sway. Indeed, the lives of the saints have borne continuing witness to the vulnerability of religious faith, its bouts of frailty in the face of this or that era's challenges. Hence the word secular: the things of a particular time. Such worldliness need not be aggressively ideological, a philosophy that directly takes on a belief in God, a lived commitment to principles and practices upheld in His (or Her or Its) name. The issue, rather, has commonly been regarded (and in letters, essays, books pronounced) as psychological rather than cultural or sociological: the tug, seemingly inevitable, of our senses, our appetites, upon the direction of our energies. God awaits us, as do the various houses of worship that insist upon and celebrate the primacy of the sacred, yet we yield to or seek outright the profane: ideas and values and habits and interests that have their origin in our earthly lives, our day-to-day desires, worries, frustrations, resentments.

Saint Paul (arguably the first Christian theologian) stressed the rock-bottom implacability of such secularism: its hold on us that stretches over all generations—until, that is, we are back to God's first chosen two, the man Adam, the woman Eve, both nakedly unselfconscious and under no threat of disappearance, extinction.

Secularism was born in that fabled "garden" of yore, when curiosity spawned knowledge. The first secularist, in a sense, was the serpent who is described as "subtle" (still no small virtue among many of us unashamed heathens), and who egged Eve on all too persuasively. In no time she and Adam were having quite a time of it—and the result, really, was the mythical birth of the mind as we know it today, countless centuries later. "The eyes of them both were opened"—a clear, sometimes scary awareness of themselves, of the world around them, of space and time: the intellect that peers, pokes, pries. But that intellect (those opened eyes) right away had to contend with a rush of emotion, an altogether new notion of themselves: "They knew that they were naked, and they sewed fig leaves together and made themselves aprons." Here is the first recorded instance of shame, and its consequences; here is a physical act (the sewing of leaves) as an expression of an inner state of alarm, regret, fear. Immediately thereafter such apprehension, prompted by an awareness of wrongdoing, is enacted, given dramatic expression: "And they heard the voice of the Lord God walking in the garden in the cool of the day; and Adam and his wife hid themselves from the presence of the Lord God amongst the trees of the garden."

Soon enough those two, now mere mortals, and so destined to die, are headed "east of Eden," where their descendants (all of us) would try to make the best of a bad deal: a major transgression had elicited a swift, unrelenting punishment (of a kind that is utterly defining both psychologically and physically), and a kind of careless abandon, as a birthright, had been taken away, replaced by suffering and more suffering, though with a new kind of mental activity, driven by an acquired moral energy (what happened when that forbidden "tree of the knowledge of good and evil" lost its aura of inaccessibility).

In the biblical chapters that follow the expulsion of Adam and Eve from the Lord's terrain, so to speak, much is made of the consequent and subsequent physical hardship, pain: floods and pestilence and drought; the hunger and illness that accompanied them. But there was, too, the subjectivity that this new life brought: human beings as exiles, as wanderers, as people paying (forever, it seemed) a price for an act of disobedience, a severe transgression that carried with it the death penalty. That inner state was, right off, marked by self-preoccupation—another first, that of a necessary narcissism as a requirement for a creature suddenly at the mercy of the elements, and with a fixed span of time available. True, after the Flood, the Lord (in Exodus) relents a bit, promises not to be persecutory in the extreme—hence the survival of humankind. But death is our fate, still. We are left to fend for ourselves, and to do so with apprehension either a constant presence or around any corner. But we are also left with a steadily increasing capacity to make the best of our fatefully melancholy situation: the freedom, and need, to explore, to experiment, to master as best we can what we see and touch. We are left, too, after that terrible Flood of six centuries duration, with a negotiation of sorts: "And God blessed Noah and his sons, and said unto them, be fruitful and multiply, and replenish the earth." A newly generous turn on the Lord's part: those people once described as "fugitives and vagabonds" were entrusted with their own earthly sovereignty. An agreement was reached, and our secular rights, privileges were affirmed: "And the fear of you and the dread of you shall be upon every beast of the earth, and upon every fowl of the air, upon all that moveth upon the earth, and upon all the fishes of the sea; into your hand are they delivered." In vivid imagery God is said to have spelled out His promise—the so-called covenant of the rainbow, a partial retraction of an earlier curse, with the implication that an ingenious humankind can survive, if it pays heed to the environment, uses it as required.

But of course the Lord did not match His gift of a subservient outside world with an offer to subdue the minds and hearts and souls of this first among creatures. Put differently, covenantal Judaism addressed our progressive triumph over a raw, threatening, potentially destructive Nature yet gave us no leeway over our thinking and feeling life. Animals can be our prey, but the animal in us prowls mightily or stealthily, as the case may be.

Not that God lost interest in our attitudes, in what we held dear, and why. The God of the Hebrew Bible is repeatedly observant and testing. One moment He seems ready to let this big shot among "living things" simply be in charge, have a time of it on the planet; another time He concentrates His moral sights on us, wants to make sure we know how interested He is in how we behave, in what we believe, and, not least, in how we regard Him. This latter supposition about God—proposed by, among others, the twentieth-century theologian Karl Barth, who saw *Him* as a seeker—by implication plays into our secular life: we are desirable enough to earn His constant interest. Our self-preoccupations are affirmed by His preoccupation with us, and that egoism (or, these days, narcissism) amounts to a veiled variant of secularism: the self of the here and now in all its ceaselessly sought affirmations, in this instance one buttressed by theology, no less.

Before Barth, there was Søren Kierkegaard, who was no stranger to psychology, even if he preferred to use it as a means of understanding our search for moral meaning, rather than our search for the less obvious, if not hidden, sides of ourselves. Kierkegaard, unlike many intellectual contemporaries of his, took seriously not only the story of Jesus but the Hebrew Bible as well—and not only the prophetic (or later) Judaism of Isaiah, Jeremiah, Amos, Micah, but the founding moments, they might be called, of that hugely demanding monotheistic faith. In *Fear and Trembling*, for instance, we are asked to consider Abraham's walk up a mountain in "the land of Moriah" with his beloved son Isaac. There God has sought him out in an apparently merciless (and inscrutable) way: the demand that a father kill his son as evidence of a compliant faith. Here are words of high drama, of staggering anxiety: "Take now thy son [The Lord insists], thine only son Isaac, whom thou lovest . . . and offer him . . . for a burnt offering upon one of the mountains which I will tell thee of. . . . And they came to the place which God had told him of; and Abraham built an altar there, and laid the wood in order; and bound Isaac his son, and laid him on the altar upon the wood. And Abraham stretched forth his hand, and took the knife to slay his son." Suddenly, though, the "angel of the Lord" calls from Heaven, tells Abraham to stop in his tracks, to spare his son, "for now I know that thou fearest God, seeing thou has not withheld thy son, thine only son from me."

For Kierkegaard such a moment was charged with a kind of moral irony almost beyond analysis or even description through man's distinctive gift, the use of words. Not that he didn't try—*Fear and Trembling* won't let go of Abraham and his willingness to follow God's direction, no matter the cost to himself, his wife Sarah, their son, Isaac. We are given, at one point, a metaphysician's abstract summary, a concept to keep in mind: "the teleological suspension of the ethical"—an occasion where our sense of right and wrong, even our ordinary sense of what we simply never could or would do, is forsaken in favor of an ascent toward a faith ultimately challenged (as opposed to a descent to the most brutish kind of criminality, callousness). For Kierkegaard our ordinary ethical standards don't apply when God calls, though in anyone's contemporary daily life (so it has been for a long time!) such an explicit summons from the Lord, or that "angel" of his possessed of speech, seems quite beyond the bounds of possibility. In a less theoretical vein, however, Kierkegaard leaves ethical contemplation for a simpler, more accessible (and affecting) narrative mode: "By faith Abraham went from the land of his fathers and became a sojourner in the land of promise. He left one thing behind, took one thing with him: he left his earthly understanding behind and took faith with him—otherwise he would not have wandered forth but would have thought this unreasonable."

Secularism is thereby acknowledged in its obviously compelling attraction—precisely the target of a God intent on a mind-boggling insistence: toss aside the loftiest of the secular, the commonsense family ties that, actually, are the bottom line, morally, for so many of us. No wonder, in Elie Wiesel's *Night* the full brunt of the Nazi horror as it got enacted in those concentration camps is realized when we learn of a boy's eventual indifference to his own father, a storyteller's personal acknowledgment that the most personal of ties, those that develop in a family, had been shattered in this precipitous downward moral collapse. But for Abraham the action was all upward: the climbing of a mountain, the hearing of a message from the heavens, the seemingly quick responsiveness on his part (he becomes a "sojourner in the land of promise"). The matter at hand, Kierkegaard reminds us, is a "heinous sin," and yet in some fashion (and without discussion or reflection) the man and husband and father Abraham becomes, with apparent effortlessness, a "knight of faith." Whence this "infinite resignation" that translated into a hand poised with a knife, ready to plunge it into a son's body? Here is a further irony: "Those . . . who carry the jewel of faith are likely to be delusive, because their outward appearance bears a striking resemblance to that which both the infinite resignation and faith profoundly despise . . . to Philistinism."

We know from Kierkegaard's *This Present Age* the posture he could summon for the philistine—the satirist's biting scorn. In that relatively brief essay he takes on, really, the Danish (and by extension European) bourgeoisie of his time, the restless yearnings of people who may go to church on Sunday for an hour or so, but who live strongly attached to a shifting assortment of possessions, projects, plans: things to own, things to do, things to dream of accomplishing. He notices the boredom that attends such activity, as if the secular world, in itself, provides little real inspiration to those who live there. Yet the alternative, a thoroughgoing commitment to the sacred, is beyond the imagining, let alone the aspiration, of most of us (certainly including, he says over and over, the multitude of professed Christians whose vows of loyalty to God, to Jesus, are regularly, loudly spoken). Indeed, for Kierkegaard organized Christianity, Catholic and Protestant alike, is one more aspect of the "philistinism," the prosaic secularism that he so evidently disdains. He needn't deign to remind us of the medieval Catholic Church, or the fat and sassy Protestant burghers whom he, a minister's son, knew by common sight. He assumes secularism as the mainstay of the Christian life for many centuries, even as he assumes that Abraham was no saintly creature, abruptly rewarded by a grateful God.

The historical surprise of a flawed father walking with his son to a destination that seemed all too final for the father, as he contemplated it, is meant to give us pause, still—no matter who we are, where or when we live. As for Isaac, we're never told what he knew, if anything, as he walked so trustingly alongside Abraham. Kierkegaard insists, though, that this was not a pair that could be quickly singled out, declared the winners of a divine moral sweepstakes: God's chosen (and most exceptional) spiritual combatants. Rather, he clothes them in a secular garb, even back then, several millennia before his time. In a sense, then, he is reprimanding his own caustic tongue, telling us that sociology and psychology, infant "sciences" in the middle of the nineteenth century, would be of no help in singling out a "knight of faith"; nor is there a course of study, or, alas, a religious practice, that secures for somebody such a spiritual station or "level" of success. Paradoxically, the secular can mask (that is, contain) the sacred—hence the mystery of faith, which Kierkegaard, with no embarrassment whatever, keeps trying to uphold, notwithstanding his cleverly modern, introspectively astute, socially watchful and discerning mind.

Kierkegaard attends carefully to Abraham's relationship with God precisely because in that encounter the assumptions of rational secularism are directly confronted, dismissed. *Fear and Trembling* takes on nineteenth-century romanticism and enlightenment, both, with a vengeance: "Abraham is therefore at no instant a tragic hero, but something quite different, either a murderer or a believer." True, by virtue of the absurd, Isaac is not at the last moment sacrificed—a decision, however, of God's, not Abraham's. We who consider that story have no real way of presuming to put ourselves in Abraham's shoes and can only, these days, "play" with such a story intellectually, as Kierkegaard did. Yet it is a biblical story and was meant to tell a sacred lesson to early secularists: God's ways are not ours, hence "fear and trembling" as a worthy response to that event, rather than an effort, say, of historical (or moral) analysis.

The thrust of Kierkegaard's essay is the unyielding disparity between the sacred and the secular. If Abraham had to surrender his son in a gesture of faith, we readers (of the Bible or of a brilliant and cranky nineteenth-century Danish theologian) have to surrender our usual (secular) assumptions about what matters and why when we try to make sense of a world utterly elsewhere. Nor was Kierkegaard unaware that a similar predicament confronted those who lived in Palestine when Jesus walked that land, taught and healed and exhorted the multitude—only to be killed in the company of thieves.

But between the time of Abraham's encounter with God on one mountain, and the time of Jesus as he preached and prophesied on another, there were additional efforts to confront the Jewish people with the demands of faith, none more important, of course, than that of Moses, who also went up a mountain to hear God's wishes—and did so at greater length, surely, than anyone else mentioned in the Bible. For pages in Scripture we learn of those conversations: they are true exchanges, and on occasion the lowly mortal one takes issue with his Lord, even turns Him around, gets Him to see things differently. Indeed, Moses and God collaborate together, plan a strategy meant to tame morally a people, bring them convincingly the Ten Commandments, of course, also bring them all sorts of other instructions, commands, announcements, recommendations. Moses is always called the great lawgiver of his people, but he was also a negotiator of sorts, a trusted emissary of no less than God, and, not least, an interpreter of the sacred for the secularist crowds of his time. He was, in that regard, a master of the details and habits and rituals that make up ordinary life; and he was constantly intent on shaping the way his fellow Jews lived their daily lives, in the hope that a people singled out by the Lord would, finally, dedicate themselves to Him in just the ways He wished.

No question he was, in secular terms, a "great man," or a "leader"—hence Freud's desire, in *Moses and Mono-theism*, to see him as the victim of parricide, a conclusion that tells a lot about a particular theorist's unrelenting determination to see things his way at all costs. Not that Freud was the first one to take the Moses story and fit it to his secular requirements. During Moses' long life (he reputedly died at 120) he surely incurred the resistance of many: the Decalogue he transmitted to his people is a demanding call to God's ways, a rebuke to man's inclinations, impulses. Moses gave his fellow Jews a divinely sanctioned collective conscience; though if there was anxiety and anger, as a consequence, there was surely the gratitude that goes with a clear-cut mandate proclaimed in the name of the highest possible authority. Here was an unequivocal monotheism, but also rules about daily living, the rights and wrongs of it. An ancient kind of secularism was confronted head-on: the great man has heard, again and again, the word of God, and in His name (not that of some tribal seer or chief) has spoken out loud and strong.

Yet even God's direct message, conveyed through a chosen intermediary (himself commanding, intriguing, a savvy but principled spokesman and negotiator) will wane in its capacity to convince, exert control. The prophetic Judaism of Jeremiah, especially, bears witness to the betrayal of covenantal Judaism at the hands of a people become all too spiritually indifferent, if not callous. The intensity of Jeremiah's denunciations (the first jeremiads!) measures the moral decline of a people, their embrace of what is convenient, momentarily satisfying: the self-indulgence of the temporal order. "Run ye to and fro through the streets of Jerusalem," the great social and cultural critic exhorts, anxious that those who read/hear his words become aware of inequity in all its garbs and disguises abroad the land. But this is a condemnation, a remonstrance in the name of religion: "Therefore, I am full of the fury of the Lord." The prophet speaks, as Moses before him, in His name: "The word that came to Jeremiah from the Lord, saying. . . . " A society gone secular, forgetful of God-given rules, laws, commandments, is vigorously chastised—and not abstractly. Repeatedly calling upon direct observation, Jeremiah is a documentarian of distant yore who regards closely and firsthand a particular fallen world: "Seest not what they do in the cities of Judah and in the streets of Jerusalem?" These are words of spiritual alarm and dismay directed with righteous vehemence and near despair: "Oh that my head were waters, and mine eyes a fountain of tears, that I might weep day and night for the slain of the daughter of my people."

As the caustic essayist or aroused moralist lets loose his scorn, he renders by implication a portrait of long ago secularism worthy of one of today's gloomy naysayers, grievously upset by a moral decline in this or that nation's public or private life. To be sure, some of our social observers are reluctant to betray even mild indignation, let alone outrage—a measure of the distance, with respect to moral conviction, that their readers/

listeners have traveled since Jeremiah's time. The lyrical heat in his statements, the raw passion he harnesses to his denunciations of an ancient secularism, tells us a lot about not only him but his intended audience: these are people corrupted, but within hearing distance, it can be said, of the very spiritual voices that were so evidently, flagrantly unheeded. In our time, among many who regard themselves as well educated and, too, philosophically inclined, ethically awake, a moralist of Jeremiah's rhetorical persuasion might be readily dismissed as all too caught up in his own "problems"—if not plain loony. Moreover, much of our influential social criticism is, naturally, secular in nature: the writer or speaker draws upon a particular civic or intellectual tradition. A good number of those who resemble Jeremiah in their words, their tone, are for many of us "fundamentalists," no compliment, despite the prime meaning of the word; or again, are consigned to the ranks of the mentally unsettled or worse.

Secularism links our age with Zion as it edged toward the time of Jesus Christ. His kind of life, for millions of us (at least in creedal expression) a continuation of prophetic Judaism, and more, a culmination of it, was unacceptable to the people of His time, and the same fate can await many who labor spiritually today. In this regard, I'd best jump from the Galilee wherein Jesus lived, spoke, to the Lower East Side in Manhattan in 1973, where Dorothy Day, a journalist, political activist, novelist, and onetime companion drinker to the likes of Eugene O'Neill, Mike Gold, John Dos Passos, Malcolm Cowley, reminisced about the perception of her that suddenly arose among some of her old friends, never mind various strangers: "I lived a Greenwich Village life for a long time. I wrote for liberal and radical journals. I didn't completely like being called 'serious,' but it was meant as a compliment. I'd gone to jail [as a suffragette] and I'd criticized the country for its indifference to the poor—and my friends encouraged me and told me I was doing a good job. When I started saying the same things, actually, but in the name of God—well, that was a different matter altogether! The first wave of disbelief took the form of worry: was I *all right*? It's hard to fight *that* one! What do you do—ask if the person who is speaking those words is *all right*? Not if you're trying to invoke the Jesus who prayed to the Lord that He forgive those who were mocking Him! I began to realize that in our secular world there's plenty of room for social or cultural criticism, so long as it is secular in nature. But I'd crossed the street, you could say; I'd gone over to those crazy ones, who speak—well, one of my old drinking friends (he taught at Columbia) called it 'God talk.' He said to me once: 'Dorothy, why do you now need "God talk" to lay into America for all its wrongs? You used to do a great job when you were a muckraking reporter, with no "religion" sandwiched into your writing.'"

By then Dorothy Day was hopelessly, in her own words (the enemy's line of thought embraced!) "a fool for Christ"—and therein a twentieth-century echo of what Jeremiah and his kind must have heard, and, to a pitch of frenzy, Jesus of Nazareth, also, as he became more and more soul-stirred, more and more skeptical of prevailing principalities and powers, and willing to take them on directly or by analogy. Those parables of his were meant to hit the listener hard, give him or her plenty of reason to look askance at what passed for the popular, the conventional, the regular or customary. What to make of one who remarks that "the last shall be first, the first last": a direct slam at secular accomplishment and power, a direct embrace of the lowly, of people more than occasionally regarded as lazy, incompetent, or worse by those on the top? What to make, further, of the company Jesus kept: those fisherman and peasants, those sick ones, hurt ones, those scorned and rebuked ones? What to make, finally, of his considerable nerve: he who invoked the Lord regularly, and who spoke in His name?

No matter one's decision with regard to Christ's eventual divinity, while here on earth for a short thirty-three years he regularly took issue, we can surely agree, with the secular world of a powerful (Roman) empire in the name of the sacred. He was a spiritually aroused itinerant storyteller, a moral evangelist of humble background, who for a while attracted a large following, probably the reason for his undoing at the hands of those with political power. Nor did he endear himself to those of his own people who had religious power; he was, in a sense, a reform Jew deeply troubled by what he saw, heard in the temple: shades of Jeremiah, of course. His death was a secular one, at the hands of the state: the doing-in of a spiritually possessed young man who came to Jerusalem, a country boy, one might say—with an accent that bespoke lowliness, with no connections to the mighty, the influential, and with a record of fomenting a kind of civil unrest. His speech was unsettling in tone, if not specific word: "I come to bring you not peace, but the sword." He did, indeed, seem to want to cut a swath through the everyday assumptions of a people now under the imperial sway of generals and their lieutenants who were hardly interested in, sympathetic to Judaism, its monotheism, its long-standing ethical traditions, so intimately connected to its history. Jesus was not the first nor the last critic of that empire's values (or of his own people's moral subjugation—his target rather than their political servitude) to be killed. Rome was not Nazi Germany or Stalin's Russia, but it knew how to enforce its sovereignty; and so, years after Jesus had died, when his followers persisted in speaking in his name, living in accordance with his precepts, they, too, were done away with, fed to devouring animals, some of them, rather than strung up on a cross.

All of that—the stuff of the Christian legend as it has survived across two millennia—would soon enough be institutionalized (hence the undiminished collective memory of a seemingly obscure and unsurprising moment in the day-to-day history of a far-flung empire's provincial life). Put differently, Jesus and his followers preceded by several generations what became Christianity: an inspired and inspiring spiritual figure, who took on a particular secular world, became in a century or two the Son of God, with buildings dedicated to the perpetuation of His name and His words, and with men and women spending their lives doing likewise in those buildings and elsewhere. But in no time that sacred mission, that organization (with rules and regulations and a proclaimed moral and spiritual authority) itself became very much part of the secular world—to the point that, in the Middle Ages, the Holy Roman Catholic Church had become in many respects an empire: rich, complacent, a player in all the intrigues of the day. Thereupon, of course, the arrival of the latter-day Jeremiahs, the necessary scolds, who railed at corruption and degradation of all kinds at the highest levels of so-called sacred communities, in the Vatican and elsewhere. But such criticism, from within or without, can't banish the essential historical irony, that in the name of an initial spiritual remonstrance of established secular and sacred power, an institution of great influence emerged, and with that development, a new kind of secularism: bishops and popes sitting down with kings and queens, and, later, lay leaders of all kinds, to decide about all sorts of secular matters.

In protest of Rome's moral corruption, a Luther would rise to say no, to demand a more rigorous adherence to the sacred. But he, too, sat with secular leaders, and in fact Lutheranism would take the proclaimed sanctity of Christianity into a new domain of the secular: the church as a pillar of the nation-state's authority. No wonder Dietrich Bonhoeffer's special agony: he saw right away Hitler's hateful secularism, but he, a Lutheran, saw his fellow Lutheran pastors embrace that version of secularism, wrap themselves in the swastika, even in the brown shirts of the street thugs who had run interference (and worse) for the rising, Austrian-born demagogue. In the end, Bonhoeffer took aim not only at Hitler but at Lutheranism as it came to such easy terms with him—the supposedly sacred proving itself, in the name of *realpolitik*, the merely secular.

Such an accommodation may strike us as disgraceful because of the morally grotesque nature of Nazism;

whereas we blink at, or simply fail to notice, the less dramatic accommodations that take place in our own more "civilized" countries, cultures. Here, for example, is Bonhoeffer writing from a concentration camp in the last year of his life (Hitler would have him killed in April of 1945, a few weeks before his own suicide):

> There still remain the so-called "ultimate questions"— death, guilt—to which only "God" can give an answer, and because of which we need God and the Church and the pastor. So we live, in some degree, on these so-called ultimate questions of humanity. But what if one day they no longer exist as such, if they too can be answered "without God"? Of course, we now have the secularized offshoots of Christian theology, namely existentialist philosophy and psychotherapists, who demonstrate to secure, contented, and happy mankind that it is really unhappy and desperate and simply unwilling to admit that it is in a predicament about which it knows nothing, and from which only they can rescue it. Wherever there is health, strength, security, simplicity, they send luscious fruit to gnaw at or to lay their pernicious eggs in. They set themselves to drive people to inward despair, and then the game is in their hands. That is secularized methodism.

The words of a prisoner who knew that death might be around any corner, and so, arguably, an exaggerated or overwrought take on those philosophers and psychologists. Still, Bonhoeffer knew that both Heidegger and Jung had made a kind of peace with the Nazis that he judged contemptible on Christian grounds, and, as already noted, he knew that the overwhelming majority of German Christendom, not to mention that nation's professoriat and its psychological healers, both lay and medical, had done likewise. From a privileged Aryan family, he might have had it otherwise, avoided the fate of an active opponent of the Nazis. Indeed, in the summer of 1939 he was in America—a visiting scholar at Union Theological Seminary, where he could have stayed through the war and where he was already celebrated for his strong, outspoken resistance to Hitler. (Bonhoeffer went on the radio to criticize Germany's "Führer" two days after President von Hindenberg made his fateful decision to appoint Adolf Hitler the Reich's chancellor, and the pastor was cut off as he tried to warn his listeners of the terrible consequences ahead for them, for their Christian faith.) As a matter of fact, when this young and already distinguished theologian decided to return to Germany, to continue to take his quite dangerous stand against the Nazis, he was himself regarded a candidate for the "help" of those very psychotherapists whom he would mention a few years later with no great admiration. In Reinhold Niebuhr's succinct words: "We worried about him; we knew how endangered he'd be, if he returned—but he *had* to go back: he was a deeply religious man, one who took Christ's life to heart, and tried to live up to it."

By the end of his life Bonhoeffer, the onetime cosmopolitan Berliner, a Lutheran in his early career by conviction, had left churchgoing for something quite else, the "Christian life" Niebuhr was trying to describe. This fearlessly decent religious philosopher and pastor, this promising scholar whose books had achieved considerable and favorable attention, felt at an utter remove from his nation's policies, practices, and thoroughly disenchanted, disgusted by his church's collaborative engagement with what he regarded as the Devil itself, the Antichrist. As one reads his late diary entries and the books he wrote against the darkening shadows of Hitler's consolidation of brute power (in the late 1930s), such as *The Cost of Discipleship*, one is carried back in time to the earliest years of the so-called Christian Era: to the "Christian life" lived by Jesus himself, and his band of followers, who risked so very much for what they held dear.

Put differently, Bonhoeffer refused the choice of exile (a step many fellow clergymen and intellectuals willingly took) because his values weren't secular. He did not, in the end, regard himself as a university teacher, as a minister, as a book-writing intellectual, as a cultivated person of many gifts and passions (he played the piano exceedingly well, wrote poetry), all of which he most certainly was—but rather as a disciple of Jesus Christ who had the responsibility and wish to risk everything, his life included, in pursuit of what Jesus (become the Christ) proclaimed, urged, died in seeking: the sanctity of faith enacted in the here, the now of a lived life. I never heard the matter put better, actually, than as Professor David Roberts, who taught at Union Theological Seminary in the 1950s, did when he tried to describe Bonhoeffer's last days and, before them, his commitments that proved fatal to him: "He lived as a *homo religiosus*, and he died a Christian martyr. There were others who died fighting the Nazis—or openly fought them in Germany, and then fled. But they were secular heroes. Even among the clergy who said no to the

Nazis—a small number, sad to say—few were as bold as Bonhoeffer. His lack of discretion tells the full story: he wasn't operating on the principles that govern most of us (practicality, probability of success in what you're trying to do, and the chances for survival); he was fulfilling a sacred calling, not making the sober and sane calculations of a secular life."

A pause—and then an afterthought put in the form of a question, which does haunting justice to a haunting Christian witness that ended on April 9, 1945, in the Flossenburg concentration camp: "People often ask what the rest of us are to make of him [Bonhoeffer], of what he did, but I wonder whether we ought not ask ourselves what his life has to teach us about *ourselves*, about how we behave and what we believe and what we do (if anything!) to indicate that what we really believe has much to do with how we live." Further on in a conversation powerfully instructive, Professor Roberts reminded us of what by then had become obvious, courtesy of his commentary, though the way he put it was original, so we students thought then, and so I still think as I remember a professor's words, written down: "God is timeless, and so is faith, and so is doubt— Bonhoeffer in his heart and mind and soul became one of the disciples of Jesus; [thereby] he jumped over all those centuries."

History tempts us, naturally, to think otherwise, and so do psychology and sociology: we all live in a particular place and time. We wonder about Bonhoeffer's emotional life, or his family's values, or the particular German philosophical and spiritual idealism that inspired him. As for his stalwart capacity to endure Nazi harassment, threats, punishment, confinement, and the constant threat of death—surely the tinge of bitterness and melancholy in his letters bespeaks a mind under severe strain, a mind trying hard to sustain itself "adaptively" in the face of a naked terror constantly exerted. But Professor Roberts wanted us to pose another possibility: that our manner of regarding Bonhoeffer was inadequate, to say the least, although thoroughly revealing about ourselves rather than the intended "subject" of scrutiny. We were, really, trying to comprehend a life fueled by spiritual energy through a way of thinking that had little to do with religious ideals as they get turned, by some, into intensely guiding principles: secular minds unable to fathom the workings (the assumptions, the yearnings, the expectations, and, yes, the worries and fears) of a mind tied significantly to the sacred.

I believe that Bonhoeffer did, indeed, leap over nineteen hundred years, embrace those desert wanderers who belonged to, not a church, an institution, a sect, but a community of kindred souls; and in a way I only began to understand what happened to him in the Delta of Mississippi in 1964, during the height of the civil rights struggle, when I was working in a so-called Freedom House in Canton, and talking with, among others, a black man, Joseph Gaines, who had wanted for years to be a minister, but who was, instead, a tenant farmer. Moreover, he was no mean critic of the very church life he sought out so hungrily on Sundays, as he once let me know in this way: "I'll be praying to Jesus, and I'll feel Him right beside me. No, He's inside me, that's it. I think the church people, they want you to come visit them, and that way you meet the Lord, and

His Boy, His Son. The trouble is, you leave, and the Lord and Jesus stay—they don't go with you. You go back to being yourself, in the state of Mississippi, in the United States of America, and it's 1964, and you've got the bills to pay, and you've got the church to pay, too—a donation every Sunday, yes sir! So, I say to myself: be on your own with God—He can be your friend all the time, not just Sunday morning. Come Monday and Tuesday and through the week to meet Him in church, or go find Him some other place—He's everywhere, if you'll only want to look. If you live with Him long and hard, you're carrying His spirit; if you think of Him but once a week you're just another—I guess you be another Mississippian!

"I'd like to be a minister, so I could know the Bible, and preach it to other folks. But in my heart, I don't believe the Lord wants me preaching on Sundays; He wants me living His way all the days of the week. I recall being little, and I asked my Pa [his grandfather] why it was that Jesus lived so long ago, and here we are, so far from where He was, the distance away, and the time, too. 'Joe,' he said, 'you got it all wrong. He is here, right near you, right inside you—if you want Him to be.' 'Sure,' I said; 'you bet,' I said; 'wow, yes sir,' I said—I want Him as near as can be. But Pa told me not so fast, young one; he told me that He's with you if you earn the right for Him to be there, and if you don't, then He's not, and you can go to church and put money in the basket and pray your head off and sing your voice out until it's gone and said good-bye, and still He won't be paying you mind, because—that's it!—you're not paying Him any mind, and it's a two-way street, sure is.

"On a good day, when I've remembered Jesus, by the way I am with my family and friends, then I'm sure He's smiling and saying, you're with Me, yes sir; on a bad day, when I'm all pouty and mean in my manners, then He's gone on to find the good souls to keep company with, and I'm just here, alone, figuring out how I can take care of mister Me, and not caring about others, and isn't that the first stop on the bus headed for hell!"

As I heard those words, I remembered Reinhold Niebuhr and David Roberts telling us students that when Bonhoeffer was at Union Theological Seminary (like Simone Weil when she was in New York), he went to Harlem to church—not in order to try to be of help to the poor, to people long humiliated, but in the conviction that Jesus was to be found there, rather than at the seminary, or the churches in the fancy parts of Manhattan. Well, of course, who is to say exactly where God is to be found? Yet, as that humble yeoman was trying to suggest, the Lord may indeed be anywhere, everywhere, may have visited people and places at all times. For some, though, He is a companion, a daily guide, whereas for others, a presence, a high presence, to be visited occasionally, be it weekly or on holidays only: a life bent on passing a kind of constant sacred muster or a life predominantly secular in its commitments. For Joseph Gaines, for Dietrich Bonhoeffer, Paul's conversion on the road to Damascus or Jeremiah's furious lamentations are not at all a far distant moment, reported in Scripture as a part of ancient history, but the stuff of daily living, without which secularity soon enough asserts its thrust, its lure, as has happened all the time and in all possible places, including, of course, the

Vatican, this or that abbey in England, the churches where hymns are sung in memory of Martin Luther.

Nor has secularism over the centuries (and within the biblical tradition) been a matter only of sin or temptation or simple acquiescence in all that plentifully *is*. As R. H. Tawney in *Religion and the Rise of Capitalism* and Max Weber in *The Protestant Ethic and the Spirit of Capitalism* have reminded us, and as Ignazio Silone likewise did, as a storyteller rather than a social theorist, religious tradition can very much connect with, even stir strongly, a secular society, give it a cadre of "believers" who work their hearts out—feverish in their compliance with business and government officials, desperately eager in their wish to show themselves godly by proving themselves, without letup, willing workers. It was, perhaps, easier for Bonhoeffer to take on (take after) the intelligentsia, the *haute bourgeoisie* of his native Germany, or for that matter, of England and the United States or Spain, three countries in which he lived for months at a time, than to take note of the ordinary working people of those countries, of any country: men and women who every day show up for work in factories, offices, whether in blue or white collars. True, for so many of us there is no choice: one works or one goes hungry. Still, the mind not only succumbs to secular necessity; the mind can make the best of a tough ordeal, even (as the saying goes) a bad thing.

"I won't tell you I'm in heaven when I'm there on the [assembly] line," a man who works in a General Electric factory in Lynn, Massachusetts, tells me in July 1972, but then follows a description of his daily efforts that shows me how sacred themes in a culture can exert themselves to the advantage of a predominantly secular life: "My both parents were—they called themselves 'God-fearing,' and they *were*! My dad would say, He's watching you, son, so you better try your best. Those three words ring in my ear to this very day, and I'm getting near a half century old: *try your best*. I guess I do. I show up early and leave late. I clock in the hours—and I bring home the bacon: that's life. Sundays, in church, I'll hear about all the troubles that came His way, to Jesus, and I say to myself: hey mister, He was the Son of God, that's what He was, and look at all that happened to Him. Can you imagine, being nailed up like that, and no one giving a hoot or a holler about you—everybody even calling you bad names? No way to end your life—He was a young man! The lesson: don't feel sorry for yourself! Don't slack off in self-pity—my mom told us four [him and his brother and two sisters] that all the time, and she got it right. So, [while on the job] I think of the sermon or one of the hymns, and I try to keep on my toes. 'Step on it!'—I'll say that to myself, sometimes out loud. You know, I'm not kidding myself: I'm just a two-bit worker in a big plant, but I'm better off than way over half the folks on this planet—hell, 90 percent, I'll bet—and it hurts me bad (kills me!) to think that I've had it easier here in this life than Jesus Christ Almighty did, the few years He came to spend with us. Go figure it out!"

After a fashion, he himself has managed to figure it all out—settle in his mind his own responsibilities as a husband, father, provider, and worker, even an employee: "I try to leave my spot [where he stands] clean, and I'll cut back on a break, if it's best for our [assembly line] team." He has also managed to connect his every-day life to his sense of what truly matters, not through a showy, talkative, self-regarding, and smug insistence on his religious faith, and not, certainly, through efforts to corral others to his way of thinking, but rather through resort to memory, meditation, observation. That is, he remembers the strongly held and asserted religious values of his parents, become his own; he calls up pas-sages of the Bible in an effort to make sense of his per-sonal life, his life as a worker; and he uses his biblical knowledge as a lens of sorts, through which he takes in what he sees in such a way that he obtains a coherent picture of what is happening around him. ("I'll be driv-ing, and something will happen—a guy is acting crazy with his car, passing, passing, and I'll remember Jesus saying, 'What profiteth?' and it all makes sense."). A worker's secular life gains coherence through his persist-ing connection to the sacred. His imaginative life even draws on the stained glass windows of the church he attends, the illustrations of the books his children read in Sunday school: "I can put myself over there [in an-cient Palestine] in my head—I'll be listening to Jesus give one of His talks, along with all the other folks. No, I hadn't thought how I'd look—be dressed [I had asked]. I guess I'm invisible to all of them; that's how it goes [in his thinking], or else they'd all notice me." In a humble, stoic, persevering life a mind crosses time and space to find the sacred, bring it home to a particular secularity.

Not that such a person is, to use Emerson's phrase, "representative man." He is the first to distinguish him-self (not in a self-serving manner) from many of his coworkers and neighbors: "Different people have different things they think of—in their spare time, when they've got time to think." Here, unpretentiously, he knows to skirt the temptation to generalize; rather, he aims to uphold a concreteness worthy of Husserl's repeated phenomenological assertion of human particularity. Still, he makes it amply clear that in the late twentieth century he belongs, to a significant degree, in the company of those who died in the first century. Sometimes, when he confesses to his "failures," to falling short of his spiritual ideals, to a quiet perplexity at what he sees around him (on television, in movies, in newspaper and magazine advertisements), I dare link him in my thoughts to Pietro da Morrone, the Benedictine hermit monk who was summoned to Rome in 1294, turned into a pope—Celestino V. In no time (a mere five months) he had abdicated, his luminous inwardness and piety, his lifelong sanctity, no help at all in dealing with the demands of papal politics. When a General Electric factory worker struggles to keep his faith, to "live as Jesus did, at least some of the time," while the rest of the time accommodating to his situation in a neighborhood, a nation, he is, with respect to such efforts, not unlike that only pope who ever quit his job: Celestino V left the Vatican to return to his hermit's life as a monk (and, soon thereafter, die). "I win, I lose," that factory worker acknowledges with a shrug, and with no claim to originality in the use of those four words, even as one suspects that the weary pope of the thirteenth century had a similar line of reasoning cross his mind as he departed the big city for the sanctuary (the sanctity) of the countryside.

It is no accident that the central character in Silone's *Bread and Wine*, Pietro Spina, is named after the Pietro da Morrone who became briefly the pope. In the novel Pietro Spina is a revolutionary on the run, hiding in the garb of a priest. The novel, in fact, renders brilliantly and affectingly the mix of idealism and pragmatism that even a principled warrior in the fight for social change must summon in his daily life. Irony abounds in the story: the hero's soulful decency, no matter that he is a hunted man, declared a criminal by the state; indeed, his sanctity, no matter his full commitment to the secular—he is an ardent socialist who wants a better world for humble workers, near penniless farmers. Pietro is hiding when he dresses as a priest, but the reader readily realizes that all too many "real" priests lack the impressive spiritual qualities Silone has given his protagonist. An utterly secular materialist bears himself nobly, earns his right to a Roman collar so often betrayed in history, as Pope Celestino knew, and as Silone first came to know as a fifteen-year-old lad, when a severe earthquake did terrible damage to Italy's Abruzzo region where he lived, the son of a peasant. In a mere eight seconds fifty thousand people were killed, and thousands more, already poor, were reduced to even further vulnerability. Under such circumstances the local bishop and his entourage promptly fled to safer territory, a secular journey, and the young boy, Tranquilli Secondo (Ignazio Silone is a pseudonym), watched that departure with surprise, consternation, disgust. Here, he knew, was a kind of lived secularism; here, as Dorothy Day once put it, was "Christ betrayed—as He has been again and again by clergymen, never mind those who attack and denounce the Church." She loved *Bread and Wine* for precisely that reason: its willingness to confound anyone looking for a clear-cut sorting of people, believers as against nonbelievers. Silone confounds, thereby, the sacred and the secular, wants us to remember the spirituality of the doubter, the crass self-interest of many who wrap themselves in the paraphernalia and claims of religious affiliation.

Once in a discussion with Dorothy Day about the very subject matter of this section of the book, the way secularism has manifested itself at various moments in religious history, she begged to disagree with my notion, then, that only recently has the secular achieved the prominence we take for granted today: "I think you underestimate *doubt* as a constant part of faith—in any century; and I think you are making too much of science (and social science) as the (recent) 'causes' of secularism. I don't deny that today there is the authority of scientific knowledge to elicit or encourage or give a kind of *imprimatur* to secularism; but for Heaven's sake, the secular world has always been 'there,' or 'here'—that's the big story of the Old Testament and the New Testament, and it's the big story, sad to say, of Christianity, both Catholicism and Protestantism. You've been talking [I had, alas] as if Galileo and Newton and Einstein and Freud have been the 'big guns' that have been shooting down religious faith, religious ties in people (in the West). To me, those folks and the people who follow their lead are part of a much longer story, and I wonder sometimes whether it isn't our conceit to think of ourselves as all that different.

"Before there were microscopes and telescopes and psychoanalysts and physicists, there were *cardinals*, there were Lutheran *bishops* who loved to 'live it up,' who had a great time for themselves, and who, I suspect, had less spirituality in them than—Einstein, who, at least, wondered about the mystery of the world and was humbled by it, all that mystery. Oh, I know—you can define 'secular' in several ways, and I suppose the same goes for 'spiritual.' I suppose that if you say that a society is 'secular,' because it's not under the authority of a church, the major influence of a church—then more societies in Europe are now secular than [was the case] in 1400 and 1500. But I'm trying to follow Saint Paul when he said 'not the letter, but the spirit,' which was what Jesus kept emphasizing, and so if the society *isn't* 'secular' because a church runs its schools and the politicians have to check things out with the people in that church, and the newspapers have to be careful in the same way—yes, that's a 'religious' nation, in a certain way, or a 'nonsecular' one, and the children growing up there may be more influenced by church doctrine as it's transmitted in classrooms. But that's only a part of the story: you can have religion betrayed from within—it happens all the time. God had a long, hard time with His chosen people, the Jews, persuading them to live in accordance with His principles, and Jesus has been betrayed over and over again by every kind of Christian church there is. I'll never forget Jacques Maritain [the Catholic theologian] telling me, 'Dorothy, I worry more about the harm done to "The Mystical Body of Jesus" by those of us who claim to be

41

devout Catholics than by the agnostic scientists and the people who believe in them.' I wasn't sure what he was getting at then, but he tried to explain it all to me, as I'm trying to [do so] now to you! I guess I want to cast a wider net with that word 'secular,' and I want to be careful that we don't let the words 'sacred' or 're-ligious'—the opposite of secular—go unexamined!"

No question, historically words such as "secular" or "secularism" or "secularization" bespoke shifts in the way people thought and acted, in the way their children were educated, in the way even property was distributed and managed:a shift from ecclesiastical power, as it was variously wielded, to what became known as temporal or civil or lay control. In a philosophical sense secular-ism also referred to the well-being of people while they lived here on this earth—as opposed to a concern for them in a supposed future state, when they would fall under the Lord's rule. But in the past, as now, how all those matters of property and politics and power and ideology, as it had access to people through words, cere-monies, mandates backed by military force, got worked into the individual minds of various men, women, chil-dren (and yes, into the minds of ecclesiastical officials, or civil leaders) would yield only to a kind of scrutiny obviously unavailable to us: those hours of inquiry that get called an interview, a recorded discussion shaped by direct questions aimed at illuminating how a "culture" settles into a particular person's thoughts, memories, as-pirations, worries, inclinations.

To be sure, the degree of *formal* secularization has ob-viously shifted over the centuries. The United States it-self is a nation explicitly founded by people who chafed under one or another kind of ecclesiastical authority: we are, it can be said, the first modern nation founded as explicitly secularist—that is, in response to societies where secularism was one of a number of competing ways of thinking. God figures in our important early political documents, but so does a temporal or civic reasoning that clearly has first legal place in our country's scheme of things. Collectively, therefore, we became, at the start, a secular nation; yet, of course, the many communities within our borders have had their own values, faiths. They were even "free" to do so in the midst of a kind of racial servitude just short of slavery as recently as 1963, so I was told, that year, in Greenwood, Mississippi, by a black woman who had her own way of talking about "secularism" in America now, or in America "back then" when her people first lived here: "I've often wondered what crossed their minds—when they just arrived to be at the mercy of all those bossmen. Who will ever know? We sure did 'take' to Jesus, though! Lord knows what our folks in Africa believed, but after we got here we got the God we know now—and there will be moments when I wonder what He thinks of all this, what's happened to us [African-American] people. Everyone talks about how you should believe this and you should believe that, and never let go of God no matter how high and mighty you become. (No worry that we're in danger of *that* happening!) But I will wonder the reverse—what He be thinking of those high and mighty folks who sit in those churches telling Him to look after them, because they're so good.

"You know what? My family hasn't ever stopped praying to God; we do it all the time, before and after we eat, and on getting up and going to sleep, all like that. We try to be God-fearing, that's one thing you can do here, no matter the bad condition we're in! We're God-fearing people, even if the whites call us those terrible names. Maybe God knows all this, what's happened in the past, and what's happening now, and so he's just waiting to pass His judgments—to say y'all colored, you've been the believers, and y'all whites, you've been the heathen folk! [It] goes to show you, what seems to be, may not be, and what God will favor and call His own is His business and will come out when He's ready, and it won't be hereabouts in Mississippi where He'll make His announcements of who's with Him, and who's against Him."

Although one might conclude that she is not being especially original—that she is speaking the received pieties of a family's life—in fact she had delivered a lecture on the difficulties that confront an observer, however learned theologically, who attempts to decide how to recognize secularism. The white folks she knew so well (whom I also got to know and interview) were at pains to express their dissatisfaction with what some of them (a minister, a school official, a lawyer) kept calling "America's secular culture." What they posed as a desirable alternative was a "Christian culture, like we once had here, before television and the movies made things bad even in our neck of the woods," so the lawyer put it. When I told my black informant what that prominent attorney had told me, she laughed heartily, said she would be praying for him, then offered this observation: "They can call themselves all they want, but (you know what?) they're in a huge lot of trouble, because it's

God who calls the shots on what they are, who they be, and so their words are just a lot of air that comes out of their big-shot mouths. I do believe they're making a mistake counting on Him as the one who'll back them up in their opinion of themselves."

Those last words rang in my ears years afterwards. I remembered them especially in 1990 at a conference at Harvard Divinity School when I kept hearing talk of "secular America" and our "secular society," and the "Christian Coalition" as it was "resisting secularism." As George Orwell reminded us, words can be used as property—and thereby we who use them can become the blind leading the blind. Secularism may be a matter of property owned, school curricula shaped in a certain direction, a culture transmitted along certain lines; but if the ultimate criterion is the relationship between all of that and *God's* judgment (rather than our judgment of His judgment), then we'd best, as that black woman suggested, take due care and pause: hedge carefully not only our personal bets (if such a wager even interests us) but also our categorical ones through which we come down this way, that way, with respect to the sacred, the profane, the religiously connected, the secularly disposed.

II

Where We Stood

1900

HISTORICAL ironies ought to give us cautionary pause as we contemplate secularism, yet cultural shifts obviously do take place over time, even if they prompt paradoxical consequences—a burst of "enlightenment" stirring an outburst of reactive nostalgia, if not a reactionary revulsion, a turn toward what was as a bulwark against what threatens to be. To contemplate a thoroughly secular Vatican, in the Middle Ages, at the height of its power across the European nations, to contemplate a slave or sharecropper population humbly, passionately, often furtively tied to the sacred, amidst a privileged, materialist white world that not rarely insisted upon turning its churchgoing into a weekly episode of self-display, is to be mindful of what William Carlos Williams, thinking about America's evolution from the seventeenth to the twentieth century, called "the zig and the zag of things," an earthy poet, through vernacular expression, bringing the Hegelian dialectic to his native New Jersey as he readied himself for the writing of his great poem *Paterson*. Individual minds vary in response to political or social changes, intellectual shifts in opinion, but those changes prompt all sorts of people to stop and think about what they believe and why, hence the accentuations of the secular or, on the contrary, the reactive flight from it.

Certainly, the second half of the nineteenth century had a decisive impact on the secularist assumptions in the West, to the point that if one wants to talk of a modern secular mind, its immediate and persuasive antecedents had come into being by the last years of the nineteenth century, the first ones of the twentieth century. It is well to remember that in 1880 Darwin, Freud, Marx, and Einstein were all alive, as were George Eliot, Hardy, Tolstoy, Dostoievsky: the giant minds of the sciences and social science that have shaped our time, and, too, the giant novelists who had examined in their different ways the secular manner of thinking that nourished the breakthrough of *An Origin of Species by Means of Natural Selection* or *The Preservation of Favoured Races in the Struggle for Life* (both 1859), or *Das Kapital* (1867), or *The Interpretation of Dreams* (1900), or the seminal four papers on theoretical physics in which the theory of relativity was proposed (1905). Darwin's work, in particular, radically unnerved thousands who held a biblical view of humankind's historical story; and to this day the implications of his thinking for biology (and even psychology and sociology) have been profound. He himself became an agnostic and saw no great overall moral or philosophical meaning in the long chronology of our being, which he regarded, rather, as a story of accidents and incidents, of chance and circumstance as they all came to bear on "natural selection." Although Copernicus and Galileo and Newton have been absorbed, so to speak, by traditional Christianity, by no means has Darwin's view of our origin and destiny been universally integrated into the teachings, the theology, of many religions that rely upon the Bible for their inspiration, their sense of who we are, where we came from, how our purpose here ought to be described. It was one thing for scientists to probe the planets, declare that this place we inhabit is only one spot in a seemingly endless number of places in an ever expanding universe, or to examine closely our body's cells, or those of other creatures; it was quite another matter to suggest that we ourselves are merely an aspect of an ever changing nature, that our "origin" was not "divine" but a consequence of a biological saga of sorts.

Meanwhile, in the Vienna of the 1890s, a young neurologist and psychiatrist was examining the mind in the way Darwin had examined the physical side of our being. Freud didn't take our thoughts at face value, any more than Darwin took at face value our present bodily nature. Freud, too, was interested in "evolution," in the way ideas and desires and habits and preferences develop in the course of their own kind of "struggle for life." He dared call upon himself, his dreams, his passing thoughts, the jokes he'd heard, remembered, told others, the turns and twists of his mind's life—and so doing, he assumed that to a degree the universal might be known through the particular with regard to the most private part of ourselves, the emotions we feel by day and, he emphasized, while asleep. Such a line of inquiry, of reasoning, had implications for psychiatry, of course, but as W. H. Auden famously noted in his memorial poem to Freud, psychoanalytic theory became "a whole climate of opinion," and as a consequence secularism gained a new hold on what once had been the prerogative of the sacred. In the Old Testament it is God who knows man, Who sees through him in his manipulative greed, in his puny, ill-fated attempts to pull this or that fast one, circumvent set religious bounds. It is God who punishes, but it is also God who listens, who interprets, who heals, especially in the New Testament, when He became man: Jesus the ever understanding one who has an eye for the troubled in spirit and, invariably, a story that helps explain what is happening, puts things in a larger (human, moral) perspective. Moreover, the institutionalization of Christ's teaching and healing ministry in the form of a Church enabled priests not only to say Mass but to attend parishioners, hear them out, marry them, baptize their children, see them through death, and, more personally, listen to their confessions, week after week.

Now, a physician was telling the world, in the first years of a new century, that he and his colleagues in Vienna, in Budapest, in Berlin knew about what was *really* being conveyed in those confessions—and in many other expressive moments hitherto the psychological domain of the clergy and, by extension, of the Lord. Today, we take for granted "pastoral counseling," but we may not realize what a displacement of sorts psychoanalysis caused when it became, increasingly, the cultural authority with respect to our mental life. A public surrender began to take place almost immediately upon the publication of Freud's first book, a rising acknowledgment that his kind of knowledge commanded not only surprise, attention, but also the respect, grudging in many instances, that goes with a physician's, a scientist's, explanations. The heated denunciations of psychoanalysis and its founder on the part of the clergy were, needless to say, both noteworthy and instructive. It is hard for some of us, at the end of this century, to realize the intensity of clerical opposition visited upon that small band of psychological investigators who lived in Central Europe. In conversations with Anna Freud I heard echoes of the harsh noise she quite clearly remembered to the end of her life: "I was a teenager when my father began to be—'notorious' might be an appropriate word, I fear. [She was born in 1895.] I recall my father talking with my brothers. They were hearing from their friends that he was controversial, that he was saying things that weren't 'right.' It was hard for all of us to know what we should do—I think that word 'right' was being used in a judgmental way, a morally condemning way, rather than as a 'scientific evaluation.' I know my father worried about the Catholic Church— it was a real 'power,' then, in the [Austro-Hungarian] empire, and it was no fun, as some of the children say these days, to incur the displeasure of priests and bishops! And we did [hear or read of that displeasure]—I can remember my father saying out loud some of what was written: they called psychoanalysis 'godless.' He nodded when he read that [allegation]—but he wasn't smiling. He was worried—though he never let his concerns hold him back from giving expression to what he believed: one way or another he got his ideas across, on paper, or in conversations. I do remember him saying this: 'They are right, psychoanalysis *is* 'godless,' it *is* 'godless materialism.'

"You know, it was his job, from the start, to understand how we behave, the reasons for the emotions we experience. He was a scientist, and he was trying to do research in an 'area' that was off-limits, you could say. It was priests who were supposed to deal with psychology, not doctors. Yes, it is true, traditional university psychology didn't stir the alarm and antagonism that came to us [I had suggested as much]. The reason was that we were much 'broader' in our outlook—we weren't studying 'reflexes' in animals or in people; we were talking about the emotions of all people, and about the conscience, and about the secrets people carry in them and inadvertently express, or reveal indirectly. This had always been the territory of religion—the priest had access to the fears and worries of his parishioners; and he was told by them of the mistakes they made, the wrongs they'd done. The priest had his confessional booth, and there my father was, with his consulting room, and his couch—this was an 'infringement,' some people called it, and it was turning 'spirit' into 'flesh,' making the spiritual a matter of mere events in the mind, each of which carried an explanation, if you looked closely and long enough."

A pause, and an unusual physical display of emotion, a vigorous shaking of the head, meant to convey the long past heat of those days, the bitterness of the accusations as they were leveled at a time and in a national and cultural setting altogether different from the one in which she and I (at Yale University in 1972) then found ourselves. But I also realized that the movement of her head was meant to convey to me a glimpse of the naysaying she had just recollected, tried to evoke for me descriptively. She herself promptly realized as much: "I think my father had a high tolerance for anxiety and fear! He was called a lot of names, but somehow he kept his wits about him, and also kept saying and writing what he believed to be true. I suspect that the reason he caused such a storm was that he was a clearheaded writer, whose ideas got across to the general public. If he'd buried them, all his thoughts, in obscure medical journals, far fewer people would have been aroused to anger. But he became a well-known writer, and *there* he was twice a trespasser—daring to step into what priests believed to be their territory, and daring to address some of their parishioners, you could say, [meaning] the men and women who bought books."

Another pause, and then a brief acknowledgment of a kind: "I suppose those who called his work 'godless' were picking up not only what he said, but his own personal beliefs. I think it's only fair to say that if 'we' can respond unconsciously to others, they in turn can do so with us! But I am repeating myself here; I am saying that it was not only what my father said, but how he said it, and where he said it. He could be blunt, and he wanted his ideas to be known outside of the universities. Anyway, he was never welcomed, in those early years, in the universities. Even late in his life, he wasn't welcomed in many of them—I know that well: after the [Second World] War, I received invitations every day, it seemed, to come and receive honorary degrees or medals or scrolls of recognition and gratitude. They were all belatedly meant for him! Finally, his work was being accepted, at least in some quarters—much less so in academic psychology and psychiatry than among people who represented the humanities, interestingly enough, and not at all, still, in some important religious circles. Even now, there is much opposition to psychoanalysis—many want to pick and choose what [of it] they like and feel free to use, as against what they have no intention of accepting, in fact, keep calling a threat to their religious beliefs or their moral principles."

With some trepidation I raised with her the matter of Freud's book *The Future of an Illusion*, a resolutely critical analysis of religious faith; it compares faith to infantile neuroses, wherein children develop fantasies for various reasons, cling to them tenaciously as if they were facts. The tone of the book is uncharacteristically harsh, even scornful, not the way Freud usually addressed readers, and the book lacks the wide range of subject matter he studied and then described for others in his elegantly written essays. Miss Freud, usually quite willing to explore whatever topic I brought up, certainly including her father's many books and articles, was herself uncharacteristically terse and, I thought, toughly dismissive of those who have had reservations about that book. She also pointedly stopped referring to her "father" and instead called him several times "Freud" (prompting me to feel that the full weight of his magisterial career was being summoned): "When Freud decided to deal directly with the question of religion, he knew he was asking for trouble. This is an almost universal matter [religious belief], and it won't yield easily (if at all!) to reason. *That* is what he meant when he spoke of infantile neurosis—he wasn't accusing anyone, so much as acknowledging what had transpired. As you know, to speak of 'infantile neurosis' in connection with anyone is to describe them as a fellow human being!"

Abrupt, flat silence—I am surprised, feel myself arraigned, lose my nerve, abandon this direction of the conversation, and quickly steer us to something far more agreeable to Miss Freud and, by then, to me: her work, at one time, with certain law professors at Yale Law School. Days later, I pick up my copy of *The Future of an Illusion.* I find it marked throughout with my responsive pencil marks, as in this section at the end of chapter 6, when Freud establishes an imaginary dialogue in order to further his point of view:

> Well then, if even obdurate skeptics admit that the assertions of religion cannot be refuted by reason, why should I not believe in them, since they have so much on their side—tradition, the agreement of mankind, and all the consolations they offer? Why not, indeed! Just as no one can be forced to believe, so no one can be forced to disbelieve. But do not let us be satisfied with deceiving ourselves that arguments like these take us along the road of correct thinking. If ever there was a case of a lame excuse we have it here. Ignorance is ignorance; no right to believe anything can be derived from it. In other matters no sensible person will behave so irresponsibly or rest content with such feeble grounds for his opinions and for the line he takes.

I read passages such as that carefully, conclude yet again that their tone is unlike what I have welcomed when in the midst of other books by the same author. I try to put myself (for a second or two, and I hope and pray with due modesty) in Freud's shoes—why such an abrupt dismissal of a subject much more complicated than he is willing to let it be? I think of Saint Augustine and of Kierkegaard and of twentieth-century individuals I've known or whose work I've studied, such as Reinhold Niebuhr, and Dietrich Bonhoeffer, and Dorothy

Day, and I find Freud's version of their interests and convictions inadequate, to say the least. Indeed, I find his approach to religion all too instructive about himself and thoroughly ironic, given the creedal nature of institutional psychoanalysis, the splits and fiercely fought disagreements, and the reverential attitude of certain psychoanalysts toward the founding father, as in Hans Sachs's book, titled *Freud: Master and Friend.* Anna Freud said as much on repeated occasions when speaking at particular psychoanalytic institutes, not quite in the way I just have, but with no wish, either, to hide her sense of things: the rigidity of belief that for a while had seized many in this new, quite prominent and influential occupation. In his epilogue to *Childhood and Society* one of my teachers, Erik H. Erikson, referred to the "talmudic orthodoxy" that he felt had descended on all too many analysts, and the analyst Allen Wheelis addressed the same matter on a number of occasions, and most especially in *The Quest for Identity.*

I bring all this up because Freud's attitude toward religion became itself an article of belief for many in my field and very much gave a particular shape to certain strains of secularism in the twentieth century almost from the start. To call upon Erikson, whose work on both Luther and Gandhi demonstrated that psychoanalytic inquiry needn't take the direction Freud pursued: "When I go back to the 1920s, I realize that those of us in [psychoanalytic] training then were declared agnostics or atheists, or if we had a religious side to us, we kept it out of anyone's hearing. Some of our teachers were already becoming oracular figures, and not just for us [students]. They were quick to point out the opposition to themselves and their ideas on the part of the Catholic Church, or the Lutheran Church in Germany; but they weren't as willing to examine their own way of looking at religious and spiritual matters—this [attitude] from people who claimed to be endlessly engaged in 'self-analysis' as well as the work they did with their analysands. What these leaders [in psychoanalysis] believed, their followers [younger analysts] also believed—and it went much further, because psychoanalysis started having an enormous impact on all sorts of important and well-to-do people, the ones who knew about it, and could afford it, and by that I mean not only that they had the money to pay for daily sessions, but they also had the time, lots of time, that it takes to have such an experience. I can see why many religious people didn't find their way to psychoanalysis at first— its assumptions weren't congenial to them. But in time its assumptions became part of—so much: the intellectual world, the movies and the theater, the world of artists and writers and journalists, and, in America especially, the psychiatric and medical world. In time, that secular world of the Western democracies was very much under the spell of what used to be called 'Freudian thought'—that phrase became an increasingly noticeable mantra!"

Needless to say, Freud's manner of approach to spirituality, to religious commitment was singularly blunt, unqualified, dismissive, and, many would argue, unknowing in its refusal even to examine a complex reflective response to our human situation with a subtlety, a nuance worthy of his own willingness in other instances to demonstrate a tentativeness in keeping with the

59

many-sided nature of what he was trying to understand. When William James examined religion in *The Varieties of Religious Experience*, he was careful to be inquiring, descriptive, rather than the scornful critic for whom psychology has become yet another weapon of confrontation, refutation. Put differently, James wrote in the tradition of European phenomenology, wherein our actions are regarded closely, conveyed to others in a language meant to render them justly, with a full appreciation of any ironies and contradictions observed. Freud, on the other hand, was predominantly analytic in his sensibility, as the name he gave to his profession certainly indicates—moreover, he was, by his own description, a conquistador, meaning a fighter who proposed to win at all costs. In the tradition of self-assured noblesse oblige, James tried constantly to be generous to those with whom he did not necessarily see eye to eye; Freud, in contrast, felt very much at the margins of a world closely connected to powerful religious institutions that saw his work (apart from his explicit writing on the subject of spiritual faith) as threatening, indeed. In 1906 James heard Freud speak in the course of his only American visit, told him that the future was his, a salutation, even an act of reverence, one cannot quite imagine being offered by Freud to another important psychological observer. When Freud was ready to acknowledge his admiration, he used the image of military struggle (in keeping, I suppose, with his notion of himself as one at constant war with various opponents: ignorance, true, but also other individuals who have claimed to know about our lives, our aspirations and concerns). In his essay "Dostoievski and Parricide" he

begins by calling *The Brothers Karamazov* "the most
magnificent novel ever written," declares "the episode
of the Grand Inquisitor one of the peaks in the literature of the world," and then this: "Before the problem
of the creative artist analysis must, alas, lay down its
arms." Were he himself examining such a train of thinking, he might raise an eyebrow, wonder why an enormous achievement, an unparalleled success, need be
turned into a "problem"—one not yet conquered by
weaponry. But his essential realization (that novelists
have, as it were, quietly, unpretentiously been there
even before he and his kind arrived, claiming victory in
the name of science) certainly is borne out in the oeuvre
of Dostoievsky (whose Grand Inquisitor argument, in
its mix of grace and agility and powerful persuasion,
seems to have taught the admiring Freud very little
when he sat down to write *The Future of an Illusion*);
that realization is also supported by the work of several
other nineteenth-century novelists, whose psychological
awareness, and refinement of perception, and whose
way of giving expression to the range of our human inwardness makes so very much of contemporary social
science research and writing pale badly in comparison.

In fact, George Eliot, all through *Middlemarch*
(1872), more than anticipates Freud: she relentlessly
examines the unconscious, uses several of her characters
to do so, and, too, clearly indicates an acute sense of
what Freud only later in his richly productive career
knew to call "ego psychology": the way we come to
terms with the unconscious through various mental ma-
neuvers. Moreover, she did not isolate psychology from
sociology or, for that matter, politics. The central figure

in the novel is, really, the town itself, its stubbornly held customs, values, but also the changes that gradually come to bear on it. The various characters in this carefully plotted story, so richly endowed with social and psychological wisdom, are meant to embody the full range of a particular, historical moment and scene—the rural England of the earlier part of the nineteenth century. But, naturally, Eliot wants us to move beyond that world, however fine and telling her evocation of it; she is in pursuit of moral knowledge of a kind that, she hopes, transcends the limits of time and place.

The author of *Scenes of a Clerical Life* summoned occasional, guarded irony for her social descriptions in that respectful group portrait of ministers and their parishioners; but *Middlemarch* is a secular story, and its church life, such as it is, offers a mere nod to ceremonial commemoration. True, at certain moments Eliot tips her hand as the onetime earnest student of religious philosophy, who actually intended, as a young woman, to write an ecclesiastical history of England. She brings us to a church; she gives us a clergyman—but through him we learn of the fast slipping hold of religious conviction on these essentially secular folk, each earnestly or warily or cleverly or mischievously trying to make do, if not make off with any and all good fortune available. At times, actually, she is more scornful, as a social critic, than Freud would dare be: a striking departure for this daughter of Robert Evans, a loyal member of the Anglican Church and the manager of a country estate, whom she, in her last, autobiographical writing, described as a country parson. Here in book 4 of *Middlemarch* is biblical life under a psychological lens that is sardonically secular: "When the animals entered the Ark in pairs, one may imagine that allied species made much private remark on one another, and were tempted to think that so many forms feeding on the same store of fodder were eminently superfluous, as tending to diminish the rations (I fear the part played by the vultures on that occasion would be too painful for art to represent, those birds being disadvantageously naked about the gullet, and apparently without rites and ceremonies)."

As if the above were not enough, the authorial voice escalates its scorn, makes a damaging connection between the far-distant past and the nineteenth-century English country scene being evoked: "The same sort of temptation befell the Christian Carnivora who formed Peter Featherstone's funeral procession; most of them having their minds bent on a limited store which each would have liked to get the most of." She quite obviously need not have used that capitalized phrase to accomplish her comparative assertion. When Dorothea, rather than the novelist directly, is speaking, we learn more gently, even wistfully, of a falling away from religion on the part of a central character in the story, an ardent idealist who first marries a biblical scholar, as a matter of fact, the older, desiccated Casaubon. At one point Dorothea tells Will Ladislaw, "I have always been finding out my religion since I was a little girl"; but she is quick to point out what has now transpired: "I used to pray so much—now I hardly ever pray."

Dorothea is not George Eliot, but neither is she unlike her in important respects—a strong intellectuality, an articulate reformist spirit, a shrewd sense of others (which does not necessarily translate into a firm grasp of one's own inner nature). Young Mary Ann Evans was a devoutly introspective Christian lady who read far and deep in not only the Bible but any number of theological sources. It took her several decades of secular London living to shed that background, and in a sense her novel *Middlemarch* tells of that transformation: a personal one that mirrored the emerging secularism of certain sophisticated precincts of nineteenth-century London. In those paragraphs above, psychological skepticism becomes an instrument of probing social analysis, which is, in turn, trumped by a contemptuously bitter designation ("Christian Carnivora") that arguably gives a clue to a writer's temporary lack of personal control. She has already more than made her point and will have plenty of opportunity to continue to develop the notion of greed as the triumphant survivor of death, and, too, of such covetousness as is ironically and routinely wrapped in the clothes of Christian worship. Yet she has to summon a biological word, "Carnivora," to seal the matter in the reader's mind—as if she has lost confidence in her own narrative ability to encompass the state of affairs at hand: the joining of public sorrow, traditionally expressed in a church, and private cupidity, not rare even in brilliant, well-educated agnostics, who surely have their particular rituals and protocols and observances to endure, while they harbor their own lustfully acquisitive daydreams, fancies.

Freud's "analysis" of the psychological sources of religious faith would strike his friendly critics as a natural outcome of a combatively argumentative, agnostic essayist's desire to strike yet another blow for Intellect or Reason over what he regarded as the murkier recesses of

our irrational life, where what we want is so often confused with what is or ought to be. George Eliot's portrayal of the mind (as opposed to her occasional social
outbursts) is as layered, textured as Freud's psychological writing at its best; she is not propounding ideology
but, rather, telling a story that allows her leeway to discuss the biggest of topics through the indirection of
human relatedness as it can be rendered in all its ambi-
guities and inconsistencies and outright contradictions
through the construction of characters and a plot in
which their thoughts and actions unfold. Even as Eliot
looked back in *Middlemarch* to the Age of Reform, the
earlier decades of the nineteenth century, when suffrage
gradually became available to more and more individuals in both rural and urban England, she also was
looking ahead to the consequences of the political and
cultural changes she was bringing to life in this most ambitious of her novels. In a sense, she is taking the measure of a world becoming more conclusively secular—
where once great and constant consideration was given
to the "image of God," now the mind of man commanded the major attention of people who may have
attended church regularly, but who looked less upward
toward the heavens than directly in a nearby mirror.

In the phrase "unreflecting egoism" Eliot captures the
breadth and depth of such secular preoccupation. She
was, of course, decades ahead of Freud, in her acknowledgment, that way, of the unconscious, its raw power
constantly assertive, no matter our notion of ourselves
as in (conscious) control of what we say or do. Her por-
traits in *Middlemarch* are unsparing in their insistence
that appearances, even those that are connected to

church attendance or high-minded acts of social generosity, don't tell the whole story of individuals or of
groups of men and women. Faith is the continual subject of her close scrutiny: the sometimes insincere faith
in God of those ministers who claim to act in His name,
but also the faltering faith of ordinary people; and too,
other kinds of faith, such as that we place in certain
professions (medicine) or institutions (the universities).
Interestingly, she reserves for a businessman, a banker,
Bulstrode, the most strenuous and affecting of spiritual
struggles. As for her physician, Dr. Lydgate, he soon
enough loses his high ideals to the demands of an all too
shallow, self-regarding wife—and does so without so
much as a moral blink. He simply settles down, accom-
modates himself to a particular marriage: "He had
gained an excellent practice, alternating, according to
the season, between London and a Continental bath-
ing-place, having written a thesis on Gout, a disease
which has a great deal of wealth on its side." Eliot portrays such an outcome, such an obvious moral decline,
not as a tragedy and, surely, not as a sin (a shortcoming
that is spiritual in nature), but as the mere manifes-
tation of a powerfully determining psychology that decisively shapes the outcome of lives. At one point she
circles around the ever present riddle of will, its relationship to social fate: "It always remains true that if we
had been greater, circumstances would have been less
strong against us." At another point, less speculative or
philosophical, she settles for a humdrum marital scene
all too worthy of the television talk shows, the self-help
books, which a century later would give us not quite the

level of access to the life of our Dr. Lydgates and our Rosamonds (his wife) that this analysis does: "Between him and her indeed there was that total missing of each other's mental track, which is too evidently possible even between persons who are continually thinking of each other."

Such a comment is not handed down in an oracular manner (as is sometimes the case in this novel more than any of her others) but is, rather, immersed in a rather casual yet careful and precise description of the way a particular couple gets along. What matters in life, we are persuaded, what gives it direction and character, has to do with how we get along with one another: one person's interests and dispositions as they connect with another person's. Our young physician is not a "good" person come to naught by virtue of a "bad" marriage; nor is the woman he chooses to marry the bearer of evil, someone who corrupts a person otherwise intended for idealism (in the mind of the author, the reader). We have, here, gone (as the saying would have us think) "beyond good and evil," be it in the biblical sense or in the somewhat alternative sense of human reflection with respect to right and wrong (theology, moral philosophy). Now it is the accidents of our various encounters and, thereafter, the implications of "interpersonal psychology" that in their sum have the final say on who and what we become.

By the same token, Dorothea Brooke and her husband Casaubon turn out to be an ironic prelude (despite all their high-and-mighty ideas, aims) to today's thoroughly commonplace "dysfunctional" marriages.

Eliot is devastating in her controlled satire as she develops that "relationship," as we know to call it. She causes us, initially, to be much taken with Dorothea, who in certain respects seems no less than an authorial stand-in; yet gradually we begin to see that a very bright and deep-thinking and far-reaching mind can also be a dim-witted one emotionally, maybe even morally. If Casaubon is meant to represent a sterile, a badly compromised and weakened religious and theological tradition, Dorothea's choice of him (her capacity to build him up, for a while, in her mind as someone he isn't) is surely intended to remind us that visions are constructed not only in the name of God but out of our ordinary human frailty. And no amount of education or intellectual brilliance will banish that frailty, hence psychology as the great leveling presence among us all.

In the first pages of *Middlemarch* Eliot shrewdly plays on the moral, if not spiritual, yearnings of her readers, not to mention of her own life as a keenly reformist observer of nineteenth-century Victorian society. We take to Dorothea immediately and compare her, with knowing favor, to her sister Celia, who seems a conventional person of no great thought, of no subtle feeling. Yet, gradually, Celia's common sense and unselfconscious decency, her seemingly "simple" life such a contrast to the pain and strain of Dorothea's introspection, begin to win us over, even as Dorothea emerges as someone too clever by half, as far less discerning in things that really count (how you live your life, with whom)—as opposed to the matters that her advanced intellect is always pondering. Eliot is comparing the old-fashioned natural piety of an earlier time (Celia) with a new kind of cultural and psychological awareness, proudly distanced from the traditional supports of church and social status. Whereas Celia will soon enough be integrated into a life as a wife, a mother, a well-to-do member of a country scene, a churchgoer, Dorothea wants to change the world and looks askance at many of its claims; hence her constantly skeptical mind that, her creator lets us know, can turn unwittingly arrogant. That is the nub of the difference, we begin to realize, between these two sisters: the ready acceptance of the past, as it has handed down its requirements, on the part of Celia, as against Dorothea's quick suspicion of so very much in that past. The latter becomes in many respects a modern person, very much on her own, sometimes to the benefit of certain people (when her intensely charitable nature seeks expression), but sometimes to her own detriment, not to mention that of others (when she swallows whole all kinds of untested new ideas, or treats those she regards as "slow" or "selfish" or hopelessly tied to the customary, the ordinary, in an instructively patronizing or dismissive fashion).

It is, finally, the customary, and the ordinary, even the lowly, who emerge from this novel with our highest regard—perhaps because they receive less attention than their "betters," and because the author has reluctantly come to realize that while her more privileged characters go about their willful and sometimes mistaken ways, these "rustics," such as Timothy Cooper, comparatively minor figures in a novel's large scheme of things, maintain their solid hold on the world's daily rhythms, enabled in their exertions not by fancy theories or highly touted new proposals but "through a hard process of feeling" that is, in turn, the result of dawn-to-dusk labor, year in and year out. "Timothy was a wiry old labourer," we are told, and he mouths a kind of refractory and earthy populism that won't yield to what is being offered in the name of secular "enlightenment," "progress," "reform." We learn through his brief appearance how easy it is to overlook people like him, or to assume the right to speak for him, or to mistake the nature of his moral bearings. He seems to resist not only the idea of progress but its specifics, such as the railroad. In fact, however, he takes the shrewd measure of what others too quickly find congenial, welcome. Whereas those with new secular ideas, in the name of politics or economics or out of "a neatly carved argument for a social benefit," urge one or another departure from what was in favor of a quite different destination, a Timothy Cooper can make quite clear his practical or moral reservations. We learn, in *Middlemarch*, how little notice, never mind admiration, he and those like him are getting, amidst the acceleration of industrial and ideological change in nineteenth-century capitalist England, even its rural precincts. Nor is the issue only one of class. Eliot is at pains to remind us that the well-to-do can join with the humble in a shrewd hesitation to embrace certain new customs and beliefs, even as both the poor and the rich can come together in an effort to break with the past, accept with satisfaction—indeed, pride—what is unprecedented, yet so promising, inviting.

Throughout the novel the old Judeo-Christian notion of "pride" as a grave instance of moral failure struggles with a new notion of pride as a necessary affirmation of one's human inclination to build, to make the
world anew. Again, with irony, the most old-fashioned
and intense, even Augustinian, self-scrutiny, is granted
to Bulstrode, a character whom another author (Dickens, perhaps) might have been tempted to caricature—
and Eliot herself may have been initially so inclined.
Certainly he is not an attractive figure at any point in
the story, and Eliot moves cautiously to unnerve us
through her presentation of his moral struggle. In the
beginning he is yet another ambitious social upstart
on the make: he gets called, for instance, "suave." We
are happily immersed in Dr. Lydgate's moral crisis, in
that of Dorothea; yet the very idea of Bulstrode's having
such a conflict seems well beyond him and, as well, his
creator, whose personal life seemed to prepare her well
for the making of characters whose evident secular
"goodness" has to be tested in various ways. In Bulstrode, however, she shows herself prepared to take a
second and more charitable (maybe "thoughtful" is
the required descriptive word here) look at the nature of
religious introspection: a smooth, canny, manipulative
banker, with a past he wants hidden, turns out to be,
however fleetingly, a sinner sweating out not only his
secular fears but his moral jeopardy. By no means,
though, does he ever become a spiritually redeemed
person. He wants the dissolute Raffles out of the way
lest he reveal what he knows, plenty damaging to a
banker who has tried hard and with considerable success to achieve not only the power that accompanies the

control of money, but a more elusive yet quite satisfying respectability: the neighborly nods of approval that count a lot during a day spent out in the world.

This episode allows Eliot to cut deep to the bone of a society fast changing from a mostly village one, bound together by values rooted in agricultural life, and by an unquestioned ecclesiastical authority—wielded constantly as an aspect of everyday existence, from baptisms to marriages to deathbed prayers and funerals—to a commercial world in which individuals rather than institutions have the predominant say: the entrepreneur, the man of business (or intellectual) agility now beholden to his own judgment, his own notions of what is desirable, possible, permissible. In the midst of such shifts not only in commerce but in sensibility, in the moral life of towns and cities, in a nation's social and cultural assumptions, all sorts of individuals struggle to consolidate their reputations, or fail quite evidently to do so. Eliot brings Dr. Lydgate in touch with Bulstrode, the doctor who is beholden to the banker, and further connects them through the potentially troublesome drunkard Raffles, whom Lydgate attends during what proves to be his final hours. Bulstrode, of course, hopes that Raffles won't pull through—that his physician won't work strenuously to pull him through. Meanwhile, awaiting the medical outcome, he goes through a spiritual crisis that evokes this characterization: "Strange, piteous conflict in the soul of this unhappy man, who had longed for years to be better than he was—who had taken his selfish passions into discipline and clad them in severe robes, so that he had walked with them as a devout squire, till now that a terror had risen among them, and they could chant no longer but throw out their common cover for safety." Such anguish naturally brings the reader closer to this man whose darker side is not heinous, and not different in kind, surely, from that of many people of substance, but whose efforts at self-improvement (not in the contemporary, superficial sense of that phrase) attest to a moral scrupulosity of some considerable strength. It is noteworthy that Eliot does not investigate Dr. Lydgate's inner life with the kind of energy she devotes to Bulstrode's—when she might well have done so: the former is taking care of the unconscious Raffles, even as he very much needs a loan from Bulstrode, and in his capacity as Raffles's attending physician gets that loan, hitherto denied him. The moral burden is placed squarely on Bulstrode's shoulders, and his response to it is constant supplication of the Lord. He prays and prays; he confronts his not so secret wishes (that Raffles die) but also is aware of the utterly self-serving nature of such a desire. He is caught, that is, between a craven opportunism and a distraught realization of precisely that. He hopes that fate (maybe boosted by a doctor's inclination not to go the last mile for someone not especially important, indeed, down-and-out) will solve this threatening crisis of exposure. Yet he holds to the earnest conviction that he dare not intervene, try to hurt the sick and vulnerable Raffles, and not only for fear of potential harm to himself but, as Eliot suggests, out of a long-standing attempt on his part "to be better than he was."

It is of no small significance that George Eliot uses words such as "soul" and "spiritual" and "prayers" in connection with Bulstrode, but not Dorothea Brooke or Dr. Lydgate or Will Ladislaw or Casaubon, other important figures in this wide-ranging chronicle, meant to be, as Henry James put it, "philosophic" in nature as well as alert to the social manners of a segment of English life. In one sentence, meant to convey a practical man-of-the-world nevertheless struggling hard with the demands of his conscience as well as his "native imperviousness," his canny wish to get successfully through yet another worldly challenge, we are told of his mind's alarm and fearfulness (as he wonders about the medical fate of a man who can hurt him) in a way reminiscent of Milton's religiously awake verse—as opposed to the shrewd, essentially secular (psychological and sociological) kind of analysis that, as a matter of fact, made the novel so appealing to the "advanced" cadre of the London intelligentsia: "Whatever prayers he might lift up, whatever statements he might inwardly make of this man's spiritual condition, and the duty he himself was under to submit to the punishment divinely appointed for him rather than to wish for evil to another—through all this effort to condense words into a solid mental state, there pierced and spread with irresistible vividness the images of the events he desired."

Why, then, is Bulstrode's essentially personal (and psychological) conflict, not unlike the many others so knowingly (in our sense of things) rendered in this novel, presented with such explicit resort to matters of the soul as well as the mind? No question, for Eliot characters such as Dorothea Brooke and Dr. Lydgate and even Casaubon are different from Bulstrode: they belong in the company of thinking people, individuals who have ideas of their own, who are not beholden to a biblical literalism once so influential. Actually, these are men and women who have no real attachment to church life; yes, they are capable of *considering* religious or even theological issues, but their daily life is essentially secular in nature. They represent the professions, the academy, the politically or socially engaged: people of "thought," of "training," for whom the past's spiritual anguish is absent; it has yielded to the intellectual and moral anguish of a secular society. In contrast, Bulstrode is of a "lower order": he is a mere businessman, an uneducated man who has been on the make, perhaps in his common life one of Eliot's "Christian Carnivora," but maybe not—they seem "higher" in social status, less connected, really, to the daily hurdle of keeping afloat (and then some) that ordinary working people must keep confronting. While Bulstrode is hardly an Isaiah, or a passionate Christian pilgrim, his moral anguish takes on a spiritual quality, and his very vulnerability, his lack of self-assurance, his social marginality, his intense fearfulness and sense of jeopardy, hearken back, as no other scene in *Middlemarch* does, to a long religious history of sinners in turmoil (not to be confused with wrongdoers in felt danger of exposure, condemnation, punishment).

In a sense, then, Bulstrode's crisis of the soul, remarkable for its singularity, enables Eliot to bid an old tradition of earnest theological introspection farewell, to give us, by implication, a forecast of the future: countless Middlemarches in which church attendance has become a social convenience or a mere duty or even a business maneuver, and in which psychology and social circumstance mean much—mean everything. She was, of course, not a theorist; in fact, she parodies theorists, mocks her own inclination to be one in her treatment of both Casaubon and Dorothea Brooke. Yet she understood the mind in precisely the way Freud did: we are told, in authorial asides, of "repressed desire," of "identity," of "unreflecting egoism," of "invisible thoroughfares which are the first lurking-places of anguish, mania, and crime." In the novel she wants to portray influential secular determinisms at work, those within us and those that come at us from the outside. With respect to the latter, every shading of class is attended, and all possible occupations, institutions brought in to the narrative. So are words such as "alienation," which (like the "unconscious") we of the late twentieth century have assumed as our very own, whereas they make themselves quite at home in this chronicle not of an immediate, late-nineteenth-century yesteryear but the by now dim past that preceded by many decades the emergence of writers such as Freud or Max Weber, not to mention George Eliot.

In the same decade, the 1870s, that gave us *Middlemarch*, another demanding novel of no mean prophetic capability appeared, George Meredith's *The Egoist* (1879), a devastatingly satirical analysis of privileged self-centeredness, and an effort, surely, to describe what was happening in England amidst its obvious economic and national successes: a boundless assertion of manipulative vanity on the part of some who had come to think of themselves as the very center of the universe—in a sense, the ultimate challenge to, defiance of, the Judeo-Christian spiritual ethic, for which such an attitude is but one more aspect of our sinful pride. Meredith was much influenced by evolutionary theory. In poem after poem Meredith emphasized our capacity to spring free of our limitations, to emerge gradually from one state of being to another. Not that such a collective fate is fore-ordained. He had read Darwin, had drawn the proper lesson, the lesson, actually, that novelists such as George Eliot and he had always known: that chance and circumstance, in all their complexity and unpredictability, determine so very much, no matter our conviction of a decisive capacity to make a difference in this life. Still, we can weigh in, exert ourselves—indeed, that is our biological and psychological and moral mandate: "Our life is but a little holding, lent / To do a mighty labour: we are one / With heaven and the stars when it is spent / To serve God's aim: else die we with the sun."

For Meredith such lyrical moments ("Vittoria," 1866) were intended to stress our potential membership in a broader community: our fellow human beings, to whom we give what we have—and so doing, achieve a kind of immortality quite unlike that evoked in churches and monasteries and cathedrals. In *The Thrush in February* (1885) he makes that point yet again; and just before he died he called the following his favorite passage of all the verse he wrote:

> Full lasting is the song, though he,
> The singer, passes: lasting, too,
> For souls not lent is usury,
> The rapture of the forward view.

Such a destiny is not exactly what the church fathers of early Christianity had in mind for us, nor their

descendants in the Catholic Church, nor those reformist pastors, theologians, kings and princes and dukes
who in their various ways gave the world the Protestant
churches. Meredith's God was an abstract one—a notion, really, of nature become Nature, and a faith, really, in an evolving human awareness, in intellectual
and moral exertion as God. In *The Question of Whither*
(whose philosophical title alerts the reader to the serious
discussion ahead) he makes this observation:

> Enough if we have winked to sun,
> Have sped the plough a season;
> There is a soul for labour done,
> Endureth fixed as reason.
>
> Then let our trust be firm in Good,
> Though we be of the fasting,
> Our questions are a mortal brood,
> Our work is everlasting.

Here is the Lord become Good; and that transformation is constantly taking place, enabled by those who do
honorable, decent work: their toil, of mind and body, a
consecration of sorts, rendered to the overall story of
humankind, which is our evolving Good, which is God.
In such an evolution, knowledge becomes Knowledge,
science is regarded as Science, and, inevitably, the sacred becomes the secular:

> Now when the ark of human fate,
> Long baffled by the wayward wind,
> Is drifting with its peopled freight,
> Safe haven on the heights to find;

Safe haven from the drawing slime
Of evil deeds and deluge wrath;
To plant again the foot of Time
Upon a purer, firmer path;

'Tis now the hour to probe the ground,
To watch the Heavens, to speak the word,
The fathoms of the deep to sound,
And send abroad the missioned bird.

On strengthened wings for evermore
Let science swiftly as she can,
Fly seaward on from shore to shore,
And bind the links of man to man.

There, in a piece of work titled "The Olive Branch" (a part of Meredith's first book, published in 1851), a young poet makes clear his conviction that somehow, through our own energies as they get usefully, thoughtfully deployed, we can soar, arrive Homeward, the Heaven of our planet become a Good Place. But a quarter of a century later, though he had not at all surrendered such a hope, Meredith was deeply troubled about possible (indeed, likely and all too evident) obstacles in such an imagined trajectory. He had taken a fuller, a more circumspect look at this human creature whose striving for knowledge he had chosen to praise, and concluded that there were other strivings at work in us, even in those who do, for sure, make this or that contribution to the world's growing body of discovered factuality. No doubt, too, he had looked around at the particular world he inhabited, one of relative comfort and accomplishment in (at the time) the richest and most powerful of nations—and seen plenty to give him concern: the craven and mean side of those who have no social or economic excuse for the way they elbow others, still, nor moral justification for the way they use their well-educated minds in the pursuit of their own purposes solely.

To take notice of such ambiguity in one's neighbors and friends and fellow citizens, and, not least, in oneself, is to risk the temptation of skepticism, first, then cynicism, then gloom. But Meredith (unlike Thomas Hardy, whose outlook in ways resembled his) was not prone to melancholy. He held steadfast, in his poetry, to a hopefulness about our prospects on this planet. He kept insisting upon our visionary side; and he never forgot how hard some people will work, how much of themselves they are willing to give, in factories and on farms as well as in libraries or laboratories. It was as if he, the versifier, owed us that realization: it was his responsibility to sing of our possibilities, our constant and heavy labor, often against substantial odds—to exult in us become exalted by virtue of our deeds.

But this poet also wrote novels and was known for his storytelling by many who had little or no acquaintance with his poems. In *The Egoist*, the most demanding and important of his fictional efforts, he didn't forsake altogether his optimism; he gave his readers a comedy—a contrast with Hardy's *Jude the Obscure*, wherein a poet's grave doubts about our future, about our capacity to manage our affairs sensibly and justly, became the energizing force in his expository writing. Meredith had no such grim intention when he constructed Sir Willoughby, who (in contrast to the humble, earnest, decent, idealistic Jude Fawley) is a rich nobleman, highly educated, quite charming, spirited and engaging, and by no means dumb either intellectually or socially (as are some others he encounters who belong to the same background he claims). Meredith is at pains not to let Willoughby have more authority than seems appropriate for a novelist who wants to mock a psychological inclination rather than explore it sympathetically. Still, the mere narration, at length, of a character's self-centeredness risks eliciting its own kind of tolerant understanding, if not pity, in the reader, even if Meredith has no affection at all for Willoughby, and the novel that tells of him has a title not meant to be laudatory, or even neutral in its significance. In a critical chapter (39), called "In the Heart of the Egoist," the philosophically mature poet tips his hand: "We are on board the labouring vessel of humanity in a storm, when cries and countercries ring out, disorderliness mixes the crew, and the fury of self-preservation divides: this one is for the ship, that one for his life." Of course Willoughby's notion of "self-preservation" is his very own: an egoist's requirement that anything and anyone in the proverbial way bend or bow out or be done with. Others are seen as desirable instruments of one's affirmation or as troubling presences precisely because they fail to defer, to placate, to oblige. "Consider him indulgently," the narrator asks of us, and then this: "The Egoist is the Son of Himself. He is likewise the Father."

This is unsettling language—it is not unlike that used in Christian theology—and Meredith has used capital letters for both Son and Father. He doesn't, though, pursue that angle of inquiry or comparison; if he had,

he'd have no doubt wanted to shift the implied meaning of the word "Egoist," to strip it of its pejorative implications, so that he could then, as the theologian Karl
Barth did half a century later, speculate on God's psychology—the utter aloneness of Him and His Son, and,
so, the Egoism that inevitably develops in Them: an
existential Egoism, or, maybe better, a transcendental
Egoism. But Meredith was not trying to leap into
Heaven knowingly, provocatively. Indeed, for him,
Heaven is right here on earth, hence the high stakes of
our behavior with one another. For God and His (only
begotten) Son to be Egoists is a matter of theological
phenomenology; for Willoughby or the rest of us to slip
that far into ourselves is a thoroughgoing slide backwards, a moral reversion: "The Egoist is our fountain-
head, primeval man: the primitive is born again, the ele-
mental reconstituted. Born again into new conditions,
the primitive may be highly polished of men, and for-
feit nothing save the roughness of his original nature."

Meredith makes no attempt to spare Willoughby a
good deal of highly critical regard and even flirts with
the word "degenerate" as a descriptive term, lest we the
readers miss the essential point of this book, a biogra-
phy of an imagined sensualist trapped irrevocably in his
own self-regard: ". . . he has entered the upper sphere,
or circle of spiritual Egoism: he has become the civilized
Egoist; primitive still, as sure as man has teeth; but developed in his manner of using them."

For the most part, in this novel, we are spared such
sweeping broadsides. The juxtaposition of "spiritual"
and "Egoism" may be confusing; the point is to stress

the rarefied or highfalutin nature of such self-preoccupation, a matter of class—though the creator of Willoughby, no doubt, might have observed the occasional
minister or teacher or doctor who would qualify as Willoughby's identical twin psychologically. We are being
reminded constantly in this novel that all the social and
cultural refinement in the world is quite compatible
with what in the Bible gets called "pride," with its
connotation of the sinful, the smug, the self-absorbed.
Meredith lacks the desire, though, to make his central
figure in any way tragic; rather, he seems to be indicating, the heart of the matter is precisely that: insofar as
one is an Egoist, one lacks the qualities that can make
for a person in some manner impressive or worthy of
serious attention, however flawed. This is a novel of
deadly superficiality, a story meant to make the serious-
minded reader (and, especially, the reader who knows of
Meredith's morally energetic poetry) shudder with apprehension, lest he or she be in the least jeopardy of
Willoughby's fate.

In 1978, at a meeting of the William Alanson White
Psychoanalytic Institute in New York City, I described
an experience I had had as a medical student at the Co-
lumbia-Presbyterian Medical Center in New York City.
I was asked to draw blood from an elderly woman
named Karen Horney who was dying of cancer. I knew
that she was a psychoanalyst, that she had authored several books which had been widely read—and that she
had little time left. I can still remember her quiet stoi-
cism as we made our rounds, trailing after the great (and
sometimes intimidating) Robert F. Loeb, the Bard

Professor of Medicine at Columbia's College of Physicians and Surgeons, and I can still remember Dr. Loeb's glancing at what she was reading, a book perched on her bedside table, George Meredith's *The Egoist*. He said nothing when he first noticed the book, and I said nothing a couple of days later when I met the same reserved but gracious lady at seven o'clock in the morning, my tourniquet in hand, and with it a tray containing syringes, test tubes, labels. Unlike some patients, Dr. Horney never flinched or murmured as I did my work; and when it was over, she thanked me, a rare event in such a line of work. She asked me a question or two about myself—where I came from, where I'd gone to college, what I'd had for a major—and when I told her I'd studied English literature, she asked me if I'd read Meredith's *The Egoist*, for which she then reached. Yes, I had; but I remembered, even then, only a few years afterwards, very little of what I'd read. She smiled, said she could understand why so little had stayed with me. I told her that, in contrast, I remembered some of Meredith's poems, and I attributed that recall to the virtues of a particular professor, Hyder Rollins, whose course on Victorian poetry I'd taken. Again she smiled graciously, nodded her head, but added a brief comment I've never forgotten: "I don't think Meredith would *want* you to remember this novel"—whereupon, I can also still remember myself thinking: for heaven's sake, then, why is she reading it, and of all times, now!

Dr. Horney seemed to know what was crossing my mind; at that time in my life I didn't realize how often individuals doing her kind of work invited the unspoken thoughts of those with whom they conversed. She spoke as if I'd actually said what I'd thought, as if she, too, had said as much to herself: "A patient of mine, a woman, kept mentioning this novel; she said it described her former husband 'to a tee.' I kept telling her I'd read the novel—I wanted to, but I never had the time. Now I do!"

I recall feeling sad then; I figured that she was nearer to death than she might want to believe, that she didn't actually have as much time as she assumed was hers. But she caught me up, yet again: she told me with no evident anxiety or fear or trembling that she might just make it through *The Egoist*, and maybe one other novel. She added that she was glad that she had the good sense to be reading fiction, not psychoanalytic journals or textbooks—and then these words, still strong in their impact, meaning, as I summon them, in their substance, from the distance of over four decades: "In this novel we are told about someone who is completely alone in the midst of all the company he keeps. That is what happens when you are an Egoist—you are deaf to anyone's avowal of love, and you have no voice of conscience addressing you. So, there is only silence."

Later that day I sat in my dormitory room in Bard Hall, looked at the Hudson River, kept hearing her in my mind say what she'd spoken earlier in that room, and wrote what I'd remembered in a letter to my brother Bill, who was then a graduate student in English literature, specializing in nineteenth-century poets, such as George Meredith. That way, and in subsequent conversations with him (he is a professor of

English now) I kept in my mind the brief encounter, so touching, even haunting, with someone whom I would later know as an important person in what became my own profession. No question, Meredith's Willoughby is beyond the heard call of others, hence his rock-bottom aloneness. Very important, he has no real conscience, as Dr. Horney was shrewd to emphasize: conscience as the voices of others who live inside us, their pleas and misgivings and worries and injunctions and admonitions all become ours to attend, to heed. In the absence of those voices, in the presence of a tenacious will geared to appetites cultivated amidst a rich life, the prepossessing Willoughby enacts his constantly insistent, exaggerated amour propre. He goes through the motions of engagement with others. He seems to struggle for the love of others, and he is a conventional person, to all appearances, not inimical to church and state, willing to defer to established customs, rules, laws. But he is the opposite of his creator's ideal—Meredith had high moral aspirations for himself and his readers: that each of us work hard on behalf of one another, that we be members of a community (village, borough, nation), an affiliation of mind and heart. These enlightened ones he celebrated: "They see how spirit comes to light, / Through conquest of the inner beast, / Which measure tames to movement same, / In harmony with what is fair. / Never is earth misread by brain: / That is the willing of her, there / The mirror: with one step beyond, / For likewise is it voice."

The title of that poem is "Hard Weather," and the poet has no doubt that it is difficult to put aside one's self, more than occasionally, in favor of a commitment to others. In *The Egoist*, he shows just how tempting that "suck of self" (a phrase coined by the novelist Walker Percy) can be, and not only for Willoughby. To make *The Egoist* a comedy is to stress the offhand, the unsurprising: the commonplace temptations rather than the singular disaster of a tragedy. A writer who is a moralist pulls his punches, lets the "inner beast" strut and swagger and seek its prey—in the hope that we readers will sweat gratefully as we take our measure of what distance separates us from Willoughby and his ilk. In a sense, I would only much later realize, Dr. Horney was getting her own distance from the "egoism" with which she constantly had to contend as a psychoanalyst. There, in the hospital, she could glimpse, at a remove, "the neurotic personality of our time," as she had described the psychological exiles and fugitives who by wrapping themselves in a host of "defenses" and "symptoms" had become substantially severed from participation in Meredith's "Earth," by which he meant Nature at its most productive: people joined in a harmony of embraced interdependence. Her patients came to her, so often, as Willoughbys, and she (like Meredith) had to take their measure but also do her best to help them out of their solipsistic ways, their belief not in God or even their fellow human beings but themselves only. Dr. Horney's phrase "our time" was meant to link the private conflicts of individuals ("the neurotic personality") with larger social and cultural developments—a linkage both Meredith and George Eliot fully appreciated, hence the "unreflecting egoism" of *Middlemarch* and the title and full text, as it were, of Meredith's novel: the Willoughbys whom a secular society (no longer beholden to the sacred) more than tolerates, encourages, as in the historian Christopher Lasch's phrase "the culture of narcissism."

Well before Dr. Horney and Professor Lasch worried publicly about the "egoism" Eliot wryly observed, Meredith sardonically evoked, the nineteenth-century poet and novelist Thomas Hardy registered a prophetic and tough and sometimes melancholy analysis of what he took the trouble to examine closely: the decline of religious conviction, spiritual faith, their replacement by a rationalism, a secular devotion to the factual, the provable, the self as our only sovereign—but at a considerable cost. In *Jude the Obscure*, his last novel (1895) he gives us a decent, aspiring country lad who gets smitten by the educational muse and takes himself to Christminster, a thinly disguised Oxford. There Jude is soon enough brought up short, disillusioned. Before he left on his pilgrimage (education as a way to God's grace), he had to "smother high thinking under immediate needs"—he and the vast majority of the world's people, still. But once he has come within the sight of this great university, where all that "high thinking" goes on, he is soon enough disappointed: "Only a wall divided him from those happy young contemporaries of his [the students] with whom he shared a common mental life: men who had nothing to do from morning to night, but to read, work, learn, and inwardly digest. Only a wall—but what a wall!"

To be sure, Hardy is remarking on class, on the way privilege separates those who have it from others, even in a university, ostensibly a place devoted to the intellect's work. But gradually the reader's sympathy for a yearning Jude (so very determined to make much of himself as a student) acquires a companion attitude, scorn for those who will have no part of the world's Judes: "He was a young workman in a white blouse, and with stone dust in the creases of his clothes and in passing him they did not even see him, or hear him, rather saw through him as through a plane of glass at their familiars beyond." Here the divide of class becomes something psychological rather than sociological: the narrator asks us to shift our attention from the unnoticed to the unobservant, from the invisible by virtue of social rank to the blind by virtue of a kind of sinfulness, which he persists in exploring. While we are told that Jude "was rather on an intellectual track than a theological [one]," we soon begin to realize that the two are not so readily distinguished, separated. Jude sees about him all sorts of reminders of Christianity—in stories, and, of course, in the form of churches, chapels. He is visiting with his own religious past and with that of his countrymen as he waits to hear whether he will be accepted for a course of study at this old university whose own past, also, is intimately connected to the history of the Christian Church in England.

Soon enough he has his much anticipated news, sent to "Mr. J. Fawley, Stone Cutter" (Hardy himself had been an artisan, a stonecutter, an architect's assistant, in his youth). He is told that he ought to remain in his "own sphere," stick to his "trade" rather than adopt "any other course." The narrator calls that "a hard slap"; soon Jude is at a bar tossing down some beer. Soon, as well, he is engaged in a broad and deep social and moral inquiry: "He began to see that the town life was a book of humanity infinitely more palpitating, varied, and compendious than the gown life. These struggling men and women before him were the reality of Christminster, though they knew little of Christ or Minster. That was one of the humors of things. The floating population of students and teachers, who did know both in a way were not Christminster in a local sense at all."

Hardy doesn't let the matter drop there, however. He has delivered, through Jude, a populist broadside, meant to expose the snobbery and insularity of a particular institution: its sanctioned arrogance and the smug egoism thereby generated in its teachers and students. He wants to go further, though, and does so by having Jude take action rather than merely mull things over with growing indignation: "The gates [of the university] were shut, and, by an impulse, he took from his pocket a lump of chalk, which, as a workman, he usually carried there, and wrote along the wall: 'I have understanding as well as you; I am not inferior to you. Yea, who knoweth not such things as these?!'—Job xii.3."

Early in the novel Jude is a "Christian young man"; he is "one who wished, next to being a scholar, to be a Christian divine." We are told that he "limited his reading [for awhile] to the Gospels and Epistles." No wonder, then, that the Bible haunts him in his hour of extreme disappointment; and no wonder that he calls upon Job, as he chalks his message on a university's walls. Jude's religious life, his deeply felt intimacy with the Bible, his hope to minister unto others in the name of Jesus Christ, his desire to learn not for learning's sake but the Lord's, comes to naught, and thereafter a life steadily deteriorates. *Jude the Obscure*, published as Freud was writing his greatest book, *The Interpretation of Dreams*, spells out a journey from religious piety, humbly pursued, to a psychopathology become a dominant aspect of daily life. Where once there was almost a naive trust in the Book of books, and all its stories, its lessons, its promises and warnings, its instances and remonstrances, now there is a growing, idiosyncratic defiance of the customary, justified by a realization of its rot, its large reservoirs of hypocrisy and pretense, its vainglory (to use a word commonly summoned back then). The second half of Hardy's novel offers betrayals, mental deterioration, infanticide, all that Freud tried to understand—his very effort to do so attentively watched, increasingly hailed, because, as Hardy noted (the point of his novel), a culture no longer powerfully, convincingly devoted to the "sacred" (with respect to its assumptions) was now becoming entranced by (what else?) the hereabouts (as against heaven and hell): the mind and its workings; society and its ills as *they* (not God's will or grace or mysterious reasons) shape our personal and collective destiny.

No question, Hardy the poet (as was the case with Meredith) struggled more privately, less stridently, to make his moral and philosophical points. For one thing, his poetry earned him less attention: he could have his vigorous say without the uproar that accompanied the appearance of *Jude the Obscure*. Indeed, the bitterness shown that novel by critics was not unlike the reception given Freud through much of his career—for daring to say what seemed so obvious and prevalent.

During his long writing life Hardy the poet constantly struggled with the biggest possible questions: what to believe, and why, and how to live, and with which day-to-day convictions? He was not afraid to use poetry as an instrument of cultural reflection. In "The Respectable Burgher on 'The Higher Criticism'" he confronts traditional biblical faith with a late-nineteenth-century scientific outlook:

> Since Reverend Doctors now declare
> That clerks and people must prepare
> to doubt if Adam ever were;
> To hold the flood a local scare. . . .

By the end of the poem the Bible's events, once invested with mystery and handed down as articles of faith, become mere stories—evidence, actually, of a superstitious past, and so this concluding self-description, if not avowal:

> Since thus they hint, nor turn a hair,
> All churchgoing will I foreswear,
> And sit on Sundays in my chair,
> And read that moderate Voltaire.

No question, Hardy, more than any of the Victorian poets (all of whom, in various ways, responded to the increasing confrontation of religious authority by rational, scientific thinking), explicitly sets aside the traditional view of God's ultimate authority in favor of an outright agnosticism. One of his poems is even titled

"God's Funeral," its message that of a reluctant but necessary farewell to religious faith as idolatry. The poet becomes a social historian, sketches the long haul of things, tells of a decisive shift in the relationship between secular knowledge and an adherence to sacred tenets:

Till in Time's stay less stealthy swing,
Uncompromising rude reality
Mangled the Monarch [God] of our fashioning,
Who quavered, sank; and now has ceased to be.

A hundred years later, we of this second half of the twentieth century would talk of a "God Is Dead" theology as if it were a new intellectual presence among us, but Hardy knew, under less favorable social and intellectual circumstances, where a scientific secularism was taking not only thinkers and writers, such as himself, but the millions of people for whom, he understood, that matter of "how to bear such a loss" was serious indeed.

In fact, he himself never quite reconciled himself to that "loss." True, he sounded the note of freethinking, contemporary candor; he gave us in verse the Bible as ancient fancy, no longer capable of holding us in real awe, no matter our persisting pretensions, protestations. In the daily clutch of things, we grab for the artifacts of Science and thereby acknowledge in our deeds what we may not want to (dare to) put into words. True, sophisticated minds, unable to accept a personal God or the immortality promised by many religions (certainly by the Christian faith), try to figure a way out of this impasse (as did Hardy himself toward the end of his life, and as do so many ordinary folk who recognize in their bones what, say, a Kierkegaard meant when he spoke of "the leap of faith," that big stretch required for the mind to make). In the midst of the darkness science both asserts and explores, we crave whatever light we can make for ourselves, even if we do so as the proverbial whistlers (or, as the expression goes, with hope against hope). Upon Meredith's death, Hardy at least allowed us (himself) this kind of afterlife:

> Further and further still
> Through the world's vaporous vitiate air
> His words wing on—as live words will.

If Hardy's rational, skeptical mind prompted a refusal of Christian faith in its customary institutional existence, and if his deeply felt social conscience, his energetic moral life, prompted his forceful confrontation, in prose and poetry, of the world's various duplicities, injustices (the phoniness he was so quick to render, mock), the part of him that, like Jude, kept hoping for a more honorable and decent world also exerted an influence on his thinking and writing, both. That being the case, he could turn utopian, or he could yearn for a God he didn't believe existed, the God of the Hebrew Prophets, the God of a Christ vividly awake to the world's various inequities, injustices. In a fascinating poem, titled "1967," he dared imagine our very recent time with some optimism:

> A century which, if not sublime,
> Will show, I doubt not, at its prime,
> A scope above the blinkered time.

Moreover, in the long haul of his life, he could not really abandon religion. His description of himself reading Voltaire can be interpreted as a provocative scientific or secular triumphalism; but one can as readily see the bleak and sad side to such a self-portrait and, too, the facetious side to a moment of lyrical sport. Here, in prose, in a work titled, no less, "Apology," he attempts a muted, tentative reconciliation: "It may be a forlorn hope, a mere dream, that of an alliance between religion, which must be retrieved unless the world is to perish, and complete rationality, by means of the interfusing effect of poetry." A determined secularist worries about our hunger for the sacred, carves out a role for the poet as one who can, as it were, lift rationalities into the heights of a hope become exalted as Hope (affirmed and celebrated through word, song, ritual in the name of "religion")—the best a guarded late-nineteenth-century seer could do for himself, for his readers: offer the secular a carefully contemplated, regulated dose of the sacred, or, put differently, remind the sacred of its distinctly limited place in the thoroughly practical, rational life that would prevail from 1900 onward.

III

Where We Stand

2000

WHEN Thomas Hardy died, in 1928, Adolf Hitler and his Nazi thugs were well on their way from political obscurity—one of a young republic's fringe groups—to major national authority. Less than five years later, the nation of Goethe and Schiller and Heine and Thomas Mann and Beethoven and Brahms, and, yes, the nation of Einstein, the nation in whose language Freud wrote, the nation of science and social science, of medicine and engineering and architecture (as in the Bauhaus movement) would be on its terrible way to the responsibility for tens of millions of deaths: on the battlefield, from relentless bombing, and, not least, in the concentration camps, whose enormous capacity for mass murder was enabled by the modern technology of a nation as "advanced" and "intellectual" as any in the world. Indeed, toward the end of the Second World War, many scientists who had fled Germany were now able to help the United States by drawing on their knowledge of theoretical physics and thereby, in a resort to applied physics, creating the nuclear bomb: science now the proven potential enabler of the entire world's destruction. Such an outcome, less than half a century after both Meredith and Hardy were here on earth, singing their faith in a growing accumulation of knowledge, would give pause to some of their heirs. The poet William Carlos Williams, for example, in *Paterson* (the first two books were published immediately after the Second World

War) worried long and hard about the historical ironies this century, then only halfway along, had visited on mankind: erudition, even in the humanities, even in poetry, could not (as with his friend Ezra Pound) offer any immunity to hate, to treason; scientific achievement could become in various ways and for various reasons an instrument of widespread death; aesthetic and intellectual refinement could prompt an indifference to social reality. No wonder, then, the vigorous, intense, unsparing, arguably overwrought assault on higher learning, on university life, in the third part of the first book of *Paterson*:

> We go on living, we permit ourselves
> to continue—but certainly
> not for the university, what they publish
> severally or as a group: clerks
> got out of hand forgetting for the most part
> to whom they are beholden.
> Spitted on fixed concepts like
> roasting hogs, sputtering, their drip sizzling
> in the fire.

How well I remember my visits, as a medical student, to Dr. Williams at his home, 9 Ridge Road, Rutherford, New Jersey—the urgent passion of his remarks as he tried to confront a young person's enthusiasm and expectations with the sober lessons acquired by a physician and poet in the course of a long life devoted to ordinary people in need of medical care and to a bravely original-minded writing of verse, of fiction, of nonfiction. As he drove (he was always pulling ahead of slow-moving cars), he told me of Joseph Goebbels, his Ph.D.

in comparative literature from Germany's august Heidelberg University; of Heidegger, the great philosopher who had embraced Nazism unapologetically; of Jung, whose psychoanalytic creativity didn't deter him from a murky involvement with Nazi-controlled psychiatry; and, again and again, of his longtime friend Ezra Pound, whose descent into madness had been so virulently mean-spirited in its character. But he didn't stop there, with the celebrated, the gifted; he mentioned the thousands of doctors and lawyers and college professors and scientists, and, alas, the ministers and priests who fell in with the Nazis, did their bidding, wore their swastikas, shouted their "Heil Hitlers!" Once, seeing me sag under all that new knowledge, and the explication of it (I had heard a running commentary of the first decades of this century), he stopped himself cold, became almost fiercely terse: "This secular mind—where it's taken us."

I didn't know where to go with that remark. As with others he uttered, I sat and listened in stunned silence, and then I asked the naive questions that told of a lucky innocence, no matter my college degree and my ongoing postgraduate education. This time, he pulled himself back from a certain destination, expressed reservations about his own remark: "I'm in deep water here—it's very complicated." I didn't know how to pursue the matter; I wasn't then privy to his line of thinking. Abruptly, we'd arrived in his beloved Paterson, and his patients were now in his thoughts—as I learned when he started telling me of one of them, a child we were about to visit at his home. Later, I wrote down the words I'd heard; and still later, while learning to be a pediatrician, and anxious to have Dr. Williams's voice "on the record," to share it through a taped interview with my fellow hospital residents at a seminar entitled "Medicine and the Humanities" in which we were participating, I would return to that same subject, and hear this: "[Through] all these years of my practice I've heard parents talk about what they want for their kids. They want everything [for them], of course, but they're no fools: they know the score, they know what's ahead. Why wouldn't they—they're living 'close to the bone.' You know what? A parent's job—a mother's, a father's—it's to teach the kid to join the club, be an American. Now, what does that mean? This isn't the America of farming and trading and the church; or of the factory life and the church. People still go to church, but the God they worship (if they do [that] while they're sitting in those pews) isn't 'The Big Man' in their lives after they leave and go home. I've seen that happen; I've watched people who have just come here from Europe figure out how to be a Catholic, lots of them, and be an American. At first it's hard, they see the conflict, and they're torn. But it doesn't take long; I'll tell you that—in no time, you've got the kids growing up in *this* country (the way it's become), and that means they hear the bells, the church bells, sure they do, but they read the [news]papers, and they listen to the radio, and they pass the stores and look at the displays—and don't forget this: so do the priests. The bells are there, but there's a lot of other noise in the air, voices with messages about buying and selling: spend and get—and work hard, so you can spend more, get more, and hey, that's the life.

"This is a here-and-now world, that's what I mean when I say 'secular'; and the religious side of it, even the moral side of it—well, there's a lot up for grabs. You want an example of what I mean? [I had appeared perplexed, even overwhelmed by the sweeping nature of his remarks, and wasn't sure what to say, or ask, in response to them.] A grandmother, a young one, who was born in Italy and came here when she was fifteen, and married and brought up a family, and now is helping her daughter bring up another one, told me a few weeks ago that it's become different going to church here than it was when she was in Italy and when she first came here. She used to sit there and talk to God, and try to figure out what He wanted, and try to please Him. Now, she says, she mostly thinks about what's going on in her life, in her kids' lives, and she asks God to make it better. You know what? She got herself so damn close to being as smart as the big-shot social critics and philosophers—she said to me: 'It used to be I prayed to God, that I would learn what *He* wanted from me, and how *He* wanted me to behave (I wanted His help to be that kind of person, the kind He wanted); but now I pray to God that He help us with this problem, and the next one—to be a Big Pal of ours! It used to be, when I prayed to God, I was talking to Him; now, it's me talking to myself, and I'm only asking Him to help out with things.'"

A long silence, as he caught his breath and watched me as I tried to figure out, in mid-twentieth-century America, at the age of twenty-seven, where we were headed in this "interview." He must have noticed that I needed some summing up, a more conceptual or analytical posture on his part, as opposed to that of the story-teller, the narrator who "merely" describes what he has seen or heard, in the hope that his listener will get the point, use it in whatever way he or she likes (including as grist for the spinning of theory). Finally, I hear this: "You see, in a secular world, you think of yourself, your family, and friends; you pray *for* yourself, your family, and friends. I don't mean that you're not being truly religious that way—I guess I'm just trying to let you know what parents have been letting me know, that there's a shift going on, there's been a shift, and they can sense it, and they're as smart as you and me and some college professor in sociology or theology, who's trying to tell his class what's happening in our country. We've gone whole hog for 'the things of this world,' and that [attitude] is what a secular life is all about, and it's part of a person's religious life, too."

I now wanted to hurry us both back to his poetry, where I felt much more at home than I had been with the direction our conversation had taken. I made reference to his poem "The Catholic Bells," its ringing affirmation of a summoning institutional presence among modest, decent people going through the rhythms of their everyday lives. Yes, he appreciated my mention of that particular poem; it had given him much pleasure to write it, and he certainly was acknowledging the authority, both joyous and grave, of a powerful religion in the affairs of those he had known so long as a home-visiting physician (in the phrase then used, a "general practitioner"). But, I was reminded, he said at the start of the poem that he was an outside observer ("Tho' I'm no Catholic I listen hard when the bells / in the

yellow-brick tower / of their new church / ring down
the leaves / ring in the frost upon them / and the death
of the flowers . . . "); and he was at immediate pains to
mention a "new church," and to connect this church to
nature's events, which, of course, would include our
human experiences:

> . . . the new baby of Mr. and Mrs.
> Krantz which cannot
> for the fat of its cheeks
> open well its eyes, ring out
> the parrot under its hood
> jealous of the child
> ring in Sunday morning
> and old age which adds as it
> takes away. . . .

Moreover, he reminds me, those Catholic bells are ringing, the poet insists, for

> the children of my friend
> who no longer hears
> them ring but with a smile
> and in a low voice speaks
> of the decisions of her
> daughter and the proposals
> and betrayals of her
> husband's friends. . . .

Here the poem moves from a portrayal of appearances
(the "painting of a young priest / on the church wall
advertising / last week's Novena . . . ," or "the lame /
young man in black with / gaunt cheeks and wearing a / Derby hat, who is hurrying / to 11 o'clock

Mass . . .") to a look beneath the surface, into the heart, if not the soul, of things to be found within the hearing distance of those bells that are both commanding yet no longer heard, meaning heeded in connection with what happens personally (we today would say psychologically) in the course of any given day. Again, Dr. Williams's "You see," spoken to me as if he couldn't take for granted that I actually could perceive what he was trying to get across in either the poem or our conversation: "You see, I'm trying to make a distinction—I was in the poem, too: that the bells are a thing of beauty, and they *register* beauty (for the observer, surely) but they don't get to the very life they were originally meant to [touch]; they're part of our *adorned* life, its loveliness, but the soul's intrigue, the battles of the mind, the lusts, the wrongs, the conflicts, the hurts and worries—that's out of their range. Maybe, you could say, out of their depth—there's no longer that deep probe of religion into the churchgoer's heart."

So it goes in this secular society, Dr. Williams was saying, as that society becomes worked into our "heart," our thoughts and assumptions and aspirations and concerns as they become our mind. Not that secularism hasn't always been a part of the thinking life of even those very much struggling for faith. Indeed, as the Psalms keep reminding us, the search for that faith is not incompatible with a search for wealth and power: David was a mighty king, he who proclaims so passionately his desire to be a faithful servant of the Lord. In psalm after psalm pride and envy and vanity rear their all too human faces—evidence aplenty of how hard it was, way back then (as now), to keep one's mind on the transcendent when the tug of the imminent was (is) so compelling. True, Psalm 8 is heralded as an avowal of God's greatness, man's insignificance. But in a way the psalmist/poet is reminding himself (and, maybe, God) that human beings have their own great authority, that they have been "crowned," that "glory and honor" are theirs. Moreover, the exaltation of the Lord carries with it an implicit skepticism worthy of our contemporary existentialists: "What is man, that thou art mindful of him? And the son of man, that thou visitest him?" Here is the scientific mind at work, trying to locate man in relation to "all sheep and oxen, yea, and the beasts of the field, the fowl of the air, and the fish of the sea, and whatsoever passeth through the paths of the seas." That same mind is indirectly asserting itself, of course, not only by God's grace, but through its own exertions of language—it is consciousness that is the psalm's subject, consciousness and its discontents, hence the inquiry addressed to the Lord, but surely an inquiry that David and others in ancient times asked of *themselves* (the secular turn of thought): who are we? who can survey this world as we do, and leave a record, through words, of our musings, our wonder, our not so thinly disguised hesitations, doubts?

A version of doubt is spoken in the brief and affecting Thirteenth Psalm, a favorite of Calvin's: "How long, O Lord? Wilt thou forget me forever? How long shall I take counsel in my soul, having sorrow in my heart daily?" Here is our twentieth-century "alienated" man, an outcry of felt abandonment, an introspection of the grief-stricken who is alone. The echo of that psalm, of course, can be heard generations later, in Jerusalem, when the Galilean teacher and healer, nailed to the cross, asks the Lord why He has forsaken a faithful believer, now so ignominiously doomed. Well before his earthly demise at the hands of an empire's local administrator, Jesus had made clear, in his moral instructions, the distinction between Caesar's "things" and those of God—a point not lost on Luther who, however, also tried to merge the two worlds by connecting the ministry to the local "caesars" (in what is now Germany) whose purposes his pronouncements amply suited. Certainly the popes whose lived splendor Luther and Calvin found so unworthy of Jesus had also figured out a way to live well (enjoy their earthly, secular time of it) and do well (commit themselves to the sacred as priests become cardinals become heads of the Roman Catholic Church).

Yet long before the excesses of Rome in, say, the thirteenth or fourteenth century—the provocations that preceded Protestantism—there was a secular hustler who prospered in Rome. A thousand years earlier, in fact, during the fourth century, when Christianity had triumphed over the "paganism" of the Roman Empire, the man we now know as Saint Augustine would begin the sixth chapter of the sixth book of his *Confessions* with these words: "I was all hot for honors, money, marriage"—a remark that, at the least, ought to give us today some historical context for the word "yuppie." Over fifteen hundred years ago Augustine's "city of man" stood strong, even as he would struggle so hard with himself to enter the "city of God." The lasting power, actually, of the *Confessions* is testimony to their psychological and moral candor. Long before Freud portrayed the mind in turmoil, in constant conflict, Augustine of Hippo looked within himself and found plenty of lust and greed and assertiveness and envy striving for expression, even as he gave us a chronicle of conscience at work, sometimes falteringly, often mightily. Hence his emergence not as a big shot, an imperial functionary with lots of people shaking in their boots at his every word, but as a priest ready (no matter the conflict, the regrets) to surrender an active sexual life with a common-law wife (they had a son) and, too, all the blandishments of a secular life available in those last years of Rome's authority. He would live to learn that the Vandals had taken Rome (410) and, indeed, were closing in on his own city of Hippo when he died (430). His, then, was a story right out of our time—the *Confessions* give us "drives" and a vigorous conscience and, not least, the ego at work, taking measure of things both within its habitat, a particular mind, and without: a still great capital city, a still inviting world of commerce and military power, not to mention a religion (Christianity) itself commanding more and more influence. That ego's willfulness, its inclination toward the sacred, would eventually settle things, prompt a decided shift in the direction of a man's energies and, not least, an account of its own workings: the ninety-three books that a bishop of Hippo was "inspecting" (cataloging, we would say) at the very end of his life.

There are, of course, empires and empires—some of them a matter of land and treasure and people and military strength, some of them a matter of beliefs held, ideas propagated and accepted, values espoused with success. Augustine laboriously wrote his manuscripts by hand, and they were just as laboriously copied by others. They did not become "books," as we know them, in his lifetime or for centuries thereafter. In this regard (the matter of culture, and of technology as it affects not only the way we live but the thoughts we have) I leap from the seventh century, from the Christian bishop contemplating at the end of his life the work he did as a writer, to the second half of this twentieth century to which we have belonged—to a conversation with Anna Freud toward the end of her life (1973), when she was willing to recall her father's way of looking at his books in the last years of his life: "More than once my father remarked that if it hadn't been for the fact that his ideas became books, and those books were read all over the world—there would not have been what we now call 'psychoanalysis.' No, he wasn't referring to the spread of his ideas, not just that. [I had interpreted her words that way.] He wrote his ideas as they came to him; he was a doctor, who was learning as he did his work with patients, and then thought about what was happening between him and them. Once his manuscripts became books, the ideas in them were out in the world—they spread, and then he got letters from others, who were interested in what he said. Soon, they were visiting him, the doctors and the teachers and the artists and the writers. Those people had a strong influence on him, on what he thought and how he wrote.

"It is usually put the other way: Sigmund Freud and his 'circle.' But as we keep saying in our clinical work, let us turn the coin over [look at the subject under discussion from another vantage point]: until others came to work with my father, he was all alone, with no sense that what he had seen and come to believe had any value to others. He needed people who could share his ideas, make suggestions, give him a sense (how is it put these days?) of 'community.' I mean by that not only 'psychological support'; I mean intellectual solidarity: colleagues who give you a feeling of 'reality,' that what you have heard, and in your own mind concluded to be true, is in turn being heard by others, who have decided that it does, after all, make some sense! Otherwise, there is a danger that the one who is coming up with the ideas will begin to feel that he is not only alone, but alone with his 'fantasies.' I suppose that may be somewhat more tolerable for novelists—though they, too, want an 'audience.' But my father was a doctor, and he had done 'research' before he began to write his book on dreams, and he very much needed to know—how shall I say it?—that he wasn't dreaming about dreams! I remember how he felt when those who read his first book began to come to him through their letters, or in visits: it all became *real*—that is, not only something in his own mind, but something that belonged to the world."

Miss Freud was saying that in our time, more than ever, the ideas of individual writers can quickly become an important aspect of the thought of millions. Thus when George Eliot gives us Dorothea's "theoretic" mind, and George Meredith gives us Sir Willoughby's limitless "egoism," and Sigmund Freud gives us an explanation of how those aspects of our human psychology, and many others, work in our daily lives, the result is a widespread public knowledge—which has its own, enormous cultural significance. The secular world is hungry for breakthroughs such as Freud achieved, lives off them, regards them as a (temporary) guiding light. Here is Miss Freud, once more, looking back as a social historian, a cultural critic, at the relationship between the emergence of her father's ideas and the use to which they were put, not in clinical settings but as instruments of instruction in how to live a life (as a body of philosophical wisdom, really): "I recall, even in the early days [of her father's work and writing], the opposition; but I also remember how surprised he was at the way—how shall I say it?—his ideas took hold, caught on fire. It's a good thing there weren't phones then: they'd have been ringing all day and night! My father was pleased, but he was thoughtful enough—he had enough distance from his own ideas—to realize that, as he used to put it, 'something larger was going on.' He meant by that—he meant people were looking to psychoanalysis for something they weren't getting elsewhere. They weren't only interested in understanding the mind; they wanted answers to all the riddles of existence.

"At first, you know, he thought that [such an interest] was a sophisticated kind of 'resistance'—an attempt to distract us, divert us, from 'depth analysis,' from psychoanalytic investigation proper, you could say, into the 'murky reaches of philosophical speculation'—that was a phrase I recall Karl Abraham [one of Freud's colleagues] using once in a conversation. But gradually we all began to see that there was something missing in the lives of people, and that the 'problem' wasn't necessarily psychological—do you see what I mean? [I nodded a bit too quickly, thereby alerting Miss Freud's never dull or apathetic psychoanalytic antennae, and prompting her to stop for a second, look directly, carefully at me—as if to suggest that, of course, there *are* some people, in and out of the psychoanalytic fold, whose way of thinking might well fit Karl Abraham's description!] My father indicated his understanding [of this social and historical development] when he used the word *weltanschauung* in connection with psychoanalysis. He wasn't being presumptuous, as some of his critics asserted. He was acknowledging that for a lot of people psychoanalysis becomes not only a 'treatment,' as the doctors would say, but something much bigger and more lasting—it's *there* for the person long after he or she has stopped being an analysand, and become someone who has been analyzed. As a matter of fact, when he [her father] wrote 'Analysis, Terminable and Interminable,' the same kind of considerations had occurred to him: for some people analysis seems to go on and on, and if it may be that something has gone 'wrong' to explain that [outcome], it also may be that what has happened has been working out quite well for the person [analysand] in question and for the analyst, too. In earlier times they would be called 'wise friends' of one another!"

In her own way, Miss Freud was echoing, on that occasion, remarks she had made in her book *Normality and Pathology in Childhood*. There she had indicated at substantial length the nature of the "search" certain parents embarked upon, throughout the childhood of their sons and daughters, for this or that "technique" to ensure optimal psychological well-being. The point was somehow to find, as she once put it, "a perfect childhood"—and then, of course, her ironic comment: "As if there ever could be such a thing—and if there were, what would be wrong then, with the children and us!"

Still, she was not inclined to overlook the possible reasons for such a "search," such a desire on the part of the well-educated and well-to-do adults of the Western, industrial nations who were the clients, if not the clientele, of psychoanalysts. In a secular society many seek "guidance" (moral as well as clinical) from doctors, from psychiatrists and psychoanalysts, rather than the clergy, hence the eagerness of so many ministers, priests, rabbis to embrace "pastoral counseling." Of course, in the early days of psychoanalysis things were different. In that regard, Miss Freud could be quite unsparingly tough on her own colleagues. For instance, she reminded them (in an address before the New York Psychoanalytic Institute) that they were doing quite well financially, and were held in very high esteem socially, culturally, a contrast with the fate of the first analysts, who had to brave a kind of professional ostracism, both intellectual and even personal in nature: the shunning of a society still monarchical and religious in its upheld tenets.

Like others who shared a profession with her, she was struggling with the way a certain kind of work can be taken up, embraced not only as something useful or helpful but as a revered bedrock of one's believing life— hence the words of her onetime analysand, Erik H. Erikson, at the end of his first book, *Childhood and Society*, when he was trying to look at the qualities that characterized (by midcentury) those who chose psychoanalysis as a profession: "the various identities which at first lent themselves to a fusion with the new identity of the analyst—identities based on talmudic argument, on messianic zeal, on punitive orthodoxy, on faddist sensationalism, on professional and social ambition—all these identities and their cultural origins must now become part of the analyst's analysis, so that he may be able to discard archaic rituals of control and learn to identify with the lasting value of his job of enlightenment."

Such a statement indicates, through the use of historically charged words (talmudic, messianic, orthodoxy) a writer's conviction that impulses and goals and attitudes once connected to Judaism, to Christianity, to institutionalized religious life, have now become connected to a profession that is prominent indeed among the secular bourgeoisie. Another psychoanalyst, Allen Wheelis, more than echoed Erikson's observations, also during the 1950s and 1960s, in an article published in the *International Journal of Psychoanalysis*, "On the Vocational Hazards of Psychoanalysis," and in his first two books, *The Quest for Identity* (a series of essays) and *The Seeker* (a novel). Wheelis was interested in the way analysts are (only for a while, one hopes) regarded as godlike by their patients (transference) and by others as well. These members of the second generation, as it were, of psychoanalysis were anxious to explore not only their profession but that world to which it had come to mean so much. Here is how Erik H. Erikson put that matter: "I came to America [in 1933] because Joan [his wife] was Canadian, and had gone to school in New York [at Barnard], and wanted to return—because we both saw what even then was happening, the rise of Fascism. We were also worried about the fate of psychoanalysis itself—it seemed to 'belong' to a relatively small group of people [analysts] and, of course, their patients. But in

America, we soon saw something else—psychoanalysis had 'spread out,' all right, broadened. 'We' were everywhere: in the movies and in the universities, and in the theater, and in public forums and discussions, much more so on this side of the Atlantic than was ever the case in Europe. I would remember wistfully my words about Vienna—where I thought 'we' were becoming 'ingrown.' Now, 'we' were 'all over the place'—including the churches and synagogues!"

Such a development had to do, ironically, with faith, though the object of faith, in "the churches and synagogues" Erikson had mentioned, wasn't God and His judgments, Christ and His teachings, or a received spiritual tradition as it has become a sacred and cherished set of beliefs, rituals: a dogma held high, called upon daily in the course of a life. Rather, the faith was (is) that of a secular mind as it has developed over the centuries, and especially in this past one: the faith we have in science; the rise of the social sciences, and their sense of entitlement with respect to the credibility extended them, the expectations entertained of them—all of that being evidence of the faith we have in ourselves, in our ability to know ourselves, gain control of things (within and outside ourselves) through such knowledge. And increasingly these recent years, these last ones of a century, a millennium, it is a faith in the capacity of the human brain (the organ that has investigated successfully all other organs) to explore itself, understand itself fully, gain operating (clinical) control over its vulnerabilities, aberrancies.

There are, clearly, important consequences to such a shift in human knowledge and, correspondingly, human allegiance. The Ego of the famous psychoanalytic triad has an increasing authority. In his more hopeful moments (some would say naive ones, some would say impossibly proud ones) Freud dared say, "Where the Id was, there shall the Ego be"—an earnest doctor's clinical dream, but maybe an exaggerated one that reflected (in the spirit of those two well-known concepts, transference and countertransference) the shared desire of patients and their doctors: the desire to have more control over desire. Eventually, Freud dared prophesy, the Id, once possessed of such hidden power, will yield increasingly to our biological scrutiny: psychoanalytic investigation a prelude to the biochemical and neurophysiological kind.

With all of the above happening, the third agency of the psychoanalytic paradigm, the Superego, has endured a shift in its overall strength, and in its relationship to the other two members of this psychological ruling junta: a diminished hold over the mind, an erosion in its capacity to shape the Ego's activity, bear down on that of the Id. It is the Superego, naturally, that has always linked us with persuasive strength, if not a decided vehemence, to the world beyond the home, the world of churches and synagogues and mosques, and, too, of "culture" in all its manifestations: the printed word, and painted canvas, and, these days, the photographs, the movies and videos and television programs of our heavily visual culture. Perhaps among individual psychoanalysts and their analysands, Freud's dictum held even in the early years of this century—an Ego increasingly enhanced, fortified, braced by "insight" may well have significantly laid low the Id. But among people influenced culturally rather than clinically by psycho-analysis, the most immediate consequence was that of an altered Superego, as Anna Freud once said (as did Erik H. Erikson, many times).

For Miss Freud, at the end of her life, such a course of events was both ironic and unwelcome: "Our first patients [who came to see Freud and his followers in Vienna and, later, Berlin, Budapest] were men and women who were the victims of self-accusation, among other things. They were men and women in whom the Superego was highly developed, to say the least—over-developed. They suffered from the judgments they had learned to hand down on themselves—for 'crimes' they had come to believe they had committed: the Superego at work! (I am simplifying, but not all that much!) Over the decades, I have seen the clinical picture change—our patients are less and less overwhelmed by the power of the Superego in their mental life. They have been brought up differently [a contrast with what was once the manner of rearing children]: they have been re-assured and complimented, and given so many things, so they know the meaning of yes, but not so much the meaning of no, and, of course, some of them have rarely, if ever, been told no—that they must *not* do this or that. Nor have they been threatened or scolded much—things were explained to them, over and over, with great professed patience, and with much assurance of the parents' love.

"I think I covered a lot of this in *Normality and Pathology in Childhood*—how, with the best of intentions, many of the most progressive and enlightened parents went out of their way to do everything in accordance with the latest psychoanalytic principles, taking care of all 'needs' and anticipating all the anxieties and fears and worries that any of us could imagine or had seen in our work—only to have, as a result, not an absence of childhood difficulties (and worse) but a whole new order of them. Gone were the children deeply afraid of doing the wrong thing, or worried that they might slip up, get into serious trouble, or bothered by frightening thoughts or nightmares, in which they step over the bounds, and get punished severely [for doing so]. Now we have, even in our younger children, what has become mentioned by more and more of us in our clinical case conferences, the 'narcissistic personality.' These children aren't afraid of being caught, judged, sentenced, and punished by their conscience, their Superego; if they are afraid of anything (and some of them seem brazenly fearless!), they are scared that they will be able to do anything, that there are no limits.

"What then will happen? I recall describing that [state of affairs] in several papers and in the book [we'd been discussing *Normality and Pathology in Childhood*]: 'When . . . the severity of the Superego is reduced, children get the deepest, most troubling anxieties of all, the fear that they can't prevail against the pressures of their own drives,' words to that effect. [They were almost the exact words she used in the book.] That is, I think, what some of our contemporary philosophers are getting at, when they talk about their existential despair? I don't mean to speak for them; I have to admit, I haven't read them much but I do read *of* them, in the papers, and I hear of them, from friends and my analytic patients— and I think they are telling us that the old Superego is no longer around for them, and for a lot of others, and they are more and more 'rational,' thanks to psychoanalysis, I would suppose, and physics and biology, all we know today, and so 'everything goes,' as the expression says, all depending on your own choice. Even if you really don't *want* it so that 'everything goes,' and even if you know the dangers—you're hard put to build a series of prohibitions. On what will you base them? (What that you can defend, that is, in a logical argument?) We've come full circle, I'm afraid [the irony of her use of that last word!]: we started out trying to use our wits to help people be less anxious, less driven by a tyrannical Superego, and we've come to the point that people are more anxious and even alarmed and fearful, but not of the Superego, but of—themselves, their 'drives,' we say, or their 'situation,' their 'existential fate,' their 'nature,' others put it. How do people say it: live long enough!"

If God is declared "dead," if the Bible is regarded as a historical text, or a series of stories, all to be deconstructed, if religion is an "illusion," and if children are seen as our big hope, our only chance of a future life (lived through them), and as ones to be encouraged, enabled, given all possible intellectual and emotional leeway—small wonder that the Superego of old is gone, with its nays and oughts, its muscled insistence on prohibitions, requirements, amplified by commandments and encyclicals and powerful preaching and hymns sung or cantors singing, by the Talmud or the words of God become man, and now part of God again, by the believed presence of a hovering Holy Ghost that, as one child said to me years ago, "can see right through you, so there's no trick you can pull that isn't noticed" (he of working-class Catholic background). All of that religious tradition is a thing of the past for more and more people, even as that boy just mentioned would go to a first-rate high school, then to an Ivy League college, and lose interest in, retain only a nominal belief in, "the Holy Ghost."

Instead, we have, as Miss Freud adduced, a still energetic Id, our lusts and resentments and angers ever upon us, and a newly authoritative Ego, blessed with insights, a growing body of knowledge, a confident sense of more of both to come—and, yes, blessed with a faith of sorts, a faith in those insights, that knowledge is all-important. I believe this, each of us says: that over time an increasingly knowing human mind will prevail over nature's various mysteries, will see us exploring the heavens, conquering one disease after another, and, not least, gaining an understanding of its own workings, the mind, at last, its own master. Under such circumstances, our scientific investigators become more than mere allies of the Ego; they bring to it a potentially ruling authority. Once the Ego was a nervous and shaky negotiator, always worried about the censorious Superego, and always assailed by the demanding Id. How to placate conscience and allow for expression of desire—a lifetime's task! Now those self-directed and self-imposed judgments of the Superego are gentler, indeed, among many of the secular bourgeoisie, not to mention among many of the rich and poor as well. Now, too, we understand our emotional life as never before and, more and more each year, our brain's biological life: a new sovereignty for the Ego. The mind's psychological and

biological investigators have become godlike for so
many of us: the "transference" that elevated psychoanalysts to seers in the eyes of their patients and at the same
time (a kind of "cultural transference") gave those individuals a broad recognition as pundits, prophets, secular
priests of sorts. The case is similar today with the neurobiologists who are exploring the brain's biochemistry,
neurochemistry, enabling a biological psychiatry of increasing credibility, competence.

Not that we have been unwilling in the past to grant
certain individuals oracular power: theologians for
some, saints for others, philosophers for still others,
soothsayers and magicians of one kind or another. More
recently, as Miss Freud and Erik H. Erikson remind us,
we have watched the secular theories of Freud become
invested with something more than enthusiastic interest, acceptance: a dogmatism, rather, that bespeaks adherence to a faith. Similarly with Marx's ideas—Lenin
the political theorist and revolutionary figure become
Lenin enshrined in a mausoleum, his every word wor-
shiped. Nor are we incapable of going down the same
road with respect to our neuro-psychopharmacologists.
Already the pill Prozac has been on the cover of our
newsmagazines, and one wonders whether some person,
at some point in time that is not far off, will address us
as a brain scientist but, soon enough, become as revered
as Freud was, accorded a degree of respect that proves as
confounding and embarrassing (and seductively inviting) as Miss Freud remembered such a development to
have been for her aging father: "Toward the end of his
life I was his secretary; I had to deal with his correspondence; and [so doing] I felt I was learning so very

much—I would say to myself that I was getting the biggest education possible. My father had become for a lot of people someone who had discovered nothing less than how the mind works, and since everyone is struggling in some way with how his or her mind works, the Dr. Freud of Vienna, and then London, was the one who had the answers—or the one who was the enemy, if you believed that only certain other people have the answers, whether they be scientists or philosophers or religious figures. So, we received lots of attention; and whether it was adulation or bitter scorn, each of those reactions, by their intensity, told us what had happened to an Austrian physician who tried to learn about how we manage our psychological affairs!"

In a polite, wry manner Anna Freud was describing herself as a witness to secular idolatry, even as she was, also, in a position to observe the envies and rivalries that can be stirred, as the expression goes, when a new kid, a whiz of some kind, arrives on the block: who are *you* to be telling others so much and, as a result, to have become the recipient of so much expressed allegiance! In a sense Freud the self-described psychological "conquistador" became, inadvertently, an investigator whose scholarship, in its reception among others, has taught us more than he ever thought was possible: the relationship of psychoanalysis to our culture as itself a means of understanding how the mind works—what we crave, how we try to manage our yearnings and apprehensions.

With God gone for so many intellectual pioneers of the last two centuries, the rest of us, as students and readers, as seekers mightily under their influence, have only ourselves left as "objects" of attention. The theologians were supplanted by the philosophers, the religiously committed philosophers by the skeptical, secular philosophers, who, in turn, have been supplanted in worldwide influence by a biologist, an economist, a psychiatrist, a physicist, each of whom (Darwin, Marx, Freud, Einstein) has an inclination to be contemplative in a particular secular way: to wonder about things, about the secrets that await our triumphs of discovery. Human beings have thus come to be seen as Promethean deities of a distinctively hardworking and limited kind, inasmuch as they possess no magic, have only their wits as instruments of newfound comprehension, and are personally all too finite in the existence they have, by mere chance, luck, found for themselves.

In the long run of Western high thought, Pascal was the great transitional figure, the one who tried so arduously and ardently to uphold the sacred, to link himself with the Judeo-Christian apologetic tradition (and especially, with Saint Augustine's mix of the cerebral and the emotional), while at the same time acknowledging quite pointedly and bravely (especially for his time, maybe for any time) the secular claims of "reason." He evidently felt these claims pressing hard on his brilliantly knowing, reflective mind, hence his willingness in the *Pensées* to declare openly his rock-bottom materialism, even as (like a figure in a Chagall painting) he hungers for transcendence, tries to defy reason's gravitational pull, leap high toward a faith that will turn those "vacant, interstellar spaces" into a believer's green pastureland. Ultimately, though, his posture is that of resignation—a secular intellectual's version, really, of Kierkegaard's resignation: like Abraham, Pascal walks toward a God he *will* believe in, no matter his every doubt, his ample measure of disbelief. Thus the well-known pensée (278) that puts the split of secular/sacred right before us (before himself) with no effort at qualification: "It is the heart which experiences God, and not reason. This, then, is faith: God felt by the heart, not by reason." The Freud who explored human subjectivity so sensitively and sensibly, both, would perhaps have been more responsive to such a way of putting the matter, less driven by that approach to the combative truculence of *The Future of an Illusion*, which, in turn, became a hymn of sorts to his own faith: a Reason hugged with no worry of idolatry, with no regard for the crimes done in its name. (He, who admired Ibsen so much, might have taken to heart the riveting message of *The Wild Duck*: that inquisitive, explorative, insistent Reason can be callous, harmful in the extreme, because illusion systematically and ruthlessly stripped from someone can bring him down completely, prompting self-destruction—yet another of the Norwegian playwright's fiercely idiosyncratic reminders posed to a secular, modern world that flocked approvingly to his plays without, always, understanding the complexity and ambiguity of their message.)

In any event, at his most determinedly secular, Pascal knew to pull no (sacred) punches: "The last act is tragic, however happy all the rest of the play is: at the last act a little earth is thrown upon our head, and that is the end, forever." Those words are a precise avowal of the heart of secularism by a spiritually passionate scientist whose writings are part of a "sacred" literary and introspective tradition but are also candid in a way congenial to Freud and Ibsen, to the scientists who are the mathematician and biologist Pascal's contemporary heirs. No wonder, in that regard, the (also French) philosopher Simone Weil (like Pascal, she was plagued by an unquenchable rationalism that wouldn't, finally, yield to the invitations of the spiritual, however desperately sought) would call upon the haunting phrase in the 282d pensée, "waiting for God," with such intense longing. In a moment of unflinching candor Pascal brushed aside so very much (not least the ceremony and ritual and educational zeal of the Catholic Church) when he dared allow this with respect to rational man: "Therefore, those to whom God has imparted religion by intuition are very fortunate, and justly convinced. But to those who do not have it, we can give it only by reasoning, waiting for God to give them spiritual insight, without which faith is only human, and useless for salvation."

Those sentences convey a degree of psychological and philosophical complexity that, in its implication, is unnervingly agnostic, a prelude, way back, to "the modern age," whereof Kierkegaard spoke, though not that of the Copenhagen bourgeoisie, whom he so roundly detested. He was a virtual stand-in for Pascal. Really, both of them are psychologists, worthy predecessors of Freud, or for that matter Dostoievsky, who famously admitted that he'd keep believing in God, no matter what—no matter the capacity of anyone to prove such a conviction "false." Faith, then, becomes something beyond any semblance of rationality, "useless" in and of itself insofar as one's ultimate future is concerned.

Therefore Abraham's blind obedience to a hope, a hope of God's grace, really, in defiance not only of rationality but of all moral sense, as rendered in *Fear and Trembling*, and therefore, as well, Pascal's "waiting," precisely the descriptive word for what Isaac and his father endured upon that hill in the ancient Middle East. All of the immediately above brings me to Walker Percy's home in Covington, Louisiana, in 1973, where we talked and talked about what he kept calling "American secularism," a version, obviously, of a larger phenomenon. But it was a version he was then regarding closely, in preparation for *Love in the Ruins*, where he took us all on, we who live now, in these last years of a century, and of the second millennium in the Christian scheme of things. In that regard, I remember his thinking of Pascal with special tenderness (and anxiety), and, of course, of Kierkegaard, whom he had read and read in the 1940s and 1950s, before his emergence as a novelist who kept trying to "illustrate" that Danish writer through the magic of storytelling. At one point Dr. Percy, a physician and metaphysician as well as a novelist, claimed this with great conviction: "The abstract mind feeds on itself, takes things apart, leaves in its wake all of us, trying to live a life, get from the here of now, today, to the there of tomorrow." He stopped—worried, I thought, that he might have gone too far.

But, in fact, he wanted to push his argument further, though with some needed qualifications: "Once we go down the path of abstraction we're taking moral risks, psychological risks. We become drunk on ourselves—full of ourselves. Sure, I'm being abstract a bit right now—I know: the sinner denouncing sin! I'm not talking about something I don't know! I guess I'm trying to weigh the risks of doing what you've got to do. We're the ones who do this—figure out the world. But there ain't no free lunch: things cost, even one of the best things we've got going for us, our ability to calculate and move from the specific to the general. People get carried away in lots of different ways, and we're usually good at spotting how the other fella is going wild, but it's harder to get that kind of distance on yourself and your kind of folks. I keep remembering Kierkegaard's gripe with Hegel—that he'd [Hegel] figured out everything, with all the theorizing he did about history and time and ideas and their impact on one another; but he left out one thing, how it goes for people from one day to another: the 'history' of someone getting through an ordinary day. Kierkegaard loved irony—he took it further: he was sardonic. He saw pretense all over the place—and he saw it in his own head: the pretense of the theorist taking on so much that he loses commonsense contact with ordinary human goings-on. We build big skyscrapers of thought, huge telescopes of visionary thought, but in our lives, we live in small bungalows or shacks.

"I know I'm being cranky about all this. I write all these metaphysical pieces, and later I'll scratch my head and try to figure out whether there isn't some other way of getting the same point across—that's when I try to tell a story. Yes, I know [I had diverted his train of thought with an abstract remark about the difference between analytic thinking and the narrative, expository impulse], it's just two different roads you take. But there are dangers in anything you do, and I think we know from our critics the dangers in fiction, about how sloppy and unimaginative and confusing and 'unformed' a short story can be, or a novel—[we have learned all that] from those critics, who are using 'the analytic mode' [alas, my words] to comment on the guy who's telling himself a story, and handing it over to the reader for its pleasure, and sure, for the message it may have wrapped somewhere inside. But who takes on the critics—I don't mean a critic who writes a review of a novel, no. [I had asked whether that was what he meant.] I mean, the limits (in general) of critical thinking, abstract thinking—well, I'm struggling here: I don't mean 'limits,' I mean pitfalls. Yes, you can say 'hazards' [I'd volunteered that word].

"Let me try this on you: we ought to stop, every once in a while, and ask ourselves who we think we are. I'm not just talking 'existentialism,' here; I think I'm talking about moral self-examination—as in exactly who do you think you *are*?! There are times when we get so full of ourselves—we've 'lost all modesty.' I recall a teacher of mine in elementary school; she'd catch us being very 'clever,' lording something we'd discovered over everyone we could lay our hands on, and she'd call us to her, and she'd say: 'Now there, Walker, you sure are smart, you're clever as can be; and you're making sure everyone in the world knows it—the trouble is, *that's* not so clever, and it's not so nice, either, because you've lost all modesty.' I think I've got it down word-for-word."

There was more, much more; a man himself quite capable of extended conceptual riffs, some of which, frankly, I had found hard to fathom ("Towards a Triadic Theory of Meaning," or "The Symbolic Structure of Interpersonal Process," or "Semiotic and a Theory of Knowledge"), was seemingly turning on himself with a certain kind of vehemence, albeit rendered with a laid-back geniality. In fact, though, Dr. Percy was worrying about all of us, how we can use our minds in such a way that we lose respect for our friends, neighbors, and family members, even: a moral or spiritual kind of awareness forsaken for a bare-bones intellectual kind that is wielded rather than simply summoned.

In time I would let Dr. Percy's words settle in my head—a shrewd arrow directed by him at the apple of knowledge become something else: the sin of pride. He was "worried sick," he had said at one point, by the inclination of many of us, himself certainly included, to take ourselves away from the concrete particulars of a lived life (the hopes and worries and fears such a life prompts) in favor of an all-too-clever kind of conceptual analysis that gives short shrift to human experience (in all its complexity) as it befalls every person who is born, lives, and knows full well of death's certainty. In his own words, a summing up of what he'd been saying, he offered this "try," a most serious look on his face: "I don't mean to demean Intellect; that's a danger—anti-intellectualism on the part of some of us who have our reasons not to be comfortable with the thinking we do. It's not thinking that's the problem—it's what comes of it; I mean, it's what we do with it, how we use it. [You] can't get to be much more of a thinker, an intellectual, a philosopher than Thomas Aquinas; he worked his mind hard so he could understand God's intentions. But today, even our theologians aren't really interested in God—and reading a lot of them, even the most respected, I'm not sure God was really very much in their minds. With all due respect, I'm thinking of your teacher [Paul Tillich]. I hope I'm being clear, and not full of myself, while worrying about a lot of folks these days for being full of their own beliefs, their own ideas. I guess I'm saying that a lot of folks believe in their beliefs, they believe in their ideas, they believe in themselves, and maybe they believe in someone's politics or some social cause: it's today's secularism. I want to add to the brew, here and now, a lot of us churchgoers—this is more complicated and pervasive than those who proclaim their belief in God on one side and those who say 'nothing doing' [with respect to religious faith] on the other side. You can attend church every week, lots of us do, and in your way of thinking, your assumptions as you go through the day, a week—they're essentially secular in nature."

We went on further, substantially longer: an intense conversation with a sincere and devoted Catholic convert who went to church every day, at least during the times I visited him. He'd often sit alone in the local Covington church for a few minutes while I'd sit on the steps outside, and an occasional friend of his, knowing me as his visitor, would say: "Waiting on Dr. Percy?" Meanwhile, (back to Pascal and Weil) he'd be "waiting on God" inside and, afterwards, would be frank to talk about how hard it can be, even in a church, to keep one's mind on "godly matters." "Oh, Walker," I'd often demur, "it's always been that way, from time immemorial—the secular undertow, surely, that existed in the thirteenth century when Aquinas wrote, and surely, as we know directly from Augustine himself, in the fourth century, and again, from Pascal's more personal, self-disclosing pensées, in the seventeenth century: "There are different degrees in this aversion to truth, but all may perhaps be said to have it in some degree, because it is inseparable from self-love." Yes, for sure, Walker agreed—he knew the whole of that one hundredth pensée almost by heart; but there have been "degrees and degrees": some times and places have been, on the whole, more connected to the sacred, some thoroughly or relatively secular.

The "ruins" of his novel *Love in the Ruins* had to do with the consequences of a progressive (in several senses of the word, maybe) secularism: people hopelessly and haplessly adrift, at a thorough remove from one another, and all too confined by their own willing gullibility, the particular train of thought that they find congenial or convincing—each self a sovereignty, and each self out to be as far in the front as possible (with respect to various rank orders, and the devil take the hindmost). Maybe it is, indeed, an ironic conceit (speaking of a secular psychology) to imagine one's own time as more distant from the sacred than other times, more consumed by a worldliness that is not an inevitable experience but a constantly upheld notion of the unqualifiedly desirable. But he was ready to risk the judgment of being blindsided by his own historical moment: yet another would-be visionary who can't quite rise above his own life's (time's) inevitable confinements. "I put the novel [*Love in the Ruins*] in the future, but of course it's only a slight extrapolation from this period we're living in right now to the years ahead that I describe— I'm using a lot of 'symbols,' I suppose you could say, to describe not so much what's coming as what we've already come to! Anyway, whatever I've done—trying to show the 'ruins' of this secular world, so madly adrift, turning here, there, and everywhere for direction, and only half-believing what it decides to hold onto for a while—Flannery O'Connor did it more pointedly in some of her stories. She had it (us!) down cold, what we're like.

"No, I don't think she was finger-pointing—she included herself in her diagnosis of our secular malaise. [I had suggested that she might have risked, at times, a righteousness become self-righteousness, much as I loved her fiction and nonfiction, loved to teach it, too.] I think she's showing you something about yourself, about me, about all of us, if she gets you feeling anxious about her *judgments*, her moral direction, her spiritual 'preoccupations' (that's the way we get back at her, use a word like 'preoccupations' that implies some damn psychiatric disorder!). You bet she's all stirred up—or wants *us* to be! She thinks we're hell-bent, and she wants to say 'fire!' not to create needless panic, but because to her way of thinking (*believing* is the word, I guess!) there *is* a fire, and we'd better take notice! But you know what? There's no danger that she's going to create a big rush to the door, the exit signs, the stairs, with lots of people falling all over each other and some getting hurt or killed. No sir, she knew most people weren't even going to notice—and I mean those 'interleckchuls' she kept parodying. She was trying to tell us what she saw in the mirror and while looking out the window—both. Somehow, she managed to get herself out of the world around her enough to give her distance on things. I tried to get that distance by pushing things hard, exaggerating a little, by saying to the reader (to myself, first): hey, look where we're going; look where we're headed—from here to there, that's where we'll be, any minute now! But Flannery didn't have to go to that kind of 'extreme.' She almost went 'back,' if anything! She took the reader into the 'earlier' time of those country scenes, with country people—and boy, what she let us know, *see*, that way!"

Of the thirty-one stories in Flannery O'Connor's *Complete Stories*, "The Artificial Nigger" was reportedly one of her favorites, maybe *the* favorite. It is a story all too easy to summarize. A sixty-year-old grandfather named Mr. Head takes his ten-year-old grandson, Nelson, by train from their backwoods home to the big city, where with a great show of self-assurance the older man plays learned guide and instructor to the innocent child. On the train, and down the strange urban streets, the saga unfolds—the supposedly wise, experienced teacher constantly pressing his knowledge on a young one both eager to learn and also intuitively aware that he is, most significantly, a foil for his grandfather's cocksure sense of himself: the know-it-all anxious to lord it over a companion who is expected to register awe and gratitude at every turn of this voyage of initiation and discovery. The story's dramatic high point takes place in a back alley of the big city. Nelson, tired as can be, has dozed off. The grandfather, worried lest they miss the train back home, awakens him with a "loud noise by banging his foot against the [garbage] can." The boy is roused all right, lurches forward "like a wild maddened pony." Soon enough he has knocked down a lady, who claims a broken ankle, calls for the police, attracts a crowd. The grandfather has cautiously trailed Nelson, is there as the boy is surrounded by unfriendly people who are awaiting the arrival of the police. Under those circumstances—the critical moment in the story—the grandfather, with the suggestive name of Head, denies any connection to the boy: "This is not my boy," and further, "I never seen him before." The rest of the story has to do with the eventual, guarded reconciliation of the two: they wander about, near one another physically, but at an utter remove psychologically and spiritually. They stumble, however, into a "plaster figure of a Negro sitting bent over on a low yellow brick fence that curved around a wide lawn." In an instant, the lost pair of wanderers, estranged from one another, make common cause, as it were, with the plaster figure: "They stood gazing at the artificial Negro as if they were faced with some great mystery, some monument to another's victory that brought them together in their common defeat." The two have happened upon "an action of mercy" and soon enough are on their way home.

Such a summary does scant justice to an allegorical narrative that is, really, in the tradition of *Pilgrim's Progress*. It is no accident, of course, that the story's protagonist is named Mr. Head, and that at the very end of the story the train which has carried them to and from the city is likened to "a serpent in the woods." Nor are O'Connor's references to light and darkness without major implication: at the start of what turns out to be a "moral mission" a "coarse-looking orange sun" appears, but in no time the two are "lost," as in *Paradise Lost,* and a heavy darkness has settled over them—to be replaced, at the end, upon their cautious, wary reconciliation, by a "moon restored to its full splendor," one that "sprang from a cloud and flooded the clearing with light."

This densely symbolic story is accessible, sustained by the down-home dialect of ordinary Southern folk whose way of putting things Miss O'Connor knew cold. In truth, the story tells of the humbling of Head—of a confident worldly Intellect (so the boy Nelson was forcefully persuaded to believe) become quite something else. At the beginning we are given the Enlightenment (though the author tips her hand, somewhat, by describing that sun as "coarse-looking," a forecast of the coarse behavior to come). For a while the callow youth learns from the ever so knowledgeable elder. What is learned has to do with human affairs, with race and class. Nelson is asked questions by his teacher, who is only too glad to correct the boy, point out his ignorance, his inadequate grasp of the reality they are jointly encountering. Again and again we are witness to the condescensions of a heady one: Mr. Head determined to exact a compliant, awestruck respect from a Nelson who is being told things but also being told off when he expresses the least doubt or misgivings, or when he displays a natural curiosity that unnerves his supposedly all-knowing mentor, a would-be intellectual authority of the first order.

At one point, in a brief exchange, Miss O'Connor manages with brilliant precision a vividly compelling, probing examination of the origins of racism: ten or twenty textbooks of social science get packed into a few

fictional lines. Nelson is being queried by his patronizing grandfather Head about "a huge coffee-colored
man" who had passed them on the train on their way
cityward. The boy doesn't give quite the answer his
teacher wants—he calls the man "fat" and "old." Finally, his teacher, having had enough, declares, "That
was a nigger"; he does so with a smug self-satisfaction
and rubs it in by remarking to a "man across the aisle"
that the person just discussed was the boy's "first
nigger." A fellow human being has now become the occasion of a child's gratuitous humiliation. The boy is
angry but can hardly turn on his powerful grandfather-
guide, who has just made matters very much worse by
calling the lad ignorant, and even moving to another
seat across the aisle—a moment that portends the
story's central thrust, that of human "alienation" as a
consequence of human pride.

What choice, then, for this boy, needlessly humiliated by his own kin now become a vain, self-exalting
"expert," all too sure of himself and all too pretentiously
insistent on letting his "pupil" learn, unforgettably,
who knows more than whom? "Nelson turned backward again and looked where the Negro had disappeared," our authorial voice tells us—and then another
"turn," this one within the child's mind: "He felt that
the Negro had deliberately walked down the aisle in
order to make a fool of him and he hated him with a
fierce raw hate; and also he understood why his grandfather disliked them." Now a youngster who has been
fighting for a modicum of self-respect from the over-
bearing Head is ready to surrender, be the apt, atten-
tive, submissive learner. Now, as today's psychology

would put it, abstractly, an "identification with the aggressor" has taken place—at a high cost, though: a boy's felt inadequacy and vulnerability has prompted him to find a scapegoat, one readily available in the "coffee-colored man" whom he originally had the innocent decency to regard as "a man," then as "a fat man," then as "an old man." Now, hustled and intimidated and cajoled and seduced by Head, the boy is ready to join the adult world; he is, as the contemporary language of psychology would have it, "socialized." Pain and self-doubt have become transmuted into hate—a grim kind of "education."

In the end Miss O'Connor offers her lesson: the democracy of misery. Now we have seen, yet again, that pride goeth before the fall. Now an intellectual arrogance has prompted an edgy distrust in this pair of blood relatives. They are estranged, confused—again, lost. Soon enough (as in the story of Christ), the young person is denied, by his grandfather and teacher, no less; and soon enough, the two, their bond seemingly sundered beyond any hope of repair, wander in the desert ("Here everything was deserted"). Yet grace will shine upon them—unexpectedly, by its very definition: a mere piece of plaster, a silly reminder of human folly and ignorance and, yes, mean-spirited arrogance offers a redemptive moment for these two troubled souls, each so alone, one through bitter disappointment, the other through a deep-down sense of his failure as a teacher, his willingness, in the clutch, to betray his grandson, rather than endure the disapproval of a crowd. The quiet resonance of this story with that of Christ, and, too, that of Dietrich Bonhoeffer, say, in this century, is all too clear, and intentional. Who deserts whom, and when and why? Who stands up for what, when, and for which reasons? The very disciples of Jesus had left his side at the end: yet another mob able to put even the morally awake into a deep sleep. As for the Christian clergy of Hitler's Germany, they truckled under overwhelmingly to the hordes Hitler so handily mobilized—with Bonhoeffer, as a consequence, very much alone at the end of his life's determined and unyielding moral vigil.

As Dr. Percy wanted me to remember, Flannery O'Connor constructed a short fiction that took sharp aim at the twentieth-century secular world she had observed so closely. She gave us our secularity, as she openly acknowledged, from a particular vantage point: "I see from the standpoint of Christian orthodoxy. This means for me that the meaning of life is centered in our Redemption by Christ, and what I see in the world I see in relation to that Christ." She was, thereby, spelling out a sacred angle of vision as hers; and so, over and over, she confounds us secular readers, who may admire her talent, her skills as a writer, her sharply astute capacity to spot pretense, hypocrisy, and, most of all, self-importance, and, in no time, mock them into an unnerving exposure—often to our discomfort, because we ourselves, late-twentieth-century secularists, are precisely the ones being portrayed by a writer who as a youth was a cartoonist, and who never lost an ability for caricature.

In the O'Connor canon, the sacred is almost beyond recognition, whereas the secular, in all its obvious triumph, is a heap of transparent, rote clichés, banalities.

In one of her best-known stories, "A Good Man Is Hard to Find," a serial killer (the Misfit) is on the loose while an American family journeys south on a vacation. Sure enough, the Misfit comes upon them and especially confronts the most senior member of the family, an elderly grandmother, presumably the repository (as with Mr. Head) of whatever wisdom is available. She tries ever so hard to "understand" this violent outsider, wants to pray for him and somehow heal him, but he is beyond her reach. He will continue on his rampage; and the reader doesn't know what to do: the grandmother's pieties ring false but tell us so much about the shallowness of the American moral landscape, as portrayed, at least, by one observer of it—whereas the Misfit's arbitrary murderousness is, of course, beyond all comprehension. Miss O'Connor has harkened back to Christ's terribly confounding and unsettling mix of explanation and warning: "I come to bring you not peace, but the sword." Yet again, that Georgian lady, even as she struggled with the devastations of a mortal illness, disseminated lupus (the very name a jolt to the imagination), was determined to strip us lean, morally: her convictions with respect to the sacred brought to bear with a mercilessly exact aim on our secular way of thinking.

In one story after another, in "Good Country People" and in "The Enduring Chill" and in "The Lame Shall Enter First," the central figure of the fictional struggle, the one who embodies our present-day values and expectations and sympathies and loyalties, the one with whom we are tempted to agree, and identify, is revealed as deeply flawed morally; in each instance it is a matter of a prideful intellect that serves its owner

poorly, makes him or her all too self-absorbed and indifferent to others, even those close by virtue of membership in the same family. As she works that theme
over, O'Connor probes what I suppose might be called
a secular progression of sorts, a "developmental psychology," a series of "moral stages," though she would surely
shun such social science talk. Still, she had keen eyes
and ears, had taken the measure of our days, ways,
hence her analysis of how the secular mind, here and
now, works.

In the beginning, she reminds us, there are the minds
eager to know, anxious to expand their awareness.
These are individuals who are sure of themselves as
teachers or thinkers, as aspiring writers or scholars or
healers: people who are quick to think of themselves as
more advanced intellectually than others, and with
some justification. They have gone to school, college,
graduate school; or they have broken with the customs
of other less worthy folks around them, the ignorant or
the superstitious, or, yes, the narrow and bigoted—and
so they are in the vanguard of thought, as compared
with their neighbors. They may be older, have had a
good deal of sobering experience in life, and therefore
with some obvious justification feel themselves a leg up
on certain others. Finally, they are men and women
who are natively intuitive, or have been lucky enough to
learn about the world through travel, and consequently
are sometimes able to distance themselves from the all
too apparent narrowness, even blindness, and assuredly
the ignorance of those nearby in one or another town.
Here, after a fashion, is O'Connor's version of the long-
heralded and, these days, much vaunted "New South":

those who, with great satisfaction and with conviction and with no little sense of personal worth, are intent on leading a region long held by others, from afar, to be benighted into a contemporary, secular "promised land." In that new Canaan money flows more widely across a long impoverished land, and, too, schools and colleges take on great meaning, and cultural pursuits (museums, orchestras, galleries, bookstores, theaters) all prosper, as do universities devoted to turning out educated businessmen, engineers, doctors, and lawyers, and, not least, future professors. All of that O'Connor attends and evokes, sometimes in a wickedly seductive and ultimately provocative (even enraging) manner: she will "build up" her assortment of artists, psychotherapists, university graduates with advanced degrees, and individuals with advanced ideas, people eager to bid good-bye to the South's racial segregation, its formerly intransigent caste system, in favor of professed "interest" in the blacks, a readiness to see them, at the least, as fellow voters, as classmates of their own kin in schools, as sharers of buses, of seats at movie houses and in restaurants—all quite promising, quite "progressive."

Yet, soon enough, this congenial expression of bright prospects yields to quite something else: an ambition for intellectual advancement, for social change, for a heightened awareness become, in their sum, a source of pride in the sense of achievements celebrated, but also in the (biblical) sense of a smugness, a congratulatory self-regard that soars. Now, hope turns to expectation—everything, in time, will be known. Science is not only a many splendored thing; it is the eventual victor in any and all confrontations with nature, with ourselves as a big part of nature, hence O'Connor's wry remark once that "mystery is a great embarrassment to the modern mind." Give us but time, and the funding, and we will clear aside those mysteries, we say or hear others say, in laboratories and classrooms, and outside them, too—a shared public notion, if not fantasy.

Meanwhile, as Erik H. Erikson observed in connection with psychoanalysis, idolatry and insistent or even punitive orthodoxy are not incompatible with such "progress" in the mind's mastery of itself and its surroundings. To repeat, Freud, ridiculing the "illusion" of religious faith, himself became an object of veneration for many, at least for a while, his every word given more credibility than he himself may have thought possible or desirable: Freudianism. Marx, similarly contemptuous of religion, became a historical figure whose picture was waved in Red Square. And in the "dictatorship of the proletariat," Stalin's rule, and other all too grim, even murderous, reminders of the way in which what got proudly called "scientific materialism" (the heart of secular thinking) became, in fact, brute and blind statism, a faith all its own imposed through relentlessly enforced indoctrination: from reflection in the name of the mind's independence to propaganda as an instrument of compulsory mass persuasion. Indeed, those of us who have done documentary work, used words and photographs and film footage to render, we hope accurately, compassionately, sensitively, and sensibly, the lives of others, have other kinds of "documentary" efforts to contemplate, lest we, also, become all too taken with our capacities, our sense of what we have done and can do and hope to do: Leni Riefenstahl's *Triumph of the Will*, of course, but no less notorious, if less powerfully effective, the mobilization of writing and photography that advanced the interests of Nazi and Soviet political and intellectual and cultural hegemony. (Not that, in more subtle or indirect ways, of course, any political and economic system, including a capitalist one, a democratic one, doesn't exert, in some degree, a shaping influence on its own citizens through the verbal and visual messages sent to them by those who own television companies, newspapers, magazines, movie studios, publishing houses.)

When Flannery O'Connor remarked that "the task of the novelist is to deepen mystery," she was, needless to say, throwing down the gauntlet to a fact-obsessed world; and on a so-called higher level, she was challenging a theory-committed world in which those facts are assembled to suit the conveniences and purposes of various concepts and the conceptualists who have promulgated them. She saw us as ever intent on proving ourselves aware of, and in progressive or potential control of, all things, and, she believed, ironically unaware of the consequences of such an outlook. True, there are, as the clichéd language of today has it, "problems" and "issues" to be (that cool, slippery word) "resolved," so any of us social scientists can be overheard admitting. But the prominent secular modes of thought, no matter their dark or dour sides, emphasize an eventual upbeat outcome—the reason, perhaps, for their "success": an embrace from a here-and-now world that worries not about Armageddon, expects not a Judgment Day, hopes not for a Heaven, fears not a Hell, but for sure counts hard and bets everything on a longer and better spell of it in this place of ours. The dream was that the heartless exploitation of the working class would give way to a world in which the state "withered away." The dream was that a searching acknowledgment of our lusts and rivalries would, through the pursuit of psychoanalysis by more and more individuals, give us a clearheaded citizenry. The dream was that physicists and biologists, their minds brilliantly set on exploring the minutest details of matter, would end up doing so all right, to the point that human life would last and last, a huge span of time at our beck and call. Nor is such optimism, today, in jeopardy, some disappointments notwithstanding. Good cheer about what we can do, what the consequence of what we do will turn out to be, is a hallmark of our time. Economists will steer us through, and psychologists, and chemists and computer technologists and research physicians, and research engineers: our "down" side will be explored and, over the generations, will recede, a consequence of (scientific) light over the murky, darker elements in this life.

For O'Connor, of course, the "mystery" to which she referred is not a matter of luck, good and bad, or of our uncertain capacity to weather unexpected obstacles put in our way by fate; she knew the mystery of evil, as well—of human "finitude," of the limits of imagination and thoughtfulness, and, very important, of reason itself, since it is something that will always emerge from our necessarily flawed minds (so she believed them to be). Put differently, she believed in God's mysteries and, with them, in the Devil, that fallen angel who nevertheless (in her eyes) has had a continuing existence, across all generations. She was not morbid, but she was not naive, and she had excellent moral vision, as attested by stories such as "The Displaced Person" and "Everything That Rises Must Converge": both of them take direct aim at various secular anticipations, at our confidence in who or what we are, at the silver lining we always find—if not the pie in the sky—as we contemplate even our troubling social reality, or the less than attractive personal qualities any of us can be found possessing. For her, an obvious irony is around the corner of any moment of achieved or fortuitous benevolence, the devil always having slippery shoes. To Freud's maxim, in the name of explorative science, that the Id's greed and tumult will give way to the Ego's confident, penetratingly effective knowledge (all wielded for the good), she would, no doubt, pose a historian's account of recent times, not to mention the observations of us made by various philosophers, theologians, novelists, poets. Surely, she'd align herself with the physicist Pascal (as in his "law of pressure"), who, like her, died at only thirty-nine, but who found time to give us this mention of the Ego, under the classificatory title of "self-love" (in his one hundredth pensée):

> The nature of self-love and of this human Ego is to love self only and consider self only. But what will man do? He cannot prevent this object that he loves from being full of faults and wants. He wants to be great and he sees himself small. He wants to be happy, and he sees himself miserable. He wants to be perfect, and he sees himself full of imperfection. He wants to be the object of love and esteem among men, and he sees that his faults merit only their hatred and contempt. This

embarrassment in which he finds himself produces in him the most unrighteous and criminal passion that can be imagined; for he conceives a mortal enmity against that truth which reproves him, and which convinces him of his faults.

Here, for Pascal, was the psychological essence of the secular mind. Even in the grim Marx, the gloomy realist Freud, the trembling experimental physicist or biologist, worried sick about what *might* happen to us, courtesy of nuclear proliferation or the emergence of new and deadly bacterial strains or viruses, there is the feisty and proud fighter who says no to such a "downer" as Pascal's comment—as he himself well knew:

He [we] would annihilate it [such a recognition of our "human Ego" as has just been described], but, unable to destroy it in its essence, he [meaning, any of us] destroys it as far as possible in his own knowledge and in that of others; that is to say, he devotes all his attention to hiding his faults both from others and from himself, and he cannot endure either that others should point them out to him, or that he should see them. Truly it is an evil to be full of faults; but it is still greater evil to be full of them and to be unwilling to recognize them, since that is to add the further fault of a voluntary illusion.

A surprising, if not stunning intellectual irony: Pascal, in the name of Christian (sacred) realism, anticipated Freud's secular realism—and then some. It is as if Blaise in the seventeenth century said to Sigmund in the twentieth: look, my dear friend, I appreciate fully (heartily, too) your desire to plumb the depths, get to the bottom of things, dispel all possible illusions; I only worry about your own. A self-described conquistador who has earned title to the word, you make the mistake of confusing particular battles with a war—no, the metaphor fails here: with, rather, a *condition*, something that *is*. I know that mention of such a notion goes against every grain of your thought. For you (as for me) the mind is full of the egoism, the narcissism you and your followers call it, that we both have explored. We differ, though, on what is possible in the future, in *any* future. For you there is knowledge as the ultimate winner, despite that narcissism, and its discontents, its dangers—if not psychoanalysis, then biochemistry, and if not that, then some other unforeseeable, triumphant turn of the scientific (i.e., secular) screw. For me, there is our human situation as it has been handed down to us from on high (forgive me if I become slyly ambiguous here, a doubter's privilege as he struggles, even so, for faith), meaning from God, or God as Nature (as part of Himself, Herself, Itself, whatever!).

You will laugh, my colleague, and say that such a viewpoint makes you, a proudly skeptical and cautious pessimist, seem positively utopian in outlook, but I must continue with this. For you secularists there is always possibility; that is, your faith in the mind's Promethean exertions and their subsequent achievements. For us, in contrast, who are secularists as well, but who strive toward the sacred, check in with it, so to speak, constantly and urgently, slouching (rather than striding) toward Jerusalem, as the poet has said of us, there is only so much possibility, because there is, as well, a certain bedrock finality to who we are, to what we seek and contend with. Round and round versions of us go, get regarded and defined (different words at different times), but in a rock-bottom sense our nature is *there*, as it has always been. We leap ahead, yes, of course, but so doing, we also return to certain inevitable and utterly fundamental qualities, situations: love and its discontents, including the "self-love" we have both discussed at such (knowing!) length; the various psychological and moral and social vulnerabilities of this life; ambition and resolve and conviction and fear and resentment and envy and jealousy and hate, and, finally, the knowledge that somehow, someway, sometime, no matter the other knowledge that has held it at bay, death will bring us to the end of this stay. That knowledge, our awareness of death, goes to the heart of our unyielding (you abhor the word, I know) humanity: an existentialism, that is, finally, in certain important respects, unalterable in its character, our illusions notwithstanding—those that go under the name of science and progress, rather than religion, meaning those that are secular rather than tied to the sacred.

IV

Where We Are Headed

WE IN the Western bourgeois world are committed, as mentioned, to the future, resolutely and consistently so. That slant, toward what is coming rather than what has been, is itself an important attribute of the secular mind. Why turn back and imagine what Pascal might have to say, based on what he has already so tellingly said, were he with us now (and especially if he wasn't, back then, a hopeful visionary with great expectations galore), when we can make prophets of ourselves, or by association, as eager, willing (sometimes, decidedly gullible) readers, part of a collective farsighted response: a culture of upbeat anticipation? Poor Pascal, anyway—so "depressed," so in need of Prozac, so immersed in the tortures (the self-torture) of an accusatory Catholicism worthy, actually, of some of the frenzied Puritan divines who began to settle America around the time he was being so "hard" on himself, not to mention the rest of us! Instead, we wear our binoculars, scan the coming years, extrapolate from what now is to what, for sure, will be, go further, give ourselves permission to run way ahead, down through more than the decades.

One such look ahead was ironically titled *Looking Backward*—Edward Bellamy's fictional effort in 1888 to envision the America of our time. He gives us a Boston both flourishing and fair-minded, the proverbial "city on the hill" of its Puritan forebears realized at last in the year 2000. He gives us a socialism that is appealing, vibrant: an egalitarian world that is a telling contrast to the Gilded Age. Now, at the start of a new millennium, the America that Henry George described in *Progress and Poverty* (1879) had given way to a country of bustling cities and towns all of whose inhabitants lived comfortable and connected lives.

When Bellamy's central character, Julian West, wakes up, scans the business and cultural life of Boston and beyond, he has sailed during his long sleep across a century and more of strife and injustice, landed safe and well on the shores of a "promised land"—with electricity and credit cards and shopping malls and a version of the radio: a novelist's uncanny capacity to imagine predictively a strikingly different life from the one he observed daily. But Bellamy's utopian story, so often hailed for the accuracy of its depiction of our contemporary habits and gadgetry, is really a moral and psychological fantasy, an idea of a nation whose citizens are kindly, contemplative, courteous, and, above all, uninterested in grabbing all they can get, no matter the consequences for others. Bellamy believed us Americans to be perfectible within, even as he saw us becoming rich; he portrays us as both just and tolerant. For him, our great lust would be for benevolence: our idealism wouldn't be deterred; our minds and hearts would flourish under such circumstances. Here is a civilized, humane Superego, well able to tame judiciously the now attenuated and discreet pressures of the Id, and an Ego free ("free at last") to pursue virtues as well as property. Meanwhile (the irony!) we, who live in the America Bellamy foretold, find *ourselves* "looking backward," making all too suggestive and melancholy comparisons between the economic and social disparities of the late nineteenth century and those of our time. To be sure, not all futurist fantasies have been confidently joyful hymns to our dreams become a realized series of breakthroughs. In the darkest hours of this century and, maybe, of all centuries, only fifty years ago, George Orwell, in 1948, gave us his well-known *1984*. There he called a halt to the Ego—the one George Eliot and Sir Willoughby in their different ways knew, the one Pascal and Freud knew, the one Pascal thought would always be, or the one Freud thought might well one day emerge. Dorothea's "theoretic" mind in *Middlemarch*, Sir Willoughby's endlessly vain mind in *The Egoist*, Pascal's portrayal of an Ego also quite self-preoccupied, though with no true conviction of its ultimate virtue, quite the contrary, and Freud's portrayal of an Ego buffeted, but also potentially capable of taking matters into its own hands (taking its owner, after all, to see a psychoanalyst: will as the Ego's great instrument of assertion, no matter an Id that resembles Pascal's description of a side of us)—all of that, in Orwell's premonitory chronicle, becomes almost irrelevant. For the time was approaching (only thirty-six years ahead, a couple of generations at the most) when the Ego as rendered by all four of those writers, two novelists, two scientists with speculative tendencies, would be mere putty in the hands of something larger than any human being, something with a momentum of its own, a strangely impersonal (and inhuman) construction of social and political reality that would have enormous, compelling, even definitive sway over all within its grasp. In essence, Orwell gave us an Ego strangely placid, imperturbable, no longer pressed by Freud's Id, no longer troubled within by Pascal's moral misgivings, no longer swollen by Meredith's version of unembarrassed conceit or Eliot's of heedless self-regard (theoretical elaboration as a variant of self-promotion), but now the property of something else: the state's (moral, political) power become for the individual a commanding and pervasive presence—the Ego as something *without*, enforcing its institutional will on the within of all those subjugated "mass-men" (Czeslaw Milosz's "captive mind").

We breathe easier these days, surely. Orwell's apprehension has not quite come true—that more and more totalitarian states would control not only the civic life of their subjects, or their economic fate, or the cultural values given expression, but their minds in a more direct and intimate way: what they think, the language they use, how they speak to one another. Of course, many of us in the social sciences and in psychoanalytic psychiatry have, perhaps, underestimated all along the impact on individuals of all that happens in the name of race, class, politics, culture as it affirms itself on the radio, on television, on the Internet, in journalism, in advertising, in the theater. It took me some time, in the course of working with children caught in political and social and racial crises, to realize that their mental life had to do not only with the relationships they had with their mothers and fathers and brothers and sisters, but with the larger world they inhabited. All the time children's thoughts and impressions and opinions and concerns and misgivings and fears are being shaped outside their homes as well as within them: in neighborhoods, and in the realm that reaches them through the television set or on-line, or as they sit watching a movie in the living room or a theater. Yet with Stalinism gone, with the terrible likes of Hitler a constantly receding nightmare, with democracies increasingly prevalent in our own hemisphere, we can assure ourselves that the "brainwashing" so often described in earlier decades of this century, and so vividly evoked, satirized by Orwell, is no longer a threat to us.

Yet Orwell may have been more pervasively and broadly prophetic than we want him to be; he may well have meant to examine across the board the nature of political and of cultural authority, their influence on a nation's citizens, and to do so as a satirist does, through the exaggerations of caricature. After all, during the Second World War he worked for the BBC; he was no stranger, then, to politics become public "information," if not outright propaganda. (The latter, of course, is always what one's enemies describe; the former what one's own side is trying to get across.) In any event, Orwell was at pains, apart from *1984*, to remind us that the language we use, the reading we favor, and what we are taught to make of that reading, has to do with a lot more than the emergence of Fascism or Communism, with their statist encroachment on private life. In "Boys' Weeklies," in "Politics vs. Literature," in "Poetry and the Microphone," in "Notes on Nationalism," in "The Prevention of Literature," he kept taking on "culture" and "political power" as they bear down on our ways of thinking, our minds. For him "the huge bureaucratic machines" that he mentions in "Poetry and the Microphone" (it was published in 1945, well before *1984* appeared) exert enormous psychological impact on our personal lives and become, in fact, overseers, even as they control so many of us, economically, politically. For him, too, Freud's Superego was not merely a consequence of family life, a "construct" that we theorists invoke as a means of referring to countless admonitions by mothers and fathers become, eventually, a child's notion of ought and naught, probably yes and definitely no. Rather, parents and children alike learn to shape their sense of the possible, the desirable, the forbidden in response to a host of institutional imperatives quite evidently and concretely transmitted to them, to all of us. A novelist rather than a theorist, Orwell nevertheless extended the psychoanalytic paradigm for widespread public consideration. In truth, he intuitively sensed what the young Willhelm Reich had noted in his work on "character types," that the mind responds significantly to the social forces of a society as well as the particular "dynamics" of this or that family, and he had also anticipated by several years Erik H. Erikson's similar line of reasoning in *Childhood and Society* (1950).

Orwell, the idiosyncratic, levelheaded agnostic and skeptic, was crankily contemptuous of "principalities and powers," including his own socialist brethren. He looked askance at the modern state, and the corporate world, and, especially, the media—so much under the control of one or the other of those two. But his picture of the future was based on gloomy conjecture rather than on substantial experience. In contrast, Milosz's *The Captive Mind* draws on a prophetic poet's daily contact with a Stalinism terribly triumphant after the Second World War. Indeed, only five years after *1984* was published, Milosz would make this crucial comparative observation in *The Captive Mind*:

> The citizen of the people's democracies is immune to the kind of neurosis that takes such manifold forms in capitalist countries. In the West, a man subconsciously regards society as unrelated to him. Society indicates the limits he must not exceed; in exchange for this he receives a guarantee that no one will meddle excessively in his affairs. If he loses it's his own fault; let psychoanalysis help him. In the East there is no boundary between man and society. His game, and whether he loses or wins, is a public matter. He is never alone. If he loses it is *not* because of indifference on the part of his environment, but because the environment keeps him under such minute scrutiny. Neuroses as they are known in the West result, above all, from man's aloofness; so even if they were allowed to practice, psychoanalysts would not earn a plum, in the people's democracies.

Here categorical assertion, even in supremely sensitive and accomplished hands, proves as inadequate as futurist fiction, such as *1984*. It is worth noting, however, that Orwell the polemical essayist (and, during the Second World War, unashamed propagandist for Great Britain, no matter his egalitarian misgivings) was shrewdly unwilling to engage in the kind of unqualified analysis that tempts Milosz in the above statement, whose simplifications, however, bear their own story:

the scarcely suppressed anxiety and anger of a private person who sees firsthand and everywhere the monolithic state "moving in," stifling any and all expressions of particular souls in favor of the rehearsed slogans, exhortative always, of officialdom. We in the West, now, have the privilege of noticing, right off, and in comfortable retrospect, the exaggerations of such a midcentury description of what Churchill's "fall of the iron curtain" meant for the psychology of millions. We can, with justification, remind ourselves repeatedly that we, too, are not immune to the strong, if less explicit and uniformed and politically engineered, influences abroad in our respective (capitalist, democratic) lands. Still, for Milosz the quantitative had become qualitative, and he surely had every right to worry: a secular, political Superego hugely watchful, able to exact a good deal of compliance from the instinctual life of a people, and able to command from the Ego every bit of responsive adherence, at first perhaps out of an edgy, reluctant awareness of *realpolitik*, and, eventually, with the unwilling, reflexic alacrity of true "indoctrination"—so the parents of Milosz's age must have worriedly foreseen as their children's fate, or that of their children's children. How long, Milosz must have wondered, would his fellow Polish citizens stay even remotely loyal in their heads and hearts, never mind their Sunday habits, to the Catholic Church, in the face of the overwhelming presence of a totalitarian regime in their lives, its authority everywhere in evidence: on the radio and television, in the newspapers and magazines, in the schools and universities, on constant public display through well-organized parades, through the sight, all the time, of the police, the army, the hovering helicopters and zooming bombers and fighters of the air force?

We know decades later that Orwell's fictional nightmare, and that of Milosz (based, again, on experience, on direct observation rather than futurist alarm) have not come to pass—a function of a political and religious struggle fought successfully in Europe and elsewhere. History is more complex than the dramatic temptations of a novelist such as Orwell permit, especially when the novelist (not unlike some of us social scientists) wants to make a provocative, singular point. Nevertheless, Milosz's sober conclusions were drawn from his acute awareness of what was, at a minimum, in the process of taking place, no matter its eventual outcome. Moreover, many thousands must have, at least partially, fallen victim to what he described, their lives witness to the psychological realization of what Orwell could only render in apprehensive speculation. Again, it was back, in Eastern Europe, a matter of degree, a struggle being waged; and no doubt about it, one has to keep insisting, the same situation of a merely *relative* independence of thought and feeling (with respect to various social and political structures) applies to our lives in the West. How significantly, as a matter of fact, did the Catholic Church influence the minds of its faithful in Poland (or elsewhere) eighty years ago, sixty years ago, never mind during the decades when commissars took on cardinals unto death for the minds (souls) of a nation's, a continent's population? Why did both Orwell and Milosz seriously underestimate the sacred as they took measure of the secular—in East and West alike? The pope's visit to Cuba, his enthusiastic reception there, tells us, yet again, of the limits of the secular, no matter its might, even as the sacred must contend constantly with secular intrusions.

In this regard, I return in my memory to a conversation I had in 1973 with Dorothy Day, in her living quarters at the Catholic Workers' St. Joseph's House, at 36 East First Street in New York City. She was reminiscing about her earlier life as a suffragette, as an ardent secular person who lived in Greenwich Village, wrote for the socialist paper *The Call,* embraced various "causes" of the time, the 1920s. Her life had changed after she gave birth to her daughter Tamar (the child of a friendship rather than a marriage): a subsequent conversion to the Catholic Church, to which she thereafter gave herself fully in mind and heart. Yet she was ever the astute observer of others, of herself, and as the author of a novel and a screenplay or two, she had trouble ignoring human complexity, paradox, inconsistency. After singing the praises of a church's traditions and values, which she didn't hesitate to describe as nothing short of "lifesaving" in their impact on her, she suddenly shifted her point of view, and with a furrowed brow offered these words: "I love sitting in church praying. I try not to let it be automatic—I try to be myself and talk to God as honestly and spontaneously as I can. I'm afraid—I'm really afraid that going to church and praying will become an automatic thing with me. I'm afraid I'll be going through the motions—that I won't be thinking, or be *myself* praying—that I'll be half conscious, daydreaming. I'm in church seeking the sacred, but I go there as a secular person. I feel split, try as I might not to be!

"I told the priest all of this [what she had at some great length been telling me, of which the above is but a part] and he wasn't happy with what I said! He reprimanded me! He said I hadn't yet learned to be a 'natural Catholic.' He said the church should be a 'regular' part of your life—you shouldn't be thinking too much about it, and be 'self-conscious' about it. Well, I wasn't ready to surrender so fast! I said, 'Father, yes, I see what you mean. But how about just 'conscious,' not 'self-conscious,' but 'conscious'? He wasn't pleased with me at all! He said he was afraid that my definition of 'conscious' is his of 'self-conscious.' He said the church has its own ways of influencing your life, and you shouldn't hold it up to secular standards—the sacred gets to you 'slow time,' and the secular 'fast time,' right away. He said I'm trying to 'force' things in church!

"I didn't want to talk with him much more about this! Maybe I'll never be able to be the 'regular' or 'natural' Catholic he wants me to be—or maybe I'll never forget what happened to some of my dear friends who became Communists [in the 1930s]. I'm not here to 'red-bait,' I never did. I could see then, and I *still* can, why they chose as they did. But I saw their minds get swept up, swept away. They criticized people for getting swept up by capitalist materialism, and then they got swept up by another kind of materialism. They seemed to lose all their independence; they said what they were supposed to say—I would be talking to them, and I could almost predict, word for word, what I'd hear coming out of their mouths! It was scary to me—not that I would necessarily disagree with what they were trying to get at. It was the *automatic* way they spoke, the instant replies, with the words and phrases I'd been hearing for years. I recall one of my friends speaking like that—I recall thinking afterwards: he's lost, his mind is gone; it's no longer his mind, it belongs to the party, and its spokesmen, and to what's decided by them, the higher-ups, here and abroad. I'm not talking about 'discipline,' here; I'm talking about believing something, the faith that you must take your orders in what you say or do, that you aren't really responsible for anything on your own, but only as part of something larger, called Communism, and your life is to be put on the line for that [ideology], in a manner that others decide, and you're in a holding pattern: you wait for those others to tell you what to do.

"I don't say it's not the same, being a Catholic, or for that matter, a devout Protestant or Jew. I'm just saying that anything is possible for any of us, that we can take religion or politics or some set of ideas, and end up living in such a way that we lose all sense of who we are—our minds no longer belong to us. I know, I know—that is what some passionate religious pilgrims say they are *hoping* will happen to them! [I had suggested as much.] But I'm hoping it's not completely the same—because God isn't here, whereas Lenin and Stalin and all those who speak in their name are very much one of us flawed, sinful human beings. I know, yes, the bishops and cardinals, the priests and nuns, are 'flawed, sinful human beings,' too. [I had made mention of that obvious point.] But God isn't that—it's the heart of the religious faith, to believe so. You know, when people ask me why I converted, *that's* what I tell them, that I was looking for something beyond this secular life, that I've lived to the full, I'll have to admit, and I found that something in a sacred tradition, and so when I go to church, I try to *live* my religion, *live* that sacred time in that sacred place, and that's what I was trying to tell the priest the other day: I get frightened I'll pick up my old secular ways in church and, while praying, just go through the motions the way I used to, when I was living in the Village and going fast, fast—always something to do, or some new idea to have, or people to meet."

She stopped, and seemed elsewhere in her thoughts, maybe visiting yet again that "secular life" to which she had just referred. I was finally beginning to understand what she had been trying to tell me—about the struggle on her part to be a believing, loyal, faithful Catholic, but not an "automatic" one. She wanted to be a believer whose *will* was part of her faith; whose *intellect* was also part of her faith; whose *passions* even, were part of her faith. She wanted, put differently, her very own, personal sacred life: her particular mix of desire (Id) and conscience (Superego) as they are handled by her "consciousness," the word she kept having in mind as she conversed with the priest, a version of Freud's Ego. She feared a surrender of her mind not to spiritual faith but to institutional authority, even as she very much felt connected to that institution's authority. It was a real tightrope she was walking, but one she very much wanted (willed, contemplated) to walk. Hers, I dared surmise, but not say, was a struggle to be a devout Catholic believer whose faith was *hers*, hers to give, as opposed to a Catholic believer who had lost a sense of herself as the one who offered her faith upward, as it were.

Again, an elusive distinction, perhaps, and one subject to interpretations (theological, creedal, psychoanalytic) other than the kind I knew then, and now, to make. Still, in her own way, I thought then, and do now, she was addressing matters that Orwell and Arthur Koestler (in *Darkness at Noon*, a book Milosz mentions in his *Captive Mind*) also struggled to comprehend. How to hold secure one's own moral and spiritual self, one's personal, reflective destiny—amidst the crushing institutional forces of the state, but also of the marketplace and, yes, the church in its decidedly secular aspect?

In the world of George Eliot and Meredith, and Freud, too, the Ego is buffeted by the ever demanding Id and a Superego of varying sway, depending on the particular person in question. None of Eliot's fictional individuals nor Meredith's are overwhelmed by a punitive conscience. Indeed, even Dostoievsky's obsessed characters, such as Raskolnikov, somehow find solace, even love, and, beyond that, a kind of redemptive sense of worth (so, too, with Dickens's dissolute ones, such as Sydney Carton). Unsurprisingly, these are individuals recognizable to us of the Western bourgeoisie, men and women not unlike Freud's patients, who also manage to find *their* kind of "redemption"—in the course of psychiatric treatment, for example, when a doctor's insights with respect to the reasons for their troubled state of mind get turned into narrative presentations on his part of their stories. That is a substantial part, actually, of what psychoanalysis is: the doctor "reads" the patient's life, assembles it into a rendered narrative, with the patient becoming, in turn, his or her reader, a listener to what an observer of himself or herself has come to know. All of this is idiosyncratic, personal: each man or woman is "driven" by particular interests, passions, a particular sense of what is suitable, what is undesirable, if not unseemly, or utterly out of order. "The mix in every patient I see is in certain important respects unique," Anna Freud once commented at the end of a challenging clinical seminar, and by "mix" she meant that human particularity: a person's life as it develops in a home, a neighborhood, a nation, in the midst of a historical time—this sum of "variables" prompting the formation of the mind's life, bearing down on it, giving it a distinctive, expressive existence.

For Orwell, the worried futurist, and Milosz, the dismayed observer, that psychological state of affairs had seemingly changed. For them, the state threatened to become not only militarily and politically triumphant, but psychologically so: the custodial Superego for millions, their Ids effectively enthralled, their Egos an instrument, pure and simple, of the state's bureaucratic manipulation. To be sure, philosophers such as Gabriel Marcel had claimed to glimpse a parallel, if not quite similar, sociological and psychological drama taking place in the advanced industrial nations of the West— so-called mass-men, individuals by the millions who are "alienated," who live for and by the slogans of a commercial world become powerfully persuasive. But totalitarian rule is quite another matter, Orwell believed, and Milosz declared out of a right as a witness to draw on comparative experiences. Milosz struggled (against the high and understandable odds of political despair) for balance, for nuance. Throughout *The Captive Mind* he wants to distinguish the inclination any of us has to one or another kind of personal, social, cultural, religious compliance (our conscience influenced by various others, by institutional life as it connects with our day-to-day experience) from the extraordinary nature of the Nazi state, the Soviet state, as they both pressed, by carefully developed design, on the lives of millions, using modern technology in a continuing public theater that made the religious theater of the past pale in comparison, and using, too, the full coercive power available to modern dictators and their fawning, fearful intimates.

Milosz starts his book, though, not with factual description but with relatively obscure literary discussion. The first chapter is titled "The Pill of Multi-Bing," which, we are told, has to do with "a curious book" that was published in Warsaw in 1932, a generation before Milosz set to work on *The Captive Mind.* The book's title is *Insatiability,* a two-volume novel by Stanislaw Witkiewicz, a Polish philosopher, who was also a painter. A phenomenologist, in the spirit of Husserl, Witkiewicz wondered what, if anything, made modern man "happy." Like many writers and artists and philosophers of the early decades of the twentieth century, he regarded civilization as a paradox: it provides both food and food for thought in substantial amounts, but it leaves many feeling insignificant, dwarfed by buildings, factories, social institutions to which they feel little affiliation, while also bereft of spiritual belief, because religion has been effectively "demythologized," not necessarily through study, reflection, argument, but by a general awareness of "science" and its conclusions that

cuts deeply, decisively into the old assertions and cer-
tainties learned in Sunday School, Hebrew School.

In *Insatiability*, the phenomenon conveyed by the
book's title is addressed through a storyteller's bold leap
into imaginative fantasy, but, significantly, of a kind
that possesses its own obvious ties to the mainstay of
credibility in the West: materialism as the one hope that
we still uphold with conviction, or that we won't cast
aside, no matter our reservations or doubts—in this instance, the materialism of the omnipresent pill, ever
ready to help us calm down, go to sleep, stay awake,
digest our food, be rid of our waste, alleviate our headaches, toothaches, stomach pains, our myalgias and
arthralgias. Milosz summarizes the thrust of *Insatiability*
by noting that it initially describes people as "unhappy
in that they have no faith and no sense of meaning in
their work." He tells the Western readers of *The Captive
Mind*, well aware of what has befallen him and his fellow Poles under the Soviet shadow, that in the pages of
Insatiability "hawkers appear in the city peddling Multi-
Bing pills." Those pills are named for a Mongolian philosopher, Multi-Bing (the long-standing European fear
of invasion from the East!), and they, not tanks and airplanes, will become vehicles of conquest: those who
ingest Multi-Bing, hitherto apathetic, perplexed, melancholy, become rather quickly "serene and happy."
People apprehensive, agitated, become calm, even-
tempered. The "dissonant music" of the past gives way
to stirring "marches and odes." Abstract paintings are
replaced by "socially useful pictures": a complete turn in
a reigning culture. (The novel's author, upon learning

that Stalin's army had invaded Poland from the east, on September 17, 1939, committed suicide.)

We are being told, right off, by Milosz, that art can foresee history, that there are clues in a culture that enable an all too accurate imaginative portrayal of what awaits us around time's corner. Armies matter, but their ultimate victory, Milosz and others have known, will depend on some solid social and psychological control over any given country's people. A writer's fantasy indicates a likely direction of history. The mind will be controlled not by a military presence, or even the persuasive influence of an ideological presence, but by dint of a mood-altering pill: people become compliant and passive in the face of history's unfolding struggles, a version of Orwell's worried prophecy, but one that specifies "neurochemistry" as the ultimate "force."

Yesterday's futurists have a way of becoming today's engineers, scientists, practical, technological experimenters. Jules Verne's *Twenty Thousand Leagues under the Sea*, the comic strip "Flash Gordon," or, for that matter, the visual and visionary ruminations of Leonardo da Vinci as he put them to paper, have become our submarines and airplanes and spaceships. Surely those machines will have their successors, and this planet will become a home base for further and farther penetrations of space by us, who will come to think of ourselves as, among other things, earth-folk, defined not only by, say, our nationalist but by our planetary origins. But right now we are not only exploring our moon and Mars and Saturn, gazing at greater stretches of the universe; we are also looking more confidently, knowingly, within ourselves—a huge jump taken this century by medical scientists. The brain, which has so successfully explored all other organs, and has, of course, imagined us doing so much, then enabled us to do so much here on Earth and elsewhere across the galaxy, is only recently, as mentioned, becoming able to understand itself with a similar kind of precision and competence. Such a development, the brain probing itself, learning to regulate itself, has also been the subject of substantial futurist speculation, Witkiewicz's meditation being one of many. Nor has an ominous, devouring, cruelly arbitrary Stalinism been the only political or economic system that has prompted such leaps of fancy with respect to the human mind: efforts, really, to conjure up a kind of "exit" for people very much threatened or vulnerable.

Perhaps the best-known novel, in that tradition, is Aldous Huxley's *Brave New World* (1932), wherein the drug "soma" figures as part of a broader scheme to strip people of their human nature, really, the strains they feel as members of a family, a workplace, a neighborhood, the worries they feel as they try to get along with their husbands or wives, their children, their bosses or employees, their fellow workers. Huxley has his laboring men and women swallowing tabs of "soma," reciting prayers; he introduces them to "hypnopedic conditioning," grants them sex on demand, and the result is a placid, quiescent employee—exactly what factory managers in our industrial nations need, want, expect of our assembly-line workers. Huxley's satire was directed at a mentality that upheld such mass production, with its human consequences. The motto for the people who live in that "new world" of his is "Community,

Identity, Stability," and the implication is that some-how, sometime ahead, through a mix of neurophysiol-ogy and political sociology we will be able to bring peo-ple around to the demands of advanced capitalism (or socialism, for that matter): turn them into willing, com-petent agents and instruments of an efficient "produc-tive society."

In a lesser literary vein, there is Philip K. Dick's *Blade Runner* (eventually made into a movie), which appeared in 1968. As the book opens, "a merry little surge of elec-tricity" is being "piped by automatic alarm from the mood organ" located near the character Rick Deckard's bed. As he awakens under such mind-galvanizing cir-cumstances, he turns to his nearby wife: "You set your Penfield too weak." He volunteers to reset it, but she wants no part of his initiative. In a few lines, the novel-ist draws on past neurological research (the Canadian scientist Wilder Penfield did pioneering explorations of the brain's functional life); he describes a future in which we manipulate our cognitive and emotional life through machines (or medicines); but he also, quite shrewdly, maybe more so than some of his "betters" among prophetic storytellers, indicates what may be left standing, so to speak, of our present psychological life, centuries from now, when all the advances in our knowledge of the brain have resulted in all those drugs and mechanical devices: namely, our own idiosyncratic, fussy, feisty selves, which, after all, may well have some say in what use we make of such a collective and avail-able "progress." Who, even then, in that future awaiting us, will use what in which manner? Human possibility will become enhanced, but human nature still could have some impact upon how (and when) that possibility is summoned: for what purposes, with whom, and how—or so a novelist not unable to leap across the generations, the centuries, even the millennia, nevertheless wants us to think. It is as if a radical futurist refuses to shed an obstinately conservative side of himself that insists on remembering our capacity as individuals to choose, to disagree as well as comply, to have our own, private opinions, attitudes, even with respect to what others eagerly embrace as necessary, salutary.

In any event, Dick's relatively recent science fiction has been followed by an utterly unsurprising *Time* cover story, titled "How Mood Drugs Work . . . and Fail," such a "news story," obviously, prompted by the increasingly "biological" nature of psychiatry. How well, in that regard, I remember the arrival of Thorazine when I was a house officer at the Massachusetts General Hospital, in the middle 1950s. How well, too, I remember one of my supervisors, Carl Binger, then editor of the journal *Psychosomatic Medicine*, telling me that there would be more and more such drugs, and that "one day" they would be (I still remember his choice of words) "elegant levers" for us doctors to grasp—a source of professional capability then way beyond the imagining of many of us. As if to give his predictive remarks a present-day sanction, Dr. Binger referred me to Freud's *Beyond the Pleasure Principle*, to this portion of it, which he let me know he knew well enough almost to quote by heart: "Biology is truly a land of unlimited possibilities. We may expect it to give us the most surprising information and we cannot guess what answers it will return in a few dozen years to the questions we have put to it. They may be of a kind which will blow away the whole of our artificial structure of hypotheses."

For Dr. Binger, the important point, then, as we conversed, was not only a coming biological ascendancy to psychiatry and psychoanalysis, and not only, too, Freud's willingness to look with some wry distance at his own ideas and, unlike some of his followers, see them in a historical context, but, most especially, his thoroughgoing hopefulness, of a kind almost immediate in its expectant expression: "a few dozen years"— that span of time from someone himself then in his sixties, a recent onlooker of a terribly destructive world war with disastrous social and economic consequences all too evident in Vienna, among other places. Still, the "first psychoanalyst," as Erik H. Erikson once called him, was quite able to foresee, within a century or so, the passing of his entire way of thinking, not to mention, presumably, the profession it had generated, "the last psychoanalyst" soon enough a personal and chronological reality. Moreover, I remember so clearly Dr. Binger's agreement with Freud's assessment of things: "You will live to see psychoanalysis hemmed in, further and further, by biology, as Freud predicted, and you will live to see sociology also bearing down on psychoanalysis." I wrote those words down as those of a psychoanalytic supervisor of mine, but at the time I had no confidence that I had ahead of me the kind of longevity Dr. Binger was positing as mine.

Yet in two dozen of those "few dozen" years Freud mentioned, I would, indeed, see the relative demise of the "orthodox" psychoanalysis I knew as a young psychiatrist in Boston; would see the increasing realization by my colleagues of the persuasive role race and class and ethnicity and nationality and culture and history all play in our mind's thinking, feeling; and would, finally, begin to see what Dr. Binger meant when, back in 1960, he spoke about "biological psychiatry" as just ahead of us. Indeed, the career of a friend of mine, who once taught at Harvard Medical School and now works at the Rockefeller Institute in New York City, is an example of how one professional life can more than accommodate itself to such a shift in a profession's direction. Torsten Wiesel was born in Sweden, was educated there, learned to be a child psychiatrist there. Eventually, however, he came to the United States and learned to do neurobiological research—for which he would win a Nobel Prize: a pioneer in biochemical and physiological and anatomical research in the human brain, assisted, of course, through the study of the brains of animals.

Another physician who has concentrated his thinking on such matters, though as a novelist rather than laboratory researcher, is Walker Percy, whose *Love in the Ruins* has already been mentioned. For all his prophecies of social collapse, moral confusion, Dr. Percy nevertheless flirts with a new science able to bring the brain's functions under closer scrutiny than is now the case. The novel is comic (in a serious, even quite sad way); the reader is offered a "lapsometer," meant to take (literally) the measure of the mind's psychological, if not spiritual or reflective, state: a neurobiological instrument that is both diagnostic and therapeutic. We are prompted to think about not only where we're headed, but where we'll soon enough be. Meanwhile, in 1997, while reading the journal *Psychoanalysis and Contemporary Thought*, I came upon an article with the title "Proposals regarding the Neurobiology of Oedipality," a title I could imagine Dr. Percy's using in mild jest a quarter of a century ago, a means (back then) of spoofing, perhaps, a bloated psychoanalytic vocabulary and an all too insipid or inadequate neurobiological one: neither field able to call upon the other in any useful way then foreseeable. But the essay is written with confidence, draws upon established research as well as speculation. We are introduced, really, to the neural networks that form the anatomical basis of our emotional life, and we are reminded that there is a developmental neuroanatomy that parallels the developmental psychology which we have learned (in certain precincts of our Western world) to call "oedipal." Put all too succinctly, nerves are acquiring their myelin just as young children are learning how to get on with their mothers, fathers.

Not that this article is meant to be a breakthrough one; there is so much we *don't* know about the development of thinking, never mind the specifics of this or that (hypothetical) "complex." But the effort, at this point, in a psychoanalytic publication to connect what Freud himself called a "metapsychology" to neuroanatomy is itself a step in what I suppose can be called an emerging biological psychoanalysis. Further along (a few more of those "dozens of years" Dr. Freud mentioned, a century or two of them, maybe), we will have some idea, at a more microcosmic level, of the neurochemistry and neurophysiology of our thinking life—and then, plausibly, the specifics (with respect to children) of maternal attachment, of rivalry, or fear in connection with fathers, will be ours to figure out in a cellular mode: the biochemistry and neurophysiology of certain localized areas of the brain.

As I say the above, I realize—the article just mentioned notwithstanding, and all the mind-altering drugs which have recently become part of the psychiatric armamentarium also notwithstanding—that we have the proverbial "miles to go," ever so many of them, before we will know about the brain what the brain has enabled us to know, for instance, about the pancreas or the kidneys or the lungs: their structure and function at a microcosmic level, a biochemical and physiological level. Still, to call upon psychoanalytic theory in a way different from that of Dr. Forsyth, an anthropologist at the University of Southern Colorado, in the above cited article on "neurobiology and oedipality," the coming centuries of this dawning third millennium will gradually give us a new kind of Ego, one with real authority, with power to act, rather than primarily react (Freud's early view of things). Sometime in this new millennium, one suspects, our space-people will multiply, the planets of this solar system will yield many of their secrets, and (who knows?) we will figure out ways to plunge into the further recesses (from our viewpoint) of the infinity that surrounds us. But we will also come into growing command of our "thoughts," our "emotions": what we call the Id and the Superego will be understood biologically and, thereafter, brought under control. Once futurists pictured the Superego as an instrument of a state's political authority, an Ego thereby endlessly vulnerable to public slogans become individual mandates, compulsions—the stuff of bureaucratic suppression, repression. Eventually, there will be an Ego able to be its own master, relatively unassailed from within and free to assert itself with an unprecedented competence that is grounded in neurochemical knowledge and its application: biology rather than state power as psychologically triumphant.

Obviously, it is impossible to know how our future psychopharmacological capabilities will effect our emotional (or social or political) destiny. The coming centuries will offer their very own version of Freud's drama, with its three well-known protagonists. But, as Freud anticipated, "mind" will increasingly become "matter," a move from metapsychological inquiry to medical applications and interventions tied to a materialist comprehension of how the brain works. Already biochemistry (in the form of lithium and other drugs) has brought manic-depressive illness under some substantial degree of control; and already the drugs that work against schizophrenia's symptoms, or, indeed, the anxieties and mood disorders of more "normal" people, have generated not only a large medical literature but a cultural response, and, too, among those who take this or that pill, a personal, introspective response—the observant Ego at work. Here, for instance, is a fourth-year medical student speaking of her bouts of anxiety and depression, her use of Prozac and Paxil, but, more generally, her sense of what the future holds for human beings as science gives them more and more leverage over nature, including their thinking and feeling lives: "Sometimes I wonder whether we won't outdo ourselves—learn how to do so much that 'we' are left behind! What do I mean? [I was quick to ask.] I don't know. The subject is too big even for words—that's what I mean! One day we'll even know how people get to speak or write—we'll be able to 'control' that the same way we control the functions of other organs, don't you think? Isn't that the logic of where we're headed? I hear neurobiologists talk about the brain's 'properties' and its 'purpose' or 'qualities' or 'functions' the way we talk about the heart, its 'purposes' and 'functions,' or the G.I. tract or the liver and kidneys—and why not! It's mind-boggling—excuse the way I put it!—but it's going to happen: we'll know the neurobiology of thinking and writing. I mean, we'll understand all that down to the level of tissues and cells and biochemistry and physiology—neurochemistry and neurophysiology way beyond anything we now know. I wouldn't even know how to think about what we'll know about all this someday: what we'll know about knowing, I guess you could say!

"One thing I wonder about—will there always be a 'me' who wonders about what she's doing, and why, or will the 'me' or the 'you' get lost in all the understanding or control we have over the way the brain works. I know I'm not being clear here—I'm being philosophical about what the biological achievements in brain research will mean for us way in the future, a few hundred years from now. Even now, there are times when I wonder where 'I' begin and all the machines and medicines stop—especially when I look at my grandmother and my mom and dad, and me! My grandmother has lived into her middle eighties, and she's lucky, she's practically never been sick. She doesn't take pills. She wakes up on her own—no alarm clock. She drives, but she prefers to walk. She *writes* letters. She has a gas stove and a refrigerator, but no microwave. She uses the phone, but she says she hates talking on it 'too long'!

"My dad—he wakes up by an alarm. He picks up messages by the phone while he's having breakfast. He has his laptop computer near him in the kitchen, and his fax. In his car he has a phone and a fax. He'll hold the wheel with one hand, and talk on the phone, or get his faxes, or dictate. He goes and talks with people all over the world, sometimes, in a teleconference place. He has an 'alarm' in his watch, to remind him that it's time to do this, or something else. He takes pills for headaches, for heartburn, for his nerves; and sometimes, to get to sleep. He flies all over and has all kind of routines to fight jet lag. For him the cellular phone and the laptop are constant necessities—like my grandma carrying her handbag, with her wallet and handkerchief and some lipstick and a small mirror!

"I'm my dad's daughter—and I rely on all the gadgets he does, and I'm sure there will be more of them in the twenty-first century. I've grown *up* with all this; my dad grew *into* it all. He remembers when the fax machine first came out; and the computers and cellular phones. He jokes—he remembers when the doctors had, maybe, phenobarbital to calm you down or knock you out! My grandma shakes her head when she hears him talk like that. Once, she said we'll all get 'lost'—we'll become 'slaves' of all the 'gadgets,' all the 'machines,' all the 'medicines they have.' 'What would happen if we had to exist without that stuff?'; she asked that, and Dad and I laughed. 'Back to nature,' Dad joked—we'd go back to our 'original state.' I kept thinking of that later; I wondered if I could get through a day if I didn't have all that 'stuff,' an alarm clock, my 'psychotropic drugs,' the fax and the computer and the cellular phone. What will it be like a few hundred years from now—will people read books anymore? Will we 'ingest' knowledge, by pill, by some machine? This sounds weird and crazy and fantastic—but my grandmother says that if she'd been told when she was my age what the world would be like when she got to be eighty-five, she'd have thought the person telling her all that had 'quite a wild imagination!' "

We both are smiling—the concreteness of that sixty or so span of years just mentioned seizes our attention, makes us time-conscious, and especially so now, in early 1997, in the last years of a century, a millennium, a time of looking forward and, as well, a time of remembering. A history of science major, now headed for a career in "research medicine," she admits to a "philosophical side" and wonders whether such a way of using the mind won't, itself, become outmoded, a relic of a distant past: "Everything is so *functional* these days. My dad says he's glad—he doesn't have any time to waste, and all of the 'gadgets' my grandmother mentions are huge time-savers. He can't imagine being without them, and I can't either. Down the line, what other 'gadgets' will become indispensable? Won't all that have an effect on the human mind? I mean, is there a limit to how fast we can think and act? It won't be long before we'll be able to 'rocket' rather than fly to

Tokyo or Johannesburg—that means we'll be places in minutes, not hours. It won't be long before we look at each other while we talk on the phone. Right now, you can reach some people anywhere—they're never 'away,' if they don't want to be. I'm just talking about the technology we have, not the technology that's coming. Maybe we'll fly to work in our 'cars'! Maybe we'll press buttons to shop—well, we already can do that. Is there a point that we'll reach—when we'll be overwhelmed, when our bodies, our brains, say 'no,' it's more than we can take? I guess things come just slow enough—the new technology—for us to get used to the latest breakthrough. But I wonder whether our ability to invent and discover won't outreach, surpass our ability to live with what we've done [built, designed, and manufactured].

"I guess if we try to imagine what it'll be like a couple of centuries from now, or at the start of the *fourth* millennium, we should try to think about our limits as well as our ability to overcome limits: I mean, the difference between what we can do with our brains in the way of figuring things out and building technology that will take full advantage of what we've figured out [on the one hand] and [on the other hand] what our brains can 'take.' I mean, I can imagine some neurophysiologist discovering *why* we need to sleep, what sleep does for the brain, and then discovering some substance that 'replaces' sleep—do you see what I mean?—and then we'd all be strutting around, telling each other that we've just added on a third of our lives to our 'living time,' because sleep isn't necessary any more. Just think of that!

You're shaking your head and smiling, but that could be happening sometime in the future—and then time itself will change: we'll be living so much longer, and we'll be awake so much longer. I wonder how it will affect us, the way we *are*, not the way we *live*, or is this kind of question, this kind of thinking, going to be obsolete, because we'll be able to 'get rid of it,' 'control' what we think as well as control 'craziness,' 'bad thoughts,' depression and anxiety?"

We are now both speechless and, in a way, exhausted with respect to our ability to think further about what has just been thought! Her mind (I *do* think) has raced so far into the future, tried to imagine so vividly where we are headed, that we have gone beyond our practical ability to fill in the blanks, so to speak—catch up with the fantasy by dealing concretely with the details, the day-to-day consequences of such an outcome. Can we eventually "program" our behavior, so that our emotions recede in significance to our cognitive life, as it connects with technology, becomes not only the heart of what we do, but the very essence of who we are? This medical student was worried about being "lost," and as she kept telling me that, I recalled Walker Percy's phrase "lost in the cosmos," a title he gave to a book of essays he wrote, but also a phrase he used to describe our sense of our situation, our condition: this creature of consciousness who through language tries to comprehend the mysteries of time and space, those two infinities in which we for a while are immersed. But one day words such as "consciousness" and "language" will also yield their meaning to biological investigation, and who can know for sure what the implications and the results of such inquiry will be for us; that is, how our sense of the world, and of our ourselves, and how our capacity to connect with others, to communicate, to ask and to tell, will all be altered!

As that student prepares to leave my university office, she asks me, casually, whether I "still believe in psychoanalysis." She is smiling, knows the irony of the inquiry, given our hour-long leap into both the darkness and light of the time ahead of us. I respond with a demurral, insist that psychoanalysis is not something to be "believed in"; rather, it is one more way of seeing things in a long chain of such that extends over the many centuries, millennia of our thinking, reflecting life. But then, she shrewdly amplifies her question and, by more than implication, corrects me. She wants me to think of psychoanalysis as a "metaphor," rather than a psychological theory, or kind of "therapy." A metaphor for what? "For people trying to get to know each other, learn from each other, for human connection," she says, and then reminds me of Martin Buber's phrase "I-Thou." She is hoping, she insists, maybe hoping against hope, she acknowledges, that amidst all the "progress" which will arrive over the generations to follow hers, all the knowledge about, yes, knowledge itself (the biology of knowledge become part of knowledge!), there will still be in those people who inhabit this planet ideas, ideals, passions (Ego, Superego, Id) that are no more regarded reductively, courtesy of biology, than they are considered reductively by many thoughtful psychoanalysts today, in the name of psychology. We pursue that matter a bit, notwithstanding her need to leave to put in time in a research lab. She worries that with an increasing rationality, grounded in a knowing command of the brain's manner of working, what we now call "love" or even "goodness" or "badness" or, ironically, "scientific research" will all be explained, defined, and put under some control: a presently wild notion that seems worthy of drugstore paperback fiction, but not beyond a comprehension based on the assumption of biochemistry and physiology as the ultimate owners, it can be said, of the brain and, just as ultimately, the property of us who, after all, have founded and built those two bodies of knowledge, whose dominion can only grow and grow as time goes by.

So it will be, we muse—an increasingly "biochemical Ego"; that is, we will extend our knowing authority over our psychological life, which is an aspect of our brain's activity. Even as the brain controls our breathing, our seeing, our hearing, it also controls our thinking and feeling, hence the future of our biological inquiry into cortical activity: a realization on our part of what takes place as we, say, do brain research. One can imagine, then, a biochemical self-consciousness: the surveillance on our part of cortical activity, of the brain's neurophysiological activity, that extends even to the research effort itself, even as now certain individuals monitor their psychological state, and what they are doing, and where, and under which circumstances, so that they may take this medication at this dose, or another medication at another dose.

The secular mind in the past lived side by side with the spiritual interests and yearnings of millions, a sacred mind. In recent centuries that secular mind has itself experienced a transformation. Once an alternative to entrenched religious life, that secularity became an aspect of individualism, as societies became less and less dominated by church life, more and more capitalistic in nature: the emergence of the bourgeoisie, with its tastes and preferences and interests very much "of this world." In this century Fascism, Nazism, Communism gave us a taste of the state as an overwhelming presence in the mental life of millions, a major presence in the indoctrinated thinking of a nation's people, especially its children (the Hitler Youth, the Komsomol). With totalitarianism on the wane, the nations of the world look ahead, now, to a future of discovery and growth rather than wars of conquest (and wars within nations), the murderous persecution of some by others. With any luck, that "discovery" will include scientific exploration of a kind that will, at last, give us knowing access to our own nature as explorers, discoverers: mind investigating brain, and, thereby, Emerson's "thinking man" a sovereign as never before in his native land, the head—able to comprehend it as he once took the measure of all those foreign territories that stretch downward from the brain stem toward the chest cavity, the abdomen.

Such a biological achievement will, in one sense, as Freud suggested, "blow away" traditional psychological and philosophical notions of human experience. Yet, as that medical student kept trying to suggest, we will, in certain important respects, still each be a self, not only the one who will master the brain, and thereby the mind, but also the one who knows hope and disappointment, love and loss: the one who can smile and cry, who can take pride in what has been achieved and see it for its limits, as a mere part of a larger story. No doubt, then, the biochemical Ego, as it were, will have its important bearing on what we can be and do, on how we live with ourselves and others, but at the same time we will surely be the mass of "biochemical processes," of "continuing neurophysiological activity," that has been plumbed as never before, but that also is capable of listening to Beethoven or Billie Holiday or Bruce Springsteen, capable of reading George Eliot or Leo Tolstoy or Chekhov or Raymond Carver or Flannery O'Connor or Walker Percy, capable of looking at Rembrandt and Van Gogh and Munch and Hopper, and capable of being such individuals, too—therein the Ego as a visitor to countless countries, a bearer of many names, an accomplished traveler able figuratively as well as literally to cross oceans, continents, time zones, ever anxious to learn more but, also, to figure out what that learning means in the larger scheme of things.

Put differently, we are the creature in whom knowing, clearly, has its greatest distinction. Other creatures know reflexively; we know tentatively, haltingly as children, then searchingly as youths, and finally, some of us, with the confident stride of, say, a Freud or of a future neurobiologist who will tell us exactly how a Freud thinks, exactly where in the brain ideas have their origin, and how they come about: the anatomy of thinking, the biochemistry of thinking. So with feeling, too—the knowing with respect to feeling awaits us: where it occurs, how it gets generated in us, and how it connects us with thoughts, ideas, interests, not to mention activities. Here, at this time, it is almost impossible for us to get *there*—to know the details and implications of a future in which we have fathomed structurally and functionally, so to speak, the nature of language, of thought, of feeling: the brain, at last, the mind's true domain. Still, the logic of materialism, and our proven capabilities as they inform our restlessly exploring nature, lead us in that direction, foretell our eventual arrival: the secular mind as ever wondering, probing, as ever intent on mastery.

In that long run of our history such knowing is, perhaps, our (secular) destiny; and yet, as some future philosopher will surely remind our triumphant biologists of the brain, there is knowing and there is knowing about the place of knowing in the course of the lived, the experienced, life: knowing and being as brothers, or sisters, but not as identical twins. Knowing is a part of being; being without knowing is, with respect to our humanity, not being. We know (and know and know); we feel, and knowing connects to that feeling, can prompt it or respond to it, so we psychiatrists notice all the time—and then there is the "leap" of action, of being carried to another kind of affirmation. Even with an almost (from our present perspective) infinite expansion of such knowing (such knowing about knowing, about feeling), we will always be, too, the creature of action, of commitment to deeds, not to mention one another, or so one hopes, even prays (the last gasp of the sacred). One prays at the very least on behalf of one's kind, though unsure, in a secular sense, to whom or what such prayer is directed, other than, needless to say, one's own secular mind, ever needy of an "otherness" to address through words become acts of appeal, of worried alarm, of lively and grateful expectation: please, oh please, let things go this way, and not in that direction—the secular mind given introspective, moral pause, its very own kind of sanctity.

A HEAD FOR
POISONING

A HEAD FOR
POISONING

SIMON BEAUFORT

ST. MARTIN'S PRESS ❧ NEW YORK

Book design by Victoria Kuskowski

Library of Congress Cataloging-in-Publication Data

Beaufort, Simon.
    A head for poisoning / Simon Beaufort. — 1st U.S. ed.
      p.   cm.
    ISBN 0-312-20549-X
    I. Title.
  PR6052.E2226H43   1999
  823'.914—dc21   99-21753
                                             CIP

First Edition: July 1999

10 9 8 7 6 5 4 3 2 1

TO MIKE SMITH

PROLOGUE

The early morning mist lay thick and white across the river, and there was a chill in the air. The young priest shivered in his thread-bare habit as he waited for the lord of the manor and his retinue to make their way through the long grass of the graveyard to the church. He glanced up, and saw that the sky was a pale, cloudless blue, heralding the beginning of yet another fine spring day. From behind him came an impatient sigh, followed by some furious muttering.

"Just a few more moments," he called softly to the waiting villagers. "They are almost here."

"We have the crops to finish planting," came the aggravated tones of Tom Ingram, a surly man given to complaining. "It is all very well for them up at the castle to roll out of their beds when they please, but while we wait here for them to deign to appear for mass, the day is trickling away."

"It is true, Father!" grumbled the parish ditcher. "We cannot stand here all day waiting for them. We have work to do in the fields while the weather holds."

"I know" said Father Adrian. "But they are here now. And Lady Pernel is with them."

He had not intended to provide this additional piece of information, but his surprise at seeing her walking towards his church with her kinsmen had startled him.

"Lady Pernel?" echoed Tom Ingram in disbelief, pushing past the priest to see for himself. "What does she want here? She never usually bothers with church."

"Keep your thoughts to yourself, Tom," warned Adrian. "If

Lady Pernel has decided to atone for her wicked ways, then it is a matter between her and God, and nothing for you to comment on."

Ingram snorted in derision. "Atone for her wicked ways! She has probably come to see whether the church has any silver worth stealing! Those Mappestones at the castle claim that there is no money to pay for our roofs to be mended, but they all live well enough on the profits from the manor. And that Lady Pernel is always dressed in clothes fit for a queen!"

There were murmurs of agreement from the other villagers, which had only just died down when the august group from Goodrich Castle entered the church. Walking with aloof dignity, they made their way to the Mappestone family pew near the chancel. Adrian waited until they had settled themselves, hoping that Ingram and his cronies would manage to keep their disapproval of yet more time wasting to themselves. Sir Godric Mappestone, the bad-tempered lord of the manor and one-time hero of the Battle of Hastings, was not a man to tolerate insolence from his villagers, and Adrian did not want trouble in his church.

The priest studied the Mappestone family as they tried to make themselves comfortable on the hard wood of the benches. Sir Godric sat in the best seat, scowling at nothing in particular and playing with the worn silver-handled dagger that he always claimed had been given to him by William the Conqueror. In his prime, Godric had been a strong, tall man with a head of thick light brown hair, but he was ageing rapidly. His hair was now grizzled, and his face was haggard and grey with the pain of some sickness that had been plaguing him for the past few weeks.

Sitting next to him was Lady Enide, his youngest child, and to Adrian's mind, the best of the whole brood. He smiled at her and she smiled back, dark green eyes dancing with their customary merriment, and her long brown plait of hair swinging jauntily down her back in the curious style that she had always favoured.

Next to her was her older sister Joan, who looked plain and shrewish next to Enide's pleasing radiance. Joan clung possessively to the arm of her husband, Sir Olivier d'Alençon, who was several inches shorter than she, and always looked as though he wished he were somewhere else.

Bringing up the rear was their infamous sister-in-law, Pernel. She leaned languorously on the eager arm of a richly dressed knight who wore, Father Adrian noted with disapproval, full battle armour complete with a broadsword. He considered asking for the weapon to be left outside the church, but he was afraid that the delay would provoke his restless parishioners to some indiscretion if more time were lost.

Pernel looked splendid that morning. Her dark eyes gleamed like bright coals, and her complexion was clear and alabaster. Luxurious tresses of raven black hair hung down her back, held away from her face by a delicate silver circlet, and her russet gown appeared to be made of the finest silk. Adrian saw Tom Ingram gaping at her with what could only be described as naked lust, and hoped Godric or Sir Olivier did not see the man ogling so.

Once the church was silent, Adrian began the mass, chanting the Latin in a clear, strong voice. He found himself unable to concentrate, and made several mistakes—not that anyone noticed. Most of the villagers were either asleep or staring out of the windows, while the company from the castle were talking among themselves in low, bored voices. Only Enide paid any attention, and Adrian was not even sure that she was concentrating as well as she might. Although she watched him, her eyes had the distant look that suggested that she was thinking about something else.

Finally, the mass was over, and the villagers fretted impatiently while the nobles made their stately way outside. Sir Olivier's shrill laughter echoed across the churchyard, accompanied by the deeper rumble of Sir Godric's voice. Adrian made his way towards them, bowing politely and wishing them good day, but although Sir Olivier nodded and Enide smiled, none of the others deigned to acknowledge his presence. Lady Pernel pretended to stumble in the grass, and clutched at the tall knight's arm while smiling coquettishly at him.

"Could your husband not come to church today, my lady?" asked Adrian, with what he hoped was a guileless smile. He saw Enide muffle a snort of amusement.

"My husband is busy," replied Pernel, eyeing the priest with dislike, not pleased to be reminded of her marriage to Sir Godric's second son while she was flirting with the handsome knight. "Sir Malger is visiting us from Normandy, and he offered to accompany me this morning in Stephen's place."

"The pleasure is all mine," said Malger with a courtly bow. His eyes glittered as he looked at her.

"Perhaps you would care to join us at the castle for breakfast," said Enide to the priest. "Sir Malger shot a stag earlier in the week, and—"

Whatever she had been about to say was forgotten as Pernel lurched towards Malger a second time. Adrian felt a surge of anger. The woman had just attended mass—surely she could at least wait until she was off hallowed ground before she engaged in unseemly behaviour with a man who was not her husband? But there was something odd about the way Pernel's arms flopped as Malger struggled to hold her upright. Then she went rigid, and Malger dropped her altogether. She fell to the floor.

Adrian's parishioners clustered around, their crop tending forgotten. Pernel began to writhe and convulse, red-flecked froth flying from her mouth as Adrian fought to hold her still.

"Fetch Master Francis the physician," he ordered Tom Ingram. Ingram made no attempt to move, but watched the scene with open-mouthed fascination.

"I think it is too late for Master Francis," said Enide, kneeling in the wet grass next to the priest, trying to help him control the stricken woman. "Pray for her, Father, quickly! She is dying!"

"She cannot be!" cried Adrian, appalled. "This is just a simple seizure. It will pass. Tom! Fetch Master Francis, and hurry!"

But Enide was right, and long before the old physician came puffing up the hill to the church, Pernel's frenzied struggles had ceased, and she lay limp and lifeless among the gravestones.

"It was a falling sickness," proclaimed Francis, with pompous confidence. "I have never seen an attack of this nature that has not been fatal. I doubt she knew much about it once it had started."

"She looked scared to death to me," said Sir Godric, looking down at his dead daughter-in-law. "Do not try to tell me she did not know what was happening to her, Francis."

The physician frowned petulantly, not pleased at being contradicted in front of the whole village. "Well, at least I can offer you one comforting thought: there are few in this parish who could benefit more from dying on consecrated ground than Lady Pernel."

"That is certainly true!" muttered Godric. "The lovely Pernel certainly led my son Stephen a merry dance while she was his wife. He will be well rid of her!"

Enide cast him a withering look for his lack of tact—no matter what Godric thought of his daughter-in-law's behaviour towards his son, it was not appropriate to discuss it over her corpse in front of the entire village. Oblivious to her displeasure, Godric strode away to shout for servants to take Pernel's body back to the castle. The others stood in an uncertain circle around the corpse, unsettled by the sudden appearance of Death among them.

"The physician is right," said Adrian in a low voice to Enide. "Lady Pernel did not exactly lead a blameless life, and she may well benefit from breathing her last on sacred ground."

"Really, Father!" exclaimed Sir Olivier, overhearing. "You slander my sister-in-law's good name with such assertions."

"What good name?" muttered Tom Ingram to the assembled villagers. "She was a devil! God took her because she had no right to set her wicked feet in His holy place!"

There were murmurs of agreement from the watching crowd, and even Pernel's two sisters-in-law seemed disinclined to argue with the sentiment. Sir Olivier spluttered with indignation, but Joan placed a restraining hand on his arm, and he said nothing more. Deciding not to wait for the servants to bring a bier, Malger lifted the body from the ground, and began to carry it to the castle. Enide, Olivier, and Joan followed in silence, and the villagers watched them go.

"I would exorcise this graveyard if I were you, Father," said Tom Ingram sagely. "The Devil has just entered it to snatch away his own!"

2 AUGUST 1100
NEW FOREST, ENGLAND

The men walked into the forest clearing, and looked around them appraisingly. The glade was a long, grassy expanse of bog and meadow fringed on all sides by a thick wall of trees. The King nodded his approval to the chief huntsman, and the man slipped away to indicate to the beaters that the hunt was to begin. The King and his companions separated, each searching for the best vantage point from which he would be able to shoot his arrows at the animals that would soon be driven towards him. The King selected a spot in the woods to the east, while his companions moved towards the marshy area in the south. Walter Tirel, Count of Poix and friend of the monarch, was surprised by the King's choice: the setting sun was slanting into the clearing, and he would be squinting into it as he took aim.

But the King's position was no business of his, so Tirel eased himself back into the scrubby bushes at the edge of the marsh and waited. After a while, the noise of the beaters began—yells and whistles and the crackle of sticks against undergrowth as men swept through the forest in a great arc, driving deer, hares, and birds towards the men who waited. Tirel inched farther back, not wanting the animals to catch sight of his red tunic and run away from him. He sighed, and turned his face to the warmth of the fading sun. It was pleasant to be out in the forest after a day of doing nothing indoors. The ancient trees were a brilliant green, shimmering in the heat of the late afternoon. Around him droned the buzz of marsh insects, audible even over the shouts of the beaters and the baying of excited dogs.

On the other side of the clearing, the King waited in eager anticipation, heart thumping with the excitement that hunting always brought to him. An arrow was already nocked in his bow, and wanted only to be drawn and aimed before it sped towards its quarry. He screwed up his eyes against the sun, and scanned the bank of trees to his right as the sounds of the beaters drew nearer. At any moment now, the beasts of the forest would begin to emerge. A few birds would come first, flapping the air in panic, feathers spiralling downwards as they flew to safety. But the King was not interested in birds. He had a household to feed, and nothing short of a stag would suffice.

A sudden frantic rustling in a tree nearby told him that a pheasant had taken flight. Not long now. The howling of the dogs was close, and he thought he could glimpse one of the beaters off to the right.

And then a deer burst out of the trees. The King's fingers tightened on the bow, and he began to draw the string back. He took his eyes off the deer for an instant, just long enough to see Tirel acknowledge that the deer was his. Meanwhile, a second stag had broken through the forest into the clearing. Tirel would get it, the King thought with confidence; the Count of Poix was, after all, one of the best shots at court.

The King's arrow sped towards the fleeing deer, and he immediately began to fumble for another quarrel. He swore to himself as the animal changed direction suddenly, and his arrow fell harmlessly to one side. He ran forward a few paces, and dropped to one knee to fire again. The sun was slanting directly into his eyes, making it difficult to see, let alone aim. Beyond the deer, the King had a fleeting impression of a man, silhouetted against the red-gold light, but then his whole attention was taken by the approaching deer.

The second arrow was never loosed. Startled, the King felt something hit him in the chest. What was it? A stone kicked up by the terrified stag? Then he found he could not breathe, and the strength ebbed suddenly from his legs. He pitched forward, his world darkening as he did so. As he toppled, he felt something drive farther into his chest, and then nothing.

The deer bolted across the clearing and disappeared into the thicket of trees on the other side. Tirel's stag, bleeding from a slight graze across its back, followed. After the animals had gone, the beaters emerged into the glade, moving cautiously, because it would not be the first time that one of them had been mistaken for game and shot in the thrill of the chase. But there was no one to be seen. Puzzled, they inched forward, calling out halfheartedly for the courtly hunters, and taking aimless swipes at the long grass with their sticks. The chief huntsman pushed past them and strode towards a flutter of yellow that he glimpsed to one side. He stopped short, and turned to the bewildered beaters, his face suddenly bloodless with shock.

"The King!" he whispered, aghast. "The King is dead!"

There were bemused glances and exclamations of disbelief, and then the other nobles in the royal hunting party began to gather, peering down at the huddled corpse of the King that lay sprawled under an oak tree. For shocked moments, there was nothing but a chaotic babble of voices, asking questions that no one could answer, and looking from one to the other with a mixture of fear and horror. Then the sound of horses" hooves caught their attention.

"That is Tirel!" cried one, pointing to where a lone horseman thundered down one of the forest tracks away from them.

"And that is Prince Henry!" exclaimed another, pointing to where the King's younger brother and two of his closest companions galloped in the opposite direction.

"But his brother lies dead!" whispered Robert fitz-Hamon, the King's oldest and most trusted friend, appalled. "How can he just abandon the body like that?"

No one answered, and all looked down at the lifeless corpse in the grass. The forest was silent and still, and the last golden rays of the sun faded and dulled across the forest clearing and the dead King.

CHAPTER ONE

JANUARY 1101
WELSH BORDERS

S ir Geoffrey Mappestone glanced around uneasily, and wondered whether he had been wise to trust the directions of his sergeant, Will Helbye, over his own vague recollections of the area. The misty countryside was silent except for the soft thud of horses" hooves on the frozen turf and the occasional clink of metal from the harnesses. He cast Helbye a doubtful look, and peered through the fog in a vain attempt to locate some familiar landmark that would reassure him he was still on English soil, and had not wandered inadvertently into the hostile territories governed by the Welsh princes.

"Are you sure your sergeant knows what he is doing?" demanded Sir Aumary de Breteuil, spurring his splendid destrier forward so that he could ride abreast of Geoffrey. "The King will not be pleased if he hears you have led me astray."

"I did not ask you to travel with us," said Geoffrey, finally nettled into irritability by the other knight's continual complaints. "If your messages to the King are so vital, why did he not send an escort for you from Portsmouth, instead of leaving you to fend for yourself?"

Aumary shot him an unpleasant look. "Secret business of state," he said pompously. "I was directed to make my appearance at the castle in Chepstow as unobtrusively as possible, in order to mask the momentous nature of the writs I carry."

Not for the first time on their six-day journey from the coast,

Sir Aumary patted the small leather pouch that was tucked inside his surcoat, a self-important smile on his face.

"You have done an admirable job," said Geoffrey dryly, taking in the other knight's handsome war-horse, exquisite cloak, and gleaming chain-mail. "No one would ever guess you are a knight of some wealth and standing."

"Quite so," said Aumary smugly, oblivious to the irony in Geoffrey's tone. "And it has not been easy, I can tell you—I have had no servants to care for my needs, and I have been forced to ride in the company of Holy Land ruffians." He looked disparagingly at Helbye and the two men-at-arms behind him who, like Geoffrey, wore the cross on their armour that marked them as Crusaders.

"I do hope you are not referring to me," said Geoffrey mildly.

He lifted his shield from where it lay over the pommel of his saddle, and slid his mailed arm through its straps. Sir Aumary was right to be apprehensive about the area, and Geoffrey was considering turning around and riding back the way they had come.

"Of course not!" said Aumary quickly, mistaking Geoffrey's precautionary action as a threat.

In contrast to Aumary's immaculate appearance, Geoffrey was clad in a hard-wearing, functional surcoat, stained with travel and with its Crusader's cross emblazoned on the back. His chain-mail was stronger, heavier, and had seen considerably more use than Aumary's, while his broadsword, Aumary knew, had edges that could slice as easily through armour as through butter. Aumary had no intention of fighting the younger knight when he knew he would lose. He turned to address Helbye, to remove himself from a conversation that was becoming uncomfortable.

"Where are we? How much farther is it to Goodrich Castle?"

"We are on the correct road," insisted Helbye, growing weary of Aumary's constant questioning. "We turned right at Penncreic; straight would have taken us to Lann Martin in Wales." He shuddered. "And the Lord knows we do not want to be there!"

Geoffrey could not agree more, and continued to scan the dense, still forest for something he might recognise. Surely, he thought, he could not have forgotten so much about his home during his twenty-year absence? The silence made him uneasy: he did not recall the lands around his father's manor ever being quite so soundless, even during the winter. His wariness began to transmit itself to Robin Barlow and Mark Ingram, his men-at-arms, and Geoffrey saw them draw their daggers. Trotting at the side of his horse, Geoffrey's dog growled deep in its throat, as if it could sense something amiss.

Suddenly, the silence was rent by an ungodly howl, and it was only the backwards start of his horse that saved Geoffrey from the arrow that hissed past his face. His raised shield protected him from the next one, deflecting it harmlessly to the ground. Behind him, Sir Aumary fought to control his own destrier, since, for all its splendid looks, it was a poorly trained beast and was whinnying and bucking in alarm at the speed of the attack. Geoffrey hauled his heavy broadsword from his belt, and wrenched his horse's head round, yelling to his men to retreat the way they had come. Barlow blocked his way, his mount insane with terror and pain from an arrow that protruded from its neck.

"Go back!" shouted Geoffrey to Aumary, Helbye, and Ingram, thinking that they might yet escape the ambush, even if he and Barlow could not. Then Geoffrey's attention was away from the bewildered soldiers, and he was fighting for his own life. Men darted from the forest, rising from where they had been crouching behind tree-trunks, or lying under piles of leaves. Geoffrey did not take the time to count them, but began to strike out, wielding his sword with one hand, and using his shield to fend off attacks with the other.

The air rang with yelling and howling, and dirty hands clawed and grabbed at Geoffrey's legs and reins, trying to drag him from his mount. He clung tightly with his knees, knowing that to fall might mean his death. A Norman knight on horseback was a formidable force, but on foot he was slow and encumbered by the heavy chainmail that protected him.

He smashed the hilt of his sword into the shoulder of the man who was attempting to hack through the straps of his saddle with a knife, and kicked another, catching him a hefty blow on the chin that sent him reeling. Seeing their comrades down, the ambushers backed away, knowing that they were helpless against the superior fighting skills of a fully armed Norman warrior. Instead they formed a circle around him, muttering menacingly and brandishing their motley assortment of weapons.

Given a moment to observe them, Geoffrey saw that they were

not hardened outlaws at all, but just villagers, nervously clutching a bizarre arsenal of ancient swords and crudely fashioned staves in a way that suggested they were not familiar with their use. He seized his opportunity, and spurred his horse forward, sending them scattering before him to escape the thundering hooves.

Meanwhile, Barlow had abandoned his dying horse, and was backed up against a tree, struggling to keep the wild stabs of his attackers" knives and hoes at bay with a sturdy cudgel. Geoffrey galloped towards him, using his sword to drive away those who did not flee from his furious advance. He hauled the gasping Barlow up behind him, and urged his horse back the way they had come, looking for his companions.

Helbye and Ingram had not managed to travel far. They were surrounded by a gaggle of triumphantly shrieking villagers, but at least they were still mounted. Without decreasing his speed, Geoffrey tore towards them, grimly satisfied as the would-be ambushers dropped their weapons and ran for their lives.

Someone was shouting in Welsh, and Geoffrey, who recalled enough of the language from his childhood to understand it, heard that it was a desperate call to retreat. He homed in on the voice, and leapt from his saddle.

It was over in moments. Seeing Geoffrey's sword at their leader's throat, the villagers immediately abandoned their fight, and the ambush fizzled out as quickly as it had begun. Breathing hard, Geoffrey waited until Helbye, Ingram, and Barlow were ranged behind him, and then studied the face of the man he held captive. The chief villager was sturdily built, and had curly black hair and dark eyes. His clothes were plain and practical, although they were cleaner and of a better quality than those of his men. He met Geoffrey's curious gaze with a hard stare of his own.

"What are you waiting for?" said Ingram in a hoarse whisper that carried to every one of the villagers who watched the scene with a combination of defeat and fear. "Why do you not strike him dead, Sir Geoffrey?"

"So I was right in my assumption when I attacked you," said Geoffrey's prisoner in poor Norman French, making no effort to disguise the loathing in his voice. "You are Geoffrey Mappestone.

I heard you were due to return from the Crusade this winter."

"I am afraid you have the advantage of me," said Geoffrey, also in Norman French, the sword still pointed unwavering at the man's neck. "I do not know you."

"Caerdig of Lann Martin," the man replied. He looked with contempt at Geoffrey's sword. "It would have been courteous of you to learn my name, since you see fit to wander uninvited on my land. This wood has been mine since your brother Henry lost his illegal claim to it in the courts."

So, they were in Lann Martin—the place where Geoffrey had least wanted to be, since he knew from his sister's letters that ownership of it was hotly contested, and that unexpected visitors were invariably dispatched long before they had time to explain their business. He shot Helbye a withering look for his incompetent navigation.

"I apologise for trespassing," said Geoffrey, addressing Caerdig. "It has been so many years since I was last here, that I no longer remember the way from Penncreic to Goodrich."

And now what? Geoffrey thought. He and his men were outnumbered at least six to one and, while he was certain he could win any fair fight, he knew he would not get far if there were archers hidden in trees or pit traps dug across the road. He saw he had two choices: he could slay each and every one of the villagers who stood in a nervous semicircle around him to ensure his safe passage, or he could negotiate a truce.

Most Norman knights would have opted for the former, but Geoffrey had no quarrel with men who had been trying to defend their village from what had probably appeared to be a hostile visit. Geoffrey was sure that Sir Aumary of Breteuil would claim that the attack on him was a direct act of aggression against the King, but while the attempted ambush of a royal messenger would doubtless not please His Majesty, retribution was for him to take, not Geoffrey.

Geoffrey had neither wanted nor enjoyed the pompous knight's company during their journey from Portsmouth to the Forest of Dene on the Welsh border, and he certainly did not feel responsible for the man. In fact, Geoffrey had hoped that Aumary would have left them long before, but Aumary knew a good thing when he saw one, and he had realised he would do well to stay in the company of the competent, intelligent Crusader knight and his battle–honed men–at–arms.

Geoffrey made his decision and gestured to the path with his free hand as he spoke to Caerdig. "If you will agree to grant us safe passage, we will leave your lands by the quickest possible route. We have no wish for more fighting."

"What?" Geoffrey heard Ingram breathe to Barlow. "We were winning! We could have had this manor of Lann Martin for ourselves!"

"Why would we want it?" Barlow whispered back, casting disparaging eyes over the gloomy forest with its matted tangle of undergrowth.

Geoffrey silenced them with a glare, and turned back to Caerdig. "We want only to return to our homes. Your dispute with my brother over Lann Martin is nothing to do with us."

Caerdig eyed Geoffrey narrowly, a humourless smile playing about his lips. "What are you proposing? That my people allow you to go free after you kill me?"

Geoffrey shook his head. "I suggest that we end this amicably, and that we each go our own way in peace."

Caerdig subjected Geoffrey to a long, appraising stare. "And how do you know my men will not shoot you as soon as you drop your sword from my throat?" He gestured to the forest path, the farthest stretch of which was swathed in an eerie grey mist. "I have archers watching."

Geoffrey gave the Welshman as searching a gaze as he had received. "You say you are from Lann Martin, and so you must be a relative of Ynys of Lann Martin. Ynys I remember very well, and he is a man whose integrity is beyond question. I will assume you have inherited his sense of honour, and will trust your word, once given."

Caerdig regarded him strangely. "Ynys was a virtuous man— before your brother Henry murdered him last summer. It seems your kinsmen have not informed you of their bloody deeds," he added, seeing Geoffrey's startled look. He sighed, and pushed Geoffrey's sword away from his throat. "But I give you my word, on Ynys's grave, that you and your men will be allowed to leave here unmolested. And as an act of good faith, I will escort you to the border myself—lest any of my men decides that he prizes revenge upon one of the filthy Mappestone brood above the honour of Lann Martin."

"Are relations between my father and Lann Martin so sour, then?" asked Geoffrey, sheathing his sword and turning to inspect his destrier.

He examined the animal carefully. War-horses were expensive, and not easy to buy: no self-respecting knight would neglect the beast that was strong enough to carry him and his many weapons into battle, would not shy from close combat, and yet was still fast enough to allow him to effect a fierce charge. There was a scratch on one fetlock, but it was nothing serious, and Geoffrey was not overly concerned. His dog materialised at his side, having emerged from wherever it had fled during the skirmish. It regarded Caerdig malevolently.

"Sour would be an understatement for our relationship," said Caerdig with a short, mirthless laugh. "And these last few months have been worse than ever. But it has not been your father's doing; it is the work of that corrupt rabble that call themselves his sons— your brothers."

He glowered at Geoffrey as though he were personally responsible.

"Does my father condone their behaviour?" asked Geoffrey, wondering whether his father could have changed so much since he had last seen him.

Sir Godric Mappestone was not a man whom anyone—his sons especially—would willingly cross. His temper and belligerence were legendary, and it was not for nothing that William the Conqueror had rewarded him so generously for his support at the Battle of Hastings and the following ruthless subjugation of the Saxons. In many ways, Geoffrey, the youngest of Godric's four sons, had been relieved when he had been sent away to begin his knightly training with the Duke of Normandy at the age of twelve. His earliest memories were of his father's black moods, when the entire household remained completely silent for days for fear that the slightest noise might bring Godric's wrath down upon them.

"Your father?" said Caerdig. "He is not in a position to do anything about your brothers."

Geoffrey's spirits sank. "Why not? Am I too late? Is he dead?"

Geoffrey had received a letter from his younger sister in October, telling him that their father was unwell. She had not made the situation sound serious, but it took months—and sometimes years—for letters to travel from England to Jerusalem, and news was usually long out of date by the time it reached its destination. This had happened with the news about Enide's own death. Because of the vagaries of travel, Geoffrey had received her letter telling him that his father was ill the same day as a curt note from his father's scribe informing him that she had died herself. By the time Geoffrey had read about her concerns for their father's health, Enide had been in her grave for at least six weeks.

He became aware that Caerdig was regarding him oddly.

"You do not know, do you?" said the Welshman softly.

"Know what?" asked Geoffrey, when Caerdig said no more, and the villagers, who had been listening, began to exchange meaningful glances.

"Your father is dying," said Caerdig bluntly. "He has been growing steadily weaker for months now, and his physician says his end is near. Rumour has it that one of your siblings is slowly poisoning him."

'What do you mean?" asked Geoffrey coldly, as Caerdig made his claim. Behind him, Helbye put a warning hand on his shoulder. Geoffrey shrugged it off, his eyes never leaving Caerdig's face. "What are you saying?"

"Easy now," said Caerdig, looking nervously to where Geoffrey's hand rested on the hilt of his dagger. "I am only repeating to you what is being said in the villages hereabouts. And any of my men here will tell you the same."

A man who wore a strange black cap stepped forward earnestly. "It is true. Everyone knows that Godric Mappestone is being poisoned—including him, although none of his attempts to discover the culprit have come to anything. However, even Godric himself knows that the most likely suspects are his own children."

"I see," said Geoffrey, deciding to dismiss the villagers" claims as spiteful gossip.

Geoffrey's vague memories of his three older brothers—Walter, Stephen, and Henry—and his sister Joan were not overwhelmingly positive, but he could not envisage one of them murdering their own father by as slow and insidious a method as poison. One of them might well dispatch the old man in the heat of the moment, but poison required premeditation and planning, and Geoffrey had his doubts. And, perhaps more to the point, Geoffrey could not imagine the aggressive Godric allowing such a thing to happen in the first place. He sensed that Caerdig and his men were simply trying to promote disharmony in the Mappestone household by attempting to drive a wedge between Geoffrey and his siblings.

"Do not believe them, Sir Geoffrey," put in Helbye. "What can these folk know about what is happening at Goodrich Castle?"

Geoffrey pushed his helmet backwards on his head to rub his nose with his free hand, and wondered whether he was wise to return to the home he had not seen in so many years anyway. His younger sister, Enide—the one who had died the previous summer—had written to him regularly since he had left, and her news from home nearly always contained some tale of a petty, but vicious, quarrel within the family. He glanced up the forest track, and seriously considered forgoing the delights of a family reunion in order to ride back to the coast and take the first ship bound for France. He realised that he had not even set eyes on Goodrich, and he was already being assailed with stories about the unpleasant dealings of its occupants.

"Sir Godric's health is important to everyone here," said Caerdig, seeing that Geoffrey was sceptical about his claim. "He is a harsh and uncompromising man, but his rule was lax compared to the havoc your brothers are wreaking. They attack us in order to harm each other."

"They still fight, do they?" asked Geoffrey distantly, still considering a quick getaway to the coast. "It seems that little has changed since I left."

"There you are wrong," said Caerdig vehemently. "Many things have changed—especially in the last few months. For example, travellers must now pay a shilling to your brother Walter to use the ferry over the River Wye."

"A shilling?" echoed Geoffrey, astonished. "That seems excessive! How can farmers pay that when they take their produce to the market at Rosse?"

Caerdig stabbed a finger at Geoffrey's chest. "Precisely! There are two courses of action open to them: they can slip across at night—at considerable risk, because the penalty for doing so, if caught, is either payment of a cow or loss of an eye. Walter prefers a cow, but he will happily accept either. Or, they can make a detour to Kernebrigges—the toll for which is only sixpence, payable to your brother Henry who has appropriated control of *that* bridge, along with the manor on which it stands."

Enide's letters had told Geoffrey enough of the greed of Walter and Henry to make him certain that Caerdig spoke the truth on that score. But he had no wish to take sides in a dispute over tolls, just or otherwise, so he changed the subject.

"I had better retrieve Sir Aumary before he breaks our truce."

Entrusting his destrier to Helbye, he walked briskly back along the grassy path in search of the older knight, the dog trailing behind him. Caerdig went too, leaving the black-capped man in charge of the villagers, while Barlow and Ingram still fingered their weapons uneasily. Geoffrey and Caerdig walked in silence, Geoffrey considering what he had been told about his father's poisoning, and Caerdig concentrating on keeping his ankles away from the dog's bared fangs. They reached the place where Aumary had been when the ambush had begun.

"Where is he?" said Geoffrey in exasperation, seeing nothing but trees and undergrowth.

"Perhaps he ran away," suggested Caerdig, amused at the notion of a fully armed Norman knight fleeing from his rag-tag village bandits.

Perhaps he had, thought Geoffrey, although even Aumary should have been able to defend himself against a badly organised attack by farmers armed with a miserable assortment of weapons.

"Aumary!" he yelled. The woods were silent, and not even a bird sang. "Damn the man! If he has gone off alone in the forest, he is an even greater fool than I thought."

Caerdig tapped Geoffrey's arm and pointed. "There is his war-horse. What a splendid animal!"

"Splendid, but skittish," said Geoffrey, leaving the path and wading through the knee-high undergrowth to where it grazed some distance away. "A destrier is of little use if it bolts at the first sign of trouble."

As he drew closer, it tried to run, but one of its stirrups had caught on a branch, and it found itself tethered. It bucked and pranced, rolling its eyes in terror as Geoffrey approached. He grabbed the reins and began to calm it, speaking softly and rubbing its velvet nose.

"Sir Geoffrey!" cried Caerdig suddenly, so loudly that the horse tore the reins from Geoffrey's hands and began cavorting again. Geoffrey shot the Welshman an irritated glance. "Here is your Sir Aumary. Here, in the grass."

Leaving the destrier to its own devices, Geoffrey went to where Caerdig knelt, and looked into the long wet nettles.

"God's teeth!" Geoffrey swore as he saw the sprawled figure of Sir Aumary lying there, face down. From between the older knight's shoulders protruded the slender shaft of an arrow. Geoffrey hauled him onto his back, but the sightless eyes and the tip of the arrow just visible through the front of his chain-mail showed that Aumary was long past any earthly help. Geoffrey swore again. Caerdig's failed ambush was one thing, but the killing of one of the King's messengers put a totally different complexion on matters.

"It was not us!" protested Caerdig, his face bloodless. "Look at that arrow. It is not ours!"

Geoffrey recalled the arrow hissing past his face at the beginning of the attack, and the one that his shield had deflected moments later.

"So someone else shot Aumary, just as you happened to be attacking us?" he said, raising his eyebrows at the Welshman. "I doubt the King will fall for that one."

"The King?" asked Caerdig fearfully. He swallowed hard. "What has the King to do with this?"

"Aumary was the King's agent, delivering dispatches from Normandy," said Geoffrey. "He met us on the ship sailing from Harfleur to Portsmouth, and informed me that he would be travelling with us because the Court is currently in Chepstow—no great distance from Goodrich, as you know."

Caerdig gazed down at the dead man in horror. "This has not gone quite the way I intended," he breathed. "I saw a band of heavily armed men riding uninvited on my lands, put it with the rumour that you were soon expected to return from the Crusade, and thought no more than that—that a Mappestone was brazenly trespassing on Welsh soil, bringing other Holy Land louts with him. Now it seems that the King's messenger lies slain on my manor."

"Seems?" queried Geoffrey, putting a foot on Aumary's back and hauling out the arrow with both hands. "It is more than just seems. What will you do?"

"What will *you* do?" countered Caerdig, watching Geoffrey inspect the bloody quarrel.

Geoffrey shrugged, rolling it between his fingers. "There is only one thing I can do, and that is to deliver Aumary and his dispatches to the King at Chepstow Castle. Sweet Jesus, man! How could you be so foolish! The death of a knight is unlikely to go unpunished, here or anywhere else. Even if it had been only me you had killed, do you think nothing would ever have been said, no reprisals?"

Caerdig shook his head slowly. "You are right: I was stupid. I did not stop to think of the consequences as I should have done. But looking at the situation with the benefit of hindsight does not help me now. I am about to be accused and punished for a murder in which I had no part."

Geoffrey declined to answer.

"But it is the truth!" insisted Caerdig. "Look at the arrow! If you can find another like it anywhere on my land, I will give you everything I own! And you know the forest laws—villagers around here are forbidden to own bows, in case they are tempted to shoot the King's deer."

"But you told me earlier that you had archers hidden in the trees," said Geoffrey. "What are they using, if not bows?"

Caerdig looked sheepish. "I was bluffing. What did you expect? You had a sword at my throat—I would have told you I had the Archangel Gabriel ready to shoot, if I had thought it would have intimidated you into not killing me. But, I repeat, none of my men own arrows like that one, or the good quality bows that would be needed to fire them."

Not wanting to debate matters further, Geoffrey shoved the arrow in his belt and began to heave Aumary's body upright to sling it across the horse. Caerdig helped, and together, after much struggling, they succeeded in securing the corpse to the saddle. Geoffrey removed the pouch of dispatches from where it dangled at the dead knight's neck, and tucked it down the front of his own surcoat.

"I am coming with you," said Caerdig abruptly, as Geoffrey led the horse back towards the path. "I will go to the King and put our case to him myself. He will listen to me, and I will persuade him to accept my reasoning as to why we cannot be held responsible for this knight's death." He glanced at Geoffrey with narrowed eyes, suddenly thoughtful. "But perhaps you put an arrow in him yourself before we ambushed you."

"With what?" asked Geoffrey, raising his eyebrows in disbelief. "A mallet? None of my men carries a bow, and Aumary was very much alive before you attacked us."

"But I cannot let a Mappestone go to the King with this tale," said Caerdig angrily. "You would have us all hanged for certain."

Geoffrey tugged the arrow from his belt and inspected it again. "This is well made," he mused, turning the pale shaft this way and that. "It is finely balanced and strong. I imagine it would be expensive."

"Quite," said Caerdig, snatching it from him to see more clearly. "And my villagers are poor—none could afford to buy such good arrows. And, of course, fine arrows are of no use without a fine bow, and I can assure you that none of my people has a bow of any kind, fine or otherwise. We are innocent of this crime, I tell you!"

"Let us assume you are right," said Geoffrey. "Then who loosed it? Why would anyone want to kill Sir Aumary of Breteuil? Despite his arrogance and self-importance, I doubt he was a man vital to the smooth running of the kingdom, or that the dispatches he carried are of great significance."

"Why do you say that?" asked Caerdig doubtfully. He gestured to Aumary's expensive chain-mail and handsome cloak. "He looks pretty eminent to me."

"Because if the messages had been as important as Aumary claimed, I am certain that the King would not have left him to his own devices in securing travelling companions from Portsmouth. He would have supplied an escort to ensure their safe arrival in Chepstow."

"And whoever killed Sir Aumary did not steal these dispatches anyway," said Caerdig, indicating the bulge in Geoffrey's surcoat. "Perhaps his death was a mistake, and the intended target was you."

"Me?" asked Geoffrey in surprise. "Why? I have been away for twenty years, and I am sure the enemies I made from stealing apples and pulling faces at old ladies have long since been forgotten. No one can wish me any harm."

"Your brothers do," said Caerdig. "So, do not expect a warm welcome from them, Geoffrey Mappestone. None of them is beyond making an attempt on your life to ensure that you never make your appearance at the castle. Word is that they think you are returning because your father will die soon, and you have come to see what is in it for you."

"I thought they might, given the way my sister has described them in her letters. But I want nothing from them. I wish only to pay my respects to my father, visit my sister's grave, and leave."

They had arrived at the clearing where Helbye chatted to the villagers of Lann Martin. The sergeant's jaw dropped when he saw Aumary's destrier and its grisly burden.

"What happened?" he cried.

"A mishap with an arrow," said Geoffrey ambiguously, tying the reins of Aumary's horse to his own saddle.

"An arrow?" echoed Helbye. He gestured to the black-capped man who stood next to him. "But I have just been listening to how the new King has been enforcing the law here in the Forest of Dene, and that no one carries a bow any more, even for shooting hares and foxes."

Caerdig gave Geoffrey a triumphant look.

"Well, Aumary did not shoot himself," said Geoffrey tiredly. "Someone killed him. And the King is going to want to know who."

Sir Aumary was not the only victim of the mysterious archer. Geoffrey saw that it had been a slender, pale-shafted arrow that had killed Barlow's horse. Like most Normans, Geoffrey had a healthy respect for horses, and he was disturbed to see one so summarily dispatched—perhaps even more than he was about Aumary. But Caerdig persisted in his claim that neither animal nor knight could have been slain by his men, and Geoffrey's own observations of the impoverished, hollow-eyed people who clustered around them suggested that if the villagers of Lann Martin had money to spare, they would not have used it to buy arrows.

The black-capped man was sent to the village to fetch a replacement mount for Barlow, and to bring two fat ponies for him and Caerdig. Aware that the sun was already beginning to turn from the pale yellow of mid-afternoon to the amber of evening, Geoffrey immediately set a course for Chepstow, forcing a rapid pace with Aumary's destrier and its sombre burden bouncing along behind.

Helbye was perfectly happy to have the company of Caerdig and the black-capped man, who was named Daffydd, and chatted cheerfully with them about mutual acquaintances from the days when Goodrich and Lann Martin had been on more friendly terms. Ingram and Barlow, who were young enough to be Helbye's grandsons, could not recall a time when relations between the two manors were less tumultuous, and complained bitterly that the two Welshmen were to travel with them to Chepstow.

"They will slit our throats in the night," grumbled Ingram.

"We will not be sleeping," said Geoffrey. "At least one of us will be keeping watch."

"I saw no one else in the forest, other than them," said Barlow doubtfully. "I do not think they are innocent of the murder of Sir Aumary. Do you, Sir Geoffrey?"

Geoffrey shrugged. "It is not for me to say. We will deliver Sir Aumary's dispatches to Chepstow, and that will be the end of it. What the King believes or does not believe about Caerdig and his men is no concern of ours."

"I have never been to Chepstow," said Ingram. "How far is it? I was hoping we would be home in Goodrich tonight. I have been away for four years now, and I am tired of travelling."

"Sir Geoffrey has been away for more than twenty," said Barlow. "So stop your whining."

"Chepstow lies perhaps eighteen miles from here," said Geoffrey. "We should reach the Great Dyke around nightfall, and from there the road to Chepstow will be good."

"I think the King will hang Caerdig," said Ingram, returning again to the subject of Sir Aumary's murder. "I cannot see that he is innocent. And it will serve him right for stealing Lann Martin from Goodrich manor. Caerdig claims he won it legally in the courts, but I wager he bribed the judges to get the result he wanted."

"I always thought, from the information in Enide's letters to me, that Goodrich's claim on Lann Martin was dubious," said Geoffrey, half to himself. "It seems just that Caerdig won his case."

Ingram and Barlow exchanged a glance of appalled disbelief at the notion that justice should enter the discussion, and Ingram tapped a finger to his temple, to indicate to Barlow that he considered his leader short of a few wits even to consider uttering such a ridiculous notion.

"Perhaps the King will reward us for bringing him Sir Aumary's killer," said Ingram after a moment, his eyes brightening. "Perhaps he will give us Lann Martin in exchange for Caerdig, and we will be able to loot it."

Both young men looked at Geoffrey hopefully. The knight sighed, and wondered, not for the first time on their long journey, whether bringing them home with him had been a prudent decision. Since Pope Urban's call for a Crusade four years before, Christian soldiers had cut a bloody swath from France to Jerusalem, killing and looting every inch of the way. Barlow and Ingram were no longer the simple Herefordshire farmers who had set out to reclaim the Holy City from the Infidel, but were ruthless, avaricious mercenaries whose bulging saddlebags were crammed with treasure stolen and cheated from the hapless people they had met along the way. Geoffrey seriously doubted their willingness or ability to return peacefully to a life of agriculture, which was what they claimed they intended to do.

He nodded at them noncommittally, and coaxed a little more speed from his horse, so that he could ride with Helbye instead. The old warrior gave him a grin, and began to chat about the old days, before the Conqueror had come to England and Goodrich had been under the control of a Saxon thegn. Caerdig and his man rode ahead of them, following a little-used trackway through the forest that Caerdig assured them led to the Chepstow road. Geoffrey's dog slunk behind them, looking this way and that for signs of woodland wildlife that might be barked at, chased, or butchered.

"Our villagers are not happy with this arrangement," muttered the black-capped Daffydd to Caerdig in Welsh, unaware of Geoffrey's knowledge of the language. "They think you are a fool to risk riding with a Mappestone and his henchmen."

"What choice do I have?" snapped Caerdig. "It is either ride with him, or have him tell the King that we slaughtered the messenger. And then Lann Martin would be given to the Mappestones for certain."

"He cannot be trusted," said Daffydd, scowling at Geoffrey.

"Who said anything about trusting him? But my uncle, Ynys, always said that Godric's youngest son was the only one of the entire brood with any honour."

"He may have been honourable in those days," argued Daffydd, "but look at him now. He has been on the Crusade, and we all know that only the strongest and most ruthless warriors survived that ordeal. Any honour they might have had when they started was battered from them long before they reached the Holy Land, so I am told."

Suddenly, Caerdig leapt into the air, and gasped in disbelief. "Hey! That dog just bit me!"

"Sorry," said Geoffrey, embarrassed. "It is a habit of his that I cannot seem to break."

It was not the first time the dog had jeopardised truces with a belated show of aggression, and with a sigh, Geoffrey dismounted and hunted around for the piece of rope he used to tether the beast when its behaviour degenerated to the point where it needed to be kept away from anything that moved. It had made Geoffrey many an enemy at the Citadel in Jerusalem with its penchant for nipping unprotected ankles. Seeing the hated tether, the dog bared its teeth at Geoffrey, and slid away into a dense patch of undergrowth. Helbye prepared to help ferret it out.

"Oh, leave him, Will," said Geoffrey, exasperated. "He will follow us in his own time."

"Well, just so long as the thing does not decide to take up residence here," said Caerdig, rubbing his heel. "I would not want it near my sheep."

"Are you Ynys's son?" asked Geoffrey, to change the subject. He suspected that Caerdig, or some farmer like him, would dispatch the dog in an instant if they knew of its history of goat and sheep slaying in the Holy Land—and they would be perfectly justified to do so.

Caerdig shook his head. "I am Ynys's nephew. But I am also his heir, and I inherited his lands after Henry murdered him last year."

Geoffrey saw he had chosen a poor topic for casual conversation. He tried again, leading his horse so that he could walk next to Caerdig. "How long has my father been ill?"

"His health began to fail noticeably last summer. Since November, he has grown far worse, and the gossip says that he will not see Easter. You have arrived home just in time—now when the Mappestone brood carve up their father's great estates, you can ensure you are not left out."

"I want nothing from him," said Geoffrey. "My mother left me her manor of Rwirdin when she died, and that will be quite sufficient for me, should I ever decide to live in England again."

Caerdig snorted with derision. "You will be lucky to get that back! Your brother Walter arranged for Rwirdin to be given to Joan as part of her dowry two years ago. Rwirdin now belongs to your sister and her husband, Olivier d'Alençon."

Geoffrey did not believe him—even Walter would not do something so flagrantly illegal—but he did not feel inclined to argue. He took off his helmet, which was beginning to rub, and scrubbed at his short brown hair with his fingers, relieved to be free of the heavy metal for a few moments. Caerdig watched him, and then reached out a hand to feel the material of Geoffrey's surcoat with its Crusader's cross on the back. It was faded now, and grimy from years of hard use, but in the brown winter countryside of Wales, it was exotic indeed.

"I have heard a lot about the Crusade," Caerdig said, "although few Englishmen took part. I have been told that the glory was great and the opportunity to amass wealth even greater."

"Then you were not told the truth." said Geoffrey, replacing his helmet. "There was no glory at all in what we did. We marched thousands of miles—sometimes in the freezing cold, and other times in the searing heat—and more of us died of disease and from raids by hostile forces along the way than ever saw the Holy Land itself. I suppose it is fair to say that there was plentiful wealth to be looted at the end of it, but when a loaf of bread costs its weight in gold, such fortunes do not last long."

"Your men seemed to have done well enough," said Caerdig, indicating Helbye, Ingram, and Barlow behind them. "Their saddle-bags are bulging."

Geoffrey grimaced, recalling the incident at the Citadel in Jerusalem involving the three Englishmen that had almost caused a riot. "That is mostly the results of some lucky betting—aided by Ingram's loaded dice—on their last night. I suppose it might buy a small plot of land, which is what they claim they want when we reach home."

"Wonderful!" muttered Caerdig, unimpressed. "Yet more English landowners with whom to fight, and farmers with whom to compete."

"I doubt it," said Geoffrey, smiling at him. "Sergeant Helbye is too old to start farming, and I cannot see the other two settling down to days of endless tilling when there is still looting to be done in the Holy Land."

"You think they will not stay, then?"

Geoffrey shrugged. "Helbye might. But I doubt he knows one end of a cow from another, so I do not think you have cause to fear his agricultural competition."

Caerdig laughed. "And you? What will you do now you are home?"

Geoffrey shrugged again. "When I was in Jerusalem, I longed for the cool, green forests of England. Now I am here, I find I hanker for the warmth of the desert sun."

"Then why did you come?" asked Caerdig. "I heard you were in the employ of the great Lord Tancred, who is Prince of Galilee. Surely you would be better in his service than here among the mud and the sheep? And the Mappestones!"

Indeed, Geoffrey had surprised himself by deciding to leave Tancred just as the powerful young Norman's fortunes were on the rise.

Tancred had not wanted him to go, and had begged, cajoled, and even threatened to make Geoffrey stay. But Geoffrey had become disillusioned with the Crusade. What had started with the noblest of ideals had quickly degenerated into a bid for power and wealth, from the highest-born baron to the humblest soldier.

When some of his closest friends were implicated in a plot to murder the ruler of the Holy City, Geoffrey had finally despaired, and had decided to leave Jerusalem. News of his father's illness had spurred him into action. He had travelled by merchant ship to Venice, and then ridden to Harfleur, where he had taken passage on a second ship that took him to Portsmouth. It was a long journey, and not without its dangers, yet Geoffrey had weathered it unscathed, and was wryly amused that he should fall foul of a silly ambush within a few miles of his home.

"You have no cause to fear competition from me either," said Geoffrey to Caerdig, tearing his thoughts away from Caerdig's attack and Aumary's death. "I will not stay long."

They rode until the last of the daylight faded, and then found a small hamlet in a clearing in the forest. The hamlet comprised little more than a sturdy wooden hall and three out-buildings for livestock, and the residents were alarmed by the sight of a fully armed knight and his retinue. Their fears were roused even more when they saw the body of Sir Aumary bouncing across his saddle.

Not surprisingly, they were reluctant to comply with Geoffrey's request for shelter for the night, but were too frightened to refuse outright. Begrudgingly, Geoffrey and his companions were offered dirty blankets and a space on the beaten-earth floor near the fire, while the horses and Sir Aumary fared considerably better in the more spacious, well-ventilated stables.

Without conscious thought, Geoffrey chose a place near the door, where he could easily escape outside if necessary and at the same time be able to watch anyone entering or leaving. The dog sniffed at the filthy blanket with sufficient enthusiasm as to make Geoffrey suspicious regarding the purpose for which it had last been used. But the night was cold, and he had used worse things to keep him warm in the past. Resting his back against the wall, he huddled into it with the dog nestling against his side, and dozed lightly. A short while later, Caerdig rose and moved nearer the fire. Geoffrey watched him in the flickering light, and did not sleep again.

CHAPTER TWO

Geoffrey was up and saddling his horse long before dawn broke the following day. The others were as keen as he was to set out and, after a breakfast of unappetising oat mash and some cold water from a nearby spring, they were off. It was still quite dark and, aware that a stumble in the darkness could damage his mount, Geoffrey led it until it was light enough to see. The Welsh ponies needed no such cosseting, and ambled along behind him, snorting and stamping in the cold morning air.

One problem that Geoffrey had not foreseen was that Aumary's body had stiffened overnight, and it was no longer possible for it to be draped across a saddle. Geoffrey was forced to buy a dilapidated cart from the people in the hamlet and put Ingram's horse to draw it, while Ingram himself became the proud rider of Aumary's destrier.

Despite the solemn nature of his mission, Geoffrey sang to himself, enjoying the crisp, clean air of early morning and the peace of the forest around him. Frost lay lightly on the winter branches, and the ground underfoot was as hard as rock. When the woodland path eventually joined the ancient foot-track along Offa's Dyke, Geoffrey let his horse have its head, and set it thundering along the side of a bubbling brook. When the horse finally began to tire, Geoffrey reined in, and slowed to a comfortable walk so that the others could catch up. He removed his helmet, and breathed deeply, relishing the feel of the sun on his bare head after the chill of the previous night.

The Dyke formed part of an old boundary between kingdoms. Some sections rose high above the surrounding land, while in other areas it made use of streams or dense outcrops of forest to mark its route. Along it ran a well-trodden path and the travelling was easy, so that by early afternoon Barlow gave a shout, announcing that he could see the great castle of Chepstow.

As they drew near, Geoffrey paused and admired the mighty fortress on its eyrie above the winding brown curl of the River Wye. Cliffs rose sheer from the water, culminating in a powerful curtain wall, behind which stood the massive rectangular stone keep itself. Geoffrey and his companions skirted the encircling wall on the side opposite the cliffs, aware that their progress was watched keenly by look-outs posted along its whole length. Trees had been felled and houses removed, so that no one could approach the castle from any direction without being seen—except for the cliffs, of course, and it would be a doomed and foolish invader who risked climbing those.

Eventually, they reached the main entrance, where there were guards in the gatehouse at ground level, as well as archers housed in the wooden gallery that ran along the top of the curtain wall. The duty sergeant heard Geoffrey's business, and then escorted them into the courtyard. As he dismounted and handed his reins to a stable boy, Geoffrey looked around him again, impressed. The keep stood in the middle of an elongated, triangular bailey. It was a formidable building, and a fine illustration of Norman strength and practicality, even though it lacked some of the refinements Geoffrey had seen in France. But decorations notwithstanding, Chepstow was a splendid fortress, and Geoffrey was not surprised that the King had favoured its constable with his presence for more than a month now.

The duty sergeant found a stretcher, and they laid Sir Aumary on it, covering him with his fine cloak. While Ingram and Barlow struggled and groaned under the dead weight, Geoffrey led the way to the keep. There was a moment of panic when Aumary almost slid off the litter as he was carried up the steep wooden stairs—the entrance, like in all Norman castles, was on the second floor, reached by a flight of steps that could be removed at times of danger, pre-senting would-be invaders with yet one more obstacle to surmount—but Geoffrey's timely lunge prevented an unfortunate incident.

Henry, King of England and youngest son of William the Conqueror, had just returned from hunting in the southern reaches of the Forest of Dene. His face was flushed from the exercise and fresh air, and he was basking in the accolades of his fellow huntsmen for having brought down a great brown stag. The stag and several fallow deer were being displayed in the hall before they were whisked off to the kitchens to be used to feed the King's sizeable household. Trestle tables laden with food lined one wall, so that the King and his men could stave off their immediate hunger until the regular meal was served later. Salivating helplessly, Geoffrey's dog aimed for them. Geoffrey caught it by the scruff of its neck, and told a squire to take it outside before it could indulge itself and have Geoffrey and his companions evicted from the King's presence.

The duty sergeant whispered something to another squire, who in turn went to the constable of the castle, the man who would decide whether Geoffrey's business was of sufficient importance with which to disturb the King. Apparently, it was not, for the constable strode forward to greet them himself, leaving the King to enjoy the company of his sycophants. He bent over the litter that had been placed at the far end of the hall, and lifted the cloak to inspect Sir Aumary's face.

"I do not know this man," he said. "He had dispatches for the King, you say?"

Geoffrey handed over the pouch that had been hidden inside his surcoat. The constable opened it, and inspected the documents it held.

"The seal is that of Domfront," he said, holding one upside down and revealing to Geoffrey that he was not a man of letters. "But I cannot imagine that these missives contain much of importance. Domfront is just a small castle in Normandy that our King is rather fond of. Was this Sir Aumary carrying anything else?"

Geoffrey raised his hands in a shrug. "The pouch seemed to be the thing of greatest value—Aumary was always very protective of it. But I admit I did not search his body for other documents."

The constable looked down at the swathed figure. "I will inform the King about this at a convenient moment. I do not think it is of sufficient merit to bother him with now. Please remain in or near the castle until I am able to arrange an audience with you."

He promptly turned on his heel and strode away, leaving Geoffrey and Caerdig with nothing to do but hope that the King would not make them wait for days. Geoffrey wanted to leave immediately, but now that he had made an appearance, he was obliged to stay until it was the King's pleasure to see him, waiting his turn with the other hopefuls who believed meeting the King would solve all their problems.

Ignoring the frustrated sighs of Caerdig at his side, Geoffrey sat on a bench and gazed around him, interested as always in architecture and art. The hall at Chepstow might be grand, he thought as he studied parts of it closely, but it was neither beautiful nor refined compared to the Saracen buildings in Jerusalem and Antioch that he had seen while on Crusade. In true Norman spirit, Chepstow was sturdy and functional, but it was most certainly not—

"And these are the men you mentioned?"

At the unexpected sound of the King's voice so close to him, Geoffrey started to his feet. He dropped onto one knee in the usual homage of a knight to a king, wondering how long the King had been watching him while he pondered the relative merits of Christian and Arab building techniques. The King gestured for him to rise.

"This is the body of Sir Aumary de Breteuil," explained the constable, gesturing to the corpse. "He was bringing you dispatches from France, but was struck down by an unknown assailant a few miles from here."

"Unfortunate," said the King, turning his gaze to Geoffrey. "And who are you?"

"This is Sir Geoffrey Mappestone," said the constable. "He claims he was with Sir Aumary when the attack occurred."

Geoffrey found himself the subject of intense scrutiny from the King's clear, grey eyes.

"Was he indeed? And did you see this unknown assailant, Geoffrey Mappestone?"

"I did not, my lord," said Geoffrey, aware that behind him Caerdig was holding his breath. "Aumary became separated from the rest of us during the attack. When we returned to find him later, his destrier was roaming loose and he lay dead in the grass."

"I see," said the King, suddenly much more interested now that he knew the dead man had owned some property. "And where is this destrier now?"

Geoffrey had heard that the King was avaricious, but he had not anticipated that his greed would be quite so transparent. "The horse has been placed in your stables."

"Good," said the King, rubbing his hands with pleasure. "Is it a passable beast?"

"It looks handsome enough, but it has been poorly trained," said Geoffrey.

It was clear Aumary's widow in France would not be gaining anything from having her husband slain in the service of the King.

"Poor training can be remedied," said the King dismissively. "Now, this man was bringing me dispatches, you say?"

The constable handed him the pouch, and the King broke the seals.

"They are accounts from my castle at Domfront," he said, sorting through them quickly and efficiently. Geoffrey remembered that the King was already being called "Beauclerc" because he, unlike most noblemen, could read and write. "It is always pleasant to learn that one's estates are profitable, but this is scarcely information for which to kill."

"Perhaps he also carried other messages," suggested the constable. "It would not be unknown for a messenger to draw attention away from something important by flaunting something unimportant."

"I suppose that must be it," said the King doubtfully. "Perhaps you will search the body for me, assuming that Sir Geoffrey has not done so already?"

Geoffrey shook his head. "Aumary only ever seemed to be concerned about the dispatches in his pouch. I assumed they were all he had—he told me they were of vital importance."

The King smiled. "The more important the messages, the better paid the messenger," he said wryly. "But what of this attack on you? Was Aumary the only fatality?"

Geoffrey nodded. "Unless you include one of my horses. This

was the arrow that killed Aumary." He held the bloodstained arrow out to the King, who inspected it minutely, but declined to take it in his own hands.

"I see," said the King after a while. "All very intriguing. Did you see your assailants?"

"I saw no archers," replied Geoffrey ambiguously, aware of the anxiety of Caerdig behind him.

"There is a Godric Mappestone who owns the manor of Goodrich and several other profitable estates to the north of the Forest of Dene," said the King, his eyes straying back to the arrow in Geoffrey's hands. "Is he a relative of yours?"

"My father."

"I see," said the King again. He looked Geoffrey up and down. "Your surcoat proclaims that you have been crusading, like my brother, the Duke of Normandy. I take it you have returned to England to claim any inheritance your father might leave you?"

Geoffrey shook his head. "I am not his heir, my lord. I have three older brothers to claim precedence. I have come only to pay my respects, and then I will be on my way again."

"Back to the Holy Land?"

Geoffrey nodded.

"I was a fourth son, you know," the King mused, regarding Geoffrey with half-closed eyes. "And now I am King of England. You should not underestimate your chances of inheritance, Sir Geoffrey. You never know what fate might hold in store for you."

"But I do not want Goodrich," said Geoffrey, more forcefully that he had intended. "Even if it did fall to me, I would decline it. I do not want to be a landlord."

"Rash," said the King, pursing his lips in disapproval. "You do not know what my wishes are in this matter, and I am your King."

Geoffrey did not imagine that the King could possibly be remotely interested in who was lord of the manor at Goodrich, but knew better than to say so. The King stroked his thick beard thoughtfully for a moment, and then gave what Geoffrey could only describe as a predatory smile.

"I am glad to have made your acquaintance, as it happens, Sir Geoffrey," he said. "There is something I would like you to do for me."

Reluctantly, Geoffrey followed the King into an antechamber just off the hall. An energetic fire blazed in the hearth, enjoyed by a selection of sleek and smelly dogs. The King nudged a few out of the way with the toe of his boot, and turned to face Geoffrey, drawing him nearer to the fire so that they would not be overheard.

At the calculating gleam in the King's grey eyes, Geoffrey's stomach lurched, and he almost hauled his arm away. Not again! he thought, with sudden despair. He had left the Holy Land and its squabbling rulers at least in part because he did not want to be dragged into their intrigues and plots, and here he was, not even home, and he was being recruited by no less than the King of England for some task that he was certain he would not wish to undertake.

"I see you do not appreciate the honour that is being bestowed upon you," said the King dryly, sensing Geoffrey's unease. "Do you not want to be of use to your King?"

Geoffrey did not, but there was no way he could say so and still be free to leave—at least, not with all of him still present and functional. He thought fast.

"I am in the service of Tancred de Hauteville, my lord," he said. "But I trained under your brother, the Duke of Normandy."

The King regarded Geoffrey keenly, and then smiled humourlessly. "I know what you are thinking. You know that relations between my brother and myself are not entirely amiable, and you think that by confessing your loyalty to him, I will release you from working for me. Am I correct?"

He was, but again, Geoffrey could hardly say so. "I only seek to warn you, my lord, lest you reveal something that you would rather a vassal of the Duke of Normandy did not know."

The King laughed. "You are wasted as a knight, Geoffrey Mappestone! You should have been a courtier. But what I am going to ask you to do for me will not compromise your allegiance to my brother. I am more concerned with a matter of security here, in England, than affairs of state in Normandy."

"Yes?" asked Geoffrey cautiously, when the King fell silent.

"Before I tell you what I want, let us talk awhile," said the King, poking at a pile of logs with his foot. "My constable tells me that you have been away from your home for some years, and so you will not be aware of some of the things that have been happening here."

Geoffrey felt that he was very well informed of occurrences in Goodrich and in England, because his sister Enide had taken care to keep him up to date with such events. Enide and Geoffrey had been close before he had left to begin his knightly training, and their relationship had remained affectionate because Enide, like Geoffrey, was literate, and they had written to each other often and at length throughout the years. Their correspondence had ended abruptly when Geoffrey had received the terse note from his father's scribe informing him that she had died. He said nothing, and the King continued.

"Your father owns a goodly tract of land when all his estates are added together. He was a loyal subject of my father, the Conqueror—indeed, it was through my father's generosity that Godric Mappestone came into possession of his lands in the first place. After my father's death, Godric transferred his allegiance to my eldest brother, the Duke of Normandy. He never fully accepted my second brother, William Rufus, as King of England."

Geoffrey swallowed hard. Godric had been playing a dangerous game if he had been supporting the Duke of Normandy over Rufus, who had been King of England before his sudden death the previous summer.

The King saw his concern and patted his arm. "Do not look so alarmed, Geoffrey. Rufus was not a popular king, and your father was right to object to his evil, unjust rule. But after Rufus had his unfortunate accident in the New Forest, many men who had favoured the Duke of Normandy above Rufus decided that *I* was the best ruler England could have. So, they abandoned their allegiance to the Duke of Normandy, and swore oaths of loyalty to me instead."

Geoffrey's unease increased. He hoped that the King was not going to order him to coax his father to abandon his allegiance to the Duke of Normandy and accept King Henry instead. Godric Mappestone was notoriously stubborn and opinionated, and it would be no more possible to persuade him to change his mind than it would be to alter the course of the sun.

"Do not fiddle with that thing!" snapped the King suddenly, as Geoffrey's hands moved nervously on the arrow. "Throw it into the fire."

Geoffrey complied, and they both watched flames lick up it, until the light wood was stained brown and then black. The King took a deep breath, and spoke again.

"I am fairly sure that your father is loyal to me." Geoffrey tried not to appear relieved. "I have also had occasion to meet your third brother—another Henry, like me—and he has assured me of his allegiance also. Your eldest brother Walter, and your sister Joan, on the other hand, have been quite outspoken against me. They claim I am a usurper, and that the throne of England really belongs to the Duke of Normandy."

Geoffrey's short-lived relief evaporated like a drop of rain in the desert, and he began to anticipate what the King was about to charge him to do with a feeling of dread. He opened his mouth to protest, but the King silenced him with a wave of his hand.

"Your second brother Stephen has kept quiet on the matter, and so I do not know where he stands. Each one of your siblings is determined to have Goodrich for him—or her—self. Now, I would not usually be concerned about the outcome of such a contest— even if the hostile Walter were to inherit, I would be able to subdue him by threatening to confiscate his land. But there is one other factor in the picture that gives me cause for concern."

Geoffrey waited, watching the yellow flames consume the arrow, and wishing that he had abandoned Sir Aumary's corpse in the forest, or better still, that he had never followed his ridiculous whim to return home in the first place.

"One of your siblings—and whether it is Walter, Joan, Stephen, or Henry, I cannot say—is poisoning your father."

"So I have been told," said Geoffrey, cleanly taking the wind out of the King's sails. "But relations between Goodrich and its neighbours have never been very congenial. The tale of my father's poisoning is probably a rumour intended to aggravate ill-feelings among my brothers and sister, which can then be used against them."

"I do not base my statements on rumour," said the King. "I base them on a letter your father sent me himself around Christmas. In it, he claimed not only that was he being poisoned but that a similar attempt had been made on your sister, too."

"Joan?" asked Geoffrey. "Then I suppose that discounts her as a patricidal maniac."

"Not Joan," said the King. "Godric's youngest child. I forget her name."

"Enide?" asked Geoffrey, a cold, sick feeling gripping at the pit of his stomach.

"That is the one! Unfortunately—or fortunately, depending on the way you look at it—this Enide died of other causes before the slow-acting poison could take her," said the King, watching Geoffrey's reaction carefully. "But the point is that someone tried."

Geoffrey rubbed the bridge of his nose, and wondered whether the King were lying to secure his cooperation. He had heard that the King was not averse to emotional blackmail when other methods were impracticable or unlikely to work.

"I am not asking you to spy on your kinsmen," the King continued in a paternal voice, despite the fact that Geoffrey knew they were the same age. "But you will surely want to know if one of your siblings is trying to dispatch your father, and if he, or she, also attempted to kill your sister."

Geoffrey stared at him uncertainly. Then Caerdig's claim—that the arrows in the forest might have been fired by one of his siblings in order to prevent Geoffrey from returning home—sprang to his mind. The King seemed convinced that there was some truth in the letter Godric had supposedly written to him, stating that he and Enide had been poisoned. Could a jealous brother also have tried to shoot Geoffrey in the forest and had killed Aumary by mistake?

The King smiled, although there was no humour in his eyes. "You are wondering what I stand to gain by your unmasking of this would-be killer?"

That question was uppermost in Geoffrey's mind, but he said nothing. The King, seeing that Geoffrey was not going to reply, continued again.

"The most powerful baron in this region is Robert de Bellême, the Earl of Shrewsbury."

He paused and studied Geoffrey to assess his reaction. Geoffrey had certainly heard of Robert de Bellême, generally considered to be one of the cruellest and most violent men in Christendom. The Earl was also vastly wealthy, and owned massive estates in Normandy, as well as sizeable tracts of land in England. Geoffrey supposed that, as lord of the little manor of Rwirdin he had inherited from his mother, the Earl was technically his overlord. He decided he would not visit Rwirdin after all, for he certainly had no wish to encounter a man like the Earl of Shrewsbury.

The King noted with satisfaction the instinctive grimace that his mention of the brutal Earl had provoked.

"Your father's manor would make a handsome addition to the Earl's estates along the Welsh border, but I am loath to see his fortunes rise too high. The Earl rebelled against my father, and he rebelled against my brother Rufus. He might do the same to me if he becomes too strong. I do not want him getting Goodrich."

"Surely that is unlikely, with so many contenders for heir," Geoffrey pointed out. "If my father were childless, it might be a different matter. But you yourself have noted that my three brothers and Joan intend to have Goodrich for themselves."

"But one, or perhaps more, of your siblings is attempting to kill your father, and you have already admitted to me that you would not stay if Goodrich were yours. I do not want a vacant landlord any more than I want a murderer as lord of Goodrich. And I certainly do not want one of the Earl of Shrewsbury's creatures in charge. And there is another thing."

He paused again, and regarded Geoffrey intently. Geoffrey sensed yet again that something was going to be said that he would rather not hear. If Henry were anyone other than the King of England, Geoffrey would have made his excuses and left. As it was, he was trapped, and obliged to listen to whatever sordid secrets the King chose to reveal.

"Do you know what happened to my brother, Rufus, in the New Forest last summer?"

Geoffrey was startled by the change of subject. "I was in the Holy Land at the time, but the story was that he was shot in a hunting accident."

Henry nodded. "He was shot, certainly. But whether by accident or design is less certain." He turned, very deliberately, and gazed at the remains of the arrow burning in the fire.

Geoffrey prudently maintained his silence. There had been a good many rumours when the news had reached Jerusalem that Rufus of England had been slain, one of which was that Henry, who stood to gain a good deal from his brother's death, was not wholly innocent in the affair. He wondered why the King was choosing to discuss this particular matter with him now.

"You seem vague regarding the details of the events of last August," said Henry. "Let me enlighten you. On the second day of that month, we were due to go hunting together, just after dawn. My brother Rufus, however, was ill. He had slept badly, plagued with nightmares, and felt unwell." He looked hard at Geoffrey. "Rather as your father has been of late."

"You believe Rufus was poisoned?" asked Geoffrey, startled. "Before he went hunting?"

Henry shrugged. "Why not? I am sure that had my brother been in his usual good health, he would not have fallen to the arrow that killed him. He would have sensed something was amiss, and moved away or called out. But I am getting ahead of myself. Because Rufus was indisposed, we did not leave to go hunting until much later—well into the afternoon. The party split, as is the custom, and my brother was left in the company of Walter Tirel, the Count of Poix."

He paused yet again. Geoffrey glanced out through the door to where Caerdig stood, wondering, no doubt, what the King and Geoffrey were finding to discuss alone together for such a long time.

"Then, events are unclear. It seems a stag was driven to the clearing where my brother and Tirel waited. My brother fired, but only wounded the animal. Tirel fired, but he killed Rufus rather than the stag. Tirel immediately fled the country, but has been roaming France ever since claiming that it was not his arrow that killed Rufus. It is assumed by many that his instant flight is a clear statement of his guilt, but I am uncertain."

If Geoffrey had been in a position whereby the King of England had been shot, and he was the only known person in the vicinity with a bow and arrows, he might well have fled himself, regardless of innocence or guilt. Regicide was a serious matter, and revenge tended to be taken before questions were asked. Geoffrey supposed that it was entirely possible Tirel had not killed Rufus, and that his flight had been nothing more than a case of instinctive self-preservation.

"I have my suspicions that the Earl of Shrewsbury might have had a hand in Rufus's death," the King finished.

Geoffrey was quite unprepared for this conclusion. Common sense told him to say nothing, but the King's claim seemed so wild that he could not help but question it.

"But what would the Earl have to gain?" he asked. "It is said that he had a greater influence over Rufus than he could ever hope to have over you."

He wondered if he had spoken out of turn, but the King only smiled. "That is reassuring to hear. I would not like my people to imagine that I consort with men such as Shrewsbury. But he has grown powerful under my brother—he owns too much land along the Welsh borders, and holds altogether too much power in my kingdom. And there is more. There are those who say that my other brother, the Duke of Normandy, is the rightful King of England, and not me at all."

Geoffrey decided that silence was definitely required over this one. The supporters of the Duke of Normandy—who included Geoffrey—had a point. There had been a treaty signed by Rufus and the Duke of Normandy, stating that the Duke should have England if Rufus died childless. Rufus had indeed died childless, and, if the treaty had been honoured, Henry should not have taken the crown.

"I am certain the Duke of Normandy plans to invade England, and snatch my throne away from me—which is why Shrewsbury is consolidating his lands along the borders here. But the Duke is barely able to rule his own duchy, let alone a kingdom as well. He will need a regent for England. And who better than his loyal servant, Shrewsbury?"

It was well known that King Henry was twice the statesman his brother the Duke would ever be, and the Duke might well reward loyalty from a man like the Earl of Shrewsbury with the Regency of England—and that would be a tragedy for every man, woman, and child in the country, given the Earl's reputation for violence. England would fare better under the harsh, but just, rule of King

Henry than that of the tyrannical and unpredictable Earl of Shrewsbury.

"So what do you want me to do?" asked Geoffrey, aware that the King was gazing at him expectantly.

"I want you to keep your father's estates from Shrewsbury at any cost. It might seem to you that Goodrich is unimportant in the battle for a kingdom. But battles have been won and lost on details. I want Goodrich in your father's name for as long as possible, and then I want his heir to be a man loyal to me. That is the essence of what I want you to do for me, and that is the reason why I brought you to this chamber—away from prying ears."

Geoffrey turned as the constable hurried towards them, triumphantly bearing aloft a scrap of parchment. "Here, my liege," he said, presenting it with a bow. "I found this stuffed down one of Aumary of Breteuil's boots."

"Ah!" said the King, scanning it quickly. "You were most astute, my lord constable, for this indeed must have been the important message Sir Aumary wished to conceal with his worthless household accounts." He waved it in the air, and then secreted it in a pouch on his belt.

Geoffrey, who had been unable to prevent himself from glancing over the King's shoulder to read what was written, wondered why the King should consider a common recipe for horse liniment so vital to his country's well-being.

It was with some relief that Geoffrey was dismissed by the King. Caerdig followed him out of the hall and into the bailey, where he grabbed the knight's arm and stopped him.

"Well?" he demanded. "What did he say? Are we free to leave?"

Geoffrey nodded, his thoughts still tumbling around in confusion.

"And?" persisted Caerdig. "What else did he say? What was he telling you away in that chamber? Did it concern Lann Martin?"

Geoffrey did not feel it was appropriate to tell Caerdig that the King had ordered him to prevent the powerful and rebellious Earl of Shrewsbury from laying hands on his father's lands—nor that the

King whole-heartedly believed the truth of the story that one of Geoffrey's siblings was trying to murder their father.

"Lann Martin was not mentioned," he said to placate the Welshman. "The King is merely concerned about some of the tales that have been circulating concerning Goodrich."

"Like the fact that your father is being poisoned by one of your brothers?" asked Caerdig.

"There is Helbye," Geoffrey said, ignoring Caerdig's question, and walking across the bailey to where his sergeant and the two soldiers stood.

"Shall I saddle up?" asked Ingram without enthusiasm, as Geoffrey approached. "Of course, the horses are tired and I have only just finished rubbing them down."

"The light is already failing and there is no more than an hour's travelling time left today," said Geoffrey, glancing at the sky. "We will spend the night here, and leave at first light in the morning."

"We have already secured ourselves some lodgings," said Helbye, clearly pleased not to be riding farther that day. "It is not grand accommodation, but it is better than a tree root in the small of the back."

Geoffrey left the others to their preparations for an evening of dice with the soldiers in the King's guard, while he went to see to his destrier. It was with some difficulty that he made the stable-boy understand that only Aumary's war-horse—not Geoffrey's—was to be transferred to the area reserved for the King's personal mounts. Reasonably satisfied that his own horse would be there for him to reclaim in the morning, he found a place to sleep and then ate a large, rich meal with some knights in the King's retinue, where he drank more than was wise.

But later, as he tried to sleep, his head swam with questions, despite his serious attempt to induce a state of drunken forgetfulness. Why had someone killed Aumary? The documents that the knight had bragged about so much had not been stolen, and neither had the scrap of parchment with the recipe for horse liniment. Had Geoffrey disturbed the killer before he had been given a chance to complete a search of the body? But in that case, why had Geoffrey not been shot, too?

Aumary was vainglorious and shallow, and Geoffrey had suspected from the start that he had deliberately lent his letters more importance than they deserved in order to enhance his standing with his fellow-travellers. It was true that the King had been pleased to learn that his castle of Domfront was turning a tidy profit, and might have rewarded Aumary well for bringing him such good news, but it was scarcely the crucial missive the knight had claimed to carry.

So, had the recipe for horse liniment been some coded message that the King alone could decipher? Geoffrey had seen that particular scrap of parchment on several occasions—Aumary had used it to wrap the cloves he constantly chewed to alleviate the stench of his rotten breath. Had this casual use of the parchment been a ploy to divert attention away from it until it could be handed to the King? Or was even Aumary unaware of the alleged importance of his clove wrapper?

Geoffrey frowned up at the wooden rafters of the bedchamber and considered. Aumary might well have thrown the parchment away or carelessly mislaid it if he had not appreciated its importance, and as a means of conveying an important message to the King, it was risky at best. The more Geoffrey thought about it, the more he came to believe that the parchment was nothing, and that the King had merely pretended to have discovered something crucial in it in order to make any onlookers think that Aumary had been killed because of a vital message.

And that suggested to Geoffrey that the King knew more about Aumary's death than he intended to tell. He had not even questioned Caerdig about the attack, and had accepted Geoffrey's concise account of the botched ambush without a single question. Did the King know, or suspect, that the attack might have been orchestrated by Geoffrey's brothers, and that Geoffrey and not Aumary, had been the intended victim?

But, Geoffrey reasoned, the King doubtless had his fingers in a good many pies, and Aumary's death was probably nothing to do with the affairs at Goodrich Castle. Since he was not going to deduce anything conclusive without more evidence, Geoffrey dismissed Aumary from his mind, and thought about his family.

Could there be any truth in the King's conviction that Godric was being poisoned? Geoffrey was reluctant to think that one of his brothers would stoop to so despicable an act as to attempt the death of their father by slow poisoning. He could very well imagine that one of them—especially the fiery Henry—might lash out in anger and kill on a sudden impulse, but the cold, premeditated act of sentencing their father to a lingering death was another matter entirely.

He took a deep breath and watched the shifting smoke, which filled the room because the chimney needed sweeping. As to the other matter—keeping the Goodrich estates from the Earl of Shrewsbury's grasping hands—Geoffrey did not imagine for an instant that any of his kinsmen would allow Shrewsbury or anyone else to take Goodrich while there was still breath in their bodies.

As his eyes closed and he finally drifted into a restless doze, he made the firm resolution that he would stay in England only long enough to ensure that one of his grasping siblings inherited Goodrich from the dying Godric—which one he did not care—and then ride for France as fast as his destrier would take him.

The copious amounts of wine he had imbibed meant that Geoffrey slept a good deal later the following day than he had intended, and the sun was already high in the sky before he emerged from his lodgings. He was not the only one—Barlow had also drunk far too much the previous night and was in no state to travel. Meanwhile, Helbye was nowhere to be found, and it was some time before Geoffrey tracked him down to a brothel near the river. And Ingram was involved in some complex negotiations to buy a donkey from one of the King's grooms and insisted that such delicate transactions could not be hurried.

It was noon before they were saddled up and ready to leave. Caerdig and his man appeared from nowhere, evidently planning on making the most of an armed escort through the outlaw-ridden Forest of Dene. Geoffrey ignored them all, and bent to check the straps on his horse's girth.

"It is high time we were back at Lann Martin," said Caerdig, glancing at the sky. "I heard in a tavern last night that the King knows all about Godric being poisoned, and is very concerned about it. King Henry does not worry for nothing, and so we should hurry before one of your kin has his way and I have some crazed murderer for a neighbour."

"Most Normans are crazed murderers," said the Saxon Ingram, not without admiration. "That is what makes them such superb warriors. I wish I were a Norman."

"Do you mean you wish you were a superb warrior or a crazed murderer?" asked Geoffrey, favouring him with a cool stare. "I do not think that one necessarily leads to the other."

His attention strayed to the scratch on his mount's leg, and he led it away from the two young soldiers to see if the animal limped. They watched Geoffrey critically.

"He does altogether too much thinking," muttered Ingram to Barlow. "He would be better thinking less and . . . and . . ."

"Killing more?" supplied Barlow helpfully.

"It is all this reading and learning that has made him like he is," Ingram continued. "It has brought him nothing but trouble. And I wager you half my treasure that it will only be a matter of time before it leads him to problems at home. His brothers are rightly very suspicious of a man with letters."

"What are you two mumbling about?" asked Helbye, looking up as he checked the buckles on his treasure bags.

"We were just saying that learning and reading is the quickest way to the Devil," said Ingram with passion, casting a defiant look at Geoffrey.

"Quite right," said Helbye sagely. "Reading is the surest way to end up in the Devil's service."

"Then perhaps you should have a word with the Pope, and inform him that most of his monks are bound for Hell," said Geoffrey mildly. "Because most churchmen can read."

Ingram glowered, and Geoffrey smiled at him, trying to coax a better mood out of the habitually surly man-at-arms. Geoffrey was popular with his soldiers, who liked his easy and pleasant manner—even if they were suspicious of his penchant for monkish pastimes, like reading. Ingram, however, was different, and had regarded Geoffrey with a deep distrust since he had first come under the knight's command—mainly stemming from his inability to understand why Geoffrey did not always leap at the opportunity to indulge in a little unprovoked slaughter or impromptu pillaging.

"Think about it, Ingram," Geoffrey said. "How would you have had reliable news from home if it had not been for Enide's letters to me? Reading and writing is not all bad."

Ingram pursed his lips and declined to answer.

"Well, *I* would not trust anything important to a letter," said Helbye firmly. "I sent a spoken message with Eudo of Rosse to tell my wife that I was coming home—Eudo was due to return here two weeks before us. I did not send her one of those evil letters for all and sundry to be reading."

" 'All and sundry' cannot read," pointed out Geoffrey. "And anyway, how do you know your Eudo of Rosse did not tell 'all and sundry' every detail in your message to your wife?"

"You wait and see," said Helbye, after a brief moment of doubt. "My wife will be waiting for me to come home, while those of you who entrusted news of your return to letters—" here he paused to eye Ingram and Barlow disapprovingly—"will find that they are not expected."

"It would probably have been better to do both," said Caerdig, sensing that here was a debate that was not the first time in the airing. "Then the letters would have reached home if the messenger had been delayed, and the messenger would have delivered the news if the letters had been lost. But Goodrich and Lann Martin are humming with the news that Sir Geoffrey is expected soon—that is why I knew who he was when he trespassed on my land—and so obviously some message or other arrived."

Bored with the discussion, Geoffrey dug his heels into his horse's flanks, and went clattering out of the castle bailey. Caerdig, about to add his own opinion regarding the virtues and drawbacks of literacy, had to urge his own mount into a gallop in order to catch up with him.

"So?" asked the Welshman, once they had cleared the cluster of shabby buildings that had grown up around the castle, and were riding through open countryside. "What did the King say yesterday? You still have not told me."

"The King believed Aumary to have been killed by unknown assailants because of a scrap of parchment the constable found," said Geoffrey, carefully omitting the fact that the vital missive had been a recipe for horse liniment. "He did not ask for details of the ambush, and seemed satisfied with the account I gave him."

"And that was?" demanded Caerdig.

Geoffrey sighed. "You heard. I said no more to King Henry than I told the constable—that Aumary was shot by an arrow as we travelled through the Forest of Dene."

"What did you tell him about me?" asked Caerdig.

"Nothing!" said Geoffrey, beginning to be impatient. "He did not ask, so I did not mention you."

"You did not tell him about my role in the ambush?"

"I have already answered that," said Geoffrey curtly. "No."

"How do I know that you were not telling the King about it while you were whispering together away from my hearing?" pressed Caerdig.

"Do you imagine that the King would allow you to ride away if he thought you were ambushing travellers in his forests?" asked Geoffrey, forcing himself not to lose his temper at Caerdig's persistence.

Caerdig fell silent, and Geoffrey led the way along the path that hugged the river. It was busy with farmers and traders going to and from the surrounding villages with their wares. Progress was slow, hampered by lumbering carts that groaned and creaked under the weight of unsold produce and that stuck fast in the clinging mud at every turn.

As they rode, a wood-pigeon suddenly flapped noisily in the undergrowth, and in an instant Geoffrey had his sword half drawn. Caerdig regarded him askance.

"It is only a bird," he said. "What were you planning to do? Run it through, like a Saracen?"

"Or shear its head from its shoulders?" called Ingram, who was riding immediately behind them.

Caerdig whipped round in his saddle and glared with such ferocity at the young soldier that Ingram blanched and fell back. Geoffrey was puzzled, wondering what there had been in Ingram's innocent jest to cause such a reaction, but decided that Caerdig had probably been irritated by the young soldier's insolent contribution to a conversation that was none of his affair.

Geoffrey put his weapon away. His reaction had been instinctive, and any of his fellow knights who had been on the Crusade would have done the same. Those who would not were long since dead.

As dusk began to fall, the shadows lengthened and the path became empty. When it was too dark to negotiate the protruding roots and muddy surface, Geoffrey turned aside and arranged to spend the night in a rickety stable owned by a forester. The forester was reluctant to extend hospitality to seriously armed soldiers, but only the foolish declined the demand of a knight, and with bad grace he supplied fresh straw and gritty, flat bread for his unwelcome guests. When he had gone to his house and left them alone, Ingram pulled a sizeable piece of cheese from inside his jerkin.

"Where did you get that?" asked Helbye in amazement. "We went nowhere near a market today."

"I hope you did not steal it from the King," said Geoffrey, fixing Ingram with his steady gaze, and remembering the trestle tables piled high with food in the hall at Chepstow.

Ingram shifted uncomfortably. "One of the serving wenches gave it to me last night. She took a fancy to a gallant young Crusader."

He grinned conspiratorially, but Geoffrey did not smile back. Ingram was playing a dangerous game, he thought—he was insolent to the knight he served, and he stole from the King. When Ingram offered him a piece of the cheese, he declined it, although no one else had any such scruples.

Later, as his men slept, Geoffrey dozed lightly, leaning against the wall with his sword resting across his knees. Caerdig began to move nearer to him, rustling through the straw. The dog opened a malevolent eye at the disturbance, growled, and closed it again. Geoffrey's fingers tightened their grip on the sword.

"I do not understand you," Caerdig said, when he had settled himself close enough to Geoffrey to avoid waking the others as he spoke. "You could have told the King that my people killed Sir Aumary, and then Lann Martin might have been yours."

"How many more times do I need to tell you?" said Geoffrey softly. "I do not want it. If I had wished to be a landlord, I could have had something ten times the size of Lann Martin in the Holy Land."

"But your brothers would have been pleased to have it for them-selves," pressed Caerdig. "What will they say when they hear that you missed such a valuable opportunity to acquire it for them?"

"They can say what they like." Geoffrey grinned at Caerdig in the darkness. "I will tell them that they should be grateful I did not tell the King what you suspected—that the arrow which killed Au-mary was actually intended for me."

"That is no laughing matter," said Caerdig severely. "You will not last long among the Mappestones if you underestimate them. My uncle Ynys underestimated them, and look what happened to him."

"What did happen to him?" asked Geoffrey. "You say he was killed by my brother Henry?"

Caerdig was silent for a moment, and Geoffrey could hear him fiddling with the buckle on his belt.

"There was a silly argument over our sheep—Henry claimed that they had broken a fence and grazed his pastureland. You know how Henry can be—he came spitting fire and demanding instant reparation. Bitter words were exchanged, and Henry threatened to kill Ynys. The next day, Ynys's body was found. He had been killed by a hacking blow from a sword—as if someone had tried to sever his head from his body."

Geoffrey suddenly recollected Caerdig's reaction to Ingram's jest—about hacking a bird's head from its shoulders—when Geof-frey had been quick to draw his sword earlier that day. Was that the reason for his curious response? Ingram had a spiteful tongue, and might have learned about the fate of Caerdig's uncle in the taverns the previous night. Geoffrey would not put a deliberately provoking remark about such a matter past the malicious man-at-arms.

Caerdig continued, suppressed rage making his voice unsteady. "Of course, there were no witnesses to the crime, and Henry denies having anything to do with it. But not many men are allowed to own swords in the woods—you know that swords are forbidden by the Forest laws—although Henry has permission to carry one. Henry has the Norman love of fighting and killing, even though he is no knight."

Geoffrey drummed his fingers on the conical helmet that lay at his side. "Was there no enquiry into the murder? Was the Earl of

Hereford informed? He is overlord here, is he not?"

"Hereford!" spat Caerdig in disgust. "He has no power in these parts. It is the Earl of Shrewsbury who is the dominant force in the border lands now."

"Shrewsbury, then," Geoffrey said impatiently. "Did Shrewsbury look into Ynys's death?"

"He did, but he lost interest when he heard Ynys had named an heir—me—and that the lands were not lying vacant. All Shrewsbury did was to warn Henry not to do it again."

"Well, Henry is unlikely to kill Ynys a second time," said Geoffrey wryly. "But it seems to me that the Earl of Shrewsbury is causing a number of problems in the border regions."

"I should say," agreed Caerdig fervently. "He has been busy bribing the Welsh princes to back him against King Henry of England, should the need ever arise. But the Earl is not a man to act unless there is some benefit to be had for himself, and there was nothing to gain from Henry's arrest for Ynys murder. It might even have had a negative effect, since the King, for some unaccountable reason, likes your brother Henry."

"What is said in these parts about the death of King William Rufus?" asked Geoffrey curiously. "It was rumoured in the Holy Land that King Henry had much to gain from his brother's sudden and most convenient demise."

"So he did," said Caerdig, startled by the sudden turn in conversation. He glanced around nervously. "But this is not a topic for wise men to be discussing in a barn with thin walls."

"Wise men do not ambush knights," Geoffrey pointed out. "But what of Shrewsbury? Is there talk that he might have had something to do with the regicide?"

"No," said Caerdig, surprised. "Nothing was ever said against Shrewsbury. Why would Rufus's death be advantageous to the Earl when Rufus liked him so? But King Henry had much to gain from Rufus's death—if you suspect foul play, do not look to Shrewsbury, look to King Henry."

Geoffrey was silent, thinking. Few people openly questioned whether Rufus's death was anything other than a terrible accident at the hands of the unlucky Tirel, although there were rumours and suspicions galore. But Tirel was protesting his innocence in France, and King Henry believed that the Earl of Shrewsbury had played a role in the death, while others believed Henry might know more of the matter than he was revealing. Who was lying and who was telling the truth? Geoffrey rubbed his eyes tiredly, and decided that he did not want to know anyway.

He wondered what were the chances of escape, if he defied the King, and rode for Portsmouth without stopping at Goodrich to see his ailing father. Godric had never had much affection for his youngest son—rare were the days when he had even recalled Geoffrey's correct name. Geoffrey had not seen his family for twenty years, and the only one who had made the slightest effort to maintain contact had been Enide. And she was dead, perhaps poisoned by the very brother or sister who may have tried to shoot Geoffrey in the forest.

He rubbed the bridge of his nose, and sighed softly. He knew it was not wise to disobey orders from a King; even if Geoffrey did manage to reach the Holy Land without being caught by the King's agents, his defiance was surely likely to catch up with him some time in the future.

Geoffrey realised with a sense of impending doom that he had little choice but to go to Goodrich, and at least be seen to be following the King's orders. A few days, or a week, should be sufficient to convince the King that Geoffrey believed that Goodrich would remain in Mappestone hands, and then he would be free to leave England—forever.

"It is late," he said, feeling that the Welshman was watching him in the darkness. "Go to sleep."

"You should sleep, too," said Caerdig, settling down in the straw. "And do not worry about me bothering myself to slit your throat during the night. Your brothers will save me that trouble, if I wait long enough."

CHAPTER THREE

Dawn the next day was misty and damp. Geoffrey rubbed the sleep from his eyes and ran his fingers through his short, brown hair to remove the pieces of straw that were entangled in it. His customary toilet completed, he went in search of something to eat, and persuaded the forester to part with another of his unappetising loaves and some tiny, sour apples. His dog had done its own scavenging, and was eating something that looked a good deal more appealing than Geoffrey's meagre breakfast. The knight considered taking it from him, but his hands still bore the scars from the last time he had attempted such a rash act, and anyway, Geoffrey already knew who would be the winner in such a contest.

He paid the forester and went on his way, the others trotting behind him. The night had been mild, and the sun of the previous afternoon had thawed the frozen ground. The path that had provided easy riding the day before was now a sticky morass of clinging mud, and their progress was slow. It was late afternoon before Caerdig stopped at a small, muddy river.

"This is where we part. My lands lie this side of the stream, and your family's start from the other bank." He hesitated, and regarded Geoffrey uncertainly. "I said I would escort you to Mappestone territory. Do you accept that I have fulfilled my part of the bargain?"

Geoffrey nodded. "Once again, my apologies for trespassing. It is what happens when you follow the advice of another, rather than trusting your own instincts."

He allowed his gaze to stray to Helbye, who immediately began to study the river, looking for the best place to cross.

Caerdig still hesitated. "You spared my life—twice if you count not telling the King the fact that his messenger was slain during my ambush. But I have kept my end of the agreement."

"So you have already said," said Geoffrey, wondering where this was leading.

Caerdig sighed. "By Welsh law, you saved me—so I might be obliged to do the same for you at some point in the future."

"That might be useful around here," said Geoffrey. "Where lies the problem?"

"The problem lies in your brothers," said Caerdig. "I swore a solemn oath to rid my people of them, and so you and I might yet find ourselves on the opposite sides of another skirmish. The bargain that we made was that you spared my life, and I would see you safely off my lands. So, now we are even."

"I see," said Geoffrey. "You are saying that next time we meet, I should assume that you are about to kill me, and act first?"

"Well, I did not mean it quite like that," mumbled Caerdig. He scrubbed hard at his face, and smiled suddenly at the amused knight. "Actually, I suppose I did. But I do not like this state of war between our families. I will not—cannot—trust any of your siblings to make peace, but I would be willing to consider terms with you. Just bear that in mind the next time you say so glibly that you want nothing belonging to your father."

With a curt nod to Geoffrey, Caerdig rode away into the gathering dusk, taking with them the mule that Barlow had borrowed after his own mount had been killed by the mysterious archer. Barlow watched them go resentfully.

"We should have slain him while we had the chance," he said. "I was expecting to feel a dagger between my shoulder blades every step of the way."

Ingram readily agreed. "We could slip after him now," he said, addressing Geoffrey. "It would only take a moment, and think how pleased your family will be when they hear we have dispensed with one of their enemies. They might even reward us."

"And so might I," said Geoffrey dryly. "But not in a way you would appreciate. What is wrong with you? We had an agreement with the man. Have you no honour?"

"Horses are worthy of honourable treatment," said Ingram, fondly rubbing the velvet nose of Geoffrey's destrier. "But not people. Especially not enemies."

And who was the enemy? Geoffrey wondered. In the Holy Land it was usually obvious, but Geoffrey was about to enter a household in which one of his siblings was poisoning his father, had attempted to kill his sister, and had very possibly tried to shoot him three days before.

He stood next to Helbye, pointing out the shallowest route across the stream. Then they went through the charade they had played out each time they had reached water on their long journey home. Destriers were far too valuable to be allowed to splash blindly through rivers where they might stumble and injure themselves, and so someone had to lead them. Helbye always offered to perform this invariably unpleasant task for his lord—rivers were often deep and usually muddy. But Geoffrey knew that Helbye suffered from aching joints, and that being wet made them worse.

Yet he also knew that the older man's pride was a delicate matter, and that he would never admit to such incapacity. So each time Helbye offered to lead Geoffrey's mount, Geoffrey declined on a variety of pretexts, ranging from a sudden desire to cool his feet to a need to stretch his legs by walking. This worked to the advantage of Ingram and Barlow, for Geoffrey could scarcely accept an offer from them after declining Helbye.

Watching the swirling black water, Geoffrey silently cursed Helbye's pride, which meant that he, and not one of his soldiers, would be fording the river on foot. He wondered what his fellow knights would think, had they known to what extent his soft-heartedness had led him.

A sudden pitiful whine gave him his excuse this time. Geoffrey's dog darted this way and that along the bank, declining to step into the chilly water, but sensing it would have to cross.

"I need to carry my dog," he said, snatching up the black-and-white animal. It was heavy, and he wondered how it had managed to gain weight on a journey that had left everyone else leaner.

Barlow climbed onto Ingram's horse, pretending not to notice Geoffrey's disapproval at the way the poor beast staggered under the combined weight of two men and their heavy baggage.

"I can take the dog," called Barlow cheerfully, holding out one hand.

"I hardly think so," said Geoffrey coolly. "Unless you plan to walk. That poor horse is overloaded as it is."

"It is *my* horse," muttered Ingram resentfully, so low that Geoffrey was not certain whether he had heard him correctly. At any other time, Geoffrey would not have tolerated such insolence from his men, but they were only a few miles from home, where the young soldiers would no longer be under his command, and Geoffrey felt he could not be bothered.

"If you will not consider your horse, then think of yourself," said Geoffrey, hoisting his struggling dog over his shoulder. "If you fall off because the horse stumbles, you will sink because your armour will drag you down. And then you might drown."

The two soldiers exchanged a look of consternation. Geoffrey was right. Although neither wore the weighty chain-mail, heavy surcoat, and hefty broadsword that Geoffrey did, their boiled leather leggings and hauberks would certainly be enough to make swimming difficult.

"We will not fall off," said Ingram, after a moment of doubt.

Barlow shivered, and his voice took on a wheedling quality. "It is January, Sir Geoffrey, and not a month for wading through rivers. Look—there is ice at the edge. And anyway, I do not want to arrive home after four years all sodden and bedraggled. What would they think of us?"

"Please yourself," said Geoffrey tiredly. He did not relish the thought of stepping into the icy water himself, but he was certainly not prepared to risk his destrier just because he did not want to get his feet wet. Taking the horse's reins in one hand and holding the whining dog over his shoulder, he stepped off the bank and into the river.

The cold was so intense it took his breath away, and he immediately lost the feeling in his legs. Helbye followed on horseback, while Ingram ignored the route they were taking and chose one of his own. The water was deeper than Geoffrey had anticipated, and swirled around his waist, tugging at his long surcoat, so that he began to doubt whether he would be able to keep his balance. He wrapped his hand more tightly round the reins, and forced himself to move faster. And then he was across, splashing through the shallows and scrambling up the bank on the other side. Geoffrey dropped the dog, which immediately began to bark at the trees, and turned to wait for Ingram and Barlow.

Not surprisingly, Ingram's horse was having problems. The weight of two riders and the pull of the deeper water chosen by Ingram were proving too much for it. Ingram tried to spur it on, but it was already up to its withers and was becoming alarmed. Geoffrey could see that it was only a matter of time before Ingram and Barlow were tipped off.

Helbye made a gesture of annoyance as he watched. "We must help them, Sir Geoffrey, or you will be forced to break the news to their families that you brought them unscathed through four years of battles, only to lose them in the river a couple of miles from home."

Geoffrey took a length of rope he occasionally used to tether the dog, and waded back into the river, cursing Ingram under his breath. Barlow was already in the water, clinging desperately to the saddle with one hand, while the other gripped his treasure-laden saddlebags. Geoffrey felt his feet skidding and sliding on the weed-clad rocks of the riverbed, and realised that the current was much stronger here than where he had crossed. He threw his rope to Ingram, who caught it and gazed at it helplessly.

"Tie it round the horse's neck," yelled Geoffrey exasperated, and wondering how someone with Ingram's speed of thinking had managed to survive the Crusade. "And let go of your bags, Barlow! Hold on to the saddle with both hands, or you will be swept away."

"No!" cried Barlow, clutching harder still at his booty. He was silenced from further reply by a slapping faceful of water.

Geoffrey hauled on the rope, urging the horse towards him. Ingram, white-faced, began to slip off his saddle, and then he fell just as Geoffrey had managed to coax the horse to shallower water. Geoffrey's lunge at his hair brought him spluttering and choking to his feet.

"Now, the next time Sir Geoffrey tells you that your horse is overloaded, you might listen to him," shouted Helbye angrily from the riverbank. "Foolish boy!"

"Where is Barlow?" asked Geoffrey sharply.

All three of them gazed at the empty saddle: Barlow had lost his grip and had been swept away, just as Geoffrey had predicted.

"Oh, no!" whispered Helbye, white-faced. "Not Barlow! His father is my oldest friend, and I promised him I would look after the lad! What will I tell him now?"

"Stay with the horses!" Geoffrey ordered Ingram, who was gaping at the swirling river in horror. "Helbye, come with me!"

He waded back to the bank, and began to run downstream, feeling even more burdened down than usual, with the lower half of his surcoat sopping wet and adding to the weight of his chainmail. His breath came in ragged gasps—the dense armour of fully equipped knights was not designed for running. He crashed through the undergrowth with the dog barking in excitement at his heels, and came to a wide pond located at a bend in the river. With sudden, absolute clarity, he recalled swimming in it as a child, and remembered that it was very deep.

He slithered down the bank and saw that, as he had predicted, Barlow had been washed into it. Geoffrey could just see him floundering just under the surface. Holding on to an overhanging branch, he slipped into the water and took a firm hold on Barlow's collar. While the young soldier flailed and struggled, Geoffrey shoved him to where Helbye waited to pull him out. The bank was slippery, and it was some moments before they were all clear of the slick mud.

Helbye fussed over Barlow, banging him on the back to make him cough up the water he had swallowed, and then gave an exclamation of disbelief. Geoffrey glanced over at them, and saw Barlow summon a weak grin, and raise his saddlebags in the air triumphantly. Geoffrey pushed dripping hair from his eyes and gave a resigned sigh.

"Well, I am glad I risked my life for two bags of treasure," he said tiredly. "But I have lost my helmet. You must have knocked it off with all that thrashing around."

"I got that, too," croaked Barlow, pleased with himself, holding up Geoffrey's bassinet with his other hand. "I saw it fall off, and I grabbed it as it sank. I thought you might like to have it back."

Geoffrey gazed at him astounded, wondering how the young man could be considering such matters when he was in imminent danger of death by drowning. It was often said that the singular outstanding characteristic of Normans was their acquisitiveness, and Barlow, whose Norman ancestry went back generations, was a prime example. Geoffrey was certain *he* would not have been so calculating under the circumstances, Norman ancestry notwithstanding. Without a word, he hauled himself to his feet, and began to walk back towards the horses. With each step, water slopped from his boots, and he was uncomfortably aware that the light breeze, which had been pleasant for unhurried riding, was now serving to chill him to the bone. He strode briskly, trying to restore some warmth to his frozen body.

When he reached the ford, he stopped dead, and Helbye, close on his heels, bumped into him. Ingram was standing alone in the centre of the clearing, gazing at Geoffrey like a cornered animal—an unappealing combination of fear and guilt.

"Now what?" muttered Geoffrey, regarding the young soldier with deep apprehension.

"I saved the destrier," Ingram squeaked. "They did not take that—they only stole your saddlebags."

The forest was silent, except for the soft hiss of the fast-flowing river. Geoffrey watched Ingram expressionlessly, waiting for an explanation. Ingram was trembling, partly from cold, but mostly from fear of Geoffrey.

"What happened?" demanded Helbye. "Where is Sir Geoffrey's saddle?"

"They came out of nowhere," wailed Ingram, not meeting the sergeant's eyes. "There were at least twenty of them. They had me covered. There was nothing I could do!"

Geoffrey looked from the shaking soldier to his destrier. His saddlebags were gone, slashed away with a knife. For a fleeting moment, Geoffrey wondered whether Ingram might have stolen them himself, but then dismissed the notion as ridiculous. Ingram knew exactly what Geoffrey's treasure had comprised, and he was wholly uninterested in the knight's collection of ancient books. Throughout the entire journey, he and Barlow had complained about their weight, while Helbye had often suggested that Geoffrey should trade them for something more saleable. But Geoffrey had shown scant interest in the riches that had attracted the other Crusaders, and his most loved possession was an illustrated copy of Aristotle's *Metaphysics*, salvaged after the looting of Nicaea.

And now it was gone. Geoffrey felt his heart sink as he realised that the thieves would not understand the value of what they had, and would probably dump the precious tome in the river when they found books and not treasure in his luggage.

Barlow approached shyly, and offered Geoffrey the smaller of the two bags that he had gripped throughout his brush with death in the river. Geoffrey was touched, knowing how keenly Barlow had guarded it and pored over it since leaving Jerusalem.

"Which way did they leave?" he snapped, interrupting Ingram's whining attempts to justify why he, a trained soldier armed with an impressive array of swords and knives, had failed to thwart the opportunistic thieves. Absently, Geoffrey took the bag Barlow proffered, and Barlow watched it go with sad eyes.

Ingram indicated where the robbers had gone by pointing. Slinging Barlow's treasure over his shoulder, Geoffrey followed the path a short distance, until his eye caught something fluttering white in the breeze. With an exclamation of delight, he scooped it up. It was the Aristotle. Nearby were his saddlebags, up-ended, and the contents rifled through. His spare clothes were gone, along with a silver chalice that Tancred had given him. But his precious books were there. Carefully, he gathered them up, and repacked them before walking back to the others.

"They took the silver cup?" asked Helbye sympathetically, after a brief glance in the bags.

"Yes," said Geoffrey dismissively. "But they left my books."

"Books!" muttered Helbye in disdain. "Never mind books! They stole that beautiful cup! Is anything else missing?"

"Just some scrolls," said Geoffrey. "They are quite fine, but of no great value. They are in Hebrew and Arabic, and the Patriarch of Jerusalem gave them to me because he said he did not know anyone else able to read them. It is a pity they have gone, because I planned to use my spare time to translate them into Latin. I cannot think why anyone would steal them, but leave the books. This Aristotle dates back more than a century, and is priceless."

"Is it?" asked Helbye doubtfully. "Well, I would not give much for it, and neither would anyone else I know. Will you sell it to some abbey somewhere?"

"Never," said Geoffrey, taking it from his bag, and running his hands over the soft leather of its bindings. "It is a work of art. Just look at these decorated capitals."

"Very pretty," said Helbye, glancing over his shoulder. "But we should not be standing around here in the cold, with everyone soaked to the skin and robbers lurking in the area. They might be back for more, since they failed to get much from you."

Barlow and Ingram needed no second bidding, and had their bags secured on Ingram's still skittish mount in an instant. When Geoffrey was slower, cold hands fumbling with the slashed straps, Helbye elbowed him out of the way to do it for him. While the sergeant cursed the damage, Ingram retold the tale in which he was now outnumbered thirty to one in the contest for Geoffrey's books. Meanwhile, Geoffrey removed his boots and poured out the water.

"Perhaps the thieves stole your foreign scrolls because they thought they might be able to sell the vellum for reuse," suggested Barlow as he waited. "They might get a few pennies for them, if it is of good quality. It would be much more difficult to use a book so."

Geoffrey supposed Barlow might be right, although he could not imagine that there was a thriving market in used vellum on the Welsh border. He let the matter drop, just grateful that his books were now back in his loving care.

"Do you still want my treasure now that you have most of yours back?" asked Barlow guilelessly. Geoffrey had forgotten Barlow's generous gesture. Despite the fact that he was still angry with him and Ingram for disregarding his advice about overloading the horse and landing them in such a dangerous situation, he could not help but smile at Barlow's transparent acquisitiveness. Barlow grinned back at him, and went to secure his returned loot on Ingram's long-suffering horse.

Geoffrey's saddle was beyond any repairs Helbye could effect without proper tools, but Geoffrey, shivering from the cold, decided he would be warmer walking anyway. Helbye was horrified.

"Take my saddle," he insisted. "You cannot make an appearance at your home after twenty years leading your own horse! You are one of the most respected knights to return from the Holy Land alive! Think of appearances."

"I do not care about appearances," said Geoffrey tiredly. "I will take a solitary chair near a blazing fire over any glorious welcome my family might give me. Anyway, it will be dark when we arrive. They will probably be asleep and will refuse to answer the door. I might have to beg a bed from you for the night, and try again in the morning."

"They will let you in!" said Helbye, shocked. "For one thing, they will imagine you have come laden with riches, and will want to secure your good will."

That was certainly true, thought Geoffrey. "Then it will not matter whether I gallop into their bailey on a battle-hungry warhorse, or walk in soaking wet. My welcome will be the same."

Helbye accepted his logic, but not happily, and mounted his own horse to follow Geoffrey along the path that led away from the river.

In front of him, Geoffrey was lost in thought. He realised he had committed several grave errors of judgment that might have cost them their lives: he should have insisted that Barlow ford the river on foot; he should have made Ingram follow the route Helbye had chosen across the water, instead of allowing him to select his own path; he should have paid heed to the dog's barking when they had reached the far bank—it was likely the animal had sensed the presence of strangers; and he should not have abandoned his destrier to Ingram's care while he tore off after Barlow—he was lucky he still had it. Such mistakes in the Holy Land might have been fatal. He wondered whether the dampness and cold were affecting his brain, or whether he was losing the skills he had acquired through years of painful trial and error.

Behind him, Ingram was still defensive about his passive role in the theft, while Barlow was full of curiosity as to who would have risked stealing from a knight.

"It must have been that Caerdig," said Barlow to Ingram.

"It was not him, but he might have sent his men," said Ingram, eager to find a culprit. "After all, he commented on our treasure while he rode with us, so he knew we had some. And he must have been aware that the ford was not safe and that we would run into difficulties crossing it."

"The ford would have been perfectly safe, if you two had listened to Sir Geoffrey," said Helbye. The two young soldiers exchanged furtively guilty glances.

"And of course, Caerdig has good reason for killing a Mappestone," said Barlow a moment later, reluctant to let the subject drop. "Bearing in mind Enide and all that."

"Barlow!" said Helbye in a low voice. "Take care what you say."

"Sorry," muttered Barlow, genuinely contrite.

"Ah, yes!" said Ingram, pretending not to hear Helbye's warning. "Enide."

Geoffrey had not been paying much attention to his men's speculations—he was still berating himself for his poor control over them at the ford—but their curious exchange caught his interest.

"Enide?" he asked, looking round at Barlow. "My younger sister Enide?"

"We are just blathering," said Helbye before Ingram could respond. He leaned forward to stroke his horse's mane. "I wonder what my wife will have cooked to welcome me home."

"Probably nothing," said Barlow, clearly relieved to be talking about something else. "She does not know exactly when you will arrive. And who is to say that the letters Sir Geoffrey wrote ever reached her?"

"I sent her no letters," said Helbye, his voice thick with disapproval at the very notion. "I sent word with Eudo of Rosse."

"What were you going to say?" asked Geoffrey of Barlow, refusing to be distracted by Helbye's clumsy attempts to side-track him. "What has Enide to do with Caerdig?"

"They were lovers," said Ingram with relish, ignoring Helbye's warning glower.

"Ingram! You have no proof to claim such a thing," said Helbye angrily. "So shut up before you say something for which you will later be sorry."

"I have proof," said Ingram, smugly confident. "We heard all about it from a soldier at Chepstow who had spent time at Goodrich last summer."

"That was nothing but gossip," snapped Helbye. "How could you trust someone like that?"

"What did you hear?" asked Geoffrey, confused by the exchange.

"Caerdig wanted to marry Enide," said Ingram quickly, before Helbye could stop him. "But her father and Ynys of Lann Martin prevented the match—"

"That is enough, Ingram!" said Helbye sharply. "This is all speculation. You have no evidence to be saying any of this."

"Enide did have a lover," mused Geoffrey, more to himself than to the others. "She wrote to me about him often, although she never mentioned his name. Was that who it was? Caerdig?"

"No," said Helbye firmly. "Caerdig did ask for her hand in marriage, apparently, but there is nothing to say that they were lovers—whatever nasty rumours were spread around about her. Caerdig was probably trying to put an end to the feud between the two manors—a marriage of convenience."

"I knew nothing of this," said Geoffrey. "Although I suppose there is no reason why I should."

"There is nothing to know," said Helbye. "Except vicious rumours and nasty lies." He glared at Ingram and then at Barlow.

"But you might have said something, Will," Geoffrey said reproachfully to his sergeant. "You know Enide was the only one for whom I really cared. If you knew something about her, you should have told me."

"I saw no point in talking about her when you would get the entire terrible story on your arrival home," said Helbye primly.

"An affair between Enide and Caerdig is not so terrible," said Geoffrey, amused.

"The affair was not the end of the matter, though, was it?" said Ingram spitefully. "What Helbye has been keeping from you is the fact that Caerdig met Enide secretly for mass one day—"

"Ingram!" barked Helbye. He dismounted, and tried to grab the young soldier, who dodged behind Barlow. "Stop this immediately!"

"Ynys and Godric had agreed not to allow the marriage between Caerdig and Enide—" said Ingram, wickedly allowing the older man to grab the merest pinch of his tunic before slithering away.

"Ingram!" yelled Helbye, making another ineffectual lunge at the grinning soldier. "Desist, or I will—"

"Or you will what, Helbye?" Ingram sneered. "We are a mile from home, and you no longer have an excuse to bully me. I will say what I like to whom I like, and you can do nothing to stop me!"

Helbye stopped dead in his tracks, and Geoffrey wondered how long Ingram had been harbouring such bitter resentment against the old sergeant. He had always been under the impression that Helbye was popular with the young men under his command. It was at Helbye's request that Geoffrey had brought Ingram home with him, although he had been under no obligation to do so. Geoffrey had done what the sergeant had asked because he liked Helbye—because he certainly did not like the malcontented, bitterly morose Ingram.

Ingram turned on Geoffrey, his eyes blazing. "The story is that Caerdig decided that if he could not have Enide as his wife, then no man should have her, and so while she was at church—"

"Ingram!" pleaded Barlow, glancing nervously at Geoffrey. "Sir Geoffrey has been good to us, and there is no need to anger him. Say no more."

Ingram ignored him, still gazing at the bemused Geoffrey with malicious defiance.

"While Enide was at mass," he continued, "Caerdig waited for her until she came out of the church, and he chopped off her head!"

Geoffrey could think of nothing to say in response to Ingram's preposterous revelation, so he turned away without giving the young soldier the satisfaction of a reply. He heard Barlow berating his friend in low tones, while Helbye was silent. Pulling gently on the reins, Geoffrey led his destrier along the grassy path towards Goodrich Castle and the small village that clustered outside its stocky wooden palisades.

Was there any truth in the story that Ingram had learned from the soldiers at Chepstow Castle? Geoffrey tried to recall what Enide had written of her lover in her letters to him, but he remembered thinking at the time that she had been remarkably miserly with the details, considering that she claimed the man was so important to her. When he had first learned of her affection, he had tried to imagine which of Godric Mappestone's unsavoury neighbours could have attracted the interest of a woman of Enide's intelligence. But his efforts at deduction had been unsuccessful then, as they were unsuccessful now.

He sighed, and turned his thoughts from the informative and affectionate letters sent by his sister to the terse messages from his father—the object of Geoffrey's long journey from the Holy Land. During the twenty years since Geoffrey had been away Godric had sent his youngest son only three letters, each one addressed to "Godfrey."

The first letter was sent a few weeks after Geoffrey had left, perhaps to ease a nagging conscience because Geoffrey had not wanted to become a warrior. His ambition had been to attend the University in Paris, and become versed in the philosophies and law. His father had regarded him in horror, and promptly booked him a passage to the Duke of Normandy on the next available ship. Geoffrey had gone happily, thinking that Paris would be easier to reach from Normandy than England, and had planned to desert his enforced duties as soon as he could. But even the best plans are fallible, and Geoffrey's repeated, but unsuccessful, bids for freedom led the exasperated Duke to pass his rebellious squire to a kinsman in Italy, where Geoffrey came into the service of Tancred de Hauteville. It was Tancred who had taken Geoffrey on the Crusade.

The second letter came the previous year, after rumours had filtered back to England that the Crusaders who had sacked Jerusalem were wealthy beyond their wildest dreams. Geoffrey's father had written a blunt demand for funds, and casually informed him that a sister-in-law had died, although he had failed to specify which one. But it was the third letter that Geoffrey remembered most clearly, even though he had read it only once before he had crumpled it into a ball and flung it into the fire.

"To Godfrey, son of Godric Mappestone of the County of Hereford. The new sheep at the manor of Rwirdin are doing well, and made four pounds and four shillings this year. These funds have been used to build a new palisade on the north edge of the outer ward of Goodrich Castle. Your sister Enide died on a Sunday at mass. Our bulls have sired sixteen calves this spring."

Given the brisk contents of the message, Geoffrey had been given no reason to assume that her death had been anything but natural—perhaps due to a fever.

He glanced back at Ingram, and saw the young soldier's eyes fixed on him defiantly. During the four years in which Geoffrey had been granted the doubtful pleasure of his acquaintance, Ingram had never been congenial company, but at least he was obedient—Geoffrey would not have countenanced taking the man into his service had he not been. He wondered what could have caused this sudden streak of rebelliousness and malice so near home. Then the truth struck him, so obvious that he smiled.

He paused when he saw that the path divided, one branch leading off to the left, and the other disappearing into a thick clump of trees straight ahead.

"Left, go left," said Helbye, pushing his way forward.

"No, straight," said Ingram impatiently.

Geoffrey was too tired to argue and too cold to stand around while the others debated. He took the left hand track, but it degenerated almost immediately into a morass of sucking mud and began to wind back on itself.

"I told you so!" gloated Ingram, tugging his horse's head viciously to turn it. "Stupid old man!"

"You keep a civil tongue in your head, or else!" growled Helbye, embarrassed that he had been wrong yet again.

"Or else what, Helbye?" Ingram sneered regarding his sergeant insolently. "What can you do to me now? We are nearly home, where I will be free from you."

"Or else I will tell everyone I meet that you ran away before the fall of Antioch," said Geoffrey mildly, fixing Ingram with a steady gaze from his clear green eyes. "And that you were nowhere to be seen during the capture of Jerusalem, although you appeared in plenty of time to join in the looting."

With grim satisfaction, Geoffrey saw the gloating fade from Ingram's face. His intuitive guess was right: Ingram's recent unpleasantness stemmed from the fear that the knight might well reveal his

cowardice in battle to the family who were about to welcome him
as a hero—Ingram's story about Enide was to ensure that Geoffrey
went thundering off to the castle immediately, so that he would not
spend time in the village until Ingram had told his story the way he
wanted it to be heard.

"You would not do that," whispered Ingram aghast. "You
would not spread lies about me!"

"Lies, no," said Geoffrey. "But who is lying?"

"You never said anything to me about this," said Helbye with
a frown. "He was supposed to be your arms-bearer both times."

As it happened, Geoffrey had not mentioned Ingram's timely
absences to anyone. Both occasions had been brutal and terrifying,
and Geoffrey had not blamed the young soldier for declining to
follow him into the thick of it. Indeed, since the lad had been so
clearly petrified, Geoffrey had much rather Ingram had run away
and hidden, rather than force Geoffrey into a position where he
would have been fighting to protect both of them.

"It seems that there are a number of things we have not told
each other," said Geoffrey, thinking about the gossip regarding Enide. Helbye looked away guilty.

"The track divides yet again," said Barlow, keen to change the
subject. His own role in the two battles had not been exactly glorious
either—to keep his promise to the lad's father, Helbye had given
him duties guarding the baggage train. "Left or right?"

"Right," said Helbye, after a moment of consideration.

"Left it is, then," said Geoffrey, throwing him a grin of devil-
ment, before making his way down the dark path. It was almost
pitch-black, and the thick clouds allowed no light from the moon
to penetrate. Geoffrey's hand went to his sword when the wind blew
in the trees, making the wood groan and creak, and Barlow and
Ingram were growing nervous.

"The soldiers at Chepstow said that outlaws live around here,"
said Barlow, casting a fearful glance behind him. "They come out
at night and murder travellers."

"Especially ones carrying treasure, like us," said Ingram forcefully.

"Perhaps you might care to say that a little louder, Ingram," said

Geoffrey. "The robbers at the far end of the woods might not have caught everything you said."

Barlow's laughter turned into a shriek of horror as something brushed past his face with a screech of its own. Geoffrey spun round, his sword already drawn, but then relaxed when he saw an owl flit away through the darkness.

"We are nearly there," he said, sheathing his weapon. "I recognise this path. Over to the left is the woodsman's cottage, and that path there leads back to Penncreic. And there," he announced with relief, seeing the familiar square shadow of the church looming in the darkness, "is Goodrich. Those lights seem to be coming from your house, Will."

"So they are," said Helbye apprehensively, peering through the gloom at the huddle of houses on the opposite hill. "It is late. I wonder what she can be thinking of."

"She must be preparing you dinner," said Barlow. "And speaking of food, I am starving! Come on, Ingram! I will race you! I wager I can get there faster on foot than you can ride."

They were off, both weaving through the trees at a speed far from safe, leaving Geoffrey and Helbye behind them. Neither knight nor sergeant made a move.

"Nervous?" asked Geoffrey, smiling at the tense old warrior beside him.

"No," said Helbye with a false laugh. "She will be pleased to see me. Are you?"

"A little," admitted Geoffrey. "I have not even arrived, and I have already been told there are rumours that my favourite sister has been decapitated by Caerdig of Lann Martin; that my manor has been given away as part of Joan's dowry; and that one of my siblings is trying to poison my father, who is so alarmed that he wrote to the King about it."

"Then maybe it is a good thing that you did not leave it any longer," said Helbye practically. "But take no notice of Ingram. He is bitter for one so young, and he has a spiteful nature."

"You think there is no truth in his story, then?"

Helbye shook his head. "When Ingram told me about the gossip he had heard, I paid a visit to the source of it myself. Ingram only had half the story. Lady Enide, it seems, was indeed slain near the church on a Sunday after mass. Needless to say, a hunt for her killer was mounted. Your brother Henry came across two poachers in the forest, they confessed, and he hanged them there and then for her murder. The claim that poor Caerdig killed her was only speculation, based on a notion put about by your brother Stephen that the poachers may have been hired by Caerdig because your father declined to have him as a son-in-law."

"Did anyone other than Henry hear the confessions of these poachers?" asked Geoffrey.

Helbye shrugged. "I do not know. But apparently there were some questions about the business for several weeks after. Caerdig was clearly a suspect, but there were stories that others might have played a role."

"Others such as whom?" asked Geoffrey, when Helbye paused.

"Someone at Goodrich Castle," said Helbye reluctantly. "A member of the family, perhaps. Or a servant. But no one really knows, and the trail must be long since cold."

"So, I am about to enter a household, one member of which may have decapitated my sister? God's teeth, Will, I would not have made this journey had I known all this!"

Thoughts tumbling, Geoffrey followed Helbye down the hill, across the small brook that bubbled along the valley bottom, and up the slope on the other side. The castle in which Geoffrey's family lived stood on the crest of the hill overlooking a great sweep of the River Wye, while the church and the small houses of the village were clustered around the outer ward to the north and west—not so close that they could be set alight and present a danger to the wooden palisade surrounding the castle, but close enough so that villagers and their livestock could flee for safety inside it should they come under attack.

Ingram and Barlow waited for them outside Helbye's house with a scruffy boy they had accosted when he had left to fetch more ale. Lights blazed from within, and the sounds of revelling could be heard from one end of the village to the other. Barlow shuffled his feet uncomfortably, and would not look at Helbye, while Ingram's thin face wore a vindictive smile.

"It is your wife's wedding day," he said to Helbye with relish.

"She thought you were not going to return," said the boy. He glanced fearfully at Geoffrey, an imposing figure in his chain-mail and Crusader's surcoat, before fixing his attention on the astonished Helbye. "We knew Ingram, Barlow, and Sir Geoffrey were coming, but no one mentioned you."

"But I sent word," protested Helbye, appalled. "I did not trust a letter—who knows who might have read it on the way—but I sent word with Eudo of Rosse."

"Eudo never returned either," said the boy. "He died of a fever on his way home."

"One up for literacy," murmured Geoffrey.

"He died in France, at a place called Venice," continued the boy, eager to please. "I learned about Venice from our priest." He looked up at Geoffrey for approbation, proud to display his pains-takingly acquired knowledge of foreign geography.

"But then again, perhaps not," said Geoffrey dryly.

Their voices had been heard by the revellers within. A screech of delight from Barlow's mother brought others running, and soon the entire village was out, clustering around the two young soldiers, and admiring their proudly displayed treasures. Barlow's mother impatiently shoved aside a proffered chalice, and hugged her son hard and long as tears rolled unchecked down her cheeks. Ingram's father, however, gave his son a perfunctory nod and immediately turned his attention to the contents of the travel bags.

Helbye's wife regarded her husband with disbelief that turned slowly to joy. She turned the sergeant this way and that, and fussed over him like an old hen. Geoffrey watched the reunions from the shadows, wondering what was in store for him in the black mass of the castle that crouched on the hill. He was certain it would not be the unrestrained delight that his men's kinsfolk expressed.

"She says she will now need to dissolve the marriage she has just made," called Helbye to Geoffrey, gesturing to where his wife spoke urgently with a forlorn figure standing apart from the celebrations, his face masked by shadow. "Will you help us?"

Geoffrey was startled. "I cannot dissolve marriages, Will," he said. "I am neither a lawyer nor a priest."

"But you can read," said Helbye, as though this would solve everything. "You can help us, and make sure we are not cheated."

"I cannot see that you will have a problem," said Geoffrey. "Especially if her second marriage has not been consummated."

Helbye blushed a deep red. "I cannot ask her that!" he whispered, aghast, loud enough to cause some amusement when several villagers overheard. "She is a woman! You do not ask such questions of women!"

"She is also your wife," said Geoffrey, laughing despite himself. "But we can do nothing about it tonight. Come to the castle tomorrow, and we will see what needs to be done."

With his horse ambling behind him, and the black-and-white dog at his heels, Geoffrey left them, and walked the last few steps to the gloomy portals of the castle. The squat gate and the black waters of the stinking moat reminded him of the day he had left. It had been early on a winter morning, so early that it was not yet light. Only Enide had ventured out to see him leave, although Joan had waved to him from a window in the hall.

Of course, his home-coming would have been very different had Enide been there to welcome him. He tried to imagine what she had looked like as a woman, although he always pictured her as the child of eleven waving him a tearful farewell from the very gate at which he now stood. He pulled himself together, impatient with his sudden, uncharacteristic flight into fancy and reminiscence. He strode over the drawbridge—someone had forgotten to raise it for the night—and knocked on the gate. There was no reply. He rapped again, using the pommel of his dagger, hearing the sound echo around the silent courtyard.

"Go away!" came a belligerent voice from within. "We have already sent a tun of ale for Mistress Helbye's wedding, and you are not getting any more!"

"I am Geoffrey Mappestone," Geoffrey called. "I have come to pay my respects to my father."

"Who?" came the voice after a moment. "There is no Geoffrey Mappestone here."

Geoffrey considered begging a bed with Helbye for the night, and returning the next day when his re-entry into his family home might not be so ignominious.

"Please inform Godric Mappestone that I wish to speak to him," he said, leaning down to haul his dog away from where it was devouring something unspeakable discovered at the edge of the moat.

"He is asleep," came the voice. "As are all honest men. Now go away, or you will find your chest decorated with the shaft of this arrow. And do not come back!"

CHAPTER FOUR

Geoffrey was tired, wet, cold, and hungry as he stood pondering the great barred gate of Goodrich Castle. He had travelled hundreds of miles for several weeks to do his filial duty to a man he had neither liked nor respected, and over the past two days he had been ambushed, subjected to an uncomfortable conversation with the King, had his most prized possessions scattered through the bushes, and forced to walk because his saddle had been slashed. Suddenly, his temper snapped.

"Enough of this!" he yelled. "Either let me in to speak to my father, or I will force an entry myself. And if you choose to direct an arrow my way, I can promise you that you will be sorry!"

A grille in the wicket door slid open, and Geoffrey was assessed by a glistening eye. After a hurried exchange of whispers and a series of grunts and bumps, the bar was removed and the gate was opened. Geoffrey was far from impressed: he had expected to be questioned, and he accepted the fact that the guards would not know him and would seek some verification as to his identity. But, despite his blustering threat, he certainly had not imagined that they would be so easily browbeaten into opening the gates in the dark to what amounted to a complete stranger.

"Come in if you are coming," mumbled the guard irritably, holding a torch aloft so that Geoffrey would not step in the deep puddle that lay under the gate. "I have sent young Julian to tell Sir Olivier d'Alençon that he has visitors."

"Sir Olivier?" asked Geoffrey, watching the guard secure the door again. "Who is he?"

"But you said you wanted to speak to him!" said the guard in an accusatory voice, almost dropping the torch in his agitation.

"I said no such thing," said Geoffrey. "I do not know this Sir Olivier."

"I supposed you to be one of his cronies, come to leech off us again," said the guard. He took a step towards Geoffrey, fingering the hilt of his sword with one hand, and thrusting the torch towards him in the other. Geoffrey was a tall, strong man, and looked larger still in his heavy chain-mail and surcoat. He also carried a broadsword and at least two daggers that the guard could see. Prudently, the man stepped backwards again.

"It is good to know that Goodrich Castle is in such safe hands," remarked Geoffrey. "I am Geoffrey Mappestone, and I have come to see my father. Not Sir Olivier, whoever he might be."

"He will be your brother-in-law, then," said the guard, dropping his belligerent manner and becoming wary. "Assuming you are who you claim. Sir Olivier is Lady Joan's husband. Joan is your sister," he added for Geoffrey's edification. He studied Geoffrey in the light of his flaring torch. "You have grown a lot bigger since you left."

"I would hope so," said Geoffrey. "I was twelve years old then."

He grew restless under the guard's brazen scrutiny, and looked around him. The gate at which he stood led to a barbican in the outer ward, a large area that was well defended by a stout palisade of sharpened tree trunks and a series of ditches and moats. A flight of shallow steps led to a wooden gatehouse and the inner bailey, also protected by a palisade. And inside the inner ward stood the great keep—a massive stone structure raised by Godric himself—and a jumble of other buildings that included stables, storerooms, and kitchens.

"Sir Olivier says you are to come in to him," called a slender boy from the top of the steps.

"Oh, marvellous!" muttered Geoffrey, anticipating the scene

that was about to ensue, where Sir Olivier would realise that he did not recognise Geoffrey and would accuse him of being an impostor. With a weary sigh, Geoffrey took his destrier's bridle and led it towards the barbican. His dog darted ahead, no doubt sensing the presence of unsuspecting chickens nearby. Geoffrey hurried to catch up with it before it could do any harm, and thrust the reins into the hands of the waiting boy as he passed.

While the dog's attention was on a discarded chicken wing embedded in the mud, Geoffrey slipped the tether over its neck, earning himself an evil look in the process. But that was too bad: Geoffrey did not want his initial meeting with his family to be a confrontation over slaughtered livestock.

"Your horse is enormous!" Julian exclaimed, looking up at it with obvious awe. "Much bigger than Sir Olivier's mount. And finer, too."

"He is also tired and dirty," said Geoffrey. "Are there reliable grooms here?"

Julian spat. "There are grooms, but they will be drunk by now. I will look after him for you. I know horses. He needs to be rubbed down with dry straw, and then fed with oat mash."

"That would be excellent," said Geoffrey, pleased that there was at least one person at Goodrich who seemed to know his business—unlike the guard. He leaned down to run his hand across the horse's leg. "And he has a scratch here that I am concerned about."

"I see it," said Julian, bending to inspect the destrier's damaged fetlock. "It needs to be washed with clean water. I will draw it from the well myself."

There was something odd about Julian that Geoffrey could not place. He was perhaps thirteen or fourteen years old, and so they could never have met. But the peculiarity had nothing to do with recognition; it was something else. However, the lad clearly had a way with horses, and Geoffrey had no reason to dismiss him in favour of one of the allegedly drunken grooms. He smiled at the boy's eager face.

"It seems you know your business, Julian."

Julian grinned back at him. "And I see you know yours. Sir Olivier never trusts me with his pathetic nag, although I am by far the best carer of horses at the castle."

"Who are you?" came a voice from behind them, hostile and angry. "What do you mean by demanding entry under false pretences? I do not know you!"

Geoffrey turned, and came face to face with a short man with jet black hair and a matching moustache. Noting the half-armour and handsome cloak of a knight at ease, Geoffrey assumed he was Sir Olivier. The small knight had drawn his sword, but let it fall quickly when the guard's torch changed Geoffrey from an indistinguishable shadow to a fully armed warrior wearing a Crusader's surcoat. Olivier looked him up and down, took stock of his size and array of weapons, and beat a hasty retreat by backing away across the courtyard. Geoffrey heard Julian giggling helplessly at the unedifying spectacle.

"Guards!" yelled Olivier, unable to control the tremor in his voice. "Seize this man! He is an impostor!"

It was not the welcome for which Geoffrey had been hoping, but it did not entirely surprise him. He strode towards Olivier, aiming to get close enough to state his name and business without having to bawl it for half the county to hear. Olivier, however, seemed to be in no mood for discussion—he promptly dropped his sword and fled up the stairs into the keep, slamming the door behind him. The guards regarded Geoffrey uncertainly, but made no attempt to do as Olivier had ordered. Clearly, neither of them wished to indulge in a sword fight with a Crusader knight whose skills would almost certainly be superior to their own.

"Oh, for heaven's sake!" exclaimed Geoffrey in exasperation, gazing at the closed door. He turned to the boy. "Julian, please inform Sir Olivier that I am Geoffrey Mappestone, and that I have come simply to pay my respects to my father. I did not imagine it would prove to be so difficult."

"I guessed who you were," said Julian, carefully passing the reins of the destrier back to Geoffrey. "They have been expecting you since your letter arrived two weeks ago, although Henry lives in hope that you might have perished on the journey."

"That is reassuring to hear," said Geoffrey. "But you had better do as I ask, before Sir Olivier orders his archers to shoot us from the windows."

"They would miss," said Julian disdainfully, but dutifully sped towards the keep where Geoffrey heard him yelling through the closed door. While he waited, Geoffrey surveyed the inner ward. Some parts were familiar, like the keep with its three floors, and the ramshackle stables. Other parts were new, like the kitchen and the housing on the well.

He glanced to where Julian was still conversing through the door, and shivered. It was cold standing in the dark, and his clothes were still wet from his plunge in the river. After what seemed to be an age, the keep door opened and a woman whom Geoffrey did not know came down the stone steps towards him, bearing the traditional welcoming cup.

"Geoffrey! At last! We were beginning to think you would never come!"

As the woman approached him, bringing with her the goblet of warm wine that was usually offered to travellers as a symbol of welcome, Geoffrey wondered whether his misgivings about returning might have been unduly pessimistic. She was smiling and, in the dark, her friendly words of greeting seemed genuine enough.

She waited while he passed the reins of his destrier back to Julian, and then thrust the cup into his hand before he was really ready. It was full to the brim, and so hot that he almost dropped it. He bit back an oath that would have been bad manners to utter at such a point, and smiled at her, wondering whether she was his sister Joan or one of his brothers'' wives. However, all the Mappestones, except Stephen, had brown hair, but this woman's luxurious mane was paler, almost beige. He decided that she must be his eldest brother's wife, Bertrada, performing her duty as the lady of the manor.

Others followed her out into the bailey, and within a few moments he was surrounded, all talking at once and asking him questions that they gave him no opportunity to answer. Bewildered, Geoffrey tried to fit the barely remembered faces of twenty years ago to the rabble of people who clustered around him.

Geoffrey's eldest brother, Walter, had been married to a wealthy local merchant's daughter called Bertrada, and the guard had already told him that Joan was wed to the cowardly Sir Olivier. After Walter and Joan came Stephen, whom Geoffrey recalled as taciturn and crafty. But none of the people who shouted questions at him in the bailey seemed in the slightest bit quiet, so perhaps Stephen had changed. After Stephen was Henry, two years older than Geoffrey, and whose overriding passions had been fighting his younger brother and killing the rats he trapped in the stables. Geoffrey wondered whether it was Stephen's or Henry's wife who had died the previous year. Perhaps she had been murdered too—like Enide.

He shook himself irritably. Such speculations would do him no good at all. He was tired and cold, and he needed time to work out who was who in his family, and how much they had changed. There was no point beginning to ask questions about Enide's death, or about who was poisoning his father, until he had allowed himself some time to become at least superficially reacquainted with his relatives. After all, he was a stranger to them, and there was no reason why they should trust him either: if there were anything untoward about Enide's death, interrogating them about it would serve only to put them on their guard.

A burly, balding man had picked up Geoffrey's saddlebags, and was testing their weight with an acquisitiveness he made no effort to hide. Geoffrey shivered again, noticing that a frost was settling, turning the churned mud of the inner ward to a rock hard consistency. The woman who had brought him the welcoming cup—Bertrada, Geoffrey had assumed—took his hand solicitously.

"You are frozen. And wet, too. We should be ashamed of ourselves! You return to us after so long, and we keep you in the cold." She led him up the steps to the keep. "How was your journey?"

"Relatively uneventful," Geoffrey replied.

He felt unaccountably nervous at being the centre of attention among so many people he did not know, and was not inclined to mention Caerdig's ambush or the death of Aumary until he was certain that one of his family was not responsible.

Bertrada laughed. "Oh, come now, Geoffrey! You travel from Jerusalem to England, and you describe the journey as 'relatively uneventful'? You must have more to say than that. You have not spoken to us for twenty years."

"Would that he had not for another twenty," muttered one man, eyeing Geoffrey with rank dislike.

Henry, thought Geoffrey immediately, regarding his third
brother with interest. Henry had changed little, although he now
wore his brown hair long and tied at the back in the Saxon fashion.
He had not grown much—Geoffrey still topped him by a head at
least. He studied Henry closer and saw a curious mixture of health
and debauchery. Henry was sturdy, and looked fit and strong, but
the red veins in the whites of his eyes and the purple veins in his
cheeks suggested that the wine fumes that Geoffrey detected on his
breath were nothing unusual.

A beautiful woman with tresses of pale gold and a delicate, almost frail figure pinched Henry's arm in a gesture of warning, and
turned to Geoffrey with a warm smile.

"We are pleased to welcome you back after so long. How long
do you plan to stay?"

"That miserable cur has just bitten me!"

Geoffrey did not need to look around to know which was the
miserable cur in question. With alarm, he saw it had slipped its tether,
and was on the loose. Fortunately, it appeared as bemused by the
gaggle of people as was Geoffrey, and had not strayed too far from
its master's protection. Geoffrey leaned down and took a secure hold
of the thick fur at the scruff of its neck, feeling a soft buzzing under
his fingers as it growled at the back of its throat. Luckily, his relatives
were making sufficient noise with their questions for the dog's feelings about them to be drowned out.

At the top of the stairs, Geoffrey was ushered into the large hall,
which had a hearth at the far end. He paused, noting that new tap-
estries had been hung, although the rushes on the floor did not
appear to have been changed since he had left. A sleepy kitchen-
maid was stoking up the fire, and it was beginning to blaze merrily.
Those servants who usually slept in the hall had been roused from
their repose and sent to the kitchens, while others scurried about
setting up a table and throwing together a meal. Geoffrey was offered
a large chair near the fire, and provided with another cup of scalding
wine. Again, it had been overfilled, and the hot liquid spilled over
his fingers and onto the dog, which leapt to its feet with a howl of
outrage.

"Unfriendly animal, that," remarked the man who had been

bitten, twisting round to inspect his ankle. "Where did you get it? Is it from the Holy Land?"

"From Italy," said Geoffrey, thinking back to when he had found the dog as an abandoned puppy some years before. There were times when he was grateful for its somewhat irascible company, although most of the time it was more menace than pleasure.

"Ah," said the bitten man, as though Italian origins explained perfectly well why a dog might bite. "If you like dogs, I have a new litter of hunting hounds. You are welcome to take one."

Geoffrey wondered how long a puppy would survive the jealous jaws of his black-and-white dog, but nodded politely, thinking he could find some excuse to decline later. The last thing he wanted was another dog.

"I would like to see our father," he said, looking round at the assembled faces, and trying to assess which one was Walter. "I hear he is unwell."

"I bet you have!" Henry sneered. "So, that is why you are here. You heard about his will and came running."

There was an uncomfortable silence, during which Geoffrey regarded Henry with dislike. He turned to Bertrada.

"Perhaps I could see him now? And then I will be on my way."

"You cannot leave us so soon!" cried the balding man. "You have only just arrived and you have told us nothing of your travels. Stay with us a while. Ignore Henry." He gave the surly Henry a brief look of disapproval, which Henry treated with a contemptuous stare of his own.

"You cannot see Sir Godric tonight, Geoffrey," said Bertrada. "He is already asleep, and he needs his rest these days. You can see him tomorrow, when you will both be fresh."

"That is a fine destrier you have," said Sir Olivier, his display of faint-heartedness at his first encounter with Geoffrey clearly forgotten—by Olivier at least. He flicked his elegant cloak behind him, and perched on the edge of the table, swinging a well-turned leg. "Was he very expensive?"

"I imagine so," replied Geoffrey. "He was given to me by Tancred."

"Tancred de Hauteville?" asked Bertrada, exchanging a look of confusion with the balding man. "Why would he do that? I was under the impression that you were in the service of the Duke of Normandy."

"I was transferred to Tancred's service nine years ago. It is by Tancred's leave that I came here. Did Enide not mention it? I wrote to tell her."

"I suppose she may have done," said the balding man, scratching at the few hairs that lay across his greasy pate. "I really cannot remember."

"She did mention it," said Olivier. He turned to Geoffrey and smiled. "You were in Italy for a number of years with Tancred, and there you also fought on the side of Bohemond, Tancred's uncle."

Geoffrey was startled that Olivier d'Alençon, whom he had never met, should be better informed about his career than the rest of his family, and was about to say so when Henry spoke.

"And why have you come back?" he demanded. "What do you want from us after all this time? I can assure you that there is nothing for you here—despite what you may have heard."

Geoffrey resented the hostility in his brother's tone, and wondered how Henry had managed to survive all these years without a dagger slipped between his ribs if he were so habitually offensive.

"I had a curious hankering to see you all," Geoffrey replied sweetly, smiling round at the assembled residents of Goodrich Castle. "And I thought perhaps I might challenge Henry to one of the fights that once gave us so much pleasure."

That should shut him up, thought Geoffrey, resting his hand casually on the hilt of his sword to add an additional threat to his words. It did. Henry glowered at him, and then strode away to sit gnawing at his finger-nails on the opposite side of the room—away from the main group, but still close enough to hear what was being said.

Geoffrey watched him go. "And I thought I might visit my manor at Rwirdin," he said, to test Caerdig's notion that it formed part of Joan's dowry. "I have never seen it, although it has been legally mine since our mother's death fifteen years ago."

There were several furtive glances, and Geoffrey had his answer.

"Yes, go," called Henry nastily from across the room. "It has a nice church. You will be able to sit in it and read about womanly things, just like you used to do."

"But you must stay here a while, first," said Bertrada, glaring at Henry. "You cannot leave us so soon after you have arrived."

There was a silence. The balding man was still regarding Geoffrey's saddlebags with impolite interest; the bitten man's attention was on Geoffrey's dog; Henry made no secret of the fact that he could not have disagreed with Bertrada more; while the golden-haired woman regarded Geoffrey with an expression he found difficult to interpret. Meanwhile, Geoffrey had reconsidered his initial hope that his visit might pass without unpleasant incidents, and was heartily wishing he was elsewhere.

Geoffrey's family stood around him as he sat in the fireside chair. He felt ill at ease as they hovered over him, and wondered whether any of them noticed how his hand rested lightly on the hilt of his dagger. Although he did not anticipate anyone—even Henry—being so rash as to attack an armed knight in as public a place as the hall, he did not feel entirely safe in their presence. He glanced down at the hot wine in his cup, noticing that no one else was drinking any. Perhaps, he realised, he should be expecting an attack from a less obvious source—especially given that his father claimed that he was being poisoned.

"What is the name of this animal?" asked the bitten man, his voice loud in the still room. He inspected Geoffrey's dog with the eye of an expert. "Is it some little-known Italian breed?"

"He does not have a name," said Geoffrey, feeling foolish. "And he is no special breed as far as I know." He hoped not: he would not like to think that there were other creatures in the world with the same unappealing traits as those exhibited by the black-and-white dog.

The bitten man nodded slowly. "Perhaps I can mate him with one of my bitches. His kind of aggression would be good for the dogs we use to patrol our boundaries. I am willing to wager that your hound is an excellent guard."

"Not really," said Geoffrey, uneasy at the notion of his savage dog being let loose on potentially valuable animals. "He only bites people he does not fear, and he flees at the first sign of trouble. He even—"

He had been about to say it had even fled when Caerdig had ambushed them, but then remembered his resolve to say nothing until he had discovered more about who might have killed Sir Aumary.

"He even what?" asked the balding man, curious.

"What happened to Enide?" Geoffrey asked abruptly, ignoring the question. "No one told me the details. I only know that she died."

There were some covert glances. "We will tell you what you want to know tomorrow," said Bertrada, standing quickly. "You have journeyed from Jerusalem to England and that is a long way, Geoffrey. I am sure you are weary."

"I have not travelled the entire distance today," said Geoffrey, not needing to be told that the mileage he had covered was considerable. "And I would like to know about Enide now."

"That is perfectly understandable," said Olivier gently. "But it is a sad tale, and one that would better be told in the morning, when you are rested."

Geoffrey made a sound of exasperation, and came to his feet fast. As one, his family took several steps backwards. He regarded them in puzzlement. Were they nervous because they were guilty of something, or because the presence of an armoured, potentially hostile Crusader knight in their hall was something that would make most people less than easy?

Henry released a malicious burst of laughter. "You are all afraid of him! Well, I am not too timid to tell him what he wants to know. Enide was murdered by two poachers, brother. I caught them in the forest. They confessed to her killing, and I hanged them. And that was that."

"Are you certain these poachers were the culprits?" asked Geoffrey doubtfully. "What was their motive for killing Enide?"

"What do you think?" Henry sneered. "Enide was an attractive woman, and she was out alone early one morning to attend mass.

When they had finished with her, they cleaved her head from her shoulders."

"But if their intention was rape, why did they kill her?" pressed Geoffrey. "And why in that manner? It is not a common mode of murder."

"I am not familiar with the way criminals think," said Henry coldly. "So I could not say. What does it matter anyway? The poachers killed her and they died for it."

"We suspected that Caerdig of Lann Martin might have been responsible at first," said the bitten man casually, as though he were discussing the weather and not the callous murder of Geoffrey's favourite sister. "We thought he might have hired the poachers to kill Enide. He had been asking to marry Enide in a feeble attempt to use her to protect his miserable estates, you see."

"Those 'miserable estates' should have been mine," snapped Henry, turning on him. "It galls me to see a snivelling coward like Caerdig trying to run them. Our mother left *me* Lann Martin, just as she left Geoffrey the manor of Rwirdin."

"But Lann Martin was not hers to leave," reasoned Olivier gently. "The arrangement that was signed by Ynys and Sir Godric all those years ago said that it would only revert to you if Ynys named no heir. And Ynys made it very clear that he wanted his nephew Caerdig to succeed him."

"Did he now?" demanded Henry, taking a few menacing steps towards Sir Olivier, who immediately retreated behind Bertrada. "It is easy for you to dismiss my rights so glibly. You would not be so smug if it were Rwirdin that Caerdig stole. That is why you married Joan, is it not?"

Olivier opened his mouth to speak, but he hesitated and his chance to respond was gone.

"If *Joan* had married Caerdig when he asked, none of this would have happened," said the woman with the golden hair who had tried to restrain Henry earlier. "It is Joan's fault that Henry lost Lann Martin and that Geoffrey has lost Rwirdin."

"Did Caerdig ask *Joan* to marry him, as well as Enide?" asked Geoffrey, bewildered by the mass of information that was coming to him in disconnected bursts.

The bitten man nodded. "Joan first, then Enide. He was deter-mined to have peace at any cost. Personally, I would prefer a state of perpetual war to marriage with either of those two!"

"Was Caerdig Enide's lover?" asked Geoffrey before he could stop himself. He realised too late that it was not a prudent question to ask out of the blue.

The bitten man did not seem surprised or offended by the en-quiry, however. He mused for a moment. "It is possible, I suppose, although I would have thought it unlikely. Enide had better taste than to take Caerdig to her bed—he always smells of leeks!"

"Are you satisfied that Henry killed the right men for her mur-der?" asked Geoffrey of the bitten man, as the others started to argue among themselves about whether Enide was or was not sufficiently desperate to succumb to the rough attentions of the leek-scented Caerdig.

The bitten man shrugged. "They confessed to the crime."

"Yes, they confessed!" shouted Henry, pushing Bertrada out of the way as he stormed over to where Geoffrey stood. "Do you think I would have extracted vengeance from innocent men?"

Geoffrey said nothing.

"Enough of this!" said Bertrada firmly, as she grabbed a table to regain her balance after Henry's rough passage. "The events sur-rounding Enide's death were dreadful, but they are all over. Let us talk of more pleasant things tonight."

"Caerdig, of course, spread rumours that one of us was respon-sible," said the bitten man, ignoring her. "But they fizzled out once Henry had hanged the poachers."

"Enough!" shrieked Bertrada.

Her voice shrilled through the hall, and silenced even Henry, who had been about to add something else. She gave Geoffrey a hefty shove in the chest to make him sit again, and fought to bring her temper under control.

"There is something else I would like to know," said Geoffrey. Bertrada glowered at him. "I am sorry, but it has been a long time, and I do not know who most of you are. Henry I recognise, but . . ." He stopped and shrugged.

The balding man smiled. "Of course. And you, too, are unfa-miliar to us, although you look so much like Enide that no one could ever doubt who you are. However, you have changed from the boy we saw off to Normandy twenty years ago."

He paused and studied Geoffrey carefully, so that it was obvious that he regretted his comment about family likeness, because he realised it had lost him the opportunity to disclaim Geoffrey as an impostor. Evidently, the others thought the same, for Geoffrey suddenly found himself the object of some intensive scrutiny.

"You *have* changed," said the bitten man, eyeing him speculatively.

"Do not try to fool yourselves," said Henry heavily. "It is obvious he is *exactly* who he claims. Look at his eyes—it is Enide staring at you! And on his chin is that small scar I made with Walter's sword when we were young."

There were reluctant murmurs of agreement, and then Bertrada began with the introductions.

"I am Bertrada, and this is Walter—my husband and your oldest brother."

She indicated the balding man with a wave of her hand, and continued.

"Joan is away at the moment, but we are expecting her back in a few days. Her husband is Sir Olivier d'Alençon."

Geoffrey rose to return the bow that served more to display Olivier's courtly manners than civility to his visitor.

"Olivier is a kinsman of the Earl of Shrewsbury, and so we are deeply honoured to have him in our family."

Bertrada's tone of voice was odd, and Geoffrey looked at her sharply, detecting undercurrents that he did not yet understand. But he certainly understood her reference to the Earl of Shrewsbury. It seemed that he could go nowhere without encountering reference to the infamous baron.

"I trained under the Earl," said Olivier, not quite nonchalantly enough to prevent him from sounding boastful. "I entered his service when I was fifteen, and was a knight by the time I was twenty—which you will know is very young. The Earl taught me everything I know."

Geoffrey thought this was nothing to be proud of, given the fact that Shrewsbury was not noted for his chivalry or his attention to the other knightly arts. Uncharitably, Geoffrey wondered how much

Olivier's knighthood had cost him, for he was certain that the chicken-hearted man whom he had encountered outside could never have lasted long in any serious battle.

As if sensing his reservations, Olivier set out to prove him wrong, reciting a list of his military successes. Geoffrey listened with growing astonishment, until Olivier mentioned his leading role in the Battle of Civitate. Geoffrey was no military historian, but he knew about the battle in which Tancred's ancestors had captured Pope Leo IX, and he also knew it had taken place almost fifty years before. If Olivier had even been born then, he would have been little more than a babe in arms.

"I see," said Geoffrey, somewhat at a loss for words after Olivier had described in detail the way in which he had pitted his few loyal troops against the superior numbers of the enemy. Olivier's eyes gleamed with fervour, and Geoffrey wondered whether he might have misheard. "The Battle of Civitate, you say?" he asked, to be certain.

"The very same," said Olivier proudly. "It was I who captured that crafty old Pope and flung him into my deepest dungeon. I kept him there for years."

"Really?" queried Geoffrey lightly. He wondered whether Olivier thought he was a half-wit to be mislead by impossible stories, or whether the small knight was trying to test his intelligence in some bizarre manner. "But I understood that Pope Leo was released as soon as he had renounced his holy war against the de Hautevilles."

Olivier shot him an unpleasant look at this contradiction. "Quite so. But he was in my dungeon first. And of course, I was at the Battle of Elgin, when King Duncan was slain . . ."

Since that battle occurred sixty years before, Geoffrey began to doubt whether Olivier was in complete control of his faculties.

"I could teach you Crusaders a thing or two. And then there was the battle of—"

"You could talk about your victories all night, Sir Olivier," said Bertrada smoothly. "But you should save something with which to entertain Geoffrey tomorrow." She turned to Geoffrey. "Now, you say you remember Henry, but this is his wife Hedwise, whom you have never met."

The golden-haired Hedwise stepped forward, smiling with the

face of an angel, although her eyes held an unmistakable glint of
something far from seraphic. "Henry has told me a lot about you."

Geoffrey was sure he had. He bowed politely over her proffered
hand, but was discomfited when she clutched his fingers and refused
to let go. On the opposite side of the room, Henry rose to his feet
at the ambiguous gesture, and Geoffrey was uncertain whether to
snatch his hand away, or to leave it where it was. For once, the dog
proved it could be of occasional value, and came to his rescue by
sniffing around her gown and then beginning to raise its back leg.
Hastily, Hedwise abandoned Geoffrey and moved away.

"That is an extraordinary animal," observed the bitten man in
some admiration. "Although you have all but ruined it. Have you
not trained it at all?"

"And this is Stephen, your middle brother," said Bertrada flatly,
indicating him with a dismissive flap of her hand. "As you may have
guessed, his main interest in life is dogs."

It was clear to Geoffrey that Bertrada's introduction was intended to be offensive to Stephen, although Stephen did not seem
to resent it. He gave Geoffrey a conspiratorial grin, and slapped him
on the shoulder in a friendly fashion. He did not look in the least
bit like the gangling eighteen-year-old Geoffrey remembered. He
was tall, although he lacked the bulk of Henry and Walter, and his
reddish hair was cut very short under his cap, so that he looked like
the soldiers who had been shorn after an outbreak of ringworm at
the Citadel in Jerusalem. And, since Henry and Bertrada had wives,
Geoffrey assumed it must have been Stephen's spouse who had died
the previous year, and whose name the Mappestone scribe had not
bothered to mention in the letter he had sent to the Holy Land.

Stephen knelt, and earned the immediate affection of the dog
by handing it something brown and nasty looking from his pocket.
Seeing the dog's attentions were occupied, Hedwise stepped forward
again, oblivious or uncaring of Henry's resentful stare.

"Henry and I were married five years ago," she said. "We already have one heir, and we are hoping another is on the way." She
patted her stomach meaningfully.

Heir to what? thought Geoffrey. As a third son, Henry's chances
of inheriting anything of value from his father were virtually negli-
gible—only slightly better than Geoffrey's.

"Hedwise. Is that a Saxon name?" he asked, searching about for a subject that would not be contentious.

"Yes, it is!" spat Henry, striding forward and dragging Hedwise away from Geoffrey. "And we are proud of our Saxon heritage!"

"You are a Norman, Henry," said Walter with a weariness that suggested this was not the first time the subject had been raised. "Being born in England rather than Normandy changes nothing."

"That is not the opinion of our King!" said Henry, standing with his legs astride and his arms folded. "And if anyone claims different, I will reveal him as a traitor!"

Geoffrey looked from Henry to Walter in bewilderment. So much for his choice of a frictionless subject. Stephen shook his head and sighed, and continued the dangerous business of tickling the dog's stomach.

"Let us not discuss Saxons and Normans tonight either," said Bertrada grimly. "Perhaps Geoffrey will tell us about the Crusades . . . "

"Why should we not discuss my heritage now?" demanded Henry. "Is it just because *he* has deigned to grace us with his presence, just as Godric is about to die? Well, I for one do not care! None of us asked him here, and none of us want him, despite the way the rest of you are fawning around him." He swung round to Geoffrey. "This manor is rightfully mine, and I mean to have it—whatever I need to do to get it!"

Geoffrey studied him thoughtfully. And did that include poisoning their father, he wondered.

Geoffrey yawned as he sat in the great wooden chair near the fireplace, and wished he were anywhere but at Goodrich Castle. Next to him, Walter and Stephen perched on stools and stretched their hands towards the flames in the hearth, while Bertrada and Hedwise affected attitudes of boredom.

"I *will* have Goodrich!" Henry declared as he paced back and forth, fuelling his anger by repeated swigs from the wine that he carried in a stained skin tied to his belt.

"How?" asked Geoffrey, genuinely curious to know why his

brother thought he would stand even the remotest chance of inheriting Goodrich over his two older brothers and Joan.

"Walter was born in Normandy, as were Joan and Stephen. I was the first to be born here and, by rights, this English manor is mine! The King himself laid claim to the English throne on exactly the same . . ." He paused, struggling to find the correct word.

"Pretext?" supplied Geoffrey helpfully.

Henry glared at him. "King Henry is like me in more than name. And he supports my claim to the manor entirely."

"He does not!" cried Bertrada, outraged. "You have never spoken to the King!"

"Oh, but I have, Bertrada," said Henry smugly, "and he sees a similarity between his claim to the English throne, and mine to the manor of Goodrich. He says he will back me in any court of law."

"How could you have met the King?" said Walter derisively. "You would never have been permitted into his presence."

"Wrong, brother. I met the King at Chepstow around Christmastime, when I took him that letter from our father."

"Rubbish!" snapped Walter. "The letter might have reached the King—although I sincerely doubt it—but *you* certainly would not have done."

"What letter was this?" asked Stephen, looking up from where he was still rubbing the dog's stomach. "I know of no letter our father sent to the King."

"Some legal document or other about Lann Martin," said Walter dismissively. "Nothing of any importance."

Geoffrey suspected that the letter had contained something rather more than petty legal niceties regarding Lann Martin. The King had received a letter from Godric around Christmas, containing details of his alleged poisoning, and it seemed as though Henry, quite unwittingly, had delivered it for him.

"Sir Olivier arranged for me to be introduced," said Henry, turning to the black-haired knight.

"Olivier?" queried Stephen, abandoning the dog and turning on the small knight. "Why should Olivier do such a thing?"

"Well, it was not me, exactly," said Olivier quickly, shooting Henry a withering glance for his lack of tact. "It was more Joan's idea."

Geoffrey wondered what the chances were of slipping unnoticed from the hall, saddling up his horse, and riding as far as possible from Goodrich and its quarrelling inhabitants. He saw exactly what was happening: Walter, Joan, Stephen, and Henry had been arguing about how Godric's estates should be divided for years, and unfortunately for Geoffrey, he had arrived at a time when these long-standing battles were intensified because of their father's impending death.

Walter was the eldest, and by rights should inherit the bulk of the manor—and since Godric Mappestone had been adding to it ever since he had been granted his initial, quite sizeable tract of land by the Conqueror, it was an inheritance worth owning. Not only did it include Goodrich Castle but it boasted several profitable bridges and fords over the River Wye, as well as the little castle at Walecford.

Joan seemed to have secured herself a decent dowry—Geoffrey's manor—in addition to a well-connected husband, but it seemed that Olivier was seeking further to improve his fortunes by adding Goodrich to it.

Geoffrey glanced at Stephen, who seemed uninterested in the conversation, although that was not to say that he was uninterested in Godric's will. As the second son, Stephen was to inherit a manor and several villages in the Forest of Dene. But there were rigid laws that applied to settlements in forests, and it was not an especially appealing inheritance. It would certainly interfere with the breeding of hounds—apparently Stephen's passion—because all dogs in the woods were required by law to have three claws removed to ensure they did not chase the King's deer. Stephen would almost certainly prefer to inherit Goodrich, but his chances of doing so while Walter lived were non-existent.

And Henry—regardless of the trumped-up reasons he might have invented for *him* to inherit Goodrich—would never do so as long as Walter and Stephen were alive.

"You probably do not fully understand the validity of my Henry's claim," said Hedwise sweetly, forcing Geoffrey to pay attention to her. "You have been away for so long that you cannot know what has been happening in our country. Well, you see, King William Rufus was killed in a hunting accident in the New Forest last August, and our new King is Henry, his younger brother."

"I have been in the Holy Land, not on the moon," said Geoffrey, smiling at her notion that he could be so uninformed. "I am not so out of touch that I do not know who is the King of England."

He could have mentioned that he had spoken with the King just two days previously, but the less she and the rest of his family knew about what the King had charged him to do, the better.

"But you do not know the basis on which King Henry holds the throne, rather than giving it to his oldest brother, the Duke of Normandy," said Henry, with his customary acidity. He kicked at a stool until it was in a position he considered satisfactory, and slumped down on it, scowling into the fire. "You have no idea of what King Henry's arguments are!"

Geoffrey most certainly did, for it had been a popular topic of conversation across most of Europe, and he had grown bored with being regaled with people's opinions on the matter. A fourth son seizing a kingdom from under the nose of a first son was not a matter that had passed unnoticed in neighbouring countries.

"William the Conqueror had four sons," began Hedwise. Geoffrey wondered if she thought he was simple, for who in Christendom did not know of the Conqueror's rebellious sons? "The eldest was Robert, who was bequeathed the Dukedom of Normandy."

"I know all this," said Geoffrey in an attempt to suppress her somewhat patronising history lesson. "I was in the Duke's service, if you recall."

"The second son was killed when he fell from his horse in the New Forest many years ago," she continued, as though he had not spoken. "The third was Rufus, to whom the Conqueror bequeathed the Kingdom of England, and the fourth was Henry, who was left no land, but plenty of silver."

"Which he increased considerably by his shady business dealings," added Walter hotly. "The man is a grasping thief as well as a usurper."

"That is treason!" yelled Henry, stabbing an accusatory finger at his brother. "Henry is our rightful King! He was born in the purple—born when his father was King. Of course he is our rightful monarch!"

"You would think that!" drawled Stephen laconically, "since it fits your own claims so cosily."

"If Henry was the rightful heir, then why did he make such an undignified dash to Westminster to have himself crowned?" demanded Walter. "Why did he not wait, and secure his older brother's blessing?" He appealed to Geoffrey. "Henry was crowned King three days after Rufus's death! Three days! You call such speed the act of a man with a clear conscience? Henry knew the throne rightfully belonged to the Duke of Normandy! Tell him, Geoffrey!"

Geoffrey did not want to be drawn into a debate fraught with such dangers. As a former squire of the Duke of Normandy, he felt a certain allegiance to him, strengthened by the fact that Rufus and the Duke had signed documents, each naming the other heir. The Duke's claim to the English throne was legal and even moral. But Henry was the man who had been crowned King in the Abbey at Westminster, and he was the man who held the most power in England. Henry also had reliable ways of discovering who was loyal and who was not, apparently, since he already knew about Walter's lack of allegiance to him. Geoffrey had no intention of taking sides in an issue that could be construed as treasonable.

"The Duke has enough to occupy him without attempting to rule England too," he said carefully. "Normandy is not peaceful, and there are many rebellions and uprisings that need to be brought under control. It is better that King Henry holds England, and the Duke holds Normandy."

"But the Duke does not hold Normandy," pounced Henry immediately. "Luckily for Normandy! When he decided to go gallivanting off on Crusade, he sold Normandy to Rufus. It is now part of King Henry's realms."

"The Duke did not *sell* Normandy to Rufus!" protested Walter indignantly. "He merely pawned it to raise funds for his holy Crusade. And he pawned it only on the assurance that he could reclaim it on his return."

"But unfortunately, Rufus is no longer here to sell it back to him," observed Stephen, looking from Walter to Henry, as if he were amused by the dissension between them. "And anyway, the Duke cannot buy it back, because everyone knows he has no money."

"Nonsense!" spat Walter. "The Duke made a profitable marriage, and has plenty of money to purchase Normandy."

"He does not," shouted Henry triumphantly. "He has squandered it all already. The Duke may be a fine warrior, but he is a worthless administrator, and he would make a worse king."

Voices rose and fell, Henry's loudest of all. Geoffrey shivered, and stretched his hands out to the fire. He was still damp, and no one had bothered to stoke up the fire since the servants had retired to bed. He was also hungry, but the food laid on the table looked greasy and stale, and anyway, he had not been offered any.

He flexed his aching shoulders, and cursed himself for ever considering something as foolish as returning to Goodrich after so many years. He looked up from the flames to the door at the end of the hall, thinking that if Caerdig had not ambushed him and Aumary had not died, Geoffrey would not have been charged by the King to investigate the mysterious happenings at Goodrich Castle, and he would have no reason at all not to stride down the room, fling open the door, and escape from his family once and for all. Even the dangers of travelling alone on the forest roads would be nothing compared to the battleground his family had created. He wished fervently that he had never set eyes on Aumary.

He tuned out the quarrelling voices, and thought about Enide, imagining how unhappy she must have been, trapped among their schismatic siblings. No wonder she had taken a lover! Had she seen Caerdig as a way to leave Goodrich, aware that her days there were numbered when someone had begun to poison her? Could Geoffrey believe Henry's claim that the poachers had confessed to her murder, or was there truth in Walter's belief that Caerdig may have hired them? Or had Henry hanged two innocent men for some sinister reason of his own?

Geoffrey stared into the embers of the dying fire, and let the sounds of dissent wash over him. He closed his eyes, and tried to imagine what Enide might have looked like. But he was tired, and almost immediately began to doze. He awoke with a start when he became aware that the hall was silent, and that everyone was looking at him.

Since he had not been listening to them, he did not have the faintest idea what he was supposed to say. He smiled apologetically, and took a deep breath to try to make himself more alert.

"See?" said Henry, favouring his younger brother with a look of pure loathing. "He does not even do us the courtesy of paying attention to what we say!"

"No matter," said Olivier, coming to sit on a stool near Geoffrey, and slapping the younger knight's knee in a nervous attempt at camaraderie. "I merely asked whether you had managed to do much looting while you were in the Holy Land."

"We heard there was looting aplenty to be had once Jerusalem fell," said Walter eagerly, his argument with Henry forgotten. "And we heard that the knights had the pick of it."

There was another expectant hush as Geoffrey looked from face to face. "I took very little," he said eventually. "I do not particularly enjoy looting."

There was yet another silence. A barely glowing log on the fire collapsed in a fine shower of sparks, and the dog snuffled noisily in the rushes, sniffing out an alarming array of unwholesome objects that it ate with a gluttonous relish.

"But there was not just Jerusalem," said Bertrada eventually. "There was Nicaea, too, and Antioch. You must have looted some of them."

Geoffrey shook his head. "Not really. These were not abandoned cities, you know—there were people living in them. In order to loot houses and shops, their owners first had to be slaughtered, and I did not feel especially comfortable with that notion."

"But you are a knight," said Olivier, clearly mystified. "You are supposed to slaughter people. What do you think knightly training is all about?"

"I have no problem with fighting armed men, but I do not like the idea of killing the defenseless."

"How curious," said Olivier, turning his puzzled gaze to Walter.

"You always were a little odd," said Walter, folding his arms and looking down at Geoffrey with a mixture of curiosity and unease. "But you have something in your saddlebags, because I felt their weight. They certainly do not contain your spare shirts!"

"Unfortunately not," said Geoffrey, thinking of the shirts' theft that afternoon. He suspected that the chances of begging a spare one from anyone at Goodrich were likely to be minimal.

"Well, what do they contain?" pressed Bertrada. "You must have some treasure, even if you were too squeamish to loot for yourself. Surely the knights shared such riches between them?"

"I have some books," said Geoffrey, unable to suppress a look of disbelief at her bizarre suggestion that Holy Land knights would share anything at all, but especially loot. "And three Arabian daggers."

"Books?" echoed Henry. He threw back his head and roared with laughter. "There go your hopes for funds to build a new hall!" he said, jabbing a finger at Walter. "And you, Stephen, will have to raise your own cash to buy that hunting dog you have been boring us with details of for the past six months! So little brother Geoffrey returns empty-handed from what was reputed to be some of the easiest looting in the history of warfare!"

"I have heard enough from you tonight, Henry," said Stephen, rising from where he had been kneeling near the fire. "I am going to bed." He turned to Geoffrey and smiled. "Despite what Henry says, it is good to have you with us again. I hope we can talk more in the morning."

He walked towards the narrow, steep-stepped spiral staircase, and they heard his footsteps receding as he climbed.

"Did you bring nothing else?" asked Walter pleadingly, ignoring Henry's renewed gales of spiteful laughter. "No jewels or golden coins?"

"I have enough to travel back to Jerusalem," said Geoffrey, although that was only because Tancred had declined to let him leave without ensuring that he had sufficient funds to return again.

"And that is it?" insisted Bertrada. "Enough coins for your passage to the Holy Land and a sackful of worthless books?"

"They are not worthless!" protested Geoffrey indignantly. "At least one of them is almost beyond value—a tenth-century copy of Aristotle's *Metaphysics*. Let me show you."

He rummaged in his bags for the text, and brought it out. Walter took it warily, as though it might bite him, and inspected the soft covers.

"Interesting," he said, despite himself. "This is not calfskin, as I would have expected. Perhaps it is goat, or some animal I have never heard of. I am told there are strange beasts in the Holy Land."

Bertrada snatched it from him impatiently and opened it. "Very nice," she said with disinterest. "How much will we be able to sell it for?"

"It is not for sale," said Geoffrey, watching her turning the pages and holding the book upside down. He had forgotten that he and Enide alone had been the literate members of the family. "Such a book could never be sold."

"Why not?" asked Olivier, looking over Bertrada's shoulder. "It is a pretty enough thing. Some woman might like it for her boudoir, or perhaps a wealthy monk might buy it."

"Well, I would not give good money for it," said Walter, watching as Bertrada handed it to Hedwise to see. "I do not see the point of owning such a thing, even if the covers are nice."

"Not just the covers," said Geoffrey, although he knew he was fighting a battle that was already lost. "Look at the quality of the illustrations and the writing. It must have taken years for someone to produce such a masterpiece."

"What a waste of a life," muttered Walter. "He would have been better breeding sheep out in the fresh air, not cooped up in some dingy cell all his days."

"It is beautiful, Geoffrey," said Hedwise softly, touching one of the illustrations with the tip of a delicately tapering finger. "I can see why you cherish such a thing."

Henry looked at her sharply and then tore the book from her hands when she returned Geoffrey's smile. Geoffrey's quick reactions snatched the precious book from the air as it sailed towards the fire. He replaced it in his saddlebag, and slowly rose to his feet. Henry took several steps backwards, and Geoffrey was gratified that even the simple act of standing could unsettle his belligerent brother.

However, once Geoffrey had demonstrated that he was going to make no one rich, his family lost interest in him, and he was abandoned to fend for himself when everyone else went to bed. He took some logs from a pile near the hearth, and set about building up the fire. He hauled his surcoat over his head and set it where it might dry, but when he came to unbuckle his chain-mail, he hesitated, recalling Henry's glittering hatred.

Easing himself inside the hearth, as close to the fire as possible, Geoffrey settled down to sleep, resting his back against the wall with his dagger unsheathed by his hand. Perhaps Henry would not risk murdering his brother as he slept, but Geoffrey was not prepared to gamble on it. His chain-mail remained in place.

When a rustle of rushes brought him to his feet in a fighting stance with his knife at the ready, it was morning, and pale sunlight slanted in through the open shutters.

"And good morning to you, too, brother," said Walter, jumping away from the weapon's reach. "Tomorrow, you can fetch your own breakfast!"

He handed Geoffrey a beaker and a bowl of something grey. Geoffrey was about to thank him, when the sound of shouting came from one of the chambers above. Walter made a sound of impatience.

"That is Stephen," he said. "He will wake Godric if he carries on so."

The shouting was followed by a clatter of footsteps on the stairs, and Stephen emerged into the hall.

"Come quickly!" he yelled. "Godric is breathing his last!"

CHAPTER FIVE

At Stephen's words, there was a concerted rush to the staircase, Bertrada jostling Hedwise as they vied for first place. And then the hall was silent again, except for the muffled thump of footsteps on the wooden ceiling above, and the occasional hiss of collapsing wood in the fire. Geoffrey sat on a stool and stretched his hands out to the glowing embers.

"You should come, too, Geoffrey," said Stephen, walking down the hall towards him. "I know Godric would like to see you before he dies. He has always liked you better than the rest of us."

"If he ever said that, it was only because I was not here," said Geoffrey wryly. "He does not usually even remember my name."

Stephen smiled. "But you wanted to see him. Come now, or you might find your journey was in vain."

Geoffrey followed his brother towards the stairs. On the way up, they met Hedwise, who was descending.

"You are too late," she said, without the merest trace of grief. "He is already dead. You called us too late, Stephen."

"He cannot be dead yet," said Stephen, startled. "You must be mistaken! He spoke to me only moments ago. I told him Geoffrey was back and he grinned at me. Then he informed me he thought his end was near and that I should fetch everyone. He cannot have slipped away so fast!"

He ran ahead of Geoffrey and disappeared into a chamber on

the uppermost floor. Geoffrey followed more slowly, pausing to glance through a door at the tiny chamber in the thickness of the wall, which he had once shared with Walter, Henry, and Stephen. It now seemed to be Walter and Bertrada's room, with plain, dirty walls and an unpleasant, all-pervading odour of stale clothes.

He reached his father's bedchamber and poked his head around the door, just in time to see Walter pulling at a ring on the dead man's finger. On the other side, Bertrada was rifling through the corpse's clothes, while Henry, Stephen, and Olivier watched them like hawks. When they saw Geoffrey, Walter turned his tugging into a clumsy attempt to lay out the body, while Bertrada pretended to be straightening the covers.

"As a mark of respect, you might consider waiting a little while before you plunder his body," said Geoffrey, unable to stop himself. Although he had seen many acts of greed during the Crusades, most men—even knights—were not usually so ruthless with their kinsmen.

"You would think that." Henry sneered. "You who could not even loot a city properly! Where is that dagger of Godric's, Stephen—the one he claims the Conqueror gave him?"

"If I knew, I would not tell you," said Stephen. "He always said that I should have that."

"Rubbish!" said Walter, abandoning his pretence of laying out the body, and beginning to haul at the ring again. "The dagger should be mine because I am his eldest son. Look in that chest, Bertrada. It will be in there."

"It is not," said Stephen. "Believe me, I have checked. The old goat has hidden it somewhere, so that none of us will be able to find it."

"Do you mean that thin, worn thing he used at the dining table?" asked Olivier disdainfully. "Why would any of you want that?"

"The hilt is silver," explained Henry. "It can be melted down and made into something else."

Geoffrey looked around the room, surprised at the changes in it since he had last been there. Gone were the practical whitewashed walls, and in their place were dark-coloured paintings depicting gruesome hunting scenes and improbably gory battles. There were soft rugs on the floor where there had once been plain wood, and the pile of smelly furs had been exchanged for a large bed heaped with multi-hued covers. He imagined that his military-minded father must have softened indeed to substitute his functional quarters for a room that reminded Geoffrey of the Holy Land brothels.

"There are a great many things to do now," said Olivier, edging towards the door. "I must inform the Earl of Shrewsbury that Sir Godric Mappestone is dead."

"You are going nowhere," said Walter, abandoning his father's hand, and leaping across the room to slam the door closed as Olivier reached it. Henry bounced over the bed, uncaring for the corpse that lay on it, and took up pulling at the ring where Walter had left off.

Walter glared at Olivier. "You will stay here until I have secured my hold on the manor. I do not want you running off to the Earl of Shrewsbury until I am ready."

"I only want to inform him about this sad death," protested Olivier in hurt tones. "And he must be told quickly, because the will is contested and he is your overlord. You might think that *you* are due to inherit, Walter, but remember what we discovered only last summer—that there is some question regarding your legitimacy. If that is true, then my wife Joan is the next in line, and although it is unusual to inherit through the female line, it is not unknown."

"But if Walter is illegitimate, the manor will pass to me," snapped Stephen. "I am the oldest legitimate son."

"But none of you will succeed!" cried Henry in wild delight, triumphantly waving aloft the ring he had wrested from the old man's finger. "I have the best claim: I am legitimate and I was born in England. And better yet, I have a Saxon wife—just like the King. My marriage will unite the Normans with the Saxons, and all these border skirmishes will be at an end!"

"I thought your border skirmishes were with the Welsh," said Geoffrey, puzzled, "not the Saxons."

No one took any notice of him as they argued with each other, so he walked to the bed and looked down at the body of his father.

"God's teeth!" he swore, the shock in his voice instantly silencing his squabbling kin. "He is not dead!"

He punched Henry off the bed and cradled his father gently in his arm. Henry staggered to his feet and advanced, eyes blazing with fury. Geoffrey looked up at him steadily, daring him to attack, and Henry, realising he would not win a physical confrontation with his taller, stronger brother, kicked the bed in frustration and thwarted anger. Geoffrey ignored his tantrum and pulled the covers up around his father's chin, realising that the chamber was fireless and chilly.

Sir Godric Mappestone, hero of Hastings and honoured warrior of the Conqueror, opened his eyes, and Geoffrey saw that he was not as near death as his family had led him to believe. He was pale and gaunt certainly, and perhaps even mortally ill, but his breathing was deep and regular and his sharp green eyes were alert and as calculating as ever.

Geoffrey studied him curiously, remembering the fiery, aggressive man who had ruled his childhood home with a rod of iron. His thick hair was solid grey, and the strong-featured face was lined with age and a life spent out of doors. His eyes held a trace of amusement, and Geoffrey wondered if his father had not feigned his "death" so that Geoffrey might witness exactly the scene that he had, with his brothers fighting over the ring and searching his body for valuables. It would certainly be an act in keeping with his crafty character.

"Godfrey, my son!" said Godric in a weak voice. "You have come back from the Crusade to see me before I die!"

"Geoffrey," corrected Geoffrey. He smiled at Godric, saddened to see the great warrior so incapacitated. He shuddered at the sickness that had reduced the mighty, blustering Godric to the skeletal figure that lay in his arm, and decided that falling in battle was infinitely preferable.

"One of my treacherous brood has poisoned me, Godfrey," muttered Godric. "With arsenic, my physician thinks. Or perhaps the fungus galerinus."

"He is rambling again," said Bertrada, from the other side of the room. "He often claims that one of us is killing him. He will be accusing you in a moment."

"She is trying to make you believe that I have lost my wits, Godfrey," said Godric with a faint smile. "But I am as sharp as I ever was. Someone has been poisoning me slowly and deliberately for months now, and I have grown more feeble each day. Did you see how they searched me for items of value, hoping I was dead? It is not even safe for me to sleep!"

"They will not do so again," said Geoffrey. "I will see that they do not."

Godric regarded him uncertainly. "You are a good boy, God-frey," he said eventually. "Even if you did harbour odd notions about wanting to be a scholar. Perhaps I should have sent Henry away instead of you—then I would not be lying here dying now."

"You think Henry is poisoning you?" asked Geoffrey, fixing his long-haired brother with a disconcerting stare. Henry was the first to look away.

"I do not know which of them it is," said Godric. "Walter and his wife, Bertrada, Joan and her husband Olivier, Stephen, or Henry and his angelic Hedwise—they all have their own reasons for want-ing me out of this world. If you had come a few weeks earlier, you might have saved me."

"You may recover," said Geoffrey, hoping the doubt he felt did not reflect itself in his voice. Whether Godric was in control of his mental faculties, Geoffrey was not qualified to say, but the knight had seen enough dying men to know when a body was beyond repair.

Godric gave a rustling laugh and closed his eyes. "I will not get better now, Godfrey. The poison has damaged my vital organs. Ask my physician about it. He will tell you."

"If you are so certain that someone wishes your death, why did you not hire a servant to prepare your food, so that no more poisons would reach you?" asked Geoffrey, certain that *he* would not have lain down and let the likes of Henry and his kin sentence him to a lingering death while he still had strength to prevent it.

"I did. But servants can be bribed, or if not bribed, then dis-patched with no questions asked."

"Torva's death was an accident," protested Walter wearily. "He was drunk, and he fell in the moat. There was nothing remotely suspicious about his demise."

Godric fixed watery eyes on Geoffrey. "And what do you think, Godfrey? Do you consider such a timely death to be mere coinci-dence?"

Geoffrey's thoughts whirled. "The man you hired to prepare your food was drowned?"

Despite his low opinion of his brothers, Geoffrey still had not convinced himself that one of them would subject their father to a death by degrees. But Torva's death seemed opportune, to say the least.

"It was an accident," insisted Bertrada. "Accidents do happen, you know."

Geoffrey looked around at his assembled relatives, seeing a variety of emotions expressed. Henry appeared to be bored, twisting the stolen ring round on his finger, while Hedwise watched him absently. Walter and Bertrada were acting as though this were a discussion that had been aired many times before, and they were heartily tired of it. Stephen seemed uneasy, although whether this reflected a guilty conscience or was merely due to the uncomfortable nature of the conversation, Geoffrey could not tell.

"Was this Torva an habitual drinker?" Geoffrey asked eventually, supposing that there might conceivably be an innocent explanation of the servant's death.

"Yes, he was," snapped Walter. "He went to the tavern every night after he prepared father's dinner. He was found dead in our moat one morning, where he had fallen as he had weaved his way home. The guards said they thought they had heard a splash, but it had been too dark for them to see anything."

"And before you ask, there was not a mark on his body," said Stephen, rather too quickly for Geoffrey's liking. "He was drunk and he drowned. End of story."

End of Torva, too, thought Geoffrey. "And did you hire another servant to take Torva's place?"

"Oh, yes," said Godric. "But I am uncertain as to whether he can be trusted. With Torva, I told him that if I became worse, I would kill him—so he had an incentive to keep me alive. But young Ine knows that I am not in a position to carry out such a threat on him. Why should he not take a bribe from the villain who is killing me by degrees?"

"Godric has been spreading these lies all over the county," said Bertrada to Geoffrey. "He even sent for the Earl of Shrewsbury, who arrived with his personal physician. Neither found anything amiss—the physician said Godric has a wasting disease, for which there is no cure."

"You have come just in time, Godfrey," whispered Godric, the softness of his voice forcing Geoffrey to lean close to hear him.

Not wanting to miss anything, the others clustered round, jostling each other to secure the best places. The old man's eyes gleamed with malice when he saw them elbowing each other just to listen to his whispered conversation with Geoffrey, and Geoffrey suspected that his father derived a great deal of pleasure from the dissension and suspicion that festered between his children and their spouses.

"Three weeks ago, when Stephen told me that Godfrey was returning, I made a new will," Godric said, just loud enough for the others to hear.

His eyes glittered as he spoke, and Geoffrey's spirits sank. He sensed he was about to hear something he would rather not know.

There was a stunned silence in the bedchamber as the old man made his announcement. Seeing he had his family's complete attention, Godric leaned back in Geoffrey's arms with a weak grin of satisfaction.

"I have made a new will," he said again.

"But the old one will stand," said Walter loudly. "No court in the land will countenance another made while you are far from sound in mind and body."

"The Earl of Shrewsbury himself witnessed it," said Godric, his grin widening as he witnessed his eldest son's consternation. "Will you tell him that he is an inadequate judge, or shall I? Godfrey, come closer. The new will is hidden in the chest at the end of the bed, under my shirts. Find it, and bring it to me."

Gently easing Godric's head onto the pillow, Geoffrey did as he was bidden, watched intently by his kinsmen. At first he thought Godric was mistaken, because he could find nothing, but when Henry grabbed a handful of shirts and shook them impatiently, a scroll of parchment dropped to the floor. There was an undignified scramble for it, which Geoffrey watched dispassionately. Since none of them could read, possession of it would do them little good.

Not surprisingly, Henry emerged triumphant from the skirmish, and broke the seal with his thick fingers. The others clustered round,

Stephen fingering a split lip, and Bertrada pushing her tousled hair back under her wimple.

"What does it say?" enquired Geoffrey provocatively, as Henry turned it this way and that in frustration.

Henry flashed him a vicious look. "Where is that lazy clerk? Norbert!" he yelled down the stairwell. "Norbert, where are you?"

Norbert the scribe appeared almost immediately, suggesting to Geoffrey that his brothers and sisters-in-law were not the only ones party to what had been happening in his father's bedchamber. He wondered how many more of the household were gathered on the stairs to listen to the unsavoury twists and turns of his family's affairs.

"Read this," ordered Henry, shoving the scroll into Norbert's hands. From the bed, Godric gave a low cackle of amusement.

"Norbert knows full well what is in it: he was present when it was drawn up—although it was actually written by that fat priest who acts as the Earl's scribe, because Norbert's writing is not all it should be. And do not think that destroying it will do you any good, because the Earl has a copy. I am not so foolish as to believe that any of you will honour my last wishes when there is wealth at stake."

"What mischief have you done?" protested Walter in horror. "You know I am your rightful heir. You have always said so."

"But I have not always been dying from poison," said Godric, his lips still parted in the smile that reminded Geoffrey of a wall-painting he had once seen of the Devil. "And anyway, you, Walter, were born out of wedlock, so you have no claim at all. Ask my brother Sigurd if you doubt my word."

"Hah!" exclaimed Henry with spiteful satisfaction.

"But Sigurd has never liked me!" cried Walter. "Of course he will support such a claim. He has always favoured Stephen."

Henry gave an unpleasant laugh that brought Walter towards him with a murderous expression on his face. Stephen interposed himself between them.

"Then the manor is mine?" he asked, prising his brothers apart. "I am legitimate, and you always said I looked like our mother. I am no bastard."

"But you are also no son of mine," said Godric, with a malice that unnerved Geoffrey. "You, Stephen, are the spawn of your mother's lover."

"Father!" intervened Geoffrey, shocked. "Consider what you say. You slander our mother's good name."

"What good name?" queried Godric, shifting his gaze from Stephen to Geoffrey. "She cuckolded me every bit as much as I was unfaithful to her. She chose my brother with whom to couple, and Stephen is the result. Why do you think Sigurd has taken such an interest in him all his life? No one could believe it is because of his appealing personality. And where do you think that red hair comes from? It is not from me—but Sigurd has red hair."

"What a pity," mused Walter to Stephen. "If I could have chosen which brother to rid myself of, it would have been Henry, not you."

"So, my claim will stand," crowed Henry triumphantly. He snatched the will from Norbert and made for the door. "I am away to see the King and to ensure that no one pre-empts me. I am legitimate, the son of Godric, and I was born on English soil. What more need be said?"

"No," said Godric, his soft voice stopping Henry dead in his tracks. "You have always claimed you were born on English soil, but you never bothered to verify it with the people who really know—your mother and myself. In fact, Henry, you were born in France, after the Conqueror's fleet had left. The Conqueror was King of England days before your mewling presence was known on English soil.

"You are right," said Henry to Bertrada, after a moment of reflection. He regarded the gloating face on the bed with a look of pure loathing. "Godric rambles; he does not know what he is saying."

"But Joan's claim would come before Henry's, regardless of where he was born," began Olivier timidly from the other side of the room.

"Remove that whining coward from my presence!" ordered Godric hotly, pointing a thin finger at Olivier. "He parades around pretending to be a warrior, and he is not fit to breathe the same air as me."

Geoffrey began to suspect that this was not the first time such a scene had been played out at his father's supposed death-bed. Godric, weak and dying though he might be, was not too frail to manipulate his children and to take sadistic pleasure from their quarrelling.

"If Walter is illegitimate and Stephen is not your son, then I am next in line," said Henry, pulling himself up to his full height. "Whether I was born in England, France, or on the Channel, matters not one bit!"

"Godfrey is the only one of my sons who cannot have poisoned me," said Godric, enjoying Henry's anger. "The new will names *him* as my successor."

"But I do not want it!" cried Geoffrey in horror, rising so abruptly that the sick man had to grab Walter to prevent himself from being tipped off the bed. "Please! I have no wish to be fettered here."

And he certainly had no wish to be the sole target for his displaced brothers" ire for the remainder of what would doubtless prove to be a very short life.

"That is quite a brilliant bit of acting, Geoffrey," said Walter bitterly as he pushed Godric back on the bed. "So now we know why your arrival home is so timely—you must have been planning this for months."

"I do not want Goodrich," said Geoffrey forcefully. "I am not interested in such things. If I were, I could have had an estate ten times the size of Goodrich in the Holy Land."

"But you have already shown yourself to be less than efficient at looting," said Bertrada. "I was in the village this morning, and I learned that even that feeble lout Mark Ingram came home with more booty than you did. I think you failed to secure your fortune there, and so have come to steal away what is rightfully ours."

"You knew all along what Godric was planning, and you contrived to hasten his end," continued Henry in the same vein. "None of us is poisoning Godric. You are!"

"Oh, Henry!" said Geoffrey, exasperated by the lack of logic. "How can that be possible? I have been thousands of miles away!"

"I know how," said Stephen thoughtfully. He turned to his brothers. "It is coincidental that Ine arrived home from the Crusade so soon after Torva died, is it not? That is because Geoffrey dispatched him from Jerusalem to do his dirty work!"

As one, Walter, Bertrada, Stephen, Olivier, Hedwise and Henry cast accusing eyes towards Geoffrey. Geoffrey regarded them aghast.

In the bed, Godric cackled in wheezy delight, and made no attempt to support the innocence of his newly created heir. While Geoffrey had anticipated that his home-coming would not be as pleasant as that of Barlow and Ingram, he had certainly not expected to be charged with the murder of his father. He took a deep breath, and fought against the unreasonable desire to run them all through there and then, and really provide them something with which to accuse him.

"No," he said firmly. "I have never heard of Ine, and I most certainly do not want Goodrich. The will must be changed back to favour Walter, as it should."

"Should it? Should it?" shouted Henry bitterly. "Well, I do not think anything of the kind!"

"Then change it to favour you," said Geoffrey, losing patience. "I do not care one way or the other. I want nothing to do with it."

"But Goodrich should be mine," said Stephen. "And I do not believe I am Sigurd's son—he would have told me if I were."

How Godric had gone from four perfectly legitimate sons to only one within a matter of moments, defied Geoffrey's imagination. He glanced down at his father, who was thoroughly enjoying the consternation and friction his revelations had caused.

"Norbert," said Stephen suddenly, elbowing Walter out of the way to grab the clerk's sleeve. "What exactly does this will say?"

Clearing his throat, Norbert began to read. " 'This is the last will and testament of Sir Godric Mappestone, lord of the manor of Goodrich, Kernebrigges, Druybruk—' "

"Druybruk?" queried Henry. "I did not know we had that."

"There is much you do not know, little brother," sneered Walter. "Continue Norbert."

" 'Druybruk, Dena—' "

"Yes, yes," said Walter, impatiently. "We know all this."

"Well, some of us do," added Stephen, with a malicious glance at Henry.

" '. . . am in sound mind and body . . .' "

Bertrada gave a snort of derision.

" 'and I leave my complete estate and all my riches to my youngest son, Godfrey Mappestone, who is in the service of the Duke of Normandy in the Holy Land. The rest of my brood can go to the

Devil. Signed this eighteenth day of the month of December, in the year of Our Lord 1100.' "

Stephen released Norbert's arm, eyes glittering with savage delight. "I thought as much! He has no legitimate son called Godfrey, and certainly none in the service of the Duke of Normandy. The old fool never could remember Geoffrey's name, and Geoffrey is now in the service of Tancred, as he told us last night. This new will means nothing at all! We can contest it!"

Geoffrey heaved a sigh of relief, grateful beyond measure that his father's long-standing lapse of memory had at last worked to his advantage.

"No!" cried Godric angrily. "The Earl of Shrewsbury will see that my last wishes are upheld! Godfrey is a nickname, and everyone will know which son I mean to inherit."

"Not I," said Stephen. "I know of no Godfrey, nickname or not."

"Nor I," said Henry.

"Enough of this," said Geoffrey. He could see his father was tiring, and he had no wish to spend the entire day arguing over a will that no one had any intention of honouring. "Contest the will if you like, but I relinquish all part in it. I will remain in Goodrich until Father . . . well . . ."

"Until he begins his journey to Hell," supplied Bertrada, glaring at the sick man.

"As you will. And then I will leave you. I do not want Goodrich, and Tancred will not allow me to stay here anyway. If ever I do return to England, I will be quite happy with Rwirdin."

"Oh, you will not like that at all," said Walter quickly, casting a guilty glance at Olivier. "It is a miserable place all surrounded by hills and forest. When I am lord of Goodrich, I will find you something better."

Geoffrey sighed. "Very well. But let us discuss this another time. Father is tiring. He should be allowed to rest."

"Causing family discord *is* tiring," said Bertrada icily. "Everyone seems surprised that he claims one of his family is poisoning him, but if they knew him as we do, the surprise would be that he has lived his sixty-six years without one of us trying it before."

"That is a cruel thing for a daughter to say," said Stephen.

"What will Geoffrey think when he hears you so callously chattering about Godric's poisoning?"

"You mean his alleged poisoning," snapped Bertrada. "We all know he is making it up. He has a wasting sickness, and is dying of purely natural causes. He is spreading these vicious rumours about us because he loves to see us fight."

"I am being poisoned just as surely as I lie here," said Godric. "My physician will provide any proof that is needed. And one of you miserable dogs is responsible!"

"How?" demanded Bertrada. "Ine prepares all your food and, despite what you are trying to tell Geoffrey about Ine being bribed by one of us, you were ill when Torva prepared it, too. You are not being poisoned; you are dying because a disease is eating your innards away."

"If you really believe what you claim, why do you not leave Goodrich?" asked Geoffrey, reluctant to continue the subject, but puzzled by Godric's seemingly passive role in his own death.

"It is far too late now," snapped Godric. "I am already too ill to recover."

"But what about earlier?" persisted Geoffrey. "Why did you not leave when you first had your suspicions? It is not as if you have no other manors in which to live."

"Two reasons, you cheeky young whelp!" hissed Godric. He was pale, and his breathing was shallow and strained. "First, Goodrich is mine, and I will not be driven out of it by some poisoner. And second, they would have followed me. They are all too frightened that one might gain an advantage over the other, and none of them dares leave my side."

"Then perhaps you should consider bequeathing everything to the Church," suggested Geoffrey, looking down dispassionately at the panting man in the bed. "That would put an end to all this wrangling, and give you some peace."

"How dare you interfere!" yelled Henry, hurling himself at Geoffrey, fists at the ready. Geoffrey side-stepped him neatly, and used his brother's momentum to send him crashing into the wall.

"Enough!" he roared as Walter and Stephen seemed about to rally to Henry's defence. His voice was loud and angry enough to stop them in their tracks and to silence Henry's groans. He glared round at them. "Our father—poisoned or not—is ill. Sick people's minds often wander and cause them to say things we would rather they did not. Either accept this, or do not come to see him. Now, he is tired, and he needs to rest—or would you kill him here and now by simple exhaustion?"

From the expressions on their faces, Geoffrey could see that they would like that very much, but reason eventually prevailed, and everyone left Godric to sleep. Geoffrey helped the sick man swallow the dregs of some wine he found stored in an impressively large metal pitcher that took both hands to lift. Godric clearly wanted to talk further, but was too weary and Geoffrey had listened to more than enough accusations for one day. He straightened the bedclothes, and stood back to allow Hedwise to feed the sick man some broth.

"You want to watch her, son," said Godric, in a hoarse whisper a little later, nodding to where Hedwise was stoking up the fire. "She has a preference for men other than her husband."

"So do I," said Geoffrey fervently, drawing a wheezy chuckle from the dying man.

The morning's squabble had left Godric exhausted, and Geoffrey sat with him for the remainder of the day to ensure he was allowed to rest in peace. He stayed in Godric's chamber, and repelled a continuous stream of visitors who were anxious that Godric might be getting better. It was tedious work, and he began to regret his offer to stay at Goodrich until his father rallied or died.

Godric's room was gloomy, a sensation enhanced by the dismal wall-paintings with their macabre themes. Whether the subject was hunting or battle, there were impossible volumes of blood, and Geoffrey wondered what fevered mind had produced such a testament to violence. He threw open the window shutters, for the room stank of dirty rushes, sickness, and paint, but Godric complained that he was cold, and refused to sleep until Geoffrey had closed them again.

Geoffrey grew restless, unused to such an extended period of inactivity, but found he was unable to concentrate on much—even on his precious books. The cheap tallow candles, which smoked and

spat and added their own eye-watering odour to the hot room, did
not provide sufficient light by which to read, and they gave him a
headache. By the end of the evening, when Hedwise came to feed
Godric his broth, Geoffrey felt sick and his limbs had a sluggish,
aching feel in them. He supposed he must have caught a chill from
his dip in the river, and went to sit near the fire, hoping the feeling
would pass after a good night's sleep.

He had already dispensed with his chain-mail—if his family attacked him as he slept, Geoffrey decided there was more advantage
in being able to move quickly than encumbered with heavy armour,
and anyway, it did not seem appropriate to be in a sickroom wearing
full battle gear. He tugged off the boiled leather jerkin he wore for
light protection, and prepared to sleep wearing shirt and leggings.

"Fetch me my scribe," ordered Godric imperiously, as Geoffrey's eyelids began to droop. "I wish to see him immediately."

"What, now?" asked Geoffrey, startled awake. "It is very late.
He is probably asleep."

"Then go and wake him," said Godric, punctuating each word
as if he were talking to a child. "Do you think I pay him to doze all
night? Anyway, he is probably off practising with that silly crossbow
of his. He thinks I do not know how he spends his free time, but I
have seen him."

"Where will I find him?" asked Geoffrey, climbing to his feet
to do his father's bidding. "Does he sleep in the hall?"

"How should I know?" snapped Godric petulantly. "I have
barely left this chamber since Christmas. How am I supposed to
know who sleeps with whom in this place?"

Geoffrey suppressed an impatient response. "I will ask Walter,"
he said, opening the door.

"You will do no such thing!" roared Godric with surprising
force. "I do not want Walter asking questions about what I plan to
do. My business is between me and Norbert, and none of my greedy
whelps—including you."

"Fine," said Geoffrey, reminding himself that Godric was a sick
man, and that grabbing him by the throat to shake some manners
into him was not appropriate. "But if you do not know where Norbert might be found, and I am forbidden to ask, how am I supposed
to bring him to you?"

"Insolent cur!" hissed Godric. "I leave you my manor and you repay me by acting with rank discourtesy! I have a good mind to disinherit you in favour of one of the others."

"I will be back in a while," said Geoffrey. Henry might have risen to Godric's baiting, but Geoffrey would not.

He closed the door on Godric's outrage and went down the stairs to the hall. It was late evening, and several lamps were lit, casting long shadows across the room. Walter sat near the fire with Stephen, arguing about the merit and flaws of some hunting dog or other, while Henry slouched in a corner, well away from them, honing a sword that already looked razor-sharp and refreshing himself from a large flagon of wine. Bertrada and Hedwise crouched together over a tapestry, straining their eyes in the poor light to add the stitches, while Olivier amused himself by watching them. At the far end of the room, a group of servants had gathered, and were listening to a travelling entertainer strumming softly on a rebec as he sang a sad ballad.

Geoffrey looked among them for Norbert, but the scribe was not there. Opening the door, he left the hall and stepped outside into the cracking cold of a January night. The sky was clear, and stars were blasted all over it. Geoffrey gazed up at them for a moment, recalling how different they had looked in the Holy Land. He took several deep breaths, and felt the residual queasiness that had been plaguing him most of the day begin to recede. Since he was out, he went to check on his destrier.

As he was walking, he saw a shadow flit from the stables to one of the outhouses. Curious, he followed, pushing open the door and peering inside. At first he thought the outhouse was in complete darkness, but there was a faint light coming from the far end. Clumsily tripping over discarded pieces of saddlery and a pile of broken tools, he made his way towards it.

Norbert sat at a crude table, his habitually pale face moonlike in the dim flame of the candle. But what caught Geoffrey's attention, and what sent him starting backwards so that he almost fell, was the bow that the scribe had aimed at Geoffrey's chest.

"Sir Geoffrey!" said Norbert, rising to his feet and lowering the weapon. "I am sorry if I alarmed you. Please come in."

On closer inspection, Geoffrey saw that the bow was quite

harmless because there was no string. Embarrassed by his dramatic response to a disabled weapon, he went to stand next to the table.

"This seems an odd item for a scribe to possess," he said, studying the bow with the critical eye of the professional. It was a wretched thing—old and cracked—and he wondered whether the effort of re-stringing it would be worthwhile.

"I grew up around here," said Norbert with a smile, gesturing to a box on which Geoffrey might sit. "I could shoot a bow before I could write, and was providing food for all my family by the time I was ten. That was many years ago, though, before hunting in the King's forests was forbidden."

"The people who live in the forest must deeply resent those laws," said Geoffrey, thinking about Caerdig and his half-starved rabble of villagers. "Especially when food is scarce."

"It is my main objection to the rule of King Henry," said Norbert, nodding.

"This bow would not present much danger to his beasts," remarked Geoffrey. He picked up an arrow that was lying on the table, noting that the wood was cheap and the balance was poor.

Norbert smiled again. "Not much danger to anyone attacking Godric's castle, either," he said wryly. "And this is one of the best that we have. I own a crossbow, but the winding mechanism is broken and the blacksmith says he does not know how to repair it. But even if we had the best bows England had to offer, it would do us no good, because there is no one at Goodrich who could hit a horse at twenty paces."

"I had noticed that the guards were somewhat lacking in military skills," admitted Geoffrey. "It surprised me, because I thought my father would be concerned that Goodrich might come under attack by all these hostile neighbours he seems to have accumulated."

"None of those are likely to attack the castle," said Norbert. "They might harass the odd traveller, and the likes of Caerdig of Lann Martin are always after our cattle, but our neighbours do not have the weapons, skill, courage, or stupidity to attack Goodrich directly."

"So, I can sleep safe in my bed tonight, then?" asked Geoffrey, raising an eyebrow.

"Hardly!" said Norbert, with a shudder. "Someone has been

poisoning your father since last spring, and someone tried to poison your sister Enide too. Goodrich is a place where you would be safer outside it than in."

"My father is demanding that you attend him immediately," said Geoffrey, reluctant to discuss poisoners and murderers with the servants. "Do you mind, or shall I say I could not find you? It is very late."

Norbert's pale blue eyes opened wide with astonishment. "I will go. But thank you for your consideration—it is more than I have been given in fifteen years from the rest of your family. They regard my learning more as a necessary evil than a hard-earned skill."

"They seem to regard our father as an evil, too," mused Geoffrey, more to himself than Norbert. "His life is a burden to them and his death will be a cause for rejoicing."

Norbert laughed quietly. "And vice-versa. Have you noticed that you are the only one who calls him 'Father'? A year or so ago, he demanded that the entire brood and their spouses call him Godric, because none of them were worthy of the right to claim him as a parent. You can imagine how they took that insult!"

Geoffrey could only shake his head over both sides in this futile feud. He stood and followed Norbert out, tripping over the same tools and discarded saddles as he had on the way in.

"Could you not find a more conducive place in which to mend your bows?" he grumbled, rubbing his chin, where a rake had sprung up and hit him.

"When it is very cold, I stay in the hall," Norbert answered over his shoulder as he walked. "But no one ever uses this building in the evenings, and I like the solitude. It is often a relief to escape from the Mapp—from people."

Geoffrey knew exactly what he had been going to say, and concurred wholeheartedly with him. He led the way across the yard and through the hall. The others looked up as he walked towards the stairs with Norbert in tow.

"Where are you going?" demanded Henry immediately, standing so abruptly that he spilled his wine. "What are you up to, fetching Norbert at this time of night?"

"Father sent for him," said Geoffrey.

"You are going to change his will," said Walter accusingly.

"You are going to make him alter the name from Godfrey to Geoffrey."

"How dare you try to cheat us!" hissed Bertrada furiously. "You have no right!"

"You are all ridiculous!" Geoffrey snapped. It had been a long day, and he felt he had already been more than patient with his relatives" accusations. "Use the few brains you were born with before you make such outrageously stupid comments! First, I can write as well as Norbert, and so do not require him to change the will—if I were so inclined. Second, who would witness this new document? Wills need two independent witnesses to be legal. Third, if I wanted Goodrich, I would take it and none of you would be able to stop me."

He stalked out of the hall and up the stairs, Norbert scurrying behind him. He forced himself to take several deep breaths to control his anger before he opened the door to Godric's room.

"Here is Norbert," he said, ushering in the clerk.

"Thank you. Now get out," said Godric viciously. "I do not want any of my brood listening to my private business with my clerk. Kindly remove yourself and shut the door."

"With the greatest of pleasure," said Geoffrey, slamming it as he left. He rubbed hard at the bridge of his nose, and then stamped up the narrow spiral staircase to the tiny door that led to the battlements, longing for some peace.

The door to the roof had not been used for some time, and Geoffrey was beginning to think he would have to rejoin his squabbling siblings in the hall, when it shot open, sending cobwebs billowing everywhere. Leaving the door swinging in the breeze behind him, he stepped out onto the parapet that ran around the top of the keep.

Battlements was too grand a term to describe the low wall that ran around the gently pitched roof. It reached Geoffrey's waist in parts, but mostly it was little higher than knee level. Geoffrey supposed that archers might be able to operate from it if the keep ever came under attack, but they would be horribly exposed each time they stood to fire. He was a passable marksman himself, although he had not taken to the bow much as a weapon and did not like to hunt, but he would not have liked shooting from Godric's crumbling parapet.

He found a stretch of wall that seemed more sound that the rest, and leaned his elbows on the top. A light wind ruffled his hair and bit through his shirt and leggings. Once alone, he felt mildly ashamed of his outburst in the hall, and of his brief flash of temper with his father. Enide's letters had been full of the contest between his siblings for control over Goodrich, and it was clear that inheritance had become such an important issue to his family that they were unable to think of little else. He knew he should not allow them to irritate him.

But what was said was said, and he would know to hold his tongue the next time. He leaned over the parapet and looked down into the bailey, three floors below. It was dark, but he could just make out the outlines of the buildings in the outer ward, while in the village beyond he could hear distant laughter as the celebrations for the return of Ingram, Barlow, and Helbye continued.

He lost track of the time he stood leaning on the wall, enjoying the peace of the evening and the pleasure of being alone. Lights were doused in the hall, and Geoffrey could hear Godric yelling furiously for something. He suspected that the old man wanted him, but he was in no mood to deal with his father's cantankerous nature that night. Bertrada had been right, he thought with a grim smile— Godric was lucky no one had poisoned him before.

"Why are you out here, all alone and in the cold?"

Geoffrey jumped in shock at the soft voice close behind him, and spun round. Hedwise stood there, laughing coquettishly at his alarm, covering her mouth with her hand and her eyes bright with laughter. Geoffrey was appalled at himself. No one could have slipped up so silently behind him in the Holy Land—and if they had, it would probably have meant a Saracen dagger between his ribs. As he had done at the ford the previous day, he wondered whether he was losing his touch. He rubbed tiredly at his eyes and told himself that he would need to take greater care if he did not want Henry or one of the others sneaking up behind him with lethal intent.

"It is peaceful here," he said in answer to Hedwise's enquiry. "Or at least it was."

Hedwise's face turned sulky. "Now, now, Geoffrey! You have no cause to be hostile to me. The door was open and a gale was blowing down the stairs. I was puzzled, so I came to investigate. No one ever comes up here—it is not safe."

Geoffrey leaned his elbows back on the wall, and she came to stand next to him.

"It should be better maintained," he said. "Supposing the castle were attacked? What does Father plan to do—kill the hostile forces with the bodies of his archers as they tumble off the walls?"

Hedwise laughed. "You are right, but we have no money for such repairs. Everyone was hoping you might provide that from your Holy Land loot. But let us not talk of such things. I am delighted you have come to visit us. I was beginning to think that I might never meet you, or that I would be an old woman by the time you returned."

"I am surprised you gave it any thought whatsoever," said Geoffrey. "It cannot be that you have gained a favourable impression of me from Henry."

"Oh, Henry!" said Hedwise, waving a dismissive hand impatiently. "I was unlucky to have such a bore foisted upon me. I did not want to marry him, but my family thought it was a good match, so I had no choice. Henry is a lout—I would have done better wed to one of the farm hands."

Geoffrey imagined she was probably right, but did not feel it appropriate to comment. Hedwise sidled a little closer to him, rubbing up against his side. When he edged away, she moved with him.

"I would have been better off with you," she continued.

Geoffrey inched away a second time. "I would have made you a poor husband," he said. "Unless you happen to like reading."

"You could have taught me," she said.

To his alarm, he felt an arm slip around his waist. Was this a genuine attempt at seduction, he thought, or was she simply trying to have him found in some dreadfully compromising position by the fiery Henry? He removed her arm firmly and turned to face her, but she was not so easily disengaged. He found one hand snaking around the back of his neck to pull him towards her, while the other one grabbed a handful of his shirt. Startled, he slithered out of her grip, and began to move towards the door.

"Come now, Geoffrey," she said, pouting at him in mock censure. "We are alone here. What harm is there in us establishing a more intimate relationship?"

"A great deal of harm if Henry were to find out," said Geoffrey. "I am in bad enough favour as it is, and I do not want to compound matters by seducing his wife."

"Will you seduce me, then?" she asked with a smile that verged on being a leer.

"I will not," said Geoffrey firmly. He had succeeded in edging round her so that he was closest to the door. "And it is cold up here. You should come inside, or you will take a chill. Women in your condition should not be fooling around on battlements in the depths of the night."

"Ah, yes," she said, leaning back against the wall and folding her arms. "I told you that I am carrying another of Henry's brats, did I? Well, let us hope it is more pleasant than the last little monster he sired. I am hoping that dog of yours will dispatch that one for me. Things looked promising yesterday, but Stephen intervened."

"Those do not seem to be especially maternal sentiments," he said, appalled that his dog might be encouraged to harm a child. "Surely your baby cannot have earned your dislike already?"

"Spoken like a true bachelor," said Hedwise in some disgust. "Believe me, Geoffrey, that brat is every inch his father. He even bears his father's name. But I did not come here to discuss Henry. I came to learn more of you."

"It is late," said Geoffrey quickly. "And I am tired. If you will excuse me, I would like to retire."

"Are you running away from me?" asked Hedwise, following him towards the door. "Such timidity does not become you, Geoffrey. No wonder you returned lootless from the Holy Land, if you are driven away so easily."

At that moment, Geoffrey would sooner have faced an army of Saracens than his brother's lecherous wife, but he said nothing. He opened the door, ignoring her restraining hands on his shirt, and clattered down the spiral stairway to the hall. Breathing heavily, he looked around. Henry was banking the fire in the great hearth, and Geoffrey heaved a sigh of relief. At least Henry had not seen him and Hedwise emerging together from the battlements and jumped to the wrong conclusion.

He walked across to the fire and knelt next to it. Henry said nothing, and Geoffrey felt a sudden sympathy for his bad-tempered brother. Henry was trapped in a loveless marriage, and was probably deeply unhappy. A fleeting notion crossed his mind that Henry might be a more pleasant person away from Goodrich, and he wondered whether he should offer to take him to Jerusalem when he left. But Geoffrey dismissed that thought instantly: Palestine would provide Henry with unlimited opportunities for his aggression and greed, and whereas Henry would doubtless thoroughly enjoy the Holy Land, the Holy Land certainly did not need yet another man like Henry.

Hedwise glided across the floor towards them, her face slightly flushed. "Godric is calling for you," she said to Geoffrey. "He said he will not sleep unless you are in the room with him."

"How did he manage before?" asked Geoffrey, making no move to stand. "Did someone else stay with him?"

"No," said Hedwise. "But he often wakes and calls out for us. We take it in turns—Bertrada, Joan, and I. He claims the poison makes his stomach crave food in the night, and so we usually have a pot of broth warming for him on the hearth. Of course, he almost always brings it back up again as soon as he has finished it."

"Really, Hedwise," said Henry in disgust. "I am sure Geoffrey does not want to hear those kind of details, and I certainly do not."

"That is because you do not have to deal with it, night after night," said Hedwise, not without bitterness. "You simply turn over and go back to sleep." She turned to Geoffrey. "Godric claims the poison is making him sick, but we are sure it is the wasting sickness he has."

From the stairwell came a tremulous cry, simultaneously pitiful and demanding. Geoffrey snapped his fingers to his dog, and stood. He sensed that if he did not go to Godric, no one would get any sleep that night.

"Thank you, Geoffrey," said Hedwise, smiling seductively. "We all appreciate your kindness."

Geoffrey gave her an ambiguous nod and made for the stairs,

aware that Henry was watching him with some suspicion. Was Hedwise determined to have Henry believe that she and Geoffrey were embarking on a relationship that was more than fraternal? And if so, why? Was it to make Henry divorce her on grounds of infidelity? On reflection, Geoffrey decided that ridding herself of Henry and Goodrich was probably was a perfectly adequate reason for Hedwise to initiate an affair with her brother-in-law. He pushed open the door to Godric's room and went to the bed.

"There you are," grumbled Godric. "Where have you been? Flirting with your brother's wife out on the battlements?"

Geoffrey stared at him. Was the old man really bed-ridden, or was he fooling them all, and secretly was as hale and hearty as the next man? But a covert glance at the gaunt skeletal figure told him that even Godric would not be able to mimic such symptoms of serious illness. A shadow glided out the room and closed the door behind him. Norbert. Was he a spy as well as a scribe? Geoffrey rubbed his eyes, and went to pour Godric some of the strong red wine he liked.

"You want to watch that Hedwise, son," said Godric, as he sipped the wine. "She has her eye on you. And believe me, to have Hedwise's eye on you is not something that will lead to pleasant consequences—for anyone, but least of all for you."

Geoffrey did not need to be told.

The following morning was grey and dull. At first, Geoffrey thought he had overslept, and that the dimness resulted from the sun already beginning to set. But after a few moments, the door of Godric's bedchamber was flung open, and Hedwise entered with the old man's breakfast. Geoffrey climbed stiffly to his feet, and went to scrub his face with the cold water that stood in a jug in the garderobe passage. He stretched, feeling his muscles aching and sore. He felt sick too, a sensation that was heightened by the nauseating smell of Godric's fish broth.

While Godric ate his soup and regaled the sceptical Hedwise with tales of his sexual prowess during his youth, Geoffrey rolled up the blanket on which he had been sleeping and stuffed it under the bed. Then he pulled on tough, boiled-leather leggings and his light chain-mail hauberk.

"Are you going out?" asked Hedwise, watching him. "Or do you always dress for the battlefield?"

"He is staying here with me," said Godric confidently. "He is merely being cautious by wearing all that armour because he is in a house of poisoners."

"I want to visit Enide's grave," said Geoffrey. "I would have gone yesterday, but I stayed with you instead."

"And you will come back afterwards?" whined Godric feebly. "You will not take the opportunity to go haring back to the Holy Land?"

It was a tempting thought. "No," said Geoffrey. "I will come back later."

"Very well, then," said Godric, waving a papery hand. "You may go."

Geoffrey buckled his sword round his waist and left, aware that Hedwise was behind him on the stairs. He did not want to resume their conversation of the night before, so he walked more quickly. So did she, and by the time they reached the hall, they entered it virtually at a run.

Walter was standing next to a roaring fire eating something from a bowl, while Stephen was feeding Geoffrey's dog. The dog, seeing it could leave with Geoffrey or continue to be fed titbits from Stephen, opted for the latter, and Geoffrey left the castle alone. Hearing footsteps behind him, he turned in exasperation, expecting Hedwise to be following him. It was Julian, the stable-boy.

"Here," the lad said, shoving a wrinkled apple and a remarkably fresh lump of bread into Geoffrey's hands. "Someone is poisoning Sir Godric, and so you are right not to take breakfast in the castle. But these are safe enough—I baked the bread myself."

"Baking is a curious talent for a stable-boy," said Geoffrey, eating the bread. It was quite salty and rather heavy, but he had tasted a good deal worse in the Holy Land.

"That is because they force me to work in the kitchens," said Julian bitterly. "I hate it there. I would rather be in the stables with the horses."

"It might not always be like this," said Geoffrey. "When you are older you might be transferred to work for the grooms if you show an aptitude for it."

Julian sighed before speeding back towards the kitchens and Geoffrey watched him go. The more he saw Julian, the more he was convinced that there was something peculiar about him. But, Geoffrey reasoned, the entire castle was peculiar, so why should he be considering a single inmate?

He strode out of the barbican, through gates where the guards were nowhere to be seen, and made for the little wooden church of St. Giles at the far end of the village. People acknowledged him as he walked—some did so fearfully, some curiously, but most were resentful, and the more people he encountered, the more Geoffrey realised that the Mappestones were far from popular landlords, and that the villagers regarded him as an extension of a family who ruled by oppression and fear.

The village was not large, and comprised parallel rows of timber-framed and wattle-and-daub houses with the church at the far end. In Geoffrey's youth, the houses had been pleasant—some had their outsides painted with washes of cream and white, others had their roofs thatched with well-tended golden straw. Twenty years on, the paint had faded to a uniform stained grey, and the thatches were shabby with weeds and nettles. The road that had been even and well drained was now rutted and thick with the human and animal waste that had been allowed to accumulate. The stench was over-whelming—even worse than in parts of Jerusalem. Geoffrey, not a squeamish man, found himself wondering what it would be like at the height of summer, when the sun would roast the fetid sludge and armies of flies would gather to feast on it.

One of the houses was better tended than the rest—its thatch was intact, and most of the black slime, which dripped down the fronts of the others, had been scrubbed away. As Geoffrey walked past it, Sergeant Helbye emerged.

"Will you help us today?" he asked, without preamble. "I came to the castle yesterday, but they would not let me in."

Geoffrey gazed at him blankly, not certain what he wanted, until Helbye's wife appeared in the doorway behind her husband.

"Your wife's second marriage," he said in sudden understanding. He had quite forgotten his sergeant's predicament. "You would probably be better seeing the priest than me, Will."

"Then will you come with us?" said Helbye nervously. "I want no misunderstandings over this. It is important."

"Yes, it is important," said Geoffrey kindly. "I am on my way to visit Enide's grave. We can go to see the priest afterwards, if you like."

Helbye gave a sigh of relief and nodded gratefully.

"I will show you Enide's spot in the churchyard," offered Helbye's wife, ducking back inside her house for her cloak. "It is difficult to find, unless you know exactly where to look."

"She is a good wife," said Helbye in a low whisper, following her with his eyes. "I would not like to lose her and have to go through all the inconvenience of finding another."

"I am sure you would not," said Geoffrey.

Helbye had talked a great deal about his wife, but Geoffrey realised that he had never once mentioned her by name. It had always been "she."

They walked the short distance to the church, and Geoffrey followed Helbye's wife through the long wet grass to a mound in the corner of the graveyard under the gnarled arms of an oak tree. While Helbye and his wife tactfully busied themselves by pulling dandelion weeds from the dry-stone wall some distance away, Geoffrey stared down at the slight bump that represented his sister's final resting place.

Geoffrey stood a long time at the foot of the grassy mound under the churchyard elm, thinking about Enide and her many letters to him. He tried again, unsuccessfully, to imagine what she might have looked like as a woman of thirty years of age. If he were honest with himself, even remembering what she had been like when he had left was difficult and, over the years, his perception of Enide had faded to a faceless figure with a plait of thick brown hair. The plait had stuck fast in his mind, because Enide had resisted the attempts of mother and sister to adopt any other style. What had initially been simple preference had soon become a matter of principle, and he knew from her letters that the plait had remained all her life.

Already weeds were beginning to creep across the grave. Geoffrey dropped onto one knee and picked at them absently, wondering what Enide would have liked him to do or say on such an occasion. A rustle in the grass made him turn, and he saw a young priest walking towards him, his black habit swirling around his legs and soaking up a good deal of early morning dew.

"Sir Geoffrey?" the priest asked, looking at the kneeling knight as he tucked his hands in his wide sleeves against the chill. "I am Father Adrian, Goodrich's vicar. I have heard much about you from Joan and Enide. Welcome home."

"Thank you," said Geoffrey. "But I wish Enide were here to say that."

"So do I," said Adrian softly. "Finding her body was one of the worst moments of my life."

"You were the one who found her body?" asked Geoffrey, climbing to his feet. Helbye and his wife came to stand nearby. "My brothers told me that she had just attended mass. What happened?"

Adrian sighed, and gazed up to where the bare branches of the trees patterned the sky. "She attended mass, and then left with the other parishioners. I stayed longer in the church than I would usually have done—there was to be a funeral that day, you see, for a woman who had died in childbirth. I lingered to say prayers for her soul, and when I came out, there was Enide, dead in the grass. Or her body, anyway."

"What do you mean by 'her body anyway'?" asked Geoffrey suspiciously.

"Not her head," explained the priest. "It was missing, and we never found it."

Geoffrey stared at the priest in horror before turning on Helbye. "What is this? No one mentioned a missing head before! You said you had told me all there was to know!"

"I thought I had," said Helbye, as surprised as was Geoffrey. "A missing head is news to me."

He glanced at his wife, but she looked away and would not meet his eyes. Geoffrey grabbed a handful of the priest's habit, suddenly angry. It had been a shock to read about Enide's death in the brief note he had been sent in the Holy Land, and it had not been pleasant to hear rumours that his sister had been murdered by decapitation. But he had assumed he had already learned the worst there was to know, and had not anticipated that there would be yet more details regarding Enide's murder that would shock him.

"What happened?" he demanded of the priest.

"Easy," said Adrian, unnerved by the knight's unexpected re-action. "I did not mean to distress you, Sir Geoffrey. I thought your family would have told you about the circumstances surrounding Enide's death."

"Let him go, lad," said Helbye, prising Geoffrey's hands from Adrian's gown. "This is a man of God you are mauling here, not some grubby Saracen."

Geoffrey released the priest reluctantly. "They did not tell me about this," he said, his voice slightly unsteady. "Where is it?"

"Her head?" asked Adrian, smoothing down his habit. "As I said, that was never found, but some of her hair lay around the corpse, cut as her head was severed."

"Then perhaps the body you found was not hers," said Geoffrey, in sudden hope, looking from the priest to Helbye. "Perhaps she is safe somewhere—a convent, maybe. She wrote to tell me that she was considering taking such a path."

"Do not vex yourself with futile wishes," said Adrian gently. "The body was Enide's, I am sorry to say. It wore her clothes and her locket—the one she told me you had given her before you left."

"Did the men who Henry hanged not tell him where to find her head?" asked Geoffrey.

"Her head was never found," said Adrian yet again. "Perhaps it was tossed into the river or buried somewhere. But either way, I am sure she rests in peace. I say a mass for her every week."

"Masses be damned!" snapped Geoffrey. "How can she rest in peace when you do not even know where part of her lies? And I am not even sure the right people died for this foul crime!"

"Then you would not be alone," said Adrian, unperturbed by Geoffrey's blasphemy. "I am certain the poachers were innocent, although I have not a shred of evidence to support such a claim. Unfortunately, by the time I learned Henry was scouring the coun-tryside looking for murderers, it was too late to stop him and urge him to caution."

Some of the anger went out of Geoffrey. "You believe Henry hanged the wrong men?"

Adrian hesitated, as though considering exactly how much he should reveal. He glanced at Geoffrey and seemed to reach a decision.

"For several weeks before she died, Enide was not well," he began. "She told me she thought someone was poisoning her, just as someone was also poisoning Godric. And at mass that morning, she seemed not herself, somehow. I do not mean I mistook her for another person," he added quickly, seeing the hope in Geoffrey's eyes. "It was more her mood. She was restless, and she did not concentrate on the mass as she usually did. It was almost as if she were expecting something to happen."

"Something did happen," said Geoffrey sombrely. "Someone decapitated her. Can you be more specific about this mood?"

Adrian shook his head. "I am afraid not. And believe me, I have given it a great deal of thought—far more than I should, when I have a busy parish to run. But I have been breaking her own wishes by speculating about this. She would not want you investigating her death."

"Why not?" asked Geoffrey. "I would want someone investigating mine, if I were murdered and two men hanged for it who should not have been."

"Would you?" queried Adrian. "Would you really want someone you loved putting themselves in peril for a deed that was done, and the consequences of which were irreversible anyway?"

Geoffrey considered. "I would not want Enide doing so, perhaps. But I am not Enide, I am a knight, and will not be so easily dispatched."

But Sir Aumary was, he thought grimly. Even wearing his chain-mail, Geoffrey would be defenceless against an attack by a good archer hidden among the trees. One clear shot, and that would be that.

"Well, Enide cared for you, and she certainly would not have wanted you to put yourself in danger by making enquiries that will lead you into danger."

"How do you know my enquiries would lead me into danger?" asked Geoffrey curiously. "Who do *you* think killed Enide?"

Adrian would not meet his eyes. "I do not know. Nor do I wish to. She was desperately afraid for her life, and her father is being poisoned even as he lies in his sick-bed. Do you not consider that sufficient warning to stay away?"

"Are you suggesting that I should stand back and allow my father to be killed under my very nose, and let my sister's murder to go unremarked?" asked Geoffrey. "I thought the Church believed in justice."

"Justice, yes," said Adrian. "But not vengeance. That is for the Lord to take, not us. Henry tried vengeance, and it is almost certain he killed two innocent men."

"I am not so hot-headed as Henry," said Geoffrey. "I will be certain."

Adrian sighed. "Then you go against my advice, and your sister's wishes. It was at her request that she was buried in this quiet corner of the churchyard. She did not want constant reminders of her to be the cause of unhappiness in her family."

"She chose this spot herself?" asked Geoffrey, aghast. "She was so certain she was going to be killed that she chose her own grave site?"

Adrian appeared flustered. "Put like that it sounds as if she knew she was going to die and we did nothing about it. But yes, she chose this spot. And she charged me to ensure that her death would not result in a bloodbath—something in which I failed her."

"It all sounds so premeditated," said Geoffrey, unsettled. "I wish I had returned before. I might have been able to do something. Why did she not ask me to come home?"

"Probably for the same reason that she would not want you trying to discover her killer now," said Adrian. "She cared for you, and she did not want to put you in danger. Look, there is nothing you can gain from investigating now. You should leave Goodrich— today. Go back to the Holy Land and forget all this. You seem more decent than the rest of your kin. Do not let them drag you down into their pit of lies and murder."

Geoffrey would have liked nothing better, but how could he leave his father in the hands of a murderer? And anyway, he had the King's orders to follow. He was silent, thinking about Enide's last few weeks of life, so certain that someone was going to kill her that she had even selected the place where she wanted to be buried. After a while, Helbye cleared his throat nervously, and Geoffrey remembered his promise to help him.

"My sergeant has something of a problem," he said.

"Yes, I know," said the priest, smiling at the burly soldier. "But it is nothing that cannot be resolved. I will draw up the papers authorising the annulment of her second marriage today."

Helbye's jaw dropped. "Is that it? Is there nothing more that needs to be done?"

"Nothing," said Adrian, still smiling. "Your marriage to her was the first one, and will stand over the second in any court of law and before God. I will give you the relevant documentation this evening."

"Useful, this business of writing," said Geoffrey to his sergeant. "But what about your wife's other husband? What will become of him?"

"Norbert?" asked Helbye's wife carelessly. "Oh, he will manage, I expect."

"Not Norbert, the scribe?" asked Geoffrey. "My father's clerk?" He recalled the forlorn figure standing away from the celebrations when Helbye had returned, his face masked in shadow.

"That's the one," said Helbye. "Norbert has always had an eye for her. The day I left for the Crusade, he told me that he would marry her if I failed to return, cheeky beggar! He was always hanging around our house, trying to get glimpses of her."

"And I suppose this is why you are always so suspicious of reading and writing," asked Geoffrey. "Because Norbert is a scribe?"

"Not at all," objected Helbye. "Writing is the Devil's skill, and only the Devil's minions learn it."

"Devil's minions like Father Adrian and me?" asked Geoffrey. He continued when he saw Helbye's embarrassment. "So, did you not want me to write to your wife in case Norbert read it?"

Helbye scratched his head. "I did not like the thought of her going to *him* to have it read. Who knows what price he might have extracted for such a service?"

"Will Helbye!" exclaimed the priest, laughing. "Norbert is not like that! He is a good enough man, and would never have made such a bargain."

"And I can assure you I would not have paid such a price," said Helbye's wife stiffly. "I would have gone to Father Adrian to have it read, anyway."

They walked back through the churchyard, Geoffrey listening with half an ear to the good-humoured banter between Helbye and his wife. Poor Norbert, he thought, abused by Godric and his unpleasant household, and thwarted in love by Helbye's unexpected return.

"There is that Mark Ingram," said Helbye's wife, pointing across the street. "He has been in the tavern asking all sorts of questions, I am told."

"What sort of questions?" asked Adrian.

"Questions about Enide Mappestone," she answered. "He seems to have it in his head that the poachers were not the ones who killed her."

"And what business is it of his?" asked Geoffrey, watching the young soldier slink along the main road in the direction of his home. Ingram, aware that he was being watched, turned, and stared back insolently before continuing on his way.

"Charming," said Helbye. "I thought his temper might improve once he was home, but evidently I am mistaken."

"I must go," said Adrian. "Old Mistress Pike has asked for last rites, and there is sickness in the tinker's family. Then I must try to persuade Walter to mend the roofs on the dairymen's cottages, because they will not survive another downpour. If he will not pay, I will have to sell the church silver to buy new thatching."

He nodded to Geoffrey, and set off up the main street. Helbye watched him go.

"Father Adrian is a good man," he said. "He works among the poor and the sick, and he is never afraid he might catch something himself. If Walter will not give him the money for his cottages, perhaps I will offer him some of my treasure."

"But Walter should pay," said Geoffrey. "He is the landlord."

"I doubt he will," said Helbye's wife. "No money for repairs has been forthcoming since Sir Godric fell ill. Walter is a skinflint!" She ignored Helbye's warning elbow in her ribs. "I do not care, Will. Sir Geoffrey should know the truth! His brother is making people's lives a misery. Look at poor Caerdig of Lann Martin, struggling to keep his villagers fed, while Walter and Henry demand high tolls each time anyone crosses the Wye! It is disgraceful!"

She turned on her heel and strode off after Adrian. After a moment of indecision, Helbye flung Geoffrey an apologetic look and hurried after her. Geoffrey rubbed the bridge of his nose. Perhaps he should have considered more carefully when he so cavalierly dismissed the notion of taking loot to his family. Goodrich Castle was clearly in need of repair, as attested by the crumbling battlements he had seen the night before, and the village was shabby and unkempt.

"Barlow!" he yelled, seeing his other man-at-arms strolling down the main street, resplendent in a new cloak and fine boots. "Where can I find a man called Ine?"

"Your father's servant?" asked Barlow, walking across to him. "He lives at the castle, but at this time of day, you will find him in the tavern. Your father is mean with his wages, and so Ine is forced to boost them by washing plates in the mornings."

"Thank you," said Geoffrey, wondering if there were a living soul anywhere in England who had a good word to say for his family—other than Adrian who, it seemed, had a good word for anyone.

The tavern was a single-roomed building at the far end of the village, with a filthy beaten-earth floor and grimy horn windows. It was chilly, and the small fire in the hearth that hissed and smoked from the wet wood did little to alleviate the cold but a good deal to reduce visibility. Geoffrey coughed, his eyes watering at the burning wood, and looked for Ine.

Leaning over a bucket of cold water in one corner was a tall, thin man with a bad complexion. He was taking greasy plates from a pile on a table, dunking them in the water, and then redistributing the remaining food with a dirty rag. Geoffrey went to sit next to him.

"Ale?" Ine asked. Without waiting for Geoffrey's answer, he went to fetch it, returning in a few moments with a large cup containing ale that was unexpectedly good.

"You are Ine?" asked Geoffrey, watching as the man dipped his cold, red hands back into the pail of scummy water.

"Yes, and you are Geoffrey Mappestone. You want to ask me if your father is being poisoned."

"Is he?"

"Ask the physician," said Ine, still not looking up. "He is away in Rosse today, but he will be back tomorrow."

"I am asking you," said Geoffrey, taking a long draught of the ale.

"I do not answer questions about that, said Ine. "As I have already told your man."

"My man? You mean Mark Ingram?" asked Geoffrey. "He asked you about Godric?"

"You know he did," said Ine, looking up for the first time, "because you told him to. But I know nothing of any poison. I told Ingram, and now I am telling you: I tasted all Sir Godric's food and his wine, but you can see that I am fit and well, and I am sure it contained nothing to make him ill. I know nothing more."

"Why are you afraid?" asked Geoffrey. "Is someone threatening you?"

"No," said Ine. "The Mappestones barely speak to me, and Sir Godric only addresses me in curses. None of them waste their time threatening the likes of me. But Goodrich Castle is an evil household, and the quicker I can escape from it the better."

"I know the feeling," agreed Geoffrey. "But in what way is it evil?"

Ine shuddered. "I could not say—only that it has an atmosphere of wickedness about it."

This line of discussion was going to get him nowhere. Geoffrey changed the subject. "What about the death of Torva? Was that an accident, as everyone believes? Or was it more sinister?"

"Torva drank heavily each night," said Ine. "And the drawbridge across the castle moat is in poor repair. It was clear someone was going to fall off it at some point. It just happened to be Torva."

"Do you believe his death was an accident, then?" persisted Geoffrey.

Ine shrugged. "Perhaps it was, perhaps it was not. But Torva was a man who asked a good many questions—because he wanted the reward Godric offered him if he could discover who was the poisoner."

"Do you think that Torva's investigations might have led to his death?"

Ine shrugged again. "I cannot say. I only know that he walked home the same way and at the same time each night, and that he was always drunk. And I know that he had been asking questions. I ask no questions, Sir Geoffrey. And from now on I will not answer them either."

Geoffrey leaned back against the wall and considered. Short of bullying Ine, Geoffrey did not think he was going to gain any more information from him. He was not sure that the man had any to give in any case, since the answers he did deign to provide seemed to be based on speculation rather than fact. But it was clear that Ine believed Torva's death was too coincidental to be an accident, and that he was fearful that he himself might go the same way if he began to investigate Godric's illness. And if Ine's suspicions were correct, then Geoffrey could deduce that someone had silenced Torva because he was coming near to the truth. Which meant that someone at Goodrich Castle had a secret that he or she very much wanted to keep.

CHAPTER SIX

Geoffrey was not inclined to eat at the castle with a poisoner lurking, so he inveigled an invitation to dine with Helbye. Helbye's wife was a considerably better cook than anyone at the castle, and Geoffrey was served the best meal he had been given since landing in England. There was a delicately spiced pigeon pie with leeks, followed by a rich custard tart with stewed apples. Geoffrey, not knowing when he might get another edible dinner, ate too much and almost made himself ill.

The meal on offer at the castle the previous day had been something that Bertrada had mysteriously called "numbles," which had transpired to be hard, stale kidneys in a powerful fish sauce. Everyone had praised the fish sauce, which had been made from a recipe of Hedwise's, while Geoffrey, who liked neither fish nor kidneys, wrestled to attain an acceptable balance between eating sufficient so as not to appear rude, but not enough to make him sick. As he finished his third helping of custard, he wondered whether he would be able to wrangle enough invitations from Helbye to avoid starving.

The large meal had made him drowsy, and he felt the need for some exercise. He strolled back to the castle, and called for Julian to saddle up his horse. Delighted to be entrusted with such a task, Julian came scurrying to obey, while Geoffrey leaned against the stable wall and wished he had not been so greedy.

As he waited, Olivier emerged from the hall, flanked by two knights whom Geoffrey had not seen before.

"Going riding?" called Olivier pleasantly, walking towards him. "We plan to trot up to Coppet Hill through the woods. It is a pleasant journey of no more than six miles there and back, and you get a fine view of the castle from the top."

"We want to exercise our war-horses, not go on some womanly jaunt," muttered one of the other knights, a squat, heavy-set man in dark chain-mail.

"Yes, of course, Sir Drogo," said Olivier hastily. "The path is good, and will put the beasts through their paces."

"I do not believe that we have met," said the second of Olivier's two companions, a man of about Geoffrey's height, with reddish silver hair and a ruddy complexion. He wore light but strong chain-mail, and his well-honed sword was no plaything like Olivier's. Despite his elegant cloak and soft deerskin leggings, he looked to Geoffrey like a man who knew how to fight.

Olivier became flustered. "Oh, dear! Forgive my poor manners. This is my brother-in-law, Sir Geoffrey Mappestone, lately returned from the Crusade. Geoffrey, this is Sir Malger of Caen and Sir Drogo of Bayeux. Like me, both are in the service of the Earl of Shrewsbury."

Malger smiled, and affected a courtly bow. "I have heard much about the Crusade," he said. "I am told the looting was beyond the wildest dreams of even the most ambitious of knights."

Geoffrey bowed in return. "I do not know about that. Many knights have very wild dreams indeed."

Malger laughed and turned to Olivier. "Where are your grooms, man? Sleeping off their dinner? Are we to wait here until nightfall for them?"

Olivier bustled away, calling for the grooms, but the hem of his expensive cloak caught in one of his spurs, and sent him staggering in the mud. Drogo and Malger exchanged a look of amusement, and Geoffrey wondered yet again how a man like Olivier had ever earned his knighthood. Meanwhile, Julian emerged with Geoffrey's destrier.

"I can do it," he said eagerly to Olivier, who was furtively brushing himself off. "I can saddle up your war-horses."

"Out of the question!" said Olivier brusquely. "And keep your hands off my animals. Ah, Ned. There you are. Saddle us up, and be quick about it."

"But not so quick that you forget to fasten the buckles properly," muttered Julian under his breath before stalking away towards the kitchens.

"Julian seems efficient enough," said Geoffrey, straightening from where he had been checking his saddle. The boy had done a good job—the straps were firm, but not too tight, and he had even polished the well-worn leather. "Why do you not trust him?"

"Never you mind," said Olivier. He rubbed his hands together, oblivious of the mud on his gloves from his tumble, and then scratched his nose. The resulting blob of filth on his face brought a second grin of amusement from his friends.

Eventually, they were ready, and the four knights set off through the village. Geoffrey was disturbed to note that their progress through the village was followed with an even greater resentment than his own had been that morning. At one point, he was certain a small boy had hurled a handful of dirt at them before being whisked into his house by his terrified mother.

Once away from the village, Geoffrey relaxed, enjoying the ride despite the cold, dull weather. Olivier chattered about a wide range of political and legal matters, although on most of them he was ill-informed, if not downright wrong. The others generally ignored him. Malger was concerned about a slight limp his horse had developed the previous day, and Drogo did not seem to be capable of rational conversation at all. He was surly, bad-tempered, and Geoffrey's suspicion that he was not quite in control of all his mental faculties was confirmed when he gave an enthusiastic grunt as Olivier praised Hedwise's rank fish sauce.

"That concoction is truly delicious," said Olivier happily. "I am indeed blessed to have been given such a sister-in-law."

Malger leered unpleasantly. "But you took your time over marrying Joan. Were you waiting for a woman like the delectable Hedwise instead?"

"Oh, no!" protested Olivier, his eyes wide and guileless. "I am more than content with my Joan. She is due back within the next two or three days, and I long to see her."

"Do you?" asked Malger uncertainly.

Unless Joan had changed a good deal from the caustic, critical woman who Geoffrey remembered from his youth, then Malger was right to be suspicious of Olivier's protestations of devotion.

"Oh, drat," said Olivier with a sigh, raising an upturned palm skywards. "It has started to rain. We must go back."

"What for?" asked Geoffrey, bemused.

"Because if we go on, we will get wet," Olivier replied with a pursing of his lips. He turned his horse around, and set it to walk back the way they had come.

Geoffrey watched him, open-mouthed.

"There goes the fearless hero of the Battle of Civitate," remarked Malger, laughing at Geoffrey's reaction. "He took a wily old Pope captive while he was only three months old, but he is afraid of a few drops of rain. What about you, Sir Geoffrey? Drogo? Will you return with him, or can you withstand a little shower?"

Drogo growled some response that Geoffrey did not understand, and spurred his horse forward. Still laughing, Malger followed, leaving Geoffrey watching the diminishing figure of Sir Olivier in amazement.

By the time Malger, Drogo, and Geoffrey had returned, the rain was persistent. Olivier hurried out to greet them, clucking and fussing over his friends" sodden surcoats and saturated cloaks. Malger and Drogo were whisked away to the hall to be offered hot spiced wine and some of the inevitable fish soup, while Geoffrey was left to fend for himself. Duty obliged him to spend the rest of the day with his father.

To pass the time, and at his father's request, he cleaned away some of the wood-smoke that had stained the dreary wall-paintings that adorned the room. Godric directed his efforts from his bed.

"You have scrubbed at it too hard," he snapped, trying to sit so that he could see better. "That part took me a week to do."

"You painted this?" asked Geoffrey, surprised that his restless, irritable father had possessed the patience to pay such attention to fine detail. "I did not know you boasted such talent."

"I suppose you think you inherited your love of the arts from your mother?" asked Godric acidly. "Well, you are quite wrong. She was like Henry, and it was her energetic spirit and fiery nature that attracted me to her. She was more warrior than many of the knights who rode with the Conqueror, and would have been at my side at Hastings had Henry not been about to favour the world with his presence. Then the battle would not have lasted so long! Your mother had a fabulous touch with the mace!"

Geoffrey, recalling the formidable woman who had easily held her own against the vile-tempered Godric, had no reason to doubt him.

"So when did you begin painting?" asked Geoffrey. "After she died?"

"Lord, no!" said Godric. "My greedy whelps would have thought that I had gone soft in the head with grief. Last spring, I decided to turn the running of my estates over to Walter and Stephen—between them I imagined they would do an acceptable job. I started this painting then, to while away the days, although I had already started to dabble with a mural here and there."

"It is . . . beautiful," said Geoffrey hesitantly, wanting to be kind, yet uncertain how best to describe the lurid, violent scenes that emblazoned the walls.

"Beautiful be damned!" said Godric, offended. "*Splendid* was the effect for which I was aiming, Godfrey! Or noble, perhaps. Beautiful is what I intended for my whore's room. You can see that if you go into the chamber across the passage. Do not look so startled, boy! Do you think I have been a monk since your mother died?"

"Of course not, but—"

"But most men do not keep their whores in the bosom of their family? Is that what you were going to say? Your mother was right about you—you should have become a priest! But you will like young Rohese when you meet her. She is a good lass."

"Where is she?"

"She is away with Joan. She performs a dual function here—or did, when I was more able-bodied. She attended me at night, while during the day she is your sister Joan's tiring-woman. She used to be Enide's maid, but Joan took her on after Enide's death. Enide—now there was a fine lass, by God! A better daughter a man could not have wished for. I would have left her the manor, had she lived."

"I wish I could have met her again," said Geoffrey, wiping sweat from his eyes with his sleeve and looking at Godric. "I last saw her when she was eleven."

"You would not have recognised her, Godfrey," said Godric, his eyes shining. "She was a magnificent woman—taller than that vicious dog, Henry, and she had more brains that all the rest of you put together. She was kind, too. My whore, Rohese, does not like this room, so Enide willingly changed with me whenever I asked, so that I could have my whore happy and not babbling that my paintings frightened her while I wanted her attention on me. What other daughter would do such a thing for her old father, eh?"

"It does seem a somewhat curious arrangement," said Geoffrey, scrubbing hard at the malevolent image of a black dog that held an equally sinister-looking black rabbit in its jaws.

"You would think that," said Godric disdainfully. "Enide held no such monkish qualms. I wish that Joan was more like her. But Joan should be back soon—she and Rohese are visiting your manor at Rwirdin."

"Joan's manor at Rwirdin, you mean," said Geoffrey, crouching down to wring out the cloth in a bucket of water and vinegar. "It seems to have been part of her dowry."

"That transaction was not legal," said Godric. "You can contest it any time you like, and no court in the land would find in favour of Joan. But, you see, Walter had to find something to entice Olivier to marry her—that wretched little man had been courting her for more years than I can remember. In fact," he said, heaving himself up on his elbows, "I remember that they started paying each other attention shortly after I sent you away."

"Olivier seems fond of her," said Geoffrey, concentrating on wiping smoke stains from the most wicked-looking pheasant he had ever seen—he had not believed that such an inoffensive bird could be depicted to appear so malignant.

"I really have no idea whether he likes the woman or not," said Godric carelessly. "But while I was away a couple of years ago, Walter decided that Olivier had dallied with her affections quite long enough, and offered him your manor as an incentive to do the decent thing."

"So I gathered."

"None of us expected you to survive the Crusade, you see, and so Walter did not think it would matter that he had illegally appropriated your inheritance. Anyway, Walter anticipated that it would rid Goodrich of the pair of them once and for all."

"But it did not, did it?" said Geoffrey. "It seems that they still spend a good deal of time here."

Godric laughed unpleasantly. "Walter's plan backfired badly, because now he has Joan *and* Olivier watching his every move like hawks. That will teach him to meddle behind my back! Still, I applaud his efforts. We were all beginning to wonder whether Irresolute Olivier was ever going to make an honest woman of Joyless Joan, although none of us blamed him for not wanting to take the plunge." He gave a dramatic shudder.

"What do you mean?" asked Geoffrey. "Olivier would not have courted her for so many years if there had not been some affection."

"You wait until you meet her," said Godric, grinning nastily. "Then you will not ask such stupid questions. Other than the fact that she is scarcely endowed with what even the most charitable of men would call a sweet disposition, she was not young and she had pursued Olivier with all the subtlety of a pack of hunting dogs after a hare for two decades. But you will see all this for yourself when she comes home."

"Why did Walter choose Olivier as her husband?" asked Geoffrey. "I was told that Caerdig requested her, and I should have thought Walter would have gained more from her marriage to him than her marriage to Olivier." And so might Joan, he thought uncharitably.

He rubbed hard at his temples where his head had started to ache, and went to pour a cup of wine from Godric's enormous jug near the bed. It was strong and acidic, and did nothing to quench his thirst.

Godric gave a sharp bark of laughter. "Poor old Caerdig would have married Henry to bring peace to Lann Martin! He is desperate for a truce."

"Is that so bad?" asked Geoffrey, pouring some water into the wine to dilute it. "But what happened to reduce Caerdig to such a state? I do not recall there being such problems with neighbours while you were more active."

"Very true," said Godric smugly. "And it is most satisfying to see Walter, Henry, and Stephen make such an appalling mess where I handled matters with ease."

"So you do not care that the good relations you spent your lifetime developing have been destroyed within a few months by Walter's niggardliness and Henry's taste for killing?"

Godric shrugged. "That is what Caerdig keeps saying. But no, why should I care? It means that people will look back on my rule with pleasure, and my memory will be revered."

"That is a selfish attitude to take," said Geoffrey, unable to disguise the distaste in his voice. "Why should Caerdig's villagers, or ours, suffer just so that people will look back with fondness on the Golden Days of Godric?"

The old man's eyes narrowed. "You insolent dog! If I were thirty years younger, I would run you through."

"You would probably try," said Geoffrey, regarding his father with dislike. "It seems to be the Mappestone way of solving problems."

"You sound just like that mewling Olivier," said Godric, returning Geoffrey's look with every bit as much hostility. "He is always trying to find a solution to problems that means he will not need to put his delicate skin in danger."

"On occasion, that might be construed as prudence," said Geoffrey, taking a sip of his wine and adding yet more water. "God's teeth, this is a vile brew! How can you drink it unwatered?"

"You are no better than Olivier is," spat Godric. "You cannot even take a man's drink without adding water. I have a good mind to alter my will again and ensure that you get nothing at all."

"I wish you would," said Geoffrey fervently. "I do not want anything from Goodrich. It is tainted with greed, selfishness, and corruption."

"Monk!" taunted Godric.

Geoffrey rubbed his head again, and admonished himself for engaging in futile arguments with a dying man. He wondered if his malady was due to the wine. He looked at the ruby red liquid in his cup, and set it down. Godric seemed very partial to it, and since the jug always stood uncovered next to the bed, it would be an easy matter for any of his family to slip something poisonous into it. He picked up the cup again and smelled it. He could detect nothing other than wine, but that did not mean to say there was nothing wrong with it. He decided to ask the physician. Godric kept exhorting Geoffrey to speak to the medical man about his alleged poisoning, so Geoffrey resolved that he would do so at the earliest opportunity.

Godric watched him examining the contents of his goblet. "Has the strong wine given you a headache?" he asked sneeringly. "Run to the kitchens, boy, and ask Mabel to give you some milk sops."

Geoffrey stared at him, and wondered whether he would end his life like Godric—bitter, mean, and self-interested, taunting his children into wishing he was dead, and loved by no one. He decided the best option was to stay single, and to volunteer for all the battles he could once he sensed he was growing unpopular. Better a death of his own choosing than of someone else's.

"So, why *did* Joan marry Olivier and not her other suitors?" he asked, to change the subject. "A marriage to the heir of Lann Martin would have brought those Welsh lands under Mappestone control, and better a man of integrity like Caerdig than a lying coward like Olivier."

"Joan married Olivier because she wanted him, and what Joan wants, Joan always takes," said Godric. "Caerdig asked for Enide, too, when he saw he was not going to have Joan. As if I would let my Enide go to the likes of him! Enide was a splendid woman! *She* did not take her wine watered!"

Geoffrey was not certain that his father's frank admiration for his dead sister was necessarily a good sign, and for the first time he began to wonder whether Enide was all he remembered. Perhaps she had changed from the happily mischievous girl he had left behind.

"So, Joan married Olivier, Enide died, and Caerdig was left with a war on his hands," said Godric gleefully. "But Caerdig will survive. He is a capable lad—not like those mewling brats who think they are mine—Walter the Illegitimate, Stephen my brother's son, and Henry the Lout."

Geoffrey turned away, repelled by the raw malice in Godric's glittering eyes. No wonder his children hated him so. Geoffrey had been home a few days, and was already considering ways to leave. He picked up the rag and began cleaning again, while Godric watched critically.

"Not so hard, boy! And you have missed a bit over there—that bishop is supposed to be wearing a golden coronet, not a crown of thorns!"

Geoffrey stood back to try to see what he meant. He had never seen anything quite like Godric's mural, and he hoped he never would again. Black was the predominant colour, with a good deal of red to depict outpourings of blood that far exceeded plausibility. Even after Geoffrey's vigorous cleaning, the painting remained dark and sullen. He scrubbed for a while longer, then dropped the cloth into the bucket and sat down, leaning back against the wall and wiping his face with his sleeve.

"This vinegar water smells foul. May I open the shutters on the window?"

"You may not!" said Godric indignantly. "I am a sick man. Do you want to kill me? Bertrada tried that back at Yuletide, but I thwarted her. She opened the window shutters in the night, hoping that I would take a fatal chill."

Before Geoffrey could stop him, Godric had embarked on yet another tale of how he had survived a murderous attack by his children. Geoffrey had already heard so many similar tales that he was inclined to believe Bertrada had been right, and that Godric's accusations were simply the desperate, pathetic attempts of a fading warrior to claim that his impending death was a result of a battle, rather than due to some invisible, sinister enemy that was eating away at his innards.

"You are beginning to concede that my suspicions have some foundation, I see," said Godric, aware that Geoffrey had not tried to dismiss his latest claim with the calm voice of reason. Geoffrey did not answer. He climbed stiffly to his feet and came to ease Godric under the bedclothes so that the old man would sleep—thus allowing Geoffrey to escape for some fresh air in the courtyard.

Godric attempted to stop him, wanting to talk, not sleep. He thrashed around, his arms flailing, causing dense clouds of particles to rise into the air that made Geoffrey cough.

"It is these vile mattresses that are killing you," he said, backing away to rub at his eye, where something had lodged. "They are filthy and full of dust."

"They make for the most comfortable bed in Christendom," objected Godric. "Your sister Enide said she always had a good night's sleep on them—when I was in her room with my whore."

"You should let Bertrada shake them out," said Geoffrey, eyes watering.

"She would steal them for herself," replied Godric. "These mattresses came from no less a person than the Abbot of Hereford. The lower one is full of straw and provides firmness, while the upper one is a mixture of hay and feathers and gives softness."

"And why did the Abbot part with such a fine bed?" asked Geoffrey, wiping his eye on his sleeve and advancing once more to make Godric lie down.

"The monks sold off his possessions after his death," said Godric. "That fine chest at the end of the bed was his, too."

His spurt of struggling had left him weak, and he was unresisting when Geoffrey straightened the covers and helped him to lie flat. The old man watched Geoffrey intently with his sharp, almost bird-like, eyes.

"You are wondering why I do not ask you to take me to safety if I am so convinced that someone is poisoning me," he said. "Well, my physician tells me it is too late, and that my innards are irreparably damaged. So, I have decided to stay here, and watch the escalating battles over my worldly fortunes. At least my last few weeks will be entertaining."

"A priest would tell you that your energies should be concentrated elsewhere," said Geoffrey, pouring some wine from the monstrous jug and helping Godric to sip it.

"Priests!" muttered Godric, finishing the wine in a single swallow. "Do not bring one of those here until I am within a hair of my death. It does not matter when I repent my sins, only that I do so. And I only intend to repent them once—I do not want to be revealing all my sins while I am alive for someone to use against me. Now, give me more wine."

After drinking, he began to cough violently, while Geoffrey knelt next to him, wiping foamy blood from his lips. Eventually, he slept, and Geoffrey slipped away to walk around the courtyard in the icy night air.

Two mornings later, Geoffrey was still asleep when Bertrada brought Godric his breakfast. She nudged him with her foot.

"Get up, will you? I will not have you here lying around doing nothing all day. We already have Olivier and his fine friends doing that—eating our food and drinking our wine."

"You mean Drogo and Malger?" asked Geoffrey, sitting up, and holding his head as an uncustomary dizziness seized him.

"Them and others," said Bertrada, slapping a breakfast tray down where Godric had to strain to reach it. "Olivier does nothing but flaunt his expensive clothes and his fine war-horse, while my poor Walter struggles here to make ends meet."

"Rubbish, woman!" said Godric. "Goodrich is rolling in money—that is why you are all so keen to get your grasping hands on my estates. Walter is just too mean to spend any of it."

Their voices drifted down the stairwell after him as Geoffrey made his escape. He donned his leather leggings and hauberk in the hall, and set off to see if Julian could find him something poison-free for breakfast. His stomach was cramped and his head swam, so that he wondered whether the poisoner had already started work on him.

Julian provided two crusts of bread and a pear that was so rotten it exploded across the floor when Geoffrey dropped it. His dog appeared from nowhere, a large ham in its jaws.

"Lord save us!" exclaimed Julian. "Bertrada has been looking everywhere for that ham!"

"Well, I doubt she will want it now," said Geoffrey, seeing that the gnawed exterior dripped with the dog's saliva.

"She will," said Julian, with utter conviction.

Geoffrey wondered what his chances were of eating with Helbye again, and determined that if Bertrada produced ham for dinner, he would not take any, especially if it had tooth marks—and even more especially if it were smothered in the ghastly fish sauce, a pot of which already simmered and bubbled evilly over the kitchen fire.

With the dog, still carrying its ham, at his heels, Geoffrey left the castle intending to visit the physician, to learn once and for all whether Godric really was being poisoned, or whether his father's mortal sickness was making him delusional. The guard at the gate also informed Geoffrey that Bertrada was looking for the ham, but declined Geoffrey's invitation to retrieve it from the dog himself.

Taking in deep breaths of fresh air, Geoffrey strode along the main street of the village, and made for the physician's house, a shabby stone building near the church. He knocked at the door, but, receiving no reply, walked to the rear where a sizeable garden was surrounded by a low wall. The garden contained neat rows of plants and several outbuildings. The sound of singing came from one of them.

Geoffrey called out, but the chanting went on uninterrupted. He vaulted over the low wall and poked his head around the door. Inside, it was dark and gloomy, and the walls were lined with an unbelievable array of bottles and phials. Bending over a flame was a small man with white hair that leapt from his head at a variety of angles. He wore the red gown of the physician, although it had seen better days, and the overfilled pockets and large number of sacks and pouches that dangled from unexpected places made him appear peculiarly shaped.

"Excuse me," called Geoffrey loudly.

"I have already told you, I will not discuss this matter," said the physician, not looking up from his work. "Go away."

"I beg your pardon?"

The physician looked up. "Oh!" he exclaimed, startled. "I thought you were that grubby Mark Ingram coming to ask questions about the poisonings at the castle again. Cheeky young beggar! As if it is any of his concern!"

"Why should he be interested in that?" asked Geoffrey, puzzled by his soldier's unseemly fascination with his family. "He has been asking questions in the tavern, too."

"He probably intends to blackmail you somehow," said the physician comfortingly. "You are Geoffrey Mappestone, I suppose, come to find out whether your father is being poisoned? Well, I can tell you, quite categorically, that the answer is yes: Godric is being murdered by degrees, just as surely as you are standing at my door."

Geoffrey rubbed his head. "What kind of poison is this killer using?"

"Come in," said the physician. "And close the door behind you." He straightened, and looked at Geoffrey with a pleased smile. "How kind. You have brought me a ham!"

Geoffrey looked to where the physician pointed, and saw that the dog had abandoned its treasure on the floor, and was scrabbling back over the garden wall. He supposed that it had discovered something else to steal, although its backward glance suggested there was something about the physician's garden that it did not like. The physician picked up the gnawed meat and placed it on a table.

"One of Bertrada's own, I see," he said gleefully. "Although I am sure she did not send it to me herself. She is always mean with her supplies, despite the fact that she knows I like her hams. What happened to this one? Have you had a go at it yourself?"

"My dog did," explained Geoffrey. "To be honest, I do not think you should eat it. It—"

"Nonsense," said the physician brusquely. "A quick rinse in clean water and all will be well. Now, what can I do for you? You are pale. Do you need a physic?"

"Thank you, no," said Geoffrey, "But I would like to hear what you have to say about my father's poisoning."

"Very little, is the answer to that," said the physician. "My name is Master Francis, by the way. Are you sure you would not like a physic? I can prepare you one quite quickly. In fact, I was thinking of making one for myself—the balance of my humours is not all it should be this morning, and I feel in need of a tonic before I go out to visit my patients today. Sit down, and I will have you feeling better in no time."

"No," said Geoffrey. "I just want to know about this poison."

"There is not much I can tell you. Godric is being poisoned. He first became aware of the symptoms last spring, and they have gradually grown worse ever since. By the summer, Walter and Stephen were running his estates completely, and so Godric had ample time in which to rest and recover. But although he did everything I told him to, he did not get better. When I first realised that he was being poisoned, I recommended that he should hire Torva to prepare and serve all his food."

"And Torva died in the moat."

"Drowned, yes," said Francis. "Torva was meticulous, and not a single morsel went past Godric's lips that Torva had not first tasted. However, while Godric became more and more ill, Torva remained healthy. About November, I was forced to confine Godric to his room. He has been growing weaker ever since, and now he cannot even leave his bed."

"Bertrada says he has a wasting sickness," said Geoffrey.

"Bertrada would," retorted Francis. "Since she and Walter would dearly love Godric to die, she has every reason to lie to you. And she is not a physician in any case. Wasting sicknesses do not have the same symptoms as poisoning—Bertrada could not tell the difference, but I can."

"What about that great vat of wine that sits by Godric's bed?" asked Geoffrey. "Could that be tainted somehow?"

"It might," said Francis. "But I do not believe it is. I have tested it several times, and Torva has been drunk on it. All this suggests that the wine is not the culprit."

"What about that horrible fish broth Hedwise keeps feeding him?" asked Geoffrey.

"That vile stuff would be enough to poison the most robust-stomached man," agreed Francis. "But again, I have conducted several tests using rats and birds, and there is nothing to indicate that the broth has been poisoned."

"Well, what else is there?" asked Geoffrey. "The stuff must be getting to him somehow."

"Most astute of you," said Francis condescendingly. "And I have been pondering the question for months, but I can come up with no answer. Your sister Enide suffered similar symptoms several times, and we thought she was being poisoned, too. But she died of other causes, and I am still no further forward in discovering the source of Godric's illness."

There was a loud bang from the bench, followed by an unpleasant smell.

"Oh, damn it all!" exclaimed Francis. "I should have been concentrating, not chatting. Now I will have to start again."

"What were you doing?" asked Geoffrey curiously, looking at

the bubbling liquids and mysterious brown powders that were neatly placed along the bench.

"Making a potion to seal wounds," said the physician. "You do not have any, do you? Only it would be good to try it out on someone."

"No," said Geoffrey, thinking that he would have to be at Death's door before he allowed something capable of exploding near any injury of his. "But do you make ink? I have run out, and it is not something that is easy to buy in Goodrich."

"I make excellent ink," said Francis with pride. "Just ask Father Adrian. It is smooth and dries slowly, so that you can leave the lid off as you write. What colour would you like?"

"Colour?" asked Geoffrey, puzzled. "Well, black, I suppose. Or brown. I want to do some writing, not illustrating."

"Pity," said Francis. "I have been experimenting with red, and I would like someone to try it and tell me what they think. And I have a beautiful azure blue."

"I want black," said Geoffrey firmly. "If my family see me writing with all colours of the rainbow, they will consider me to have lost my wits and will lock me away."

Francis laughed. "They might! I make paints, too. It was I who supplied the pigments for your father's wall paintings."

If Geoffrey had supplied the paints for Godric's violent foray into art, he would have kept quiet about it. He smiled politely.

"Here they are," said Francis, gesturing to several buckets of pitch-black paint. "I suppose they will never be used now. It is a pity, because they were expensive to concoct. I use only the finest compounds."

"Such as what?" asked Geoffrey dubiously.

"Such as pitch, certain oils and refined pig grease, lead powder, various herbs to bind it. For my yellows I use saffron. For my reds I use pig's blood."

"Pig's blood is not expensive," said Geoffrey, crouching down to inspect the pots.

"No, but saffron is," said the physician. "And I add saffron to all my colours except the blacks and the browns. I use a little of Hedwise's famous fish sauce in those."

"No wonder they smell so unpleasant," said Geoffrey, standing up. The thought of Hedwise's fish sauce made his stomach churn, and he thought he might be sick. He walked quickly outside, and took some deep breaths of fresh air.

"I told you that you looked pale," said the physician, following him. "You should have taken the physic I offered you. What ails you?"

"Hedwise's fish sauce," said Geoffrey, smiling ruefully. "I have never liked fish, and it seems to feature in every meal the castle has to offer."

"Hedwise is proud of that fish sauce," said Francis. "And her fish broth. I am not interested in the broth, but the sauce is an excellent thickener for my paints."

"Please," said Geoffrey with a shudder. Although he did not like fish, he ate it if he had to, and it did not usually make him ill. He wondered what secret ingredient Hedwise added that seemed to please everyone else, but left him gagging.

Godric was asleep again by the time Geoffrey returned, and so the knight decided to go riding while he could. Olivier joined him and they cantered towards Coppet Hill again, Olivier chattering like a magpie, and boasting in ever greater detail about his role in the Battle of Civitate. He had just reached the climax when a sudden rustling from the undergrowth silenced him. Geoffrey carried a lance, and he drew it out of its holder when he heard the unmistakable snuffling of a wild boar.

Boars were large animals and could be dangerous, especially when frightened or enraged. Fortunately, the one that ambled towards them was neither, although Olivier took one look at it and sent his horse crashing blindly through the undergrowth to escape. Geoffrey and the wild boar watched the fleeing knight in bemusement, and parted to go their own ways without a blow being exchanged. The boar was more interested in the juicy roots that were growing around the base of a tree, and Geoffrey did not feel inclined to drive his lance into the contentedly foraging animal as most knights would have done.

He reached the top of the hill, and sat for a long time gazing across the rolling countryside that spread out in front of him. In the distance, he could see the dense forest and tatty rooftops of Lann Martin, while Goodrich Castle dominated the land with its great tower of grey and brown stone, and its wicked wooden palisades.

His mind wandered back to twenty years before, when he and Enide had climbed the hill together to escape the bullying attentions of their older siblings. For the first time since learning about her horrible death, Geoffrey became aware of an acute sense of loss and his stomach contracted with a dizzying sense of grief. He felt the ground tip and sway in front of him, and quickly dismounted before he fell, clutching the reins for support and trying to bring his emotions under control.

Who could have killed Enide? And why? Was it the same person who Francis the physician seemed so sure was killing Godric? Would one of his brothers or their wives really poison their father? Or was it Joan and the cowardly Olivier, desperate for more lands to pay for Olivier's extravagant lifestyle and scrounging friends?

Eventually, the pounding in his head lessened, and he began to feel better. He mounted his horse again and set it galloping across the smooth turf of the hilltop, enjoying the sense of power and speed as he gave the beast its head. When it was spent, he reluctantly turned it around and headed towards Goodrich.

As he rode, the light drizzle turned into a persistent downpour. Hot after his exertions, Geoffrey enjoyed the feel of cool rain on his face, although he was less keen on the sensation of cold water trickling down the back of his neck as the heavy drops seeped through his armour. Julian came racing out to meet him, and flung himself into his arms. Geoffrey was startled and somewhat embarrassed.

"Whatever is the matter?" he asked, bewildered. "Julian, please! People are looking at us!"

"Olivier told me a boar had got you," the boy sobbed. "He said it was the biggest one he had ever seen, and that it felled your horse and was mauling you. He is waiting for the rain to stop so that he can take Walter and Henry to collect your body."

Given Olivier's penchant for fabrication, Geoffrey supposed he should not be surprised by the tale, but it was cruel to upset a child needlessly.

"Nothing happened," he said, gently disengaging himself. "Like Olivier himself, the boar was more interested in food than in fighting."

Julian rubbed a hand across his face, and took the reins from Geoffrey to lead the destrier into the stables, still snuffling. Geoffrey strode across the bailey to where Olivier was watching two servants slaughter a goat.

"It was harsh of you to upset Julian like that," he said, trying to keep the anger from his voice.

Olivier looked at him in astonishment. "You are alive! Did you kill that great monster, then?"

"I did not," said Geoffrey shortly. "But you should have checked your facts before telling the boy that I was dead."

Olivier regarded him blankly. "What boy?"

"Julian," said Geoffrey impatiently. "And, incidentally, you really should let him deal with your destrier. He is much better than your grooms."

"He is also a woman," said Olivier. He put his hands over his mouth in horror. "Dash it all! I promised Joan I would not tell."

"A woman?" asked Geoffrey in confusion. "What are you talking about? Have you been drinking?"

"No. I should not have spoken. Ignore me."

"What do you mean, a woman?" demanded Geoffrey, taking a hold on the small knight's arm. Olivier stiffened with fright.

"I cannot tell you," he said, his voice a pleading whisper. "Joan would skin me alive."

"I will skin you alive if you do not," threatened Geoffrey.

Olivier licked his lips nervously and eyed Geoffrey up and down, assessing whether the knight or his sister presented a more serious threat. He swallowed hard and seemed to come to the conclusion that while Joan might be more dangerous, Geoffrey was a more immediate problem. He began to speak quickly, keeping his voice low so that the servants would not overhear.

"Julian is really named Julianna. She is a pretty little thing under all that dirt, and Joan feared for her . . . her . . ."

"Virginity?" asked Geoffrey bluntly.

"Well, if you put it like that, yes," said Olivier prudishly. "Godric was a bit of a devil for the women before his illness, and Joan did not want Julianna to go the same way as Rohese—whore today, gone tomorrow."

He chuckled at his nasty joke, but sobered when he saw Geoffrey did not share it. He hastened to explain further.

"Joan did not want Julianna to fall into to the same situation, and so she is training her to be a pastry chef. Julianna dresses like a boy so that she will be safe from unwanted male advances."

So that explained why he had always thought there was something a little odd about Julian, Geoffrey realised. Her gait was not quite right for a boy, and she was sharper and more cynical than was usual for stable-boys.

"But Godric is hardly in a position to seduce Julian," he said. "The man is confined to his bed."

"But Walter, Henry, and Stephen are not," said Olivier. "And they are every bit as dangerous. Poor Julianna would be with child before she was halfway across the bailey with them around. As soon as Godric is dead, we will leave Goodrich—assuming of course that we do not inherit—and we will take Julianna and Rohese with us. Then they can live safely with us."

"This does not sound like Joan," said Geoffrey, unconvinced. "Has she softened, then, as the years have passed?"

"I doubt it," said Olivier proudly. "She is as stalwart and bold as she ever was. But you do her an injustice, Geoffrey. Under her harshness, she is a deeply caring woman. Who else would strive to keep a pretty maid from seduction by her brothers?"

"Enide?" asked Geoffrey.

Olivier gazed at him in disbelief. "Hardly! But because Julianna is a woman, you can see why I am reluctant to allow her near my war-horse."

"Not really," said Geoffrey. "My horse cares neither one way nor another about the sex of its grooms. Julian is very good. I prefer him to the others."

"Her," corrected Olivier. "Well, each to his own. But I believe very strongly that women should not be allowed near horses. Horses are for men."

"I dare you to say that to Joan," said Geoffrey, amused.

Olivier paled and scurried away, leaving Geoffrey laughing. He went up the stairs to the main hall, and opened the door. Inside, his family were gathered around the hearth together. When they saw Geoffrey, their faces took on expressions of astonishment and acute disappointment.

"Olivier said you were dead," said Walter accusingly, as though Geoffrey had no right to prove the small knight wrong. "We were going to fetch back your corpse."

"He told us that you were killed by a boar," agreed Stephen, raising his eyebrows questioningly at Olivier, who had nervously followed Geoffrey into the keep.

"We should have known better to have listened to that snivelling coward," said Henry, slamming a pewter goblet down on the table in an undisguised display of bitter frustration as he glowered at Olivier. "I thought it was too good to be true!"

"Well, I am pleased to see you alive and well," said Hedwise, casting a defiant glance at her husband. "Come and sit by the fire and dry your wet clothes."

Avoiding her outstretched hand, Geoffrey sat on a stool near the hearth, where Bertrada sullenly handed him a beaker of scalding ale, her resentful looks a far cry from her attempts to ingratiate herself with him a few nights earlier, when she had believed that he had been loaded down with loot. Making no attempts to disguise their blighted hopes at his unexpected return from the grave, his relatives ignored him and he sat alone, sipping the bitter brew and listening to Olivier tell Stephen about the massive boar they had encountered, which had escaped Olivier's sword by the merest fraction. The tale was so far removed from events as Geoffrey recalled them that he began to wonder if they had even shared the same experience.

Geoffrey's brief moment of ease did not last long, because Godric began clamouring for him, claiming that someone had tried to suffocate him while he slept. It took a long time to calm him, and the sick man only agreed to rest when Geoffrey promised not to leave.

Later that evening, Geoffrey was awoken from where he dozed restlessly next to the fire by the sound of his father's voice.

"They killed Enide, you know."

Godric was wide awake and regarding him with bright eyes. Geoffrey must have been more deeply asleep than he had thought, for his mind was sluggish. He gazed uncomprehendingly at Godric, wondering whether he had misheard him.

"They killed Enide as well as poisoning me," said Godric. "And they killed Torva. All for this—for Goodrich! I wish that I had never set eyes on the place! Old Sergeant Helbye's sons do not cluster round him like vultures waiting for his corpse—because he has nothing to give them. It was after Enide was murdered that they began to poison me in earnest. She knew how to keep the family in order, and when she died, they turned on me more viciously than ever."

"It is late," said Geoffrey, refusing to be drawn into that kind of discussion. "You should not be saying such things, or you will give yourself bad dreams. Go to sleep." He stood stiffly, and stretched.

"You will never make a good knight," said Godric critically, changing the subject as he did when conversations were not proceeding as he intended. "Look at the state of you! Your chain-mail will rust if you do not look after it and keep it dry."

"How can I keep it dry in England?" asked Geoffrey. "It rains all the time."

"I wish I could see your destrier, Godfrey," said Godric, suddenly wistful. "The cowardly Olivier informs me that it is a handsome beast."

"He is handsome enough," said Geoffrey, pulling off his surcoat and hanging it on the hooks in the garderobe passage to dry. "But perhaps a little too independent-minded."

"He should suit you very well, then," said Godric. "But you are trying to distract me. I was telling you about Enide. I thought you said you were fond of her."

Geoffrey paused as he unbuckled his chain-mail, but did not reply.

"Why they should kill her is beyond me," mused Godric. "You have some loose links there, Godfrey: you should mend them before you next go out. The castle was a much more pleasant place when Enide was in it."

"There are vile rumours about her death," said Geoffrey. "Ingram told me that Caerdig had killed her." He stopped, and rubbed the bridge of his nose, disgusted that he had allowed himself to embark on speculations about Enide's death with his father after he had determined that he would not do so. Such a conversation would scarcely lead to a peaceful night's slumber for Godric, and would only serve to make the old man more paranoid than ever.

"Perhaps Caerdig did kill her," said Godric. "Someone did— she did not cleave her own head from her shoulders."

Geoffrey sighed. "But Henry assures me he hanged the culprits."

"So he claims," said Godric bitterly. He made a sound of ex-asperation. "Stop fiddling, Godfrey, and come and stand where I can see you. Now, I know you do not believe that I am being poisoned, and I accept that. I am beyond caring for myself, but Enide I loved dearly. Find who killed her for me, Godfrey, and I promise that I will never ask anything of you again."

"If you will make another will and leave me out of it, I will do what I can," said Geoffrey. "Meanwhile, I am wet. Can I borrow a shirt? I have lost all mine."

"Then you can buy some new ones," snapped Godric, his wheedling tone instantly superseded by his customary evil temper. "Just because you think I am about to die does not mean that you can have the clothes from my person. You are just like the others— all clamouring for the dagger that the Conqueror gave me. Well, they shall not have it. None of you shall. I have hidden it away, and no one—not a single living soul—knows where I have put it. And you shall not have the clothes from my poor body until I am gone."

"I do not intend to walk around the castle in your nightshift," retorted Geoffrey, eyeing the garment that Godric's "poor body" wore. "I want to borrow a shirt. I only have one, and it is wet and probably needs to be washed."

"Yes, it does," said Godric, eyeing him distastefully. "What do you mean by coming into your poor father's death chamber wearing a dirty shirt?"

"Can I borrow this one?" asked Geoffrey, holding one of the ones stored in the chest at the end of the bed.

"I suppose so," said Godric reluctantly. "And take some clean hose, too. Yours are really quite disgusting. Hedwise will wash them for you. But in return, will you do what I ask? Enide did not deserve to die, and her death must not go unavenged. She was being poisoned too, but the villain responsible decided he could not wait, and struck off her head as she came out of the church. I envy her in a way, for I would rather die from a sword blow than by slow poisoning."

"Even if you are right," said Geoffrey, "what can I do now? I have asked questions, and discovered nothing."

He dropped his sodden shirt onto the floor, and pulled the dry one over his head.

"I will provide you with a list of suspects that you can interrogate. First, there is Henry, who hated her as he hates you—because you are more clever than he is. Then there are Walter and Bertrada. It was Enide who discovered Walter was illegitimate. I would have kept it from him, just for a peaceful life, and—"

"How could Enide discover such a thing?" asked Geoffrey, startled. "And anyway, I do not believe that Walter was born out of wedlock. Someone would have mentioned it long before now, if it were true—especially you."

"I have a chest where I store old documents," explained Godric. "I cannot read, so I had no idea what was in it. Enide was sorting it out for me one day, and she found the evidence."

"What evidence?" asked Geoffrey tightly, sensing that Godric was about to make him very angry.

"A writ giving Walter's birthdate, and a certificate with details of my marriage to your mother. The dates do not tally. And there are also documents that prove I was away at the time of Stephen's conception, so that I could not possibly have sired him without supernatural help. Enide came to tell me what she had learned. While I was explaining—perhaps more loudly than I should have done— my other villainous whelps overheard."

"And so poor Enide had information thrust upon her that made her a danger to Walter and Stephen?" said Geoffrey coldly. "No wonder you think she has been done away with! How could you have kept such documents? Why did you not burn them?"

"Easy for you to say!" snapped Godric. "You can read—you would know which ones were which. There are important writs in that chest. How could I be certain that I was not destroying one of those?"

"You could have asked Norbert," said Geoffrey, unappeased. "Your clerk. That is why you employ him, surely? To read and write for you?"

"I could not trust *him* with such delicate information!" said Godric, appalled. "He would have used it to his own advantage."

"Unlike you," pointed out Geoffrey bitterly. "What a mess all this is. Where are these documents now?"

"Enide destroyed them," said Godric.

"But by then everyone knew of the existence of these writs and their contents anyway, so technically, Enide should not have been a greater risk than anyone else," said Geoffrey, trying to reason it all out. "So that still does not explain why someone chose to kill her."

"You will have to work that out for yourself," said Godric. "I cannot tell you everything. And do not leave Joan and Sir Fearful out of your reckonings, either. Poor Enide's head was severed with a sword, so perhaps that snivelling coward performed the foul deed."

Geoffrey's thoughts whirled with confusion. Was there even the most remote grain of truth in what Godric had just told him? Or was it simply a ploy to make Geoffrey remain at Goodrich and take on the manor? He rubbed his head where his helmet had chafed it, and went to the heavy pitcher that stood on the floor for some wine. He slopped some into a cup, and took a gulp. He resisted the urge to spit it out again: seldom in his life had he tasted anything so bitter and vile that was not medicine.

He looked dispassionately at Godric, who lay in his bed staring up at the ceiling. He raised the cup to his lips again, but even the smell of the powerful brew was too much. He slammed it down on the windowsill, and fought the desire to snatch up his sword, and race down to the hall to dispatch the whole lot of them.

CHAPTER SEVEN

Geoffrey awoke with a start to see Hedwise towering over him. His momentary consternation that she had come for him was relieved when he realised she was only bringing breakfast to Godric.

"That is fine. Now go," Godric said forcefully as Hedwise set a tray on the chest at the foot of his bed. Hedwise glowered at him and then gave a soulful look to Geoffrey before pulling the door shut behind her.

"You will have to beware of that vixen today, lad," Godric said with a leer. "Henry has gone off hunting with Olivier and his friends, so she will be on the prowl and you just might be the prey."

Geoffrey felt groggy and sluggish and was concerned that Hedwise had been able to enter the room without waking him. In the Holy Land, any knight who slept so deeply would risk never waking at all, and Geoffrey prided himself on his ability to snap awake, to be alert and ready for a possible attack. The fact that it was Hedwise who had managed to slip past his defences made it just that much more potentially problematic.

He did not relish the prospect of spending an entire day indoors with his father, but given the alternatives—Hedwise unrestrained or his family still inflamed by Godric's changed will—he decided to continue his cleaning of the paintings, while hoping to glean some information from Godric that might help solve the mystery of Enide's murder.

As it turned out, it was Geoffrey who did most of the talking, entertaining—and at the same time disappointing—his father with tales from the Crusade.

"It seems to me that you have fallen in with the wrong crowd, Godfrey," his father mused in some disgust that evening. "You say this Tancred of yours actually tried to protect those people on the Dome of the Rock? It was lucky that the Duke of Normandy and Bohemond and the others were not so womanly, or the whole Crusade might have turned back before it reached Constantinople."

Geoffrey was not sure if that would have been such a bad thing. He was about to say so when the door burst open and Walter strolled in, Bertrada and Olivier at his heels. Behind them were Stephen and Hedwise, walking rather more closely together than was usual for a man and a woman not married to each other. Walter made himself comfortable by the fire, while the others clustered around the bed, eyeing Godric speculatively, assessing whether the old man was continuing his remorseless decline in health, or whether the worst had happened and he was rallying. Godric eased himself up onto his elbows, simultaneously gratified by and uncomfortable with the attention.

"What do you lot want, and what is all that racket?" he complained, as through the window came the sounds of shouting from the courtyard below, mingled with the snorting of horses and the jangle of weapons. Walter threw open the shutters and leaned out.

"It is the Earl of Shrewsbury!" he exclaimed in surprise. "What is he doing here?"

Everyone looked at Olivier. "His visit has nothing to do with me," said the small knight defensively.

"Joan," said Walter heavily, still peering out of the window. "Joan is with him. She must have told him that Godric was near his end. Is that true Olivier?"

"It is nothing to do with me," the small knight repeated, playing with the hilt of a highly decorated dagger with which Geoffrey would not have deigned to peel fruit, let alone carry at his side. "But Godric was very ill when she left a week ago. I imagine she thought he had not long for this world."

"But Godric seems to have rallied somewhat now," said Bertrada, looking hard at Geoffrey, her tone suggesting that this was not good tidings.

"I suppose the Earl has brought the copy of this wretched new will of Godric's," said Walter. He pursed his lips, and looked at Geoffrey. "Are you sure *you* did not send for him?"

"I most certainly did not," said Geoffrey.

The Earl of Shrewsbury was one of the last people Geoffrey would invite anywhere. If the King were sufficiently worried to recruit Geoffrey to ensure that the Earl was kept away from Godric's inheritance, then Geoffrey would just as soon not meet the Earl at all.

Godric's eyes gleamed in anticipation of recriminations and arguments to come. "You had better attend to Shrewsbury, then," he said to Walter. "And send Rohese to me."

Walter opened the door, and held it open for Geoffrey to precede him.

"Not a chance," said Geoffrey, sitting near the fire. "The black-hearted Earl is your guest, not mine. I will stay here and ensure that father rests."

Stephen walked towards the door, and there was an almost comical jostle as he and Walter tried to be the first one out to greet the Earl. The others followed, leaving Geoffrey alone with Godric.

It was not long before laughter and other sounds of gaiety drifted up from the hall, as the Earl and his retinue were treated to a welcome quite different to the one Geoffrey had received. A sound from the doorway caused Geoffrey to glance up from where he was helping Godric to sip some of his strong red wine. A woman stood just outside the door, beckoning to him. Reluctantly, Geoffrey went to see what she wanted.

"I see your taste in clothes has not improved since I last saw you," she said, putting her hands on her hips and surveying his borrowed hose and shirt with some amusement. "You always were a ruffian."

"Joan?" Geoffrey asked, subjecting his older sister to the same meticulous attention as she had given him. Her thick, curly brown hair was dusted with silver, and her slender figure had thickened since she had reached her forties. But she still possessed the restless energy that Geoffrey remembered, and the hard lines around her mouth suggested that time had honed, rather than softened, her domineering tendencies. He had entertained hopes that he might fare better with Joan than with his brothers in terms of civility, but such rashly held fantasies were rapidly dismissed.

"Of course I am Joan," she retorted. "Who else is left, bird-brain? You have met our esteemed sisters-in-law Bertrada and Hedwise, and surely even you can see that I am not Enide risen from the grave!"

Geoffrey winced. For the first time since he had met him, Geoffrey felt sorry for Sir Olivier.

"Where is Rohese?" came a querulous voice from the bed.

"She will be with you as soon as she has warmed herself from the journey," called Joan. "And before you say it, she will do better by the fire than tumbling about in this chilly hole with you." She cast a disparaging glance around at Godric's room and shuddered. "This place reminds me of a whore-house!"

"Well, you should know!" shouted Godric furiously. Joan threw him a contemptuous glower, and began to walk down the stairs.

"The Earl of Shrewsbury has ordered that you attend him in the hall," she said over her shoulder to Geoffrey as she left.

"Then the Earl of Shrewsbury can go to the Devil," retorted Geoffrey. "I am not his vassal, especially since Walter seems to have used my manor of Rwirdin to secure Olivier d'Alençon for you."

Joan paused and glared at him. "You should have been here, then, if you wanted Rwirdin so much. You cannot cheerfully leave our father and poor Walter to run your estate for you, and then swan back and demand it on whim."

"Their stewardship of my manor has made a good deal of money for our father and poor Walter," said Geoffrey acidly. "I do not think you will hear them complain."

"Well, Rwirdin is mine now and you cannot have it back," said Joan in a tone that suggested that, as far as she was concerned, the topic was laid to rest for good. "Now, do not be foolish and make an enemy of the Earl. He is waiting for you."

"Then he can wait," said Geoffrey, walking back into his father's chamber. "I do not care if I make an enemy of the Earl or not—I do not plan to be here long enough for that to matter."

Joan stamped back up the stairs. "Do not be stupid, man! Do you know nothing of the Earl and his reputation?"

"Enough to know I do not want him as any acquaintance of mine," said Geoffrey. "So, you can tell him to take his orders and—"

"Sweet Jesus, Geoffrey!" whispered Joan, casting an anxious glance back towards the stairs. "Do not play with fire in our house! If you will not come for yourself, then come for your family. We have no wish to draw his wrath down upon us!"

"I did not invite him here, you did," said Geoffrey, as Stephen appeared behind Joan.

"What is keeping you?" Stephen demanded of Geoffrey. "The Earl is becoming impatient. Not only that, but your dog has just bitten him. You had better come and explain its foreign manners before he has it run through."

Reluctantly, Geoffrey followed his brother and sister down the stairs, and his resolve to leave Goodrich as soon as possible strengthened with each step. At the far end of the hall, seated comfortably in front of a blazing hearth was Robert de Bellême, the Earl of Shrewsbury, laughing loudly at some anecdote that Olivier was telling him— probably his bold encounter with the wild boar. Despite his reticence, Geoffrey was interested to see in the flesh the man whom much of England and Normandy held in such fear. He was not disappointed. Geoffrey was a tall man, but the Earl was immense. Even seated, he dominated the hall. Falling to his shoulders was a mane of sparse grey-black hair, and his eyes were like tiny pieces of jet in his big, red face.

As Geoffrey walked closer, the Earl stopped laughing and affixed him with eyes that, on closer inspection, were reptilian. Geoffrey was not a man easily unsettled, and he had faced more enemies than he cared to remember, but there was something about the Earl's beady gaze that transcended any malevolence he had encountered before. He had a sudden conviction that King Henry's suspicion that Shrewsbury might have had a hand in the killing of William Rufus might not have been so outlandish after all.

He paused in front of the hearth and looked down at the Earl, before kneeling and rising so soon again that his obeisance was only just within the realms of courtesy. The Earl continued to regard him, and the hall was silent as everyone waited for the great man to speak.

"So," he said eventually, tearing his eyes away from Geoffrey's steady gaze, and looking him up and down. "You are Sir Geoffrey Mappestone, newly returned from the Crusade." His voice was deep and powerful, and Geoffrey could well imagine it directing the many battles that he was said to have fought and won.

The Earl continued when Geoffrey did not reply. "You do not look like a knight. Where is your chain-mail?"

"I was about to retire for the night," replied Geoffrey coolly. "I do not usually wear it to bed."

Olivier's imprudent laughter was silenced by a flick of the Earl's expressionless eyes. "I see," he said. He took a hearty swig from the goblet he held and changed the subject abruptly. "Your sister tells me your father is near his end. You have timed your return well."

"It was not timed at all," said Geoffrey. "And he is not as ill as everyone seems to believe."

He was certainly not too ill to consider a romp with his whore Rohese, thought Geoffrey. He looked at the assembled people and wondered which one she was—a woman brave enough, or feeble-minded enough, to serve both Godric and Joan.

"Really?" asked the Earl in a voice so soft it was sinister. "Your brothers are not under that impression, and so I have taken the liberty of bringing my personal priest to give Sir Godric last rites."

He snapped imperious fingers, and a fat priest slid out from the ranks of the courtly retinue to disappear up the stairs.

"Thank you," said Geoffrey politely. "That was a kindly thought."

The Earl looked startled. "No one has called me kindly for many years—if ever. But tell me, Sir Geoffrey, how was the looting in the Holy Land? Did you bring many items of value home with you? Might I see them?"

"He brought nothing but a sackful of books," said Henry, spite-fully gesturing to Geoffrey's saddlebags near the Earl's chair.

"And three Arabian daggers," added Walter helpfully.

"Books?" asked the Earl, confused. "Whatever for? Do you intend to renounce your worldly ways and take the cowl now you are home? I understand many knights have done so."

"Absolutely not," said Geoffrey. "I intend to return to my lord Tancred de Hauteville in the Holy Land as soon as possible."

"Are you asking us to believe that you have made a dangerous journey of several weeks" duration, simply so that you can turn around and go back?" asked the Earl with arched eyebrows.

"Believe what you will," said Geoffrey, shrugging. "It is the truth."

Out of the corner of his eye, he saw Stephen gesturing desperately to him, urging him to be more polite, while the rest of his family appeared horrified by his disrespect to the Earl. But Geoffrey had no intention of being interrogated about his personal affairs by Shrewsbury or anyone else. If his family did not care for his attitude and threw him out of the castle, then so much the better—it would be an excellent excuse to escape the obligations imposed on him by the King, and the whole household could murder each other to their hearts" content.

"Well, you are here now," said the Earl, sitting back in his chair, his eyes never leaving Geoffrey's face. "So, I suppose we had better make the best of it. How would you like to join my service for a few months? I can always use a good knight."

Geoffrey was taken aback, and he was reminded of the murders he had solved in Jerusalem, when he had been recruited to the task by more than one of the warring princes who held power there. He had vowed that he would never allow himself to be put into a similar situation again, and since he was already under orders from the King, the Earl of Shrewsbury was out of luck.

"Thank you, no," he said, forcing himself to be civil. "I will not be in England long, and anyway, I am already in the service of Tancred de Hauteville."

"But I was given leave to understand that you are a knight in the retinue of the Duke of Normandy," said the Earl, looking at Stephen briefly before bringing his cold eyes back to bear on Geoffrey. "What has possessed you to abandon the Duke and flee to the service of another?"

"It was on the orders of the Duke that I went to Tancred," said

Geoffrey, nettled by the implication that his loyalties were cheap, "although I fail to see what concern that is of yours."

The sharp intakes of breath from the Earl's courtiers and the horrified faces of his family suggested that Geoffrey's answer might have been less than prudent. For several moments, the Earl did nothing but stare at Geoffrey, his expression unreadable.

"I meant no offence," the Earl said finally, although his tone was anything but conciliatory. "I asked merely because the Duke is a good friend of mine, and I always look to the interests of my friends. But we waste time here, Sir Geoffrey. I called you to me for two reasons. First, so that I could see you and make my own assessment of Godric's youngest son. And second, so that you could make reparation to me for the nasty nip I have suffered from that evil beast you call a dog."

Geoffrey's heart sank, and he looked around for the animal.

"Have no fear," said the Earl. "I have not ordered it to be dispatched. Yet. But what have you to offer me in recompense for my wound, other than books, of course?"

"Just advice," said Geoffrey, as determined that the Earl should not intimidate him into offering compensation as the Earl was to have it. "Dogs bite. Stay away from them."

This time, there were no sharp intakes of breath: Geoffrey had gone too far. Blood drained from the Earl's face as he rose from his chair, his big body taut with anger. He advanced on Geoffrey, his thick fingers resting lightly on the hilt of his sword. Geoffrey cursed himself for dispensing with his chain-mail and weapons. He was never without them while out on patrols, and the situation at Goodrich ever since he had arrived was every bit as dangerous as was chasing Saracens in the desert. He did not back away as the Earl drew nearer, but he was tense, ready to leap to one side if the Earl were to haul his gigantic broadsword from his belt.

"What about one of these Arabian daggers, my lord?" asked Walter hastily, hauling them from Geoffrey's saddlebags. Once out, he eyed them dubiously. "What peculiar-looking things!"

The Earl had been close enough to treat Geoffrey to wafts of his bad breath but, intrigued by the puzzlement in Walter's voice, he turned abruptly to inspect the daggers. Geoffrey forced himself to breathe normally, and looked around quickly to assess which of the

Earl's assortment of knights and squires he might most easily over-power to grab a weapon. Olivier's two friends, Malger and Drogo, were present. Malger appeared amused by Geoffrey's behaviour, but Drogo was clearly outraged. Neither of them would present an easy target, but nearby was a scrawny clerk who carried a handsome sword at his side. Geoffrey edged closer to him, surreptitiously look-ing for any buckles that might interfere with his snatching of it.

Meanwhile, the Earl turned the Arabian daggers over in his hands, admiring the craftsmanship and balance. Stephen darted to-wards Geoffrey while the Earl's attention was taken.

"For God's sake, Geoffrey! Do you want to be slain here and now in front of us all?" he hissed. "Do you know nothing about the Earl of Shrewsbury? He will kill you as you stand—just as I have seen him kill others, and for less serious crimes than insulting him! And think of us. I, for one, do not wish to join you in a heap of mangled limbs on the floor of my own hall."

Geoffrey had heard enough of the Earl to know that the scene Stephen envisaged was not as far-fetched as it sounded. He sighed. He had returned to England to escape some of the bloodshed that was a part of daily life in Jerusalem, and he had no wish to be the cause of his family's massacre at the hands of the tyrannical Earl of Shrewsbury. If anyone were to dispatch them all, Geoffrey would rather it were himself—for the murder of Enide, or the poisoning of his father, or even for the death of Aumary, shot in the forest by the mysterious archer.

"Do the Saracens really use such barbaric weapons?" asked the Earl, still examining the weapons with intense interest.

Geoffrey fought back the urge to ask why the dagger should be considered barbaric, while the small mace that dangled from the Earl's waist was not.

"The Saracens sometimes use long, curved swords, too," he answered, aware of Stephen's relief that Geoffrey had decided to be civil.

The Earl jerked his thumb back quickly and looked at the blood that oozed from a cut there.

"How sharp they are! This makes two wounds I have suffered at your hands, Geoffrey Mappestone."

"Daggers are of little use if they are blunt," said Geoffrey, heartily wishing the Earl had done himself a more serious injury. "I had intended them as gifts for my brothers, but I have come to the conclusion that they will be safer from each other without them."

While the Earl roared with unexpected laughter, Walter, Henry, and Stephen craned forward to see the weapons that might have been theirs. Walter's face was a mask of disappointment when he saw the jewelled hilts and finely engraved scabbards, although Henry gave the impression he would not have taken his anyway.

"And what of your sister?" demanded Joan. "Or do your fraternal instincts not stretch to the females in the family?"

"You have my manor at Rwirdin," retorted Geoffrey. "Is that not enough?"

The Earl laughed again and clapped his hands in delight. "What an extraordinary family! Your quarrels never cease to amuse me, and now it seems that they will be livelier still with Sir Geoffrey's ready wit. Tell me, how is it that this manor of Rwirdin seems to have become the matter for such dispute? It is a small place, I understand, and not rich."

Walter looked uncomfortable, and Joan defiant. Stephen intervened

"It belonged to our mother, along with the village of Lann Martin," he said. "When she died, she willed Lann Martin to Henry, and Rwirdin to Geoffrey."

"Why?" asked the Earl. "Surely her property should have reverted to her husband after her death?"

"Our father, foolishly, agreed with our mother that Lann Martin and Rwirdin would keep his two youngest sons" greedy eyes from the rest of his property," said Stephen. "He applauded the fact that she had thought to provide for those of his children never likely to inherit Goodrich."

Henry stepped forward angrily, but the Earl was no longer interested. "I like these daggers," he announced, waving one around experimentally. "They are unusual. And I like the unusual. Which one will you give me, Sir Geoffrey?"

"Take them all," said Geoffrey carelessly. He had not planned to keep them anyway, and was not concerned whether they found a home with his brothers or the Earl. It was also clear that the Earl would glean far more pleasure from taking them without Geoffrey's blessing than with it, and Geoffrey did not want to give him any such satisfaction.

"You should not be incautious with your wealth, my brave knight," said the Earl in mock admonition. "I will take two of these fine weapons, and leave you the third. Who knows? You might need it to buy me off another time."

He handed the smallest one back to Geoffrey, who wondered idly what the chances were of plunging it into the Earl's black heart and still leaving the hall alive. He suspected that if he could achieve the former, the latter would be little problem, for the Earl did not seem to rule his retinue on the basis of his integrity and godliness, and Geoffrey decided that most of them would probably be thoroughly glad to see the back of him. Drogo would almost certainly object, but Geoffrey was confident he could overpower the slower, older knight easily enough, given a sharp broadsword. Malger, meanwhile, was more pragmatic, and would almost certainly opt for whichever direction appeared to be the most profitable—he was therefore unlikely to fight Geoffrey over the Earl's death.

"I hear you have made the acquaintance of the King," said the Earl conversationally, still admiring his new acquisitions. "Chepstow is a splendid castle, is it not?"

"What?" said Walter, narrowing his eyes. "Geoffrey has never met the King."

Geoffrey's heart sank.

"Visiting the King was his first stop, I am told," said the Earl, feigning surprise. "Really, Sir Geoffrey! Did you not mention to your brothers and sisters as important an occasion as an audience with King Henry?"

"It did not seem relevant," said Geoffrey tersely.

"You took him the body of that poor knight who was killed," pressed the Earl. "Sir Aumary? Was that his name?"

"Yes," said Geoffrey. He had little choice now but to be open, or his brothers would begin to suspect him of even more skullduggery. "Aumary was killed in an ambush in the Forest of Dene. Since he was bearing dispatches for the King, I thought I should take them to Chepstow as quickly as possible—Aumary told me they were important."

"And were they?" asked the Earl.

"I have no idea," said Geoffrey. "I did not read them. They were sealed."

"Were you not in the least bit curious?" pressed the Earl, clearly not believing a word of it. "Did you really not have the remotest idea about what was in them?"

"It was none of my business," said Geoffrey. "I try to stay away from the affairs of kings and rulers wherever possible. It is safer."

"But I am told you can read," the Earl insisted. "Did you not glance over the King's shoulder to see what was the nature of these vital messages that had put you to so much inconvenience?"

So that was it, thought Geoffrey. Aumary's messages to the King was why the Earl was so keen to meet him—the Earl had heard that the King had received dispatches from France, and he wanted to know what was in them. Since Geoffrey had no intention of telling the Earl or anyone else about the King's recipe for horse liniment, continuing to feign ignorance was by far the most prudent course of action.

"I did not read the messages," he said firmly, "and the King most certainly did not give them to me to peruse. Perhaps the constable might know—he was present when they were opened."

"I have already asked him, and he told me to ask you," said the Earl smoothly. "But never mind. They cannot have been that important, or the King would have provided Aumary with an escort—and he travelled alone, I understand. But here comes my priest. Is the end near for Sir Godric, Father?"

The priest gave his head a jowl-cascading shake. "Not for a while yet, my lord, although I have given him last rites lest his end should come upon him unexpectedly. He is sleeping, and I am certain he will wake again tomorrow."

"Good," said the Earl, rubbing his hands together briskly. "But I am tired. I had expected to stay at Monmouth tonight, but I thought I should come here instead given that Godric is soon to be dead. I will take your chamber, Walter. The rest of you," he said, waving a contemptuous hand at his grovelling retinue, "can fend for yourselves."

After the Earl had swept up the stairs, followed by his squires, his knights and clerks began to argue among themselves as to who was to sleep where in the hall. Geoffrey was about to return to Godric's chamber when Walter caught his arm furiously.

"What is this about you meeting the King? Who was this murdered knight—Sir Aumary—and who ambushed you? You have said nothing about all this before."

"It was none of your affair," said Geoffrey, freeing his arm impatiently.

"You lied to me," said Bertrada coldly. "You said your journey from Jerusalem was uneventful, and now I hear that you had an ambush to contend with—hardly a non-event, even for a fighting man like you."

"And what else did you tell the King?" demanded Henry, standing in his way to prevent him from leaving. "I suppose you thought he might help you wrest Goodrich from us. Well, he would not, because he believes it should be mine. He told me so himself."

"Rubbish!" spat Walter, almost beside himself with rage. "Goodrich will be mine because I am the oldest."

"I heard about the brush that Geoffrey had with our neighbour," said Stephen. "Mark Ingram gave me the details. He said that Caerdig ambushed you when you were almost in Lann Martin."

"What?" exploded Henry. "You fought with Caerdig? Why does the Welsh weasel still live? Call yourself a knight? Why did you not run him through?"

"Because then his men would have killed me," said Geoffrey. "And anyway, when I had him at the tip of my sword, he was unarmed."

"So?" demanded Henry. "What has that got to do with it?"

"Well done, Geoffrey!" said Walter scathingly. "You have a God-given chance to rid us of one of our most bitter enemies, and you throw it away."

"Why did you not tell us about it?" asked Stephen. "I am not questioning your decision to spare Caerdig's life, only that you did not inform us of an ambush so close to our home."

"Perhaps I was wrong," said Geoffrey. "But I did not want to arrive here after twenty years claiming that I had been attacked by one of your neighbours."

"What kind of excuse is that?" yelled Henry, incensed. "I could have had Lann Martin, to add to Goodrich when it is mine."

"Goodrich will never be yours," shouted Walter hotly. He lurched suddenly, and Geoffrey realised he was well on the way to being drunk. Doubtless being intoxicated was the best way to deal with an unexpected and wholly unwelcome guest like the Earl.

Stephen sighed as they began to argue again. "I have had enough of this. I have a bitch in the village that is about to pup, and I would like to check all goes well. Good night, brothers."

He turned on his heel and walked away. Not wanting to be left with Walter and Henry, who had made no effort to stop squabbling, Geoffrey followed him outside. The gate between the inner and outer wards stood wide open, and Stephen strolled through it, whistling as he went. There were no guards at the barbican gate, and Geoffrey could hear him shouting to be let out. Geoffrey swung round suddenly at a noise behind him, and did not relax much when he saw Malger standing in the shadows.

Malger frowned when he saw Stephen calling for the sergeant on duty to wake so that he could leave. "I do not feel the Earl is particularly safe here. I think I will post my own guards for as long as he stays."

"That is probably wise," agreed Geoffrey. "I could take this so-called fortress single-handed."

He decided not to add to Malger's concerns by saying that he almost had—when he had blustered his way into the castle on his first night home, and the only resistance he had encountered was an aborted challenge from Sir Olivier and a few surly questions from the guards.

Malger strode away, shouting to men who lounged in the bailey, and set about establishing his watches. It would probably be the first time Goodrich had been in secure hands since Godric had taken to his bed, Geoffrey thought.

It was cold wearing only his father's tatty shirt and patched hose, and he was glad to go back inside. He reached the door just as the first heavy spots of rain began to fall. Stephen would get wet. Walter and Henry were still arguing bitterly, unaware that they were providing entertainment for the Earl's retinue who listened with undisguised amusement to the increasingly furious exchange.

Geoffrey left them to it, and went to his father's room, taking a candle from a sconce on the stairs so that he could see where he was going. The dog slunk from under a table, and went with him, uncharacteristically subdued. Geoffrey wondered whether the Earl had kicked it.

He started back as someone emerged on the stairs above him, and cursed yet again for allowing himself to be caught weaponless within the treacherous walls of Goodrich Castle. A young woman stepped out of the shadows, her face tear-stained.

"I thought you were Sir Olivier," she said unsteadily.

"Do I look like a peacock—all feathers and no courage?" he demanded, and was immediately sorry. He had no right to take out his residual anger at the Earl on someone he had never met.

The girl gazed at him with large, troubled eyes. "I am Rohese. You must be Sir Godfrey."

"Geoffrey. And you are my father's . . ." He had been about to say whore.

"Chambermaid, yes. But Godric will not be able to save me!" She began to cry.

"Save you from whom?" asked Geoffrey, confused. "Sir Olivier? I cannot see that he would present much of a threat to anyone."

"Not Olivier. *Him.* The Earl!" Her voiced faded to a horrified whisper.

"Ah."

"Will you help me?" she pleaded, clutching his arm, and gazing up at him with wide eyes that leaked tears. "Do not let him take me, Sir Godfrey. Joan says that if he wants me, I have no choice but to go to his bedchamber."

Geoffrey studied her. She was tiny, and had a delicate heart-shaped face with large blue eyes. Tendrils of golden hair escaped from the veil she wore over her head, and his heart softened when he saw she was only about sixteen.

"But what can I do?" he asked. "The Earl, it seems, is a law unto himself—what the Earl wants, the Earl takes."

"I will die rather than let him have me!" she said, with a frail attempt at courage. "Give me your dagger. I will kill myself here and now!"

"You would be better justified in using it on the Earl," said Geoffrey. "Is he expecting you?"

"He is in his chamber, and Joan said she would send Sir Olivier for me if I did not go to him of my own accord." She swallowed noisily as footsteps sounded on the stairs below.

"Rohese?" called Sir Olivier softly. "The Earl is waiting."

Rohese gave a noise halfway between a groan and a sob, and almost swooned against the wall. Geoffrey took her by the wrist and hauled her into Godric's room, closing the door behind them. Now what? he thought, looking around and wondering what he had let himself in for. Godric's chamber was likely to be the first room that would be searched if the Earl's amorous intentions were serious. There were few places Rohese could hide—unless she could fit down the garderobe shaft—a desperate option, but one that Geoffrey had employed himself on occasion before he had grown too large. But Godric's chamber was on the top floor, and even if Rohese survived the fall, she was likely to drown in the foul, sucking mud that comprised much of the castle moat.

Olivier's footsteps were coming closer, and Rohese gazed at the door in mute terror. Geoffrey hauled open the chest at the foot of the bed and bundled her inside. He was sitting on it and buckling to his waist the Arabian dagger that the Earl had rejected when Olivier entered.

"Have you seen Rohese the whore?" Olivier asked, lifting the covers of Godric's bed to peer underneath it.

"Is she back then?" Geoffrey asked. "That is good news. My father has missed her."

"Well, he can have her tomorrow," said Olivier, going to the tiny room at the far end of Godric's chamber to look down the garderobe shaft. "But tonight, the Earl would like her. Damn it all! Where can she have gone?"

"I take it the opportunity to revel in the pleasure of the Earl's company is less than appealing to her?"

"What nonsense are you talking?" mumbled Olivier. "If you are asking whether she wants to go to him, that is wholly irrelevant. Do you mind standing? I want to look in that chest."

"I have been sitting on it," said Geoffrey. "How could she have climbed inside without my noticing?"

"I had not thought of that," said Olivier, scratching his head. "Help me look for her, Geoffrey. The Earl will be wanting me to stand in, if I cannot find her!"

Geoffrey gazed at him, and wondered what kind of man the Earl was.

"I meant by supplying Joan," said Olivier hastily. "And she will not approve of that!"

"I doubt the Earl would make much progress with Joan if she were not willing," said Geoffrey, certain that his assertive sister would not stand for any nonsense—unless she viewed the arrangement positively, of course. He stood, and looked under Godric's bed, and then went to check the garderobe shaft.

"She is not here," said Olivier, slumping down on the chest. I wonder where she could have gone."

"Perhaps she has hurled herself off the battlements," suggested Geoffrey. "I might, if the alternative was a night with the Earl of Shrewsbury."

"You would not last a night with him," said Olivier with conviction. "You would be unable to keep a civil tongue in your head, and he would run you through long before dawn."

"I had noticed that the Earl seems to prefer sycophants over people with independent minds," said Geoffrey, smiling as Olivier looked blankly at him. "But you had better go and find Rohese, or you will have to answer to Joan."

"Lord, yes!" said Olivier, hurrying from the room.

"You are playing a dangerous game, Godfrey," said Godric, lifting his head from the pillow, where he had been pretending to sleep. "Do not make an enemy of the Earl. He is barely on this side of sanity, and I would not like to imagine you in his clutches."

Geoffrey sighed. "So I have been told several times recently."

He opened the lid of the chest, and helped Rohese out. She ran to Godric and buried her head in the folds of his nightgown, sobbing softly.

"You have been decent over this," said Godric, stroking her hair, and looking up at Geoffrey. "None of the others would dare risk the Earl's wrath over a serving wench."

"We have not won yet," said Geoffrey. "They will be back, and we need to find another hiding place."

He glanced around the bare room, and began to reconsider the garderobe option.

"She can slip between my mattresses," whispered Godric. "They will not look there, and better a little discomfort than entertaining the Earl."

"Better a good deal of discomfort, I should say," muttered Geoffrey. He heaved the light, upper mattress high enough for Rohese to climb underneath it, and let it down gently. "Do not lie that way, you will suffocate. Keep your head this end. Good. And if father will keep his legs to the left, you might yet survive the night un-Earled."

He was just tucking in the bedcovers when the door was flung open and Olivier marched in, flanked by Drogo and Malger.

"Does no one ever think to knock before entering?" Geoffrey demanded angrily. "This is my father's bedchamber. He is ill, and does not need you bursting in every few moments."

"My apologies," stammered Olivier, disconcerted by Geoffrey's display of temper. "But the Earl has sent us to search again. I have looked down the garderobe, Drogo," he added as the thick-set knight went towards it.

"Why? Does he not trust you to carry out as simple a task as searching a room for a whore?" asked Geoffrey acidly. "For God's sake, man, you have looked once already. Where do you think she might be? Between the floorboards? Blending in with the wall-paintings?"

"Even a whore would have problems blending in with those," muttered Malger, eyeing them disparagingly. "Drogo, look in the chest."

Drogo flung open the lid of the chest, and began to stab around in it with his sword.

"Oh, well considered, Sir Drogo," said Geoffrey facetiously, sitting on the edge of the bed and hoping he was not crushing Rohese. "If she were hidden there, you would be presenting the Earl with a whore with ventilation for his night of debauchery."

Drogo whipped his sword out of the chest and he made towards Geoffrey menacingly. Malger intercepted him, and held him back only with difficulty.

"Not now, Drogo," said Malger, glowering at Geoffrey. "But

we will not have long to wait, given his insolent tongue. How he survived the Earl tonight is a mystery to me."

"Are you leaving?" asked Geoffrey as the trio made for the door. He tore the bedcovers away from Godric, revealing the emaciated body that lay helpless underneath. "Are you sure you would not like to inspect my father, lest he has his whore secreted inside his nightgown? Perhaps she lies underneath him. Shall I lift him for you?"

Drogo was across the floor in an instant, hauling his hunting knife from its scabbard. But Geoffrey was quicker by far, and when Drogo felt the tip of Geoffrey's Arabian dagger pricking his throat he stopped dead, breathing hard, his small eyes blazing with a mixture of fear and anger. Gradually, he lowered his weapon, and took a step backwards. Geoffrey made no move to follow, but kept his own dagger raised.

"The whore is not here, as you can see," he said softly. "Now, my father is tired, and he needs his rest. He would appreciate some peace, entertaining though your company has been."

Without a word, Drogo turned and stalked out. Malger snapped his fingers at Olivier.

"Come, Olivier. We should be organising the guards on the gatehouse, not chasing a whore. Surely your wife can find her? Meanwhile, I want archers on the palisade—if this miserable hole can supply us with any, that is."

Olivier watched Malger leave, and then turned horrified eyes on Geoffrey, his naked fear very much at odds with his knightly attire. He said nothing, but shook his head despairingly at Geoffrey and scuttled after his friends, closing the door behind him. Geoffrey dropped the dagger to his side.

"God's blood, Godfrey, you *do* play a dangerous game!" said Godric admiringly, reaching out a feeble hand to try to pluck the bedcovers back over him. "But have a care, boy. I did not leave you Goodrich so you could hold it for a week—you would do well to be more prudent around the Earl and his henchmen. And whatever you do, do not let Joan catch you hiding my whore. She would skin you alive."

Geoffrey rubbed his eyes, knowing very well that Joan would be none too pleased if she was forced to spend a night in merry debauchery with the Earl because her brother had secreted Rohese

away. He smiled at the notion, and went to help Godric with his
blankets. Rohese's head appeared at the bottom of the bed.

"I would stay there tonight, if I were you, Rohese," said Geoffrey, suddenly weary. "Can you manage? Can you breathe under
there with all that dust?"

She nodded tearfully, and ducked out of sight.

Godric sighed, and turned a face that was grey with fatigue to
Geoffrey. "By the Devil, I am tired. Fetch me a cup of that wine,
Godfrey."

The massive jug had been refilled, and was so heavy that it was
easier for Geoffrey simply to dip the goblet in it and draw some out,
than it was to pour. He helped Godric take several small sips, and
settled him down for the night, pushing him to the left side of the
bed for Rohese's comfort. When Godric slept, Geoffrey hunted
around for a spare blanket, wrapped himself up in it, and lay on the
floor near the fire, placing the Arabian dagger near his hand. Within
the last hour, he had made himself new enemies, and it always paid
to be cautious. The dog settled next to him, its head resting on its
paws.

Geoffrey had scarcely begun to doze when the door opened yet
again, and Hedwise slipped in with Stephen behind her. Wearily,
Geoffrey pulled himself back from the brink of sleep and sat up.
Would they never leave him alone? Hedwise held out a bowl to
him, which Geoffrey accepted with some caution.

"In all the confusion of the Earl arriving, we never offered you
anything to eat," she said, softly so as not to waken Godric. "But
here is some fish broth to last you until morning."

"And here is some wine," said Stephen, holding out a bottle.
He began to hand the bottle to Geoffrey, but then took it back to
break the seal for him. "There. This is excellent wine, but the seals
are sometimes difficult to remove. I would not like to think of you
here with a bottle of wine that you could not open."

"I am sure I would have managed," said Geoffrey, for whom
awkward seals were never a problem. "But thank you."

Stephen gave a sudden laugh. "Forgive me—I do not mean to

be patronising. I am sure a man who forced the walls of the Holy City would have no problems undoing a bottle of wine. Perhaps tomorrow we can open one together. I would like to hear more about the Crusade."

Geoffrey nodded, and examined the bottle. Marks in the glass suggested that it had come from France, and was a far cry from the bitter local brew that was usually consumed at Goodrich. He smiled at Stephen to show his appreciation.

"Did you see your dog?" Geoffrey asked, politely interested in what was clearly Stephen's main love in life.

"I am just going there now," said Stephen. "I had not reached the barbican before it started to rain, so I came back for a cloak. Then I remembered you, stuck here with Godric, and I thought you might need something to help you sleep."

"Thank you," said Geoffrey again.

Stephen prepared to leave. "Enjoy the wine, Geoffrey," he said. "But do not touch that foul brew father likes. It will poison you."

Geoffrey glanced at him sharply, but Stephen's attention was caught by the way the lamplight shone through Hedwise's nightshift, and he could not tell whether his brother's words had a deeper meaning or not.

"You should not have let everyone know that you came home lootless," said Hedwise, laughing down at Geoffrey. "Then you would not have been so neglected in favour of the Earl."

That, Geoffrey thought, was probably true. He returned her smile, and sipped the broth. Not surprisingly, it smelled strongly of fish, and Geoffrey had to force himself not to show his distaste. It had been kind of her to think of him, and Geoffrey had no wish to alienate yet another member of his family by declining a gift brought out of consideration for him. He took a mouthful of the wine to mask the flavour, but either the wine also had the taint of fish about it, or the broth had done irreparable damage to his sense of taste.

Stephen gave him an odd salute and left, flinging his cloak around his shoulders as he went. Hedwise closed the door behind him and came to sit next to Geoffrey.

"Finish the broth, Geoffrey," she said. "Or you will be wasting away." She smiled at him, her eyes dark in the candle-light, and edged a little closer. Pretending to reach for the wine, Geoffrey moved away, but it was not long before her leg was rubbing against his.

"Hedwise . . ." he began.

"Hush," she said, putting a finger on his lips to prevent him from speaking. "Let us enjoy these few moments together without words. Drink the broth."

Geoffrey took a second tentative sip, fighting not to gag at the unpleasant, almost bitter taste, and washed it down with a swallow of wine. Hedwise moved closer yet, squashing Geoffrey against the wall. He wondered whether her attraction to him was a case of simple lust, or whether she was working to put him in some dreadfully compromising position in which Henry would certainly attempt to kill him for adultery.

He was in the process of extricating himself from her encircling legs, when the door opened yet again, and Walter lurched in, supported by Stephen. Hedwise sprang away guiltily, and Walter eyed them blearily for a moment, while Stephen gave a knowing smile and said nothing.

"I am dispossessed," slurred Walter gloomily. "First, my manor is about to go to another man on the basis of some trumped-up claim of illegitimacy, and second, I have even been ousted from my own bedchamber."

He dropped a blanket on the floor next to Geoffrey, and slumped on it, wafting wine fumes all over the chamber.

"Move over, little brother. There is enough room near this fire for two. Or should I say three?" He leered at Hedwise. "But I am not sleeping while that thing is in the room," he added, indicating Geoffrey's dog with a sideways toss of his head that almost toppled him over.

The dog, sensing it was the focus of attention, rose, and walked towards Walter, wagging its tail hopefully. Walter made a sudden movement with his hand to repel it, and it jerked backwards, knocking into Geoffrey. Fishy soup and wine alike spilled onto Geoffrey's shirt sleeve.

"I will take him," said Stephen, flicking his fingers at the dog as he had seen Geoffrey do. "And this time, I really am going to visit my pupping hound, Your dog can come with me."

"He will not go out in the rain," said Geoffrey, shaking his arm to remove the worst of the spillage from his sleeve. "He—"

Without so much as a backwards glance, the dog followed Stephen from the room, wagging its tail and snuffling around him in a friendly manner never bestowed upon Geoffrey. Geoffrey could only suppose that Stephen must have something edible secreted on his person.

"Good," said Walter, as Hedwise went too, closing the door behind her and leaving them with the light from the flickering fire. "I am exhausted. Finish that broth or Hedwise will be mortally offended. She is quite justifiably proud of that fish soup."

He watched Geoffrey take another sip, screwing up his face against the strong, fishy flavour. Hedwise's mortal offence was just too bad, Geoffrey decided. He made a pretence at draining the bowl to satisfy Walter, and then tipped the remainder down the garderobe shaft as soon as Walter's eyelids began to droop. As soon as Walter was asleep, he began some impressive snoring that had their father tossing and turning restlessly.

Geoffrey placed the empty bowl on the hearth and tucked the blanket around his oldest brother, although he could see that Walter was a far beyond caring about any such tender ministrations. Geoffrey took a sip of wine to rid his mouth of the taste of fish, but, if anything, Stephen's brew was worse. Since the bottle suggested it was wine of some quality, Geoffrey could only assume that it must have gone sour on its long journey from France. He set it virtually untouched back on the hearth by the bowl, and sat next to Walter, watching the flames flickering in the fire. He felt sick and his stomach hurt, and the mere thought of fish broth almost brought it all back up again.

He pulled his surcoat tighter around him against the cold, and listened to the sounds of Olivier's noisy search for Rohese in all manner of improbable places. A picture of the Earl's face swam before him, the dark face twisted with loathing, so that Geoffrey felt disinclined to sleep, although he was bone weary. In the end, he rose and moved the chest from the end of the bed against the door, reeling from a sudden wave of dizziness as he did so. Satisfied that anyone trying to enter the room would now make sufficient noise to waken him, he slipped into a deep sleep.

'What have you done? How could you? Are you some kind of monster to do such a vile thing under your father's own roof?"

Geoffrey was vaguely aware of strident voices, and of someone prodding him hard with the toe of a boot. The shouting seemed very distant, and he was certain it could have nothing to do with him. He settled back to sleep again.

"Oh, no you don't! Come on! Wake up!"

The voices became more insistent, and Geoffrey felt himself being pulled upright. Then he was jolted awake with a start as a bucket of icy water was dashed over him. He gasped in shock, trying to force his eyes to focus on the people who surrounded him.

"That did the trick!" announced Henry grimly, flinging the bucket into a corner. "He is all yours."

He stepped back to reveal the Earl of Shrewsbury behind him. Geoffrey squinted up at them, wondering why the light was lancing so painfully into his eyes. He tried to stand, but his legs were like rubber, and would not hold him up.

"Stay where you are," said the Earl sharply. "Now. Tell me why you saw fit to murder your own father. He was dying anyway. You only had to wait a short while longer."

Geoffrey thought he was in the depth of some dreadful nightmare, and tried to force himself awake. But a vicious kick from Henry when he did not answer convinced him that he was indeed awake, but that he might be better dreaming.

"Do not just sit there!" yelled Henry. "The Earl asked you a question and is expecting a reply."

Geoffrey tried to speak, but his tongue felt as though it belonged to someone else and the sounds he managed to produce made no sense to anyone, least of all to himself.

"What is the matter with him?" demanded the Earl, glaring at Henry. "He was not so inarticulate when he bandied words with me last night. Has he been at the wine?"

"I should say," said Stephen from his father's bedside, hefting up the enormous jug. "This flagon was filled to the brim with the strong red wine Godric likes only yesterday, and it is now completely empty." He used both hands to tip it upside down, lest anyone did not believe him.

Their voices buzzed in Geoffrey's head, and he began to feel sick. He took a deep breath, and tried to speak a second time.

"What has happened? Why are you all shouting?"

They stared at him. "Who would not shout after coming to find Godric most foully murdered?" demanded Walter, eyeing him angrily. "And I believed you the other day, when you told us that you did not approve of the slaughter of unarmed people!"

"What are you talking about?" asked Geoffrey, bewildered. "Who murdered Godric?"

"He is feigning innocence," said Henry, striding over to Geoffrey, and hauling him to his feet. "Come and see your handiwork!"

Geoffrey reeled, and grabbed at the Earl to prevent himself from falling over.

"He does not smell of wine," said the Earl, standing back as Stephen hurried forward to relieve him from Geoffrey's embrace. "Are you certain he is drunk?"

"He downed the wine to rid his brain of the unpleasant memory of what he has done," said Henry harshly. "Look there, Geoffrey. Now what have you got to say for yourself?"

Geoffrey gazed down at the sprawled corpse of Godric Mappestone with a confused jumble of feelings, the strongest of which was nausea. Godric had been stabbed in the chest, and whoever had killed him had done so with Geoffrey's Arabian dagger—the one of the three that the Earl had declined to take the night before. Geoffrey closed his eyes in despair, but opened then again when the blackness threatened to overwhelm him.

"The chest was against the door," he said weakly. "How could anyone enter?"

"What chest?" demanded the Earl. "You mean that one?"

He pointed to the chest that stood at the end of the bed, where it had been before Geoffrey had moved it. Had Geoffrey dreamed that he had dragged it across the floor to the door? But there were fresh scratches on the floor, where the heavy box had slightly damaged it. Was it Walter who had killed Godric in the night, and who had then moved the chest back to its original position so that he could leave? And had Rohese witnessed the murderer, and was she still hidden between the mattresses? Geoffrey felt he could hardly look with the Earl watching.

He tugged one arm free from Stephen and rubbed it across his face. He felt as though he were suffocating from the heat of the room, and yet he felt icy cold.

"Can we go outside?" he asked, thinking that if he did not, he might well be sick. "I cannot breathe in here."

"He does not like to be in the same room as his victim," said Walter. "What do you say, Stephen? Shall we leave Bertrada to lay Godric out and adjourn to the hall?"

"I am not laying him out!" declared Bertrada indignantly. "He has been murdered!"

"It is not contagious," said the Earl dryly.

In Goodrich Castle, Geoffrey was not so sure. Taking advantage of their bickering, he shrugged off Stephen's restraining hands, staggered towards the door, and lunged down the stairs. Once in the hall, he weaved his way unsteadily across it, making for the door.

"Do not let him escape!" yelled Henry, in hot pursuit, although the only person in the inner ward to hear was Julian, who saw Geoffrey and hurried forward to help him.

"I knew it!" she exclaimed, as Geoffrey slumped heavily on the bottom step, unable to walk any further. "I was certain you were not the kind of man to kill Sir Godric as he slept. You have been poisoned, just like he was!"

"I most certainly have," said Geoffrey pulling his knees up in front of him and resting his swimming head on his arms. "But by whom? And was it the same person who killed my father?"

"Well, I should say so!" said Julian with conviction. "It is unlikely that there are two poisoners in the castle. Enide was also poisoned, of course, but she never did find out who did it."

"Now you have had some fresh air, do you remember anything else?" asked the Earl, coming over to where Geoffrey sat.

He leaned against a wall, nonchalantly inspecting his fingernails, but lurking in the depths of his eyes was a black malice. Joan, Stephen, and Godric had been right when they had advised Geoffrey against making an enemy of the powerful Earl of Shrewsbury, and he wished he had given their advice a little more thought before dismissing it in such a cavalier manner.

"You are in quite a predicament, Geoffrey, so you had better hope you recall something useful," put in Bertrada helpfully.

"I went to sleep after Walter did, and I remember nothing until you woke me this morning," said Geoffrey. "Although Hedwise and Stephen brought me some broth and wine that Walter was most insistent that I finished."

He looked from one to the other, trying to see whether any of them betrayed themselves by guilty glances, but they stood with the light behind them, and his vision was still too blurred to see any incriminating looks anyway.

"So, are you saying that you slept through the murder?" asked Bertrada with heavy sarcasm. "Is that what you are telling us?"

"Yes," said Geoffrey. "But Walter was there, too. Did he see nothing?" Or did he commit murder was his unspoken thought, recalling the moved chest.

"When I woke, I tried to rouse you, but you were slumbering too deeply," said Walter. "Quietly, so as not to wake Godric, I came downstairs for breakfast. It was Bertrada who raised the alarm, when she took Godric his morning ale."

"Was our father dead when you left the room?" asked Geoffrey. "And did you move the chest?"

"Chest? What chest?" demanded Walter belligerently. "You keep talking about a chest, but the only box in Godric's room is the one at the end of the bed, and there was no need for me to move that. And of course father was alive when I left this morning. It was not *I* who drank so much that I lay insensible through his murder!"

That was not strictly true, Geoffrey knew. Walter had drunk a good deal the night before, and was virtually unconscious by the time Stephen had helped him stagger into the room.

"But did you actually look at father in the bed?" pressed Geoffrey. "Was he sleeping?"

"I have already told you," said Walter, becoming impatient. "I did not want to waken him early, so I left quietly. I did not go and poke at him—but since I would have heard anyone kill him in the night, of course he was still alive when I left."

"But you did not actually *see* that he was still living," insisted Geoffrey.

"What is this?" demanded Henry furiously. "Godric was

found dead after Walter had left him alone with Geoffrey. He was slain with Geoffrey's own knife, and we let him ask such questions of his innocent kin? Why, his guilt shines through every pore in his body! We should hang him now, and rid ourselves of a murderer!" He stepped towards Geoffrey, and drew a dagger from his belt.

As Geoffrey tried to pull free of Henry, alarmed at the extent to which the poison seemed to have sapped his strength, the Earl strode forward and pushed Henry away, sending him reeling with little more than a flick of his hand.

"You are quite wrong, Henry," he said. "Geoffrey's guilt is far from clear—yet. It is obvious that he drank himself insensible on the wine that was missing from your father's chamber, as any fool can see from the state of him now. But that in itself speaks of his innocence of the murder. He can barely walk, and I do not think he could have slain Godric while he was so incapacitated."

Geoffrey looked at Julian, wondering if she might announce that he was not drunk at all, but suffering from the effects of some insidious poison. But Julian had already decided whose side she would take in the battle between the brothers, and she said nothing.

"But who else could have done it?" Henry asked, still fingering his dagger. "And do you not think it a coincidence that Godric has been brutally murdered so soon after *Geoffrey* returned, and after *Geoffrey* spent the night alone with him?"

"But Geoffrey has spent other nights alone with Godric," Hedwise pointed out. "And anyway, last night they were not alone. Walter was with them."

Henry whirled around with murder in his eyes. "So now you want to blame Walter? How is it that you are suddenly so protective of Geoffrey? Is he more to you than just a brother-in-law?"

Geoffrey wondered what kind of supernatural being Henry imagined him to be, if he believed that Geoffrey could seduce his brother's wife and kill his father within the space of a few hours— and still manage to drink enough strong red wine to render a garrison insensible. A wave of sickness washed over him, and he held his breath, not wanting to throw up over the Earl's feet.

"What is clear is that someone would very much like me to believe that Sir Geoffrey is the culprit," said the Earl softly. "And I do not appreciate being misled. I do not appreciate it at all."

He looked at each member of the assembled Mappestone clan in turn, silencing their bickering every bit as effectively as a volley of arrows would have done.

"It seems to me that what has happened is this," the Earl continued. "Sir Geoffrey drank himself into oblivion, and then someone seized the opportunity to slip into Godric's chamber and kill the old man while Geoffrey was incapacitated. This someone seems to have selected Geoffrey's Arabian dagger so that he would be implicated."

"Geoffrey's dagger was selected, because it is Geoffrey who used it," said Henry sullenly.

"Really?" said the Earl silkily. "But perhaps it is *you* who is the culprit, Henry. After all, it was *you* who pointed out the dagger first, and you are clearly keen for me to allow you to hang Geoffrey as the killer. Is that because you do not want to give him time to prove his innocence and your guilt?"

Henry paled and made to answer, but apparently could think of nothing to say that would adequately refute the Earl's accusations.

"And you, Walter," said the Earl, swinging around to face him. "It seems that you cannot prove that Godric was not killed while you, too, were in his chamber. Who says that you did not slay him while Geoffrey lay insensible? Or even that your loyal wife, Bertrada, did not do it for you?"

"But what would we have to gain from that?" protested Bertrada. "Godric was dying anyway!"

"You are right," said the Earl, after a moment of consideration. "In which case, it must be that the plot simply aimed to hurt Geoffrey. I was right in my initial assumption—someone wants him accused of murder. Now, which of you might mean him harm?"

He looked around again. Walter and Stephen met his gaze; Henry did not. Bertrada fiddled with a loose thread on her gown, while Hedwise appeared bored by the entire business, and was staring into the distance. Joan glowered at Geoffrey, while behind her, Olivier fingered his moustache nervously. On the fringes, the Earl's knights, Malger and Drogo, exchanged meaningful glances.

"Which of you has something to lose?" asked the Earl, studying the Mappestones as a cat might watch a mouse. "I imagine that you all think you do. Did Sir Godric inform you that he had made a new will, and that he passed a copy to me for safe-keeping? Not that he distrusted you, of course."

"That new will can never stand up in a court of law," objected Bertrada. "It was made while the old man was far from well in mind or body!"

"Well, that does reflect rather poorly on me as a witness, then, does it not?" said the Earl sardonically. "Do you think I am incapable of making such a judgment?"

Bertrada swallowed hard, and was silent.

"Godric's new will is damaging for the greedy hopes of all his offspring," said the Earl smoothly. "He claimed that Walter is illegitimate, and that Stephen is the son of his brother Sigurd. Henry maintains that only a Mappestone born in England should have Goodrich—which Godric tells me Henry was not—so that rules him out. And that leaves only Geoffrey."

"No. It leaves me, too," said Joan briskly. "There are precedents in law for a woman to inherit, and I intend to exploit them."

"You are quite right," said the Earl. "And you made your case most prettily to me last night. But there is a factor that none of you have taken into account in all this."

"What?" demanded Henry, more roughly than was prudent with a man like the Earl. "We have debated this issue for years. I believe we have left no stone unturned."

"I am sure you do," replied the Earl sweetly. "But I made some enquiries about the relationship between your father and mother before they were married, and I discovered that they shared the same grandfather. Such a marriage cannot be considered sacred under the laws of God and the Church—consanguinity is a serious matter, you know, and kingdoms have fallen for less. Anyway, I applied to the Church to have Godric's marriage annulled—for the good of his soul and that of his wife."

He paused to look around at them, enjoying the stunned expressions on their faces. Geoffrey was certain that the souls of Godric and his wife were the last things on the Earl's mind. The Earl saw the doubt in his eyes, and gave the faintest of smiles before continuing.

"Quite by chance, the news that the Pope had agreed to the annulment came the day Godric himself summoned me on account of his claim that he was being poisoned by one of his family."

He paused again, aware that he had the undivided attention of his small audience.

"Godric was distressed by this information, of course, but he made another will immediately."

"But who could be his heir?" cried Stephen. "It seems we are now all his illegitimate offspring!"

"He did what many of my loyal subjects have done," said the Earl. "He left everything to me."

CHAPTER EIGHT

I f Geoffrey had not felt so dreadful, he would have laughed at the
expressions on the faces of his brothers and sister. All went from
shocked disbelief to cold fury within the space of a few moments.

"But we have seen this new will," said Walter, the first to recover himself sufficiently to speak. "It says that Godric has bequeathed everything to Geoffrey."

"To Godfrey," corrected Stephen. "In the service of the Duke
of Normandy."

The Earl raised querying eyebrows. "And who might this Godfrey be?"

"There is no such man," said Stephen. "It—"

"Then this other will is of no consequence," said the Earl dismissively "And it is quite irrelevant, anyway." He snapped his fingers
and his fat priest hurried forward. "Here is the will Godric made in my
presence, citing me as sole beneficiary. Would you like to read it?"

"Geoffrey will," said Walter, stepping forward and snatching the
parchment from the fat priest's damp fingers. He thrust it at Geoffrey,
and everyone waited. Geoffrey tried to make the black lines on the
parchment stay still long enough for him to read them, but they
wriggled and swirled and threatened to make him sick.

"I cannot," he said, dropping his head back onto his arms, and
letting the parchment flutter to the ground. Walter retrieved it, and
turned it this way and that helplessly.

"I thought he was literate," said the Earl, turning to Joan in surprise. "You told me that he could read and write in several languages."

"Enide always said he could," said Bertrada, "although I never saw any evidence of it myself. Perhaps he has been deceiving us all these years."

"Just like he has deceived us by hiring Ine to poison Godric," said Stephen bitterly.

"Are you accusing him of hiring a poisoner as well as stabbing Godric?" asked the Earl sternly. "I thought I had just told you that I do not appreciate people trying to mislead me. If you have evidence for your charges, then let me see it. If not, you will desist from your wild accusations."

Stephen was the first to look away from the Earl's piercing gaze.

"I have no evidence," he admitted. "But I have my suspicions. Geoffrey is a liar—you just saw that he cannot read when he has always pretended to us that he can. And he returned to Goodrich solely so that he could claim to be this Godfrey in the service of the Duke of Normandy."

"Of course he can read," snapped Joan. "Show them, Geoffrey!"

"Geoffrey thought *he* was this mythical Godfrey, did he?" asked the Earl, ignoring her. "Well, it does not matter that he cannot read for you. Your clerk will do that later. The will you hold is a copy, by the way: the original is safely in Shrewsbury. Now, I am sure you will not be so rash, nor so ungrateful for my protection all these years, as to hurt my feelings by contesting the will?"

"But what will we do?" asked Bertrada in a small voice. "Where will we go?"

"To Rwirdin, I suppose, if Sir Geoffrey will have you there," said the Earl. "What you do is really none of my concern, and I honestly do not care. But I want you out of my castle, and off my land within a week. I shall be back then to take possession, and I will deal harshly with anyone who is still here."

"But this cannot be happening!" cried Walter, still clutching the offending piece of paper. He leaned down and jerked Geoffrey's head up by the hair. "For God's sake, man! Read it before it is too late!"

The Earl made a hasty, crab-like movement to one side as Geoffrey's stomach protested against the sudden movement.

"Have a care, Walter," he said angrily. "He was almost sick over me, and these boots cost me a fortune. And whether he reads it or not will make no difference: it will say the same thing whoever reads it to you. The manor is mine. Now, let us not part on bad terms. I would like your congratulations on my new acquisition before I leave."

He stood, hands on hips, displaying the fine cut of his clothes, and waited.

"Do not make an enemy of a man like the Earl of Shrewsbury," said Geoffrey, squinting up at his brothers and sister. "Do you not know of his reputation?"

The Earl eyed him sharply, and then laughed. "Is that what they advised you last night? I wondered what Stephen was muttering about. So, it seems I have him, and not you, to thank for my Arabian daggers. In which case, you are still in my debt, Sir Geoffrey Mappestone. I would take the third dagger, but I think I will decline, given its recent use. I will claim something else in due course, when the fancy takes me."

If the Devil does not take you first, thought Geoffrey, wishing he had aimed a little more accurately at the Earl's expensive boots.

"I wish you well," muttered Walter bitterly, seeing that the Earl was not going to leave until he had his satisfaction. He gave a clumsy bow, and was away, tugging his wife behind him. One by one, the others followed suit, leaving to make their way back to the hall, presumably to engage in another of their violent discussions.

"And you, Sir Geoffrey? Will you not offer me your felicitations?" asked the Earl smoothly, leaning down to look Geoffrey in the eye.

"I wish you as much joy of Goodrich as it has brought me," said Geoffrey.

"That is ambiguous!" said the Earl, with arched eyebrows. "But I have come to expect as much from you." He coughed gently. "You realise, of course, that you owe me your life?"

"Really?" asked Geoffrey without conviction. "And how is that?"

"Despite what I said to Henry, you are still my prime suspect for the murder of Godric." When Geoffrey did not answer, the Earl continued. "Your pretence of drunkenness is nothing more than that—how can you be drunk, and yet not smell of the wine you consumed? But I saved you from Henry's vengeful hands anyway. You would have been kicking empty air by now, had I not intervened."

This was very possibly true, thought Geoffrey. "But unless you are prepared to settle for a book, or the dagger that murdered my father, I have nothing that would interest you," he said.

"There is always Rwirdin," said the Earl casually. "Of course, it is nothing like the prize of Goodrich and its castles and bridges, but it is well situated for hunting in the Forest of Dene, and it is a pretty place by all accounts."

"It seems you do not need my permission to take it," said Geoffrey, nodding to the copy of the will that Walter had hurled to the ground in a futile display of temper.

The Earl could always fake wills, as he had appeared to have done to secure possession of Godric's lands. Had the Earl also ordered one of his henchmen to slip up the stairs in the dead of night and slay the dying Godric too? After all, it would save him the inconvenience of returning later to present his claim, after Godric had died a natural death.

The Earl gazed at him with his beady eyes. "You are more astute than I gave you credit for. Yes, I will take Rwirdin if the fancy takes me. But I am inclined to let you keep it for a little while longer, for two reasons. First, I do not want your treacherous brothers and sisters hanging around my court claiming that they are homeless, and demanding that I take their brats into my household. And second, you were once in the service of the Duke of Normandy, and he is a man for whom I feel some kinship."

"I do not understand," said Geoffrey, wishing the Earl would leave, so he could lie down and sleep. "Why should my association with the Duke stay your hand?"

"There will be a time when the Duke will come to England to claim what King Henry has stolen from him—the crown. I have not yet decided whom I will support, but at this point in time, the Duke has a greater hold over my loyalties. You might well be here—the Duke will need every fighting man he can muster, because King Henry has grown powerful."

"You spared me from being hanged because you anticipate that I will fight for the Duke of Normandy against the King of England?" asked Geoffrey, stupefied by the convoluted logic.

"Put like that, it sounds a little crass," said the Earl, smiling. "But you have grasped the essence of my argument. Of course, should I decide to fight for King Henry, you will need to make another choice. But that is an issue for future discussion. What will you do now? Will you visit your manor at Rwirdin?"

"Rwirdin was Joan's dowry," said Geoffrey. "It is no longer mine."

"But Joan's possession of it is illegal, and would never stand up in a court of law. So, Sir Geoffrey, I am still your liege lord, and you had better expect to encounter me again. And, despite the little agreement we have just made, if you have not learned the folly of your insolent ways by then, I will kill you."

"If I do not kill you first," whispered Geoffrey to himself, watching the Earl stride across the courtyard to where his retinue awaited him.

'Sir Geoffrey!" cried Helbye, hurrying across the yard shortly after the Earl and his cavalcade had gone. "What is all this I hear about Sir Godric being dead and Walter being dispossessed? What will happen to the village if the Earl of Shrewsbury comes to Goodrich?" He stopped short when he saw Geoffrey, and knelt beside him in horror. "Lord save us, lad! What have they done to you?"

"They poisoned him," said Julian, appearing from nowhere. "Just like they did with Enide."

"Enide?" echoed Helbye. "My wife says she was beheaded, not poisoned. And who would want to poison Sir Geoffrey? You are out of your wits, boy!"

"They poisoned Enide too, just as they poisoned Sir Godric," insisted Julian. "She tried to find out who and why, and it was then that she was murdered."

"I feel dreadful, Will," mumbled Geoffrey.

For the first time, he truly believed his father's claims that some-one at the castle had been poisoning him. He could think of no reason—other than poison—that could be responsible for the way he felt at that moment. He put his head in his hands.

"Did you take much ale or wine last night?" asked Helbye, sitting back on his heels and regarding Geoffrey sympathetically.

"None at all," said Geoffrey. But that was not true, he recalled. He had drunk some of the wine Stephen had brought him before he had fallen asleep. He vividly recalled Stephen breaking the seal on the wine to offer it to him. But had he? What if the seal had already been broken and the poison already added? Was Stephen the poisoner, then? Or was the toxin contained within Hedwise's revolting broth, which Walter had insisted that he finish? Or perhaps the poisoner was Malger or Drogo, or even the Earl himself—who was reputed to be familiar with such potions. Thinking was making Geoffrey's head ache, and he rubbed it, longing for sleep.

"You must not sleep until you have seen the physician," said Julian firmly, trying without the least success to pull the knight to his feet. "We will go to see him now. He will make you feel better."

Helbye took Geoffrey's hand. "You are very cold—perhaps the lad is right. I saw the physician entering the house of Father Adrian on my way here. It is not far. Come on."

Helped by Helbye, Geoffrey staggered to his feet and made for the gatehouse. The ground tipped and swirled, and he felt inclined to sit again, but after a moment, the dizziness receded and he began to walk more steadily.

"Where are you going?" demanded Henry from the top of the stairs to the keep. "Fleeing the scene of your crime?"

Without a backwards glance, Geoffrey was past the gatehouse and down the steps leading to the barbican. The guards opened the wicket gate to let him pass, slamming it shut behind him. Once outside, Geoffrey slackened his pace, leaning against Helbye as his shaking legs threatened to deposit him in the mud of the village's main street.

The church was not far, and Geoffrey followed Julian slowly through the overgrown graveyard to the priest's house, a tiny structure set well away from the road and surrounded by neat vegetable plots. While Julian darted inside, Geoffrey let himself slide down the wall, all but exhausted after his efforts.

"Come inside," came a kindly voice. "The grass is wet and is no place for a sick man to be sitting."

"I am not sick," said Geoffrey, squinting up to see the young priest standing over him, clad in his threadbare black habit. "I was well enough yesterday."

"Well, come inside anyway," said Adrian, helping him to his feet. "You should rest."

"Those at the castle have poisoned him," announced Julian, leading the way into the priest's small but clean house.

"Really? Just as they are doing to his father, then," came another voice. It was Francis the physician, sitting at Adrian's table and enjoying a cup of ale. He stretched out a hand to feel Geoffrey's forehead, and frowned. "This is odd. You should be hot, not cold. And your lifebeat is sluggish when it should be faster. This is not the same poison that afflicted your father and Enide."

Geoffrey could think of nothing to say. Did that mean that there were two poisoners in his family, each with a supply of something deadly? Or perhaps it was only one person, experimenting with a different toxin when supplies of the first grew low?

"I suppose you did not think to bring a sample of what you ate and drank last night?" asked Francis, not overly hopeful. "What is that on your sleeve?"

Geoffrey looked at the pale brown stain, and recalled the dog knocking into him and spilling the soup and the wine. Impatient with his sluggishness, Francis grabbed his arm, and smelled the material cautiously.

"Ah!" he exclaimed with great satisfaction. "I thought so! Ergot!"

"Ergot," mused Geoffrey blearily. "The fungus called St. Anthony's fire?"

"Yes, indeed," said the physician, impressed. "Enide said you were a man of learning. I thought Godric might be suffering from ergot poisoning, since it can take many months to kill a man, but his limbs were healthy, and, as you will know, ergot causes the skin to die over time. But the concoction used on you was intended to have a more immediate effect." He pointed to Geoffrey's sleeve. "This is strong. No wonder you feel unwell!"

"But it is not the same poison as that used on my father?"

"The one used on Sir Godric is of a more insidious nature. I still cannot identify it, although I have laboured many nights with tests and experiments."

"Sir Godric is dead," Helbye informed him bluntly. "He was murdered last night."

Priest and physician gaped at him. "That cannot be true," said Francis eventually. "Why should someone want to kill Godric? He has only a few days left to him anyway. What happened?"

"He was stabbed with my dagger during the night," said Geoffrey, wondering if they, like his brothers, would immediately assume his guilt. "I was asleep in the same room, but heard nothing until awakened by my family this morning, and by then, my father was dead."

"I must attend his body," said Adrian, standing and beginning to collect together the items he would need to give last rites. "He died unshriven."

"The Earl of Shrewsbury's priest attended him before he died," said Geoffrey.

"How did the Earl know to send a priest?" Francis pounced. "Did the Earl slay Sir Godric, then? Those two have never seen eye to eye."

"Not so loud!" exclaimed Adrian in alarm, going to the window to look out. "The Earl does not like you, either. Now that Godric is dead, you will need to guard your tongue."

"No more than do you," retorted Francis. "But you have not answered my question, Sir Geoffrey. Do you know who killed poor Godric as he lay dying? Was it the Earl? Or did one of Godric's sons, or even that harpy, Joan, finally lose patience with their subtle poison and do away with him?"

Geoffrey shook his head, and then leaned his elbows on the table to hold it with both hands as his world buzzed and blackened at the sudden movement. "I have no idea," he said weakly.

"Do your business, physician," said Adrian, nodding towards Geoffrey. "Or you will lose another patient today."

"There is no danger of that," said Francis practically. "He has already survived the worst the poison can do, or he would not have woken at all this morning. I will make him a brew of pennyroyal, mint, and honey, and he must drink as much of it as he can, to wash the poison's residues from his body."

"Well, go on, then," said Adrian as the physician made no move to prepare the potion.

Francis stood, rummaging around in his ample collection of pouches for the herbs he wanted. There were so many of them that Geoffrey wondered whether he might be made ill a second time through a case of simple misidentification. Eventually, the physician set a large bowl in front of him.

"Drink this—all of it—and then sleep. By the time you wake, you will feel better. Probably."

He gathered up his pouches and strode from the room. Geoffrey looked doubtfully at the bowl in front of him, wondering whether Francis's brew might inadvertently complete the task where someone else had failed.

"Drink it," said Adrian, smiling at his hesitancy. "Francis would never harm Enide's favourite brother, and he is a good physician, despite his eccentric appearance."

"No, thank you," said Geoffrey, pushing the bowl away from him. He stood to leave, disgusted that he had allowed Julian to lead him into yet more potentially hostile territory.

"Then at least sleep here for a while," said Adrian. He raised his hands as Geoffrey began to object. "I will not force you to stay, but I imagine you will be very much safer in my house than at the castle. And your sergeant can watch over you, if that will make you feel more comfortable."

"If you will not listen to the physician, then take the advice of the priest," said Helbye, pushing Geoffrey towards a bed in an alcove at the back of the room. "And I will be here, Sir Geoffrey. I will not leave you to the mercy of that murderous brood up at the castle."

Geoffrey wanted to examine his father's body, to see if he might uncover some clues regarding the identity of his killer. And there was Rohese, too. Was she still buried in the dank depths of Godric's mattresses? If so, Geoffrey needed to talk to her, for surely she must have seen or heard something during the night. But he knew that he would never be able to walk up the hill again, and even if he did, he was in no state to do battle with Henry or one of the others if they refused to let him in. He sank down on the bed, thinking that a short doze might restore his strength, and was asleep before Helbye had finished fussing over the covers.

When he woke, it was dark, and he was aware of low voices coming from the people who were huddled around the table. Cautiously he raised his head, and saw Adrian, Francis, and Helbye deep in conversation. Julian, who had been sitting near Geoffrey, stood when she heard the rustle of straw from the bed.

Julian's movement attracted the attention of the others, and Helbye came towards him, his face anxious. Warily, Geoffrey sat up, relieved that the paralysing dizziness seemed to have gone and that the strength was back in his arms and legs. He stood.

"You deserve to feel atrocious for not taking the medicine that I so painstakingly prepared," admonished Francis severely, referring, Geoffrey assumed, to the casual way he had flung a few powders into the bowl of warm water. "But it seems you have recovered without it anyway. And I have more good news for you. I believe I can prove you were not your father's killer."

"I am grateful someone can," said Geoffrey, going to sit on the bench at the table next to Father Adrian. "How have you acquired this proof?"

"As a physician, I have access to a certain knowledge of the dead," began Francis, a touch pompously. "After I left you, I went immediately to inspect poor Sir Godric's corpse. None of your kinsmen had seen fit to lay it out in a decent manner, so I was able to inspect the scene of crime undisturbed, as it were. He was slain by a single wound to the stomach."

"But he was stabbed in the chest," objected Geoffrey. "I saw the knife there myself."

"Did you, now," said Francis thoughtfully. "Well, that clears something up, at least. As I was saying, the fatal wound was to his stomach. I imagine he would have died reasonably quickly from blood loss, but certainly not instantly. The knife, however, was embedded in his chest—as you yourself have attested."

"I do not understand," said Geoffrey.

He shook his head as Adrian offered him some ale. The priest took a deep draught from the beaker, and offered it a second time. Somewhat sheepishly, Geoffrey accepted, for his throat was dry and he was even more thirsty than he had been at times in the desert.

"How did the knife move from his stomach to his chest?"

"Well, it did not do it on its own," replied Francis facetiously. "The wound in the chest had been inflicted *after* Godric had died. I can tell such things by the amount of bleeding—wounds bleed little or not at all after death, and there was virtually no bleeding from the injury to Godric's chest, unlike the gash in his stomach."

"So someone killed my father with a fatal, but not immediately effective, wound in the stomach, and then stabbed him in the chest after he was dead?" asked Geoffrey doubtfully. "That does not sound very likely."

"Likely or not," said Francis haughtily, "that is how it happened. Now, the blood was still sticky although the body was cool. I estimate that Godric died sometime around dawn, or, more probably, a little earlier."

But that did not help Geoffrey very much at all, because it did not tell him whether his father had died before or after Walter had risen and left. If he had died after, then Walter was probably as innocent of the murder as was Geoffrey. But if he had died before, then there were three possibilities. First, Walter, like Geoffrey, was drugged in some way to make him sleep through it—although he had not seemed ill that morning; second, Walter had killed Godric while Geoffrey slept, and had left Bertrada to discover the corpse; or, third, Walter had not killed Godric, but was complicit in his murder at the hands of another. And, despite Francis's claim, Geoffrey could not see how the physician's evidence proved that Geoffrey was not responsible.

Francis appeared to read his mind, for he smiled, and leaned across to dilute Geoffrey's ale with water from a jug from which Julian had been drinking.

"Avoid wines and strong ales for a day or two—the body will need time to recover. But you are interested in proving your innocence in all this, I see. Very well, then. I am almost certain that the poison used on you was some kind of poppy powder mixed with a tiny amount of the juice of ergot. You were not given enough to kill you, although whether by design or chance, I cannot be certain."

"Chance would be my wager," said Helbye with conviction. "Someone does not want you at the castle, lad. Whoever poisoned you wanted you dead, not sick."

Geoffrey was thoughtful. Someone had gone to some trouble to ensure that his dagger was used to kill Godric, and that he was still in the room when the body was found. Was it because—as the Earl had claimed—someone had wanted him accused of his father's murder? Or was Helbye right, and the poisoner had actually wanted him dead? He sighed, not knowing what to think, or where to start looking for answers.

He turned to Francis. "Were the wound in Godric's stomach and the wound in his chest caused by the same implement?"

Francis's hitherto smug expression faded. "I did not think to look. How could I have forgotten to test for something so obvious?"

"No matter," said Geoffrey. "I can look myself." He drank more of the watered ale. "But you still have not explained your reasoning that the murderer was not me."

"Next to the hearth was an opened bottle of wine and an empty bowl. Both contained the unmistakable aroma of poppy and ergot. You have already told me that you consumed something before you slept and, judging from your condition when you came to me, you could not possibly have been in a fit state to kill Sir Godric before dawn. The poppy would have had an effect almost immediately, and you were still under the ergot's influence when you came here this morning."

Geoffrey did not consider Francis's logic to be without its flaws, especially since the bowl was empty because he had tipped Hedwise's broth down the garderobe shaft, and he certainly would not wish to hang his defence in a court of law on such a fragile thread. But at least it served to gain him another ally—two, if he included the priest Adrian, and, in a place like Goodrich, allies might mean the difference between life and death.

He rubbed his eyes, and tried to make some sense out of the evidence Francis had provided him. "So both the wine and the broth were treated with ergot?"

"Not just ergot," said Francis pedantically. "There was poppy powder, too."

"Why bother with two poisons?" asked Geoffrey. "It seems that the poppy powder would have served its purpose alone."

"There are a number of possibilities," said Francis. "Ergot in large quantities is fatal, but the poisoner probably did not want you wandering about the castle waking everyone as you died publicly—hence he or she added the poppy so that you would slip away quietly. Or perhaps each was the preferred compound of a different poisoner."

"You mean that two people at the castle tried independently to poison me last night?" queried Geoffrey incredulously. "I know I am not popular with my brothers and sisters, but I do not think anyone but Henry holds genuine murderous intentions."

"I think you overestimate your claim on your family's affections," said Adrian sombrely. "I heard in the village this morning that Godric presented a copy of his latest will to you, naming you as his sole beneficiary. You have been away, so you cannot know the importance to which the inheritance of Goodrich has soared among your brethren. Walter, Bertrada, Stephen, Henry, Olivier, and even Joan and Hedwise would not hesitate to kill to get Goodrich."

The priest's words were far from comforting, and it was with some gratitude that Geoffrey accepted Helbye's offer of a bed by his hearth that night. The knight huddled near the embers, twisted slightly to one side to avoid the drips that came through the roof from the rain outside, and thought about what he had learned. There was no question whatsoever in his mind now that Enide had been the victim of some foul plot, the prize of which was the inheritance of Goodrich. She had known about the documents that proved Walter's illegitimacy and that claimed Sigurd, not Godric, was the father of Stephen. The poachers Henry hanged had been innocent.

Godric claimed that Enide had burned the documents. Had she? Or had she kept them for some reason of her own? If the latter were true Geoffrey knew exactly where she would have hidden them, and resolved to look the following day. Was that why Adrian noticed that she had been distracted the morning of her death, or was her lack of concentration because she had arranged to meet someone—Caerdig perhaps? And why did someone poison her, but not fatally, if the intention was to secure her silence?

He rubbed his head, and took another sip of the water Helbye had left him. He was horrified at the notion that two members of his family would try independently to poison him the same night. After all, he had been to some pains to convince them that he did not want Goodrich. Of course, they had not believed him, and had even concocted some distorted story about him bribing Ine to return from the Holy Land to poison Godric.

Geoffrey frowned in the darkness. The physician had said that he had detected ergot in both the wine and the broth. Geoffrey tried to remember what little he knew about ergot. It was a fungus that poisoned crops, and prolonged or large doses caused gangrene. Godric had no gangrene, so did that mean that the person who had poisoned Godric was different from the person or persons who had poisoned Geoffrey?

A dim memory also told him that ergot was supposed to have a fishy flavour. The fish broth had certainly tasted fishy, and the smell had made him feel sick. But then, he recalled, so had the sip of wine that he had taken afterwards. So, had someone wanted him to take the poison sufficiently desperately to tamper with both broth and wine? Was it Stephen, who brought the bottle? Was it Hedwise, who made the broth? Was it Walter, who had insisted Geoffrey finish the broth or risk offending Hedwise? Or was it someone else, knowing that wine and broth would be taken to Geoffrey, and using Stephen, Hedwise, and Walter as innocent participants?

Geoffrey remembered Rohese. Perhaps she might have seen or heard something, assuming that she had remained in her hiding place, and had not emerged to kill Godric in his sleep. But that would mean that she probably also poisoned Geoffrey, and he was only too aware that she had had other, far more immediate, matters on her mind than taking the time to indulge in poisoning and murder. And in any case, if Rohese were going to poison anyone, it was far more likely that it would have been the Earl.

And how did the Earl fit into all this? Geoffrey could not imagine that Godric had made a will citing the evil Shrewsbury as sole beneficiary, and he did not believe that Godric would accept an annulment of his marriage without mentioning it to his children—it would have been exactly the kind of revelation he would have relished making. And if that were true, then the will that the Earl had flaunted earlier that day was a forgery.

Geoffrey shivered, and moved nearer the fire. Was King Henry right, and the Earl had taken part in the killing of King William Rufus for some dark purpose of his own? The Earl openly professed to be a supporter of the Duke of Normandy—as long as it worked to his advantage. Perhaps King Henry was right, and Shrewsbury was indeed aiming to consolidate his holdings on the Welsh border so that he could aid the Duke to take England.

He yawned. It was very late, and he sensed he would make no further sense from his thoughts that night. He drew the rough blanket round his shoulders and lay down, still watching the flickering flames.

During the night, it had rained hard, and the ground outside Helbye's house was thick with mud. Declining the sergeant's offer of company, Geoffrey walked up the hill and hammered on the gate to the barbican. The guard let him in, and watched him walk towards the inner gatehouse. It was still early, and the guard in charge there was still asleep. Thinking that *he* would never tolerate such laxness in a castle surrounded by hostile neighbours, Geoffrey scrambled over the wooden gate and dropped lightly down the other side. Malger had been right to put his own soldiers around the castle walls the night the Earl slept in Goodrich.

Geoffrey's dog appeared from nowhere, and came to snuffle round him, greedy for its breakfast. A little guiltily, for he had forgotten to feed it the day before, Geoffrey found a large soup bone in the kitchens. The dog wrapped slathering jaws around the stinking delicacy, narrowly missing Geoffrey's fingers, and slunk away to gorge itself in peace. Geoffrey was in the act of taking a piece of cheese from the pantry when he remembered the ergot, and decided against it.

"It is all right," said someone behind him, so close that it made him jump. "I had some of that last night, and I am still here."

At first, Geoffrey could not see from where the voice came, and thought that someone was playing a game with him. Either that, or the ergot had hallucinatory qualities that the physician had failed to mention. He bent to peer under the table.

"Julian? What are you doing there?"

The girl emerged slowly, her eyes red and puffy from crying, and went to cut Geoffrey some cheese. She sniffed wetly, and rubbed her nose on her hand before using it to pass Geoffrey the cheese. Geoffrey hesitated a moment before taking it, but supposed he had eaten far worse during his years as a soldier, and anyway, he was hungry. Julian disappeared into a storeroom, and reappeared with some stale bread and a pitcher of milk.

"Milk?" asked Geoffrey dubiously. "That is what children drink. Is there no ale?"

"I expect so," said Julian. "But it will be sour, and at least I know this cream cannot be poisoned, because I have just milked the cow myself."

That was enough to satisfy Geoffrey. He swallowed his prejudices along with the milk, and even decided it was preferable to sour ale, and certainly not so hard on a stomach still sore from the abuses of the previous day. The bread was gritty and made from cheap, poorly ground flour, but the cheese was surprisingly good—smooth, and yet with a pleasant, tart flavour.

"So, what is wrong?" Geoffrey asked of Julian as he ate. "Has Sir Olivier declined your services with his splendid war-horse again?"

Julian shot him a nasty look. "I cannot find my sister," she said. "I think they may have killed her and hidden away her body."

Geoffrey looked up sharply, slopping the milk over his leg. Realisation came slowly to him. "Oh, Lord," he said in horror, his breakfast forgotten. "Rohese?"

The girl nodded. "She was your father's chambermaid."

That was one way of putting it, thought Geoffrey. He abandoned the bread and cheese to the dog, which, having secreted the bone somewhere sufficiently foul for no other living thing to want it, was on the look out for something else. Geoffrey burst out of the kitchen and raced across the yard. Reaching the door to the keep, he slowed, opening it quietly. The servants still slept, or were beginning to wake, and were talking among themselves in sleepy voices. No one paid him any attention as he walked across the hall and ran up the stairs, Julian at his heels.

"Stay there," he ordered as he reached Godric's chamber, closing the door to keep her out. He did not want Julian to see what he was afraid he might find. He went to the bed and gazed in horror.

Godric still lay as he had done the previous day. Dry blood stained his nightshirt and the bedclothes, although Geoffrey's Arabian dagger had been removed, and lay on the bed next to the body. Geoffrey raised a shaking hand to his head. Until now, the death of Godric had seemed unreal, for his brief glimpse of the corpse the day before was only a hazy memory in his drugged mind. He had credited Walter and Stephen, and even Joan, with some degree of decency, and had not imagined that they would leave their father unattended for an entire day.

He took a deep breath, and forced anger to the back of his mind. His fury at his siblings could come later, but Rohese could not wait—assuming she had not suffocated already. He hauled up the mattress tentatively, half expecting to find yet another corpse to add to Goodrich's death toll. It was with considerable relief that he saw the bed was empty.

A loud sniff from outside reminded him that Julian was waiting. He covered Godric with a sheet and went to let her in.

"I thought she might be here," he said vaguely.

He rubbed the bridge of his nose. So, what did Rohese's disappearance tell him? That the Earl had found her after all, and had stolen her away while Geoffrey was lying in his drugged stupor? That she had fled the castle after killing his father? Or that she had simply hidden somewhere else until she was certain it was safe to come out?

"Rohese would not be in this room!" said Julian accusingly, her eyes brimming with tears. "They searched it at least twice when they were looking for her. You should know—you were here too, caring for your father!"

She began to weep, first silently, and then her voice rose to heart-wrenching sobs.

"Hush," said Geoffrey, embarrassed. "Someone will hear you."

"I do not care!"

At a loss to know how to comfort her, Geoffrey closed the door, and made her sit on the chest, handing her a piece of cloth in which to blow her nose. She took the cloth and wiped her eyes with it, and then ran her sleeve across her nose.

"She is dead!" Julian wept. "No one has seen her since *he* came!"

"Who? The Earl?"

Julian nodded miserably. Geoffrey looked down at her and wished he could offer the child the assurances she needed, but who knew what had gone on in Godric's chamber after Geoffrey had swallowed the poisoned broth? Or was it the wine that had done the damage?

"She probably found somewhere else to hide," he said, hoping he sounded more confident than he felt. "I know the Earl did not find her before I went to sleep, so perhaps he never found her at all."

Julian sniffed again, and looked at the bed. Her expression of grief turned to one of horror. "Is *he* still there?" she asked in a whisper. "I thought he would have been taken to the chapel by now."

"So did I," said Geoffrey. "I will take him this morning, but first—"

He was arrested in the act of removing the cover, to begin the process of preparing his father's body, by a sudden, terrified shriek from Julian.

"Whatever is the matter?" said Geoffrey, half-angry and half-alarmed by Julian's medley of unexpected noises.

"Do not lift that blanket!" pleaded Julian. "There is a corpse underneath it."

"I know," said Geoffrey dryly. "It is my father's."

"But he is dead!"

"Corpses usually are," said Geoffrey. He looked at the girl more closely. "What is the matter with you? Have you never seen a dead man before?" He had seen so many that the notion that a child might find one unnerving had failed to cross his mind.

Appalled, Julian shook her head. And then gave another scream, leaping from the chest and dashing to the opposite side of the room to stand cowering against the wall.

"Now what?" cried Geoffrey, bewildered. "Pull yourself together, Julian, for God's sake. My brothers will be here in a minute, thinking I am committing another murder!"

"This room is haunted!" whispered Julian, beginning to shake uncontrollably. "Sir Godric's ghost walks here!"

"Are you sure there was nothing wrong with that milk?" asked Geoffrey doubtfully. "Because something seems to have addled your wits. It is not—"

He broke off as a slight but unmistakable thump came from the chest. Taking his sword from a peg on the wall, where he had hung it two nights before, he stepped forward and flung open the lid.

Two hostile eyes greeted him, glowering out from among Godric's motley selection of mended shirts and well-patched cloaks.

"Mabel!" exclaimed Julian, startled.

"Of course it is me!" snapped Mabel, glaring at the girl. "Who else did you expect?"

"I thought you might be Sir Godric," said Julian in a small voice.

"Sir Godric is dead!" snapped Mabel, standing, and putting her hands on her ample hips. She was a large woman, well past the bloom of youth, and her thick golden hair was dull and coarse. Her skin, which might once have been soft, was tough looking and leathery from an outdoor life.

"Mabel, the dairymaid?" asked Geoffrey, searching distant memories for a youthful face that might have weathered into the one that glowered at him now.

"Mabel, the buttery-steward, actually," she replied tartly. "I have not been a dairymaid for many a year. And I will have you know that my butter and cheese is sought after as far away as Rosse."

"I trust you do not usually make them in the presence of corpses?" asked Geoffrey mildly, lowering his sword and regarding the angry woman steadily.

She flushed. "I came to lay him out," she said, waving a strong red arm at the bed.

"Then why were you in the chest?" asked Geoffrey. "Looking for a shroud?"

The woman held up her hand, and Geoffrey saw she held a sheet—grey from use and frayed in parts, but clean, nevertheless. "I brought one with me. I hid in the chest because I thought you were one of them—one of those others."

Geoffrey appreciated the sentiment, but her explanation still left many questions in his mind. He said nothing and waited.

"I see you do not believe me," she said, but not in a way that suggested she was particularly concerned. She pushed past him, and made for the bed. Julian leapt back with a cry.

"Foolish child!" said Mabel, although not without kindness. "There is nothing to fear. Come here and look. See how peaceful his face appears? No one can poison him now. Dear Sir Godric is far from the reach of his evil kinsmen at last."

Julian declined to look, and instead fixed her gaze on Geoffrey. "Mabel was your father's whore before Rohese became his chamber maid."

"I was not his whore!" objected Mabel loudly. "I was his companion. For years—ever since his wife died. I came to his chamber almost every night to . . ." She gestured expansively.

"Discuss cheese and butter?" asked Geoffrey, beginning to see the humorous side of the situation.

One of Enide's letters had mentioned that his father had a penchant for one of the dairymaids years before, and it seemed as though his affection had been a long-term proposition—until Mabel had been displaced in favour of the younger, and distinctly more attractive, Rohese.

Mabel glowered at him. "Sometimes we talked about dairy products," she said, arching her eyebrows haughtily. "Sir Godric was fond of my cheeses."

And so here was another potential killer, thought Geoffrey, his amusement fading: Mabel, the rejected lover of many years, who fed her master the cheeses he so liked. Had Godric been mistaken, and it had been Mabel, not his offspring, who had been slowly poisoning him?

Julian fled to the far side of the room when Mabel hauled away the sheet that Geoffrey had placed over Godric. On the floor, Geoffrey saw a bucket of clean water and some cloths.

"Did you bring those?" he asked, pointing to them.

"Of course I did," Mabel snapped. "How else am I supposed to wash his poor murdered corpse?"

"I still do not understand why you hid in the chest when we came," said Geoffrey. "If your intentions here are honourable, why should you feel the need to flee?"

"I told you," sighed Mabel. "I thought you were one of the others. They never did approve of the fondness your father entertained for me, and they would have thrown me out."

"What makes you think that I will not?"

"You at least covered him with a sheet, which is more in a few moments than that brood managed over an entire day. Anyway, they might have accused me of stealing his ring. And I do not have it. You can search me if you like," she added with a sway of her hips.

"Thank you, no," said Geoffrey hastily. "And if you refer to the ring that he wore on his right hand, Henry has it." He recalled vividly Henry wresting the ring from what he had believed to be Godric's corpse some days before.

"Has he, now?" said Mabel harshly. "I might have known! Sir Godric always said he wanted me to have that. But no matter. I want nothing from the Mappestones anyway. Come nightfall, I will be away, and I will never return to these parts again. There is nothing to keep me here now. One sister died in childbirth at the end of last summer, and the other died of an ague just a month ago. Her poor corpse was not left in peace, though. Walter said it was dogs, although around here, who knows?"

"Your sister's grave was desecrated?" said Geoffrey, bewildered by her wide-ranging monologue.

"I do not know about that, but it was disturbed, and it looked as though someone had been poking around in it a few days ago—since you returned, in fact."

"Well, it was not me," said Geoffrey firmly.

"Did I say it was?" demanded Mabel, hurling Godric's stained nightshirt on the floor at his feet. "But I have heard strange things about you—that you read books and make secret signs on scraps of parchment with inks. Master Helbye told me about it."

"It is called writing," said Geoffrey. "And literacy does not automatically lead to grave-robbing."

"I said nothing of grave-robbing," said Mabel belligerently. "I said that my sister's grave had been disturbed, but I did not dig it up to make sure she was still in it. Walter said he thought some dogs had scratched up the surface."

It was not an uncommon occurrence, especially if a family was poor, and unable to pay a grave-digger for a sufficiently deep hole.

"Or maybe it was that Earl of Shrewsbury," said Mabel darkly. "I have heard even worse things about the likes of him than of you.

It is said that he dabbles in the black arts, and he may have needed to rob a grave for some wicked spell he was casting."

"So, what will you do if you leave here?" asked Geoffrey, not wanting to pursue *that* topic of conversation when the castle was full of people who might inform the Earl that nasty things were being said about him. "Where will you go?"

"I have been offered the position as cheese-maker at Monmouth Castle, and I intend to leave as soon as Godric is laid out. My roof leaks and that miserly Walter will not pay to have it mended."

Geoffrey sat on the chest and watched her, while Julian wrapped her arms over her head and crouched against the wall, out of hearing and out of sight.

"You are fond of him still?" he asked, noting the gentle way in which her rough, red hands stripped the corpse of its bloodstained hose.

She sighed softly, and would not look at Geoffrey. "I will always be fond of Sir Godric," she said. "No one understood him like I did. And that Lady Enide was worst of all. She hated the arrangement I had with him."

"Enide did? Are you certain? I was led to believe she was the most understanding of them all when it came to his whores . . . I mean his companions."

He recalled Godric's pleasure as he recounted Enide's sympathy in his courting of Rohese, even giving up her own bedchamber so that Godric could seduce the girl in more conducive surroundings.

"She encouraged that Rohese all right," said Mabel, vigorously scrubbing at the blood that stained Godric's stomach. "But she made life so difficult for me that Sir Godric was obliged to tell me about the door. Oh!" Her hands flew to her mouth, and she gazed at Geoffrey in horror.

"What door?" asked Geoffrey, interested.

"No. Nothing. I mean window." Mabel was clearly no liar. Her belligerent manner dropped, and she became flustered.

"What door?" asked Geoffrey again.

"No!" said Mabel firmly. "I will not tell you. Sir Godric made me promise that I would never tell anyone about it. Especially one of you!"

"But Sir Godric is dead, Mabel," said Geoffrey. "And you might

be able to help me catch the person who killed him if you tell me
what you know."

"Do you think so?" asked Mabel, uncertain. She looked down
at the still features of Godric. "No. You are only trying to make me
give up my secret. You are not interested in his killer—you only
care about his wealth, just like the rest of them."

"I am very interested in who killed him," said Geoffrey softly.
"He was my father. And I do not care about his wealth."

Mabel regarded him long and hard. "That nice Sergeant Helbye
says you only returned to pay your respects to Sir Godric. And young
Barlow and Ingram have been telling everyone how you threw away
so many chances to go looting because you have no taste for killing."
She paused, and continued her searching look at his face. "All right,
I believe you."

"Good," said Geoffrey, leaning back against the wall and folding
his arms. "Then will you help me catch my father's murderer?"

"Oh, no," said Mabel. "That would be far too dangerous. But
I will tell you about me and Godric and Enide. That might help."

She cleared her throat importantly, and perched on the edge of
the bed. On the other side of the room, Julian pulled her hands from
her ears and listened.

'I took up with your father the summer after your mother died,"
Mabel began. "That was fifteen years ago now. All was well at first.
I think your brothers and sisters were just glad that I was able to
soothe his ill-temper from time to time. But about a year or so ago,
Enide began to object. She made life very difficult for us, and waited
for me on the stairs to prevent me from going to him, urging him
to take Rohese instead. In the end, Sir Godric told me about the
door, but he said I should never tell another Mappestone about it,
no matter what happened."

She paused, and Geoffrey could see she was already having second thoughts about breaking her trust.

"Why did Enide take against you after so many years?" he asked,
to distract her from her dilemma.

Mabel shrugged. "She said I was too indiscreet, and that Sir

Godric should take up with a woman who lived in the castle and who could come to him when he needed her, rather than having to send a servant to the village to fetch me. And my husband did not always approve of that, anyway," she added.

Geoffrey could see his point. Was that why Enide had been so accommodating over the business with the chambers, then? he wondered. To encourage Godric to make use of Rohese in the chamber opposite, rather than send for Mabel in the village?

"And the door?" he asked.

Mabel pursed her lips. "It was the only way I could get to him, but Sir Godric charged me never to come to him if there was anyone who might see me using it. He said word might get out to his neighbours that the keep of Goodrich Castle contained a secret entrance."

"Where is it?" asked Geoffrey.

Mabel hesitated yet again, gazing at Geoffrey's face as though she might be able to read there what were his true intentions. Finally, just when Geoffrey was beginning think he might have to think of better reasons to persuade her, she spoke.

"Come on, then. I will show you. Julian can wait outside while I do it, and make certain no one comes in and sees what we are doing."

When Julian hesitated, reluctant to miss out on something that sounded so intriguing, Mabel put her hands on her hips, and Geoffrey bundled the girl out of the chamber and closed the door. Mabel led the way into the garderobe passage, and poked around at a wood-pannelled wall behind some shelves at the far end, where Godric had kept a few gowns and some rusty pieces of armour. She gave a hard tug and, with a groan, the entire wall slid back to reveal a dark passageway. Geoffrey shuddered, and closed it.

"Is that all you are going to do?" Mabel asked angrily, opening it again. "I betray a trust made to a man who lies foully murdered, and all you do is give it a quick glance and shut the door?"

Geoffrey appreciated how it looked, but nothing, not even the most ferocious of battles, could evoke in him the blind terror that could a tunnel or a cave. He had once been supervising an under-mining operation while besieging a castle in France, and the whole structure had collapsed while he was still inside. He recalled every moment of the hours spent trapped in the tunnel, with water slowly rising and the air growing thinner and thinner, not knowing whether he would ever be rescued. The black slit in the thickness of the wall in Godric's garderobe held less appeal for him than an army of Mappestones.

"Where does it lead?" he asked.

"Go down it and see," said Mabel. "If you are afraid of the dark, here is a torch."

Several torches and kindling on a shelf just inside the tunnel suggested that Godric's secret door had been used relatively frequently.

"Who else knew of this?" Geoffrey asked, taking the kindling from her and replacing it before she could light it. "Besides you and my father?"

"Enide knew—long before I did. I suppose Sir Godric told her. But none of the others knew, as far as I am aware. Sir Godric tended to trust only her."

"But was there anyone outside the family who knew?" pressed Geoffrey. "One of the servants, maybe? Or Norbert the clerk?"

Mabel let out an explosive bark of laughter. "Of course not poor old Norbert! Sir Godric trusted him even less than he trusted his sons. I believe no one at the castle knew, but he did have visitors sometimes. Once or twice, Sir Godric sent me off early, and I saw others entering after me. I do not know who they were. Sir Godric was always very careful that they were not seen."

Geoffrey looked at the sinister passageway and swallowed hard. Godric might well have told Rohese about it, especially if he had seen that Geoffrey had been drugged, and would no longer be able to protect her. It was very possible his father's young whore was down there now, too frightened to leave, and he knew he should go to see. But the passageway would be too low for him to stand upright, and probably too narrow for him to walk without turning sideways. As he stood looking, he could feel the cold, damp breath of the tunnel oozing out around them, filling the garderobe passage with a rank, musty smell. He closed the door firmly.

"I will explore it later," he said vaguely. "It—"

He was interrupted by loud voices outside the bedroom door. Mabel scurried from the passage, and began laying out Godric again just as Henry burst in, followed by Walter and Stephen. Julian slipped in behind them, her eyes darting everywhere for evidence of Mabel's door. Geoffrey hoped the astute Stephen would not notice what the girl was doing.

"What have you been up to, all alone in here with father's corpse?" Henry demanded.

He strode forward, as though he would lay hold of Geoffrey to shake the truth out of him, but made a hasty diversion when he saw the effects of the poison had worn off, and that Geoffrey would certainly no longer accept any manhandling from his smaller brother.

"He is not alone," said Stephen, eyeing Mabel with amusement.

"Geoffrey! You should be ashamed of yourself!" cried Walter, aghast. "Seducing our father's whore while his corpse is barely cold."

"Excuse me!" said Mabel angrily. "What do you take me for? I am not for any man to take!"

"Well, Mabel," said Stephen pleasantly. "To what do we owe this pleasure? You vowed never to set foot in Goodrich after our father's preferences changed to younger women."

"I came to do for his poor corpse what you would not," said Mabel, scrubbing furiously. "Sir Godric and I had our good times and our bad ones, but I wanted to see him properly prepared for his funeral, and I knew you lot would not bother."

"You came to search for the ring you claim he promised you, more likely," said Joan, appearing suddenly in the doorway. "I looked for it myself, but someone had beaten me to it."

"Henry took it," said Stephen. "Before Godric was even dead."

"Liar," spat Henry. "I gave it back to him."

Geoffrey was sure he had not, and moved away from the bed and his bickering relatives. He sat by the ashes of the fire, and gave a sigh. His head began to ache, and he felt sick again, as always seemed to happen when he set foot in his father's chamber. He started suddenly, astounded at his sluggishness in putting together the facts that had been staring him in the face almost from the moment he had arrived at Goodrich. Godric had hired two food-tasters to assure him that no one was poisoning his meals, and the physician had found no poisons in what Godric had eaten. But the toxins were not in the food at all: they were in the room!

Geoffrey had heard of poisons being put in clothes and materials, and Godric's bed had always made Geoffrey cough and his eyes water. Had someone been placing some kind of poisonous powder in the bed, so that it would kill Godric as he lay in it, the poisons wafting into the air around him each time he moved—and the weaker Godric grew, the more he would be forced to stay in bed, and the longer the poison could work on him. That was it! Geoffrey grew more certain as he considered it. Geoffrey had been told that Godric had been confined to his bed around November, and had simultaneously taken a turn for the worse.

So, Geoffrey now knew something that the physician had been unable to deduce. He knew how his father had been poisoned when all the food had been carefully checked. He decided that he would ask the physician to see whether he could find traces of the poison in Godric's mattress. His elation subsided as quickly as it had arisen. He knew how Godric had been poisoned, but he still did not know who had done it. Julian came to sit next to him, sniffing and rubbing her nose against an already slimy sleeve.

"You look sick again," she said in a low voice. "Do not let on to Henry, or he will take advantage of it and kill you." She reached for the bottle of wine Stephen had given Geoffrey two nights before, and offered it to him. "Drink some of this. It might make you feel better."

"God's teeth, Julian!" muttered Geoffrey. "Do not give me that. It contains the poison that almost dispatched me the last time."

"It cannot," protested Julian. "The seal is not broken. How can it be poisoned if the seal is intact?"

Geoffrey stared down at the bottle. Julian was right. He looked around, but it was the only bottle in the room. It was, without doubt, one of the same kind that Stephen had brought him, and before Julian had picked it up, it had stood next to the bowl in which Hedwise had brought the broth. Geoffrey leaned over and picked up the bowl. It was clean: someone had washed it. Geoffrey frowned, and looked at the bowl and bottle thoughtfully. It seemed that the murderer was taking great care to cover his, or her, tracks.

CHAPTER NINE

Once Geoffrey's squabbling relatives had left Mabel to her business and she and Geoffrey were once more alone in Godric's chamber, Geoffrey went to examine his father's body. The wound in the stomach was small, although deep, and had penetrated an area that Geoffrey, who had seen many battle injuries, knew would be fatal because of the great veins there. But the wound to his chest was larger, and Geoffrey could come to no conclusion other than that it had been made by the one Arabian dagger that the Earl of Shrewsbury had declined to appropriate. The smaller wound, however, had not. Geoffrey made a search of the room, but could find no other weapon. He sat back and considered, watching as Mabel carefully combed Godric's hair and beard.

It seemed clear to Geoffrey that whoever had stabbed Godric in the stomach was probably not the same person who had knifed him in the chest after he had died—it was unlikely that someone would wait at the scene of the crime before attacking him a second time with a different knife—and the physician's evidence implied that the second injury had been inflicted later, after Godric had taken some time to die from the wound to his stomach.

So, was the person who had poisoned Geoffrey the same as the person who inflicted the fatal wound on Godric? Or did that honour go to the person who had stabbed the already-dead Godric after his death with Geoffrey's dagger?

Geoffrey rubbed his head, and then went to open a window, leaning out to inhale the fresh, cool air. As he leaned, he saw a deep, red stain on the outside wall that disappeared into a tapering tail on the grey stone. He inspected it closely. It was wine, and a good deal of it. Geoffrey could only suppose that it was the wine that had been in Godric's massive jug, and that someone had tipped the stuff out of the window to make it appear as though Geoffrey had drunk it before, after, or during the murder of his father. It was also possible that the ergot-tainted brew had gone the same way.

So, that explained one mystery, he thought with satisfaction, before returning his attention to the murder of Godric.

Geoffrey knew he had dragged the chest across the floor to the door, so that anyone entering the room would have made sufficient noise to awaken him—and he would have woken had he not been drugged when the killer had appeared to kill his father. Meanwhile, his dog, which would have growled at a night intruder, had been whisked away by Stephen. During the night, someone had moved the chest back to its usual position at the end of the bed. Was Walter responsible for that, lying when he claimed to have slept the whole night undisturbed? Or was he telling the truth, and had heard nothing?

But Walter would need to be an unnaturally deep sleeper not to have been awoken by the sound of the chest being moved. Geoffrey chewed his lip. But perhaps Walter was a man who could sleep through anything—he had not woken when Geoffrey had put the box there in the first place, and there was the fact that he had been very drunk.

Or was the culprit Stephen, who had brought drugged wine for Geoffrey to drink, and who had made sure the dog would not cause a disturbance by taking it to his own room for the night?

Or was the killer Hedwise, who had provided Geoffrey with the rank fish soup? Geoffrey rubbed his chin. Not Hedwise—the chest was heavy, and he doubted that a woman of her slight build would have had the strength to move it, at least not without considerable effort.

And who else knew about Godric's secret passage? Despite Mabel's claim that she was the only one in the castle who knew of its existence, Geoffrey was not so sure. He suspected that once he knew the answer to that question, he would have the solution to his father's murder. He looked around the gloomy room, wondering what he should do first. He supposed he should see to the safety of Rohese, and explore the passageway to see if she were hiding there. But even the thought of entering the slit of blackness brought him out in a cold sweat.

As soon as he had helped Mabel to wrap Godric in the grey sheet she had brought, he left her to complete the finishing touches to her handiwork, and poked his head around the room of the door opposite. This was the chamber that Enide had shared with Joan when Geoffrey had been a boy. He had assumed that Enide would have had it to herself once Joan had married Sir Olivier—although Godric had suggested that she had shared it with Rohese.

Geoffrey rubbed his chin thoughtfully. Bits of the mystery were beginning to fit together: Enide had occasionally slept in Godric's room—in Godric's bed—and she was said to have been poisoned, too. Therefore, it was the bed that had made both her and Godric sick. Geoffrey himself had only felt ill after he had spent some hours in Godric's chamber—after the insidious poison had been given enough time to work on him.

No one was in Enide's old room. Judging from the clothes that hung on pegs along the walls, Joan had reclaimed it, and was currently sharing it with Olivier. Geoffrey ducked back outside to the stairs, listened hard for a few moments, hearing the inevitable cacophony of raised voices in the hall, and felt reasonably confident that everyone else was otherwise engaged. Then he went back to Joan's room and softly closed the door.

He looked around. Godric had apparently been to work on Joan's room, too, because the walls were decorated with an aggressive swirl of greens and yellows. On closer inspection, Geoffrey saw that the design was a vine that sprouted vivid golden flowers and supported a veritable host of insects and birds. Joan—or someone—had made an attempt to hide some of the mural by adding new pegs for clothes, and one wall had been whitewashed. But Godric had intended his decorations to last, and the fanciful beasts could still be seen through the new paint, giving the impression that they were being observed through a heavy mist.

Realising that the longer he stayed, the more likely he was to be caught red-handed snooping in Joan's chamber, Geoffrey went quickly to the bed. Making as little noise as possible, he heaved the straw mattresses away to reveal the bare stones behind. He crouched down, and began to poke about with his dagger. Many years ago, he and Enide had prised a stone out of the wall when they had been bored and restless one winter afternoon, and behind it they had hidden their treasures—small, childish things that they did not want Henry to steal.

Geoffrey smiled when he saw that no attempt had been made to seal up the hole again, and that the stone slipped out as easily as it had so many years before. The gathering of dust on the floor in front of it suggested that it had not been used for some time, and he began to think that he might have been wrong after all, and that Enide had discovered some new hiding place for her secret things.

He lay flat on the floor, and thrust his hand into the hole as far as it would go. He grimaced in disgust when a dead mouse was the first thing his fingers encountered, but then he felt something else—something that had the unmistakable crackle of parchment. Carefully, he drew it out, and then groped in the hole again, this time discovering a small leather pouch. When he was satisfied that there was nothing else, he slid the stone into its place, and shoved the mattresses back against the wall again. Slipping his findings—other than the mouse—down inside his shirt, he opened the door a crack, and listened carefully.

Voices were still raised in bitter dispute in the hall, some of them almost screaming. The debate was sufficiently loud that Geoffrey did not hear the soft step of a leather shoe on the stairs below. He was just closing Joan's door behind him, when he came face to face with Hedwise.

"Sir Geoffrey!" she exclaimed, smiling impishly. "Were you looking for something particular among your sister's belongings?"

"Nothing particular, no," he replied, angry with himself at being caught after all his precautions. "But my father told me that I should admire the wall-paintings in Enide's room, and I thought I should view them before Joan hides them with whitewash."

"Yes, Joan does hate those murals," said Hedwise, still smiling mischievously. "Sir Godric was all set to decorate the hall with his version of the Battle of Hastings, but Joan would not let him."

That was probably a blessing, thought Geoffrey.

"Well," he said, making to step around her, "I think she was wise."

"I think so, too," said Hedwise, moving slightly so that Geoffrey was obliged to rub against her as he tried to slip past. "But what is this? What do you have here?"

One slender arm darted out to grab what Geoffrey had hidden in his shirt. He was quicker, and had caught her hand before she could pluck out the documents he had discovered.

"Hedwise!" Olivier's shocked voice echoed around the confines of the narrow stair well. "What are you doing?"

"I was just talking to the brother I have recently met," said Hedwise, turning her seraphic smile on the diminutive knight.

Olivier melted before her onslaught of charm, and grinned stupidly at her. Geoffrey made to walk away, but Hedwise quickly stepped in front of him again.

"Perhaps you will consider a walk with me in the meadows below the bailey," she said, smiling beguilingly at him. "It seems that the castle is always so full of arguing and fighting that we never have the chance for normal conversation."

"Good idea," said Olivier immediately. "I will just fetch my cloak."

Geoffrey rubbed his hand over his mouth to prevent Hedwise from seeing his amusement. "I have a lot to do," he said. "Enjoy your walk with Sir Olivier."

"If you do not come with us, I will tell Henry that you have stolen documents from Joan's room," she said in a low, careful voice. She gazed at him, and Geoffrey found himself staring into a pair of hard blue eyes in which lurked no trace of the angelic quality they usually exuded.

"Tell him," said Geoffrey with a shrug. "But he will not be able to take them from me."

"He always said you were a brute," she said, pouting at him. "I was prepared to give you the benefit of the doubt, but it appears as though I should have trusted his judgment after all."

"Perhaps you should," said Geoffrey, shoving past her and making his way towards Godric's room.

Hedwise's ambiguous attitude toward her husband's determined

efforts to have Geoffrey hanged for murder made Geoffrey very uneasy. Goodrich Castle seemed to ooze an atmosphere of menace, and
Geoffrey, although not a man easily unsettled, felt vulnerable. He
pulled his boiled-leather leggings over his hose, and struggled into a
light chain-mail tunic—not the one that reached his knees, which
he used for travelling and battles, but one that might nevertheless
deflect a blade aimed at his back. Over this, he drew on his padded
surcoat, and buckled his sword to a belt at his waist.

Mabel sat next to Godric's body and watched him.

"That passageway is narrow," she said eventually. "You will
never get down it with all that on. You will get stuck."

Geoffrey was unable to prevent a shudder. "Where did you say
this tunnel comes out?" he asked, thinking that the entrance to the
other end might not be so hideous, and that he might yet avoid
entering the sinister black slit.

"Down by the trees near the river. But you will not find it unless
you know where to look. Godric could not have kept it a secret for
so long if its exit was obvious."

In his heart of hearts, Geoffrey knew this was true, and it was
becoming increasingly apparent that he was not going to be able to
escape exploring the tunnel. He wondered whether Julian might go,
but the girl had kicked up such a fuss when she had seen Godric's
corpse that Geoffrey was sure that she would be inconsolable if she
stumbled upon the body of her sister down there.

But Geoffrey had other things that he needed to do, and was
thus able to postpone the unpleasant task of investigating dank and
poky tunnels until later. He knew he should read the documents he
had found in Enide's hiding place, and he wanted to ask the physician
to test the bed for poison before the killer removed all traces of it—
just as he had with the fish-soup bowl that had been wiped clean,
and the bottle of wine that had replaced the one that Geoffrey had
sipped from. And Geoffrey knew that he should send a message to
the King, informing him that he had failed in his duty, and that the
Earl of Shrewsbury now had Goodrich manor to add to his domains.

With Enide's documents still tucked inside his shirt, he clattered
down the stairs intending to visit the physician first, and then to look
in the woods near the river to see if he could find Rohese—if she
had escaped the Earl by running away down the tunnel, the woods

at the other end seemed as good a place as any to start a search. He deliberately did not allow himself to admit that the tunnel itself was probably a better point to begin looking.

He reached the hall, and collided with a servant who was scurrying to carry a basket of bread to the trestle tables that were being set up for the mid-day meal. Geoffrey's dog made an appearance as the bread scattered, and by the time the agitated scullion had retrieved the food from the filthy rushes, the basket was considerably emptier than it had been.

"Geoffrey!" called Bertrada from the far end of the hall. "We are about to dine. I am sure you would like to join us."

Geoffrey was sure he would not, and gave an apologetic wave of his hand before striding towards the door. He was intercepted by Stephen, coming in from outside and bringing a brace of pheasants with him.

"My hunting hounds got these," he said proudly, slinging them onto a bench. As quick as lightning, Geoffrey snatched them up again, and his dog's expectant jaws snapped into thin air.

"I will take him with me next time I go," said Stephen admiringly, leaning down to ruffle the dog's thick fur. "He is quick and he learns fast. He would make an excellent hunter."

"But you would never benefit from it," said Geoffrey, handing the pheasants back to Stephen. "You would never see anything he caught, and it would be more than your life is worth to try to wrest it from him."

"Give him to me for a week," said Stephen, smiling a challenge. "I will prove you wrong."

Geoffrey had serious misgivings. He did not want the animal to acquire any further skills that would render it more difficult to control, and he was certain that Stephen would be unable to quench the hard spark of self-preservation and greed that guided the dog in all things. Stephen draped his arm around Geoffrey's shoulders in a friendly fashion, and gestured to the table at the far end of the hall.

"Please, eat with us," she said. "If the Earl was serious in his command for us to pack up and leave Goodrich in a few days, then this might be one of the last meals we have here together."

"No, thank you," said Geoffrey. "I have a great deal I need to do."

"Such as what?" asked Stephen. He eyed Geoffrey's chain-mail and surcoat. "Does this mean that you are thinking of leaving us?"

"I plan to leave as soon as I can," said Geoffrey.

"Then you should spare a few moments to dine with your family," said Bertrada, walking down the hall to take his arm. "You have scarcely seen us at our best since you returned, and we do not want you harbouring an unfavourable impression until you visit us again after another twenty years."

It was a little late for such concerns, but Geoffrey had questions he very much wanted to ask certain members of his family—such as whether Walter had heard anything during the night of Godric's murder and, if he could manage to do it discreetly, who were the people who might have access to ergot and poppy powder. Geoffrey yielded to the insistent tugging of Bertrada's hands on his arm, and followed her back down the hall.

The Mappestone family dined at the table near the hearth, at the end of the hall farthest from the door. As Godric's youngest son, Geoffrey's place had usually been far distant from the centre of power in the middle. This had suited Geoffrey well, for he had not wanted to be overly close to the irascible and unpredictable Godric, and being set apart from his siblings had meant that he and Enide had been left pretty much to their own devices and conversations.

But Bertrada had decided differently, and Geoffrey found himself placed between her and Walter in the seat of honour. He glanced at Henry, wondering how he would take such an affront to his dignity, but Henry merely met his eyes and then looked away. Geoffrey was immediately on his guard. They wanted something from him.

Walter passed him a tray containing lumps of undercooked meat, first spearing a piece for himself with his hunting knife. Geoffrey took a smaller portion, supposing that, unless the entire tray were poisoned, it would be safe to eat. The same was true of the bread, although Geoffrey was mildly concerned about the tumble it had taken in the lice-infested rushes that lay scattered on the floor.

While Walter fell upon his meat as though it were the last he would ever devour, Bertrada entertained Geoffrey. She told him about the successful harvest the previous year, and a little about the uneasy relations with the landlords whose estates bordered their own.

"It is all the doing of the Earl of Shrewsbury," said Henry, from where he sat farther down the table. "Before he came to power, relations were strained, but not so vicious."

"I do not think so," said Walter, gesticulating with his meat and splattering grease across the table. "He is trying to ensure that all the landowners in these parts unite with a common purpose, and so he wants them to be friends with each other, not enemies."

"And what might that purpose be?" asked Geoffrey. Defence against the Welsh, he wondered, or consolidating the border lands ready to fight for the Duke of Normandy against King Henry?

"It is not yet forty years since the Conqueror took England," said Stephen. "But despite all the castles he built and the fact that virtually all positions of power in the country are held by Normans, the kingdom remains uneasy. And it will do for a generation yet."

"But the problems of a kingdom are not concerns of ours," said Bertrada, bored. "What is our problem, of course, is the fact that we have lost Goodrich."

There was a silence, broken only by the sound of Walter's teeth cracking the bones on his piece of meat, followed by some furious slurping as he sucked the grease from his fingers.

"We need to consider what we should do about it," said Stephen. "I, for one, do not believe that the battle is completely lost yet."

He reached inside a pouch at his belt, and drew out a crumpled piece of parchment. It was the will that the Earl of Shrewsbury had presented to the startled Mappestones, claiming that he, and none of them, was Godric's heir. Stephen smoothed out the parchment, and then handed it to Geoffrey. Everyone—Walter, Bertrada, Stephen, Henry, Hedwise, Joan, and Olivier—watched intently.

Geoffrey took the parchment and read what was written there. It stated that Godric, as lord of various manors, was of sound mind and named the Earl of Shrewsbury as the sole successor to his estates, because his sons were the offspring of an annulled marriage. At the bottom of the writ was Godric's unmistakable sign—a Latin cross, representing a sword, surrounded by a circle—and the seals of the witnesses, who were the Earl himself and his knight Sir Malger of Caen.

Geoffrey finished reading and looked up.

"Well?" asked Walter. "What does it say?"

"Exactly what Shrewsbury said it did," said Geoffrey. "It names him as the sole beneficiary of all Goodrich's estates and bears Godric Mappestone's mark. Surely you must have asked Norbert to read it to you?"

"Norbert has left us," said Stephen. "Since he clearly knew of this will, yet did not see fit to warn any of us about it, it seems he has decided to flee. He has not been seen since the Earl departed."

Geoffrey did not blame Norbert. It would not be pleasant to be faced with the scheming Shrewsbury on the one hand, and the thwarted greed of the Mappestones on the other. He wished he had joined the clerk and was even now riding through the countryside on his destrier, miles away from Goodrich and its murderers and squabblers.

"But is the will a forgery?" demanded Henry.

Geoffrey shrugged. "I could not possibly say. What do you think? You must have seen Father make his mark many times. Does it look genuine to you?"

Stephen snatched the parchment back and all three brothers pored over it before giving their considered opinions: Henry thought it was forged; Walter believed it to be genuine; and Stephen was not prepared to say.

"You should think about the timing of all this, though," said Geoffrey, musing as he speared another piece of meat with his dagger.

He lifted his goblet to his lips, but then set it down again, untouched. While he could be reasonably certain that the meat was probably untainted—everyone without exception had taken a piece and eaten it before Geoffrey had touched his—he was not so sure about the wine.

He leaned back, thinking. "Our father sent a message to the Earl of Shrewsbury a few weeks ago to say that he was being poisoned, and that he thought the culprit was one of you."

"Vicious, evil lies!" spat Bertrada.

"The Earl duly arrived," Geoffrey went on, ignoring her, "and Father seems to have regaled him with information about the question of Walter's legitimacy and Stephen's paternity."

Walter rose to his feet. "I will hear none of this at my table—"

Henry sneered. "It is not your table and it never will be. I have the better claim—"

"If we do not put aside our differences and listen to Geoffrey, none of us will have a claim," snapped Stephen, his voice uncharacteristically loud. "Sit down, Walter, and pay attention. Geoffrey, forgive us. Please continue."

"Father seems to have informed the Earl that neither Walter nor Stephen had a legitimate claim to Goodrich for various reasons. We know this because the Earl mentioned it himself. Father stated that he wanted to make a new will citing his heir as Godfrey in the service of the Duke of Normandy."

"You will never have Goodrich!" yelled Henry, leaping up with his dagger in his hand. "How can you listen to this, Stephen? He is thinking that he can secure our help to get Goodrich for himself!"

He made a threatening move towards Geoffrey, but stopped uncertainly when Geoffrey also rose to his feet, his hand on the hilt of his sword. Stephen imposed himself between them.

"If you cannot listen without interrupting, then leave us," he said sharply to Henry. "Time is running out. We have six days before the Earl comes to claim Goodrich, and I do not want to spend that time listening to you ranting and raving. You have nothing new to say!"

Henry's face flushed a deep red and he looked murderous. Joan intervened.

"Do sit down, Henry." She sighed, exasperated. "How can I eat with you glowering and squawking like a fiend from Hell? Carry on, Geoffrey. I am interested in what you have to say, even if Henry is not."

"Father said he made a will citing Godfrey as his heir," reiterated Geoffrey, sitting again and casting Henry a contemptuous look. "He said there were two copies. One he kept in the chest at the end of his bed—that was the one that Henry found and that Norbert read aloud to you all the day that Father pretended to be dead—and the other was placed in the safe-keeping of the Earl himself."

"But we know all this," said Stephen, when Geoffrey paused. "What is it that you have concluded from it?"

Geoffrey held up the parchment that proclaimed the Earl as heir. "Father could not read. Therefore, he would not know what he was signing, and only had it on trust that the will contained what he had dictated."

"Are you saying that the Earl simply substituted his own name for Godfrey's and Godric just signed it anyway?" asked Walter in disbelief.

"It is certainly a possibility," said Geoffrey. "How would Father know he was being misled? He could not read the thing himself."

"But Norbert was there," said Stephen promptly. "Norbert would have told him if the will had said that the Earl was to inherit, and not one of us."

"Would he?" asked Geoffrey. "Why?"

There was a silence as they tried to think of an answer. Geoffrey continued.

"Father did not trust Norbert, and has certainly not given him cause to be loyal. And you did not treat him kindly, either. I saw you push and yell at him when you called him to read the will Henry found. Norbert is a clerk, an educated man, and yet you deal with him like you would a scullion."

"So?" demanded Henry, uncomprehending. "He earned no better from us. All he ever did was hang around Will Helbye's wife and make a nuisance of himself."

"But my point is why should he risk the wrath of a man like Shrewsbury to tell people who have despised his talents for years that they are about to be disinherited? Why should he?"

"Norbert!" shouted Henry, rising yet again. "I will kill him! He has betrayed us!"

"And," Geoffrey went on, "you have just told me yourselves that Norbert has not been seen since the Earl left. Something of a coincidence, would you not agree? I did not read the will that Henry found in Godric's chest the day he pretended to die, because you did not let me see it. Who knows what it really said—or whether Norbert even read what was really there?"

"He took a risk, then!" said Stephen. "Supposing we had given it to you—he would have been uncovered as a liar. You would have seen the name of the Earl and not Godfrey."

"But who would you have believed had I contradicted him?" asked Geoffrey, shrugging. "Your father's clerk of many years' standing, or me, who none of you trust?"

"You have a point," said Bertrada. "We would not have believed you over Norbert. I would have assumed that you were lying to get possession of the will—to run off to a court to state your claim before we could contest it."

"And if you recall, Norbert was very quick to come to Father's chamber after you called him," Geoffrey continued. "I thought it was because he was interested in eavesdropping on your quarrel for amusement, but I suspect it was because he was anxious about the will, and he wanted to hear what was happening regarding it. I assume none of you have the will? The last time I saw it, it was in Norbert's hands in Father's bedchamber."

There were several shaken heads.

"So, the will the Earl handed us is legal and not forged after all?" said Stephen, disappointment writ large on his face as he gazed at the parchment on the table.

Geoffrey shrugged. "The situation I have just outlined is only one of several possibilities. Another is that Norbert is innocent in all this, and that Father really did make a will naming Godfrey as his heir. And Father told me that Norbert did not write the will, but that the Earl's priest was the scribe. Watch."

He drew a quill and ink from the pouch at his side, and began to draw on the wooden table. The others crowded in on him, jostling to see what he was doing. Carefully, he copied Godric's mark, making it identical to the one on the will.

"What is this?" cried Walter, aghast. "Are you a forger now?"

"I wish we had known this before," said Joan, inspecting the two marks closely. "Such a talent in the family might have come in useful."

"What is your point, Geoff?" asked Stephen. "What do these marks prove?"

"That the Earl's scribe might have written two wills stating that Father's heir was to be Godfrey. Then father would have added his mark to the bottom of each of them after Norbert had read them through to ensure all was correct—the Earl kept one and Father kept the other. At a later stage, the Earl's scribe might have made yet *another* will, stating that the heir was the Earl himself, and simply copied Father's mark onto it, just as I have done. While handwriting is distinctive and can be difficult to copy, a simple sign like this one is easy enough, as I have just shown."

"This is dreadful," cried Walter. "You are saying that either the Earl has made out an entirely new will and has had his clerk forge Godric's mark at the end of it, or he deceived a man on his deathbed to sign something he did not intend."

"Does that sound so out of keeping with Shrewsbury's character?" asked Geoffrey. "From what I hear of the great Earl, this shows him acting with great chivalry. He could have ridden in, slaughtered the lot of you, and had Goodrich anyway."

"Not the Earl!" cried Olivier, taking part in the conversation for the first time. "He is a man of honour and integrity!"

Everyone gazed at him in astonishment, and then turned their attention back to the will without bothering to comment. Geoffrey wondered whether they were being entirely prudent in discussing how the Earl could have committed forgery or deception in front of one of his kinsmen. Once again, Geoffrey vowed to complete his business at Goodrich as quickly as possible, and leave. He certainly intended to be on the road long before the Earl rode in to claim his ill-gotten gains—and that would leave him less than six days to uncover the identity of the killer of his father and sister.

"There is another possibility, too," said Stephen, picking up the parchment and tapping it against the table. "And that is that the Earl had *both* wills with him when he came visiting two nights ago. He said one of the reasons that he allowed Joan to persuade him to come was that he wanted to see Geoffrey, and I wonder whether he was undecided which of the wills he was planning to reveal."

"What do you mean?" demanded Henry. "None of what you have just said makes sense."

"I mean that the Earl would be taking a grave risk by openly forging a will, and the King watches him like a hawk for any such moves. It would have been safer for the Earl if he could have used Godric's real will—the one citing Godfrey as heir. The Earl wanted to know what kind of man Godric's youngest son was, and how long he would be staying before leaving again for the Holy Land. We all know that the Holy Land is a dangerous place, and I am sure Geoffrey would not have been allowed to leave Goodrich without making a will himself. And guess who the beneficiary would have been in the event of his death?"

"But even that would not have been necessary," said Joan thoughtfully. "The property of a man who dies without legal issue reverts to his liege lord—in our case, the Earl of Shrewsbury."

"But Geoffrey, although expressing a wish to return to the Holy Land, was not the malleable man for whom the Earl had hoped," said Stephen, nodding agreement.

"What?" snapped Henry. "Speak in words a man can understand, for God's sake."

"It was Geoffrey's insolence to the Earl that decided him on which will he was going to reveal," explained Stephen. "If Geoffrey had not been belligerent to the Earl, Goodrich would still be in the family—the Earl was forced to use the forged will, because he knew he would not be able to make Geoffrey do anything that he did not want to do—like make a will and leave Goodrich to him."

"Oh, well done, Geoffrey," said Walter wearily. "You have lost us our inheritance!"

"Just a minute," said Geoffrey, startled. "Goodrich still would not have been mine. All of you denied that I could be this Godfrey of Father's will."

"That was before," said Bertrada. "Circumstances have changed. It is better that Goodrich should fall to you than that greedy Earl. At least we can negotiate with you."

"Negotiate be damned!" spat Henry. "I will not parley over Goodrich with him!"

"You stand a far better chance of getting something from Geoffrey than you do from the Earl," said Hedwise. "So shut up and listen."

"All this is beginning to make sense," said Joan. "Except for one thing. You keep saying that *I* invited the Earl here. I can assure you that I did not. He paid me a visit while I was seeing to affairs at Rwirdin, and questioned me vigorously about our father's health and the time Geoffrey was expected back. Then he told me we would travel here together. His visit was no chance drop-in, but part of a planned itinerary."

Geoffrey escaped from the dinner table as soon as he could, and went to check on his horse in the stables. The castle buzzed with activity: the Mappestones, in a rare display of cooperation, had agreed upon a plan to try to see what might be done to prevent the Earl from seizing their inheritance. It had been decided that Henry and Stephen were to take a message to the King, informing him that the Earl had seized Goodrich, and Hedwise was to ask a relative in the service of the Abbot of Glowecestre, whether the Earl really had lodged a claim to annul Godric's marriage on the grounds of consanguinity.

Meanwhile, Bertrada and Joan were to continue packing to be ready to leave should the King fail to come up with a solution, and the Earl arrived to take possession of Goodrich. Walter was to arrange Godric's funeral and then hunt for Norbert—to determine from the clerk whether the will was forged. And although nothing was said, Olivier, being a relative of the Earl, was not to do anything. He was even prevented from visiting the stables with Geoffrey, lest he sneak out and inform the Earl that plans were afoot to thwart him.

Geoffrey was free to do as he pleased, although, as only Joan had been bold enough to say, it would not be taken kindly if he were to leave, because without Geoffrey how could the Mappestone claim to Goodrich stand? Geoffrey agreed to stay for another six days, although he determined that he would not be there to greet the Earl. He smiled to himself, grimly amused that whereas only a few hours before, each and every one of his family had been desperate for him to leave, now they could not afford to let him go.

In the stables, Julian assured him that she had taken good care of the destrier, and he asked her to walk the animal around the outer ward a few times—partly to exercise the horse, but mostly to prevent her from spending the afternoon weeping over the missing Rohese.

Julian sniffed and snuffled, grateful to be entrusted with such a task, but clearly fretting over her sister.

"But if you are going out, you will need your horse," called Julian, as he strode away to visit the physician.

"I am only going to the village," Geoffrey replied. "There is no need for a horse."

"You are a funny kind of knight," said Julian, eyeing him doubtfully. "Sir Olivier would never leave the inner ward on foot. He says walking is undignified."

"All knights do not think the same way as Sir Olivier," said Geoffrey, although he suspected that a good number of them did.

He did not want a horse with him as he explored the woods. Firstly, and perhaps most importantly, the great destrier might do himself an injury on the uneven surfaces. And secondly, it would be impossible to take a horse into the kind of places Rohese might hide.

He left Julian and strode out of the barbican. It was early afternoon, and a pleasant day for January. The sun shone from a cloudless sky, and the ground underfoot was hard with a light sprinkling of frost. His leather-soled boots skidded on the icy wood of the drawbridge that spanned the moat, and his sword accidentally bumped against the dog, which was trotting at his heels. With a yelp, it shot off down a path that cut parallel to the moat. Geoffrey sighed with exasperation, knowing that unless he found it, there would be livestock slaughtered and hell to pay. Reluctantly, he followed it.

The moat was a great, wide crevasse, which was hewn from the living rock to present a formidable barrier before any would-be attacker ever reached the palisade. In parts, refuse thrown from the castle and periods of rain had turned it into a morass of thick, evil-smelling muck. Geoffrey grimaced in distaste and hurried on, glancing up at the sturdy stone walls of the keep as he did so.

He stopped. In a great dark red triangle below Godric's window was the stain of the wine that someone had thrown out—so that it would appear that Geoffrey had drunk it. The mark was so large that it could only have come from the contents of Godric's huge jug. Glancing around to ensure that he was not being watched, Geoffrey scrambled down the steep side of the moat near the path, and picked his way across the marshy bottom to the other side.

He began to poke about among the weeds with his sword, searching for he knew not what. He found several items of discarded clothing that were brown and hard with age, and one or two of the paint pots that Godric had been using to despoil his room. Hidden deep in a patch of nettles was something metallic. Geoffrey bent to pick it up. It was a knife with a long thin blade, and a hilt that was worn smooth with use—and it was one that Geoffrey recognised instantly. It had belonged to Godric, who had claimed that he had been given it by the Conqueror himself, and it had been one of his most prized possessions. Geoffrey's brothers had squabbled over it when they mistakenly thought that Godric was dead. He wondered what had possessed the old man to toss it from his window, until he inspected it more closely and the answer became horribly clear.

Recent rains had washed the weapon, but under the hilt, traces remained of the blood that had stained it. Geoffrey recalled the small wound in Godric's stomach, and gazed down at the knife. Here, then, was the weapon that had inflicted the fatal wound on Godric. Someone had hurled it from the keep after he was dead, along with the wine. Geoffrey looked at it for a few more moments, before dropping it back where he had found it. He supposed he could have taken it back to the others, but could not be sure that they would not accuse him of stealing the stones out of it, or worse, of using it to kill Godric. He did not want to be found with it on his person.

He plodded his way back through the muck, and climbed up the rocky bank near the path. He was greeted by two friendly brown eyes and a wagging tail, as the dog wound energetically around his legs, interested in the smell of offal on his boots. He retraced his steps back to the drawbridge, and then walked into the village to visit the physician to ask him to test Godric's bed for traces of poison. Francis was not at home, and rather than waste the day waiting for him to return, Geoffrey left the main street and wandered towards the river, to the woods that stood behind the castle.

It was not long before he realised that Mabel had been right, and that his task was hopeless. Geoffrey explored every inch of the palisade that ran along the northern rim of the castle's outer ward, and found nothing. Godric had not intended for his fortress to have an easily breached back door, and so Geoffrey supposed that he should not be surprised. But he was disappointed, nevertheless, because he knew that if he did not find Rohese soon, he would have no alternative but to brave the tunnel.

When the shadows began to grow long and the sun sank in a great ball of orange, Geoffrey abandoned his search, and turned towards home. He was almost back on the path, when he tripped and stumbled over the partly hidden root of a tree. Swearing, he righted himself, only to come face to face with a quivering arrow embedded in a thick trunk inches from his face; it had missed him only because of his clumsiness.

He ducked back down among the bushes and listened intently. Somewhere off to his right, he heard the sound of a twig snapping as someone trod on it. He began to creep towards the sound, careful to keep his head below the bushes. He heard another noise, the rustle of footsteps in frosty leaves. He edged closer, his own progress all but silent. And then he glimpsed him—a man with a bow weaving in and out of the trees, moving cautiously. Abandoning stealth, Geoffrey was up and tearing through the undergrowth after him. The man partly turned, saw Geoffrey bearing down on him, and fled in the direction of the path that ran along the river-bank.

Geoffrey was not attired for racing through bushes. His surcoat flapped around his legs and snagged on branches. Also, his leggings and mail tunic were heavy, and weighed him down. His breath came in ragged gasps, but he was gaining on the bowman nevertheless. The man stopped and turned, bringing his bow up as he did so. The arrow, loosed more in the hope that it would slow Geoffrey down than to hit its mark, sped harmlessly to the left, and cost the archer valuable moments. Geoffrey could sense the panic in the man, who forced himself into a desperate spurt of speed as he neared the path.

Without breaking speed, Geoffrey ducked to the right as the arrow hissed past, and hurtled after him, knowing the would-be killer was almost within his grasp. He was close enough to see the man's breath billowing out of his mouth in the cold winter air.

And then disaster struck. A small donkey-drawn cart was already on the track, lumbering along it towards the village. The archer tore across its front to disappear into the bushes that lined the river, causing the donkey that drew it to buck in fright. Geoffrey, following fractionally later, went crashing into the side of the cart, toppling it and its driver over into the litter of dried leaves and dead twigs that lay along the river-bank. Geoffrey lost his footing, and his momentum took him flying head over heels to land sprawling in a frozen patch of mud on the other side.

His vision swirling from the tumble, Geoffrey hauled himself up onto his hands and knees just in time to see his quarry disappearing into the shrubs that grew profusely along that part of the river bank. Geoffrey tried to scramble to his feet, but his senses swam and he fell to his knees again. As he did so, the bowman glanced fearfully backwards, so that Geoffrey had a fleeting impression of his face, before he disappeared into the dense undergrowth that led to the water's edge. Geoffrey rubbed his eyes, trying to clear his vision, realising with a lurching disappointment that he had not seen enough to recognise who it was who had almost succeeded in killing him.

Trying to catch his breath, Geoffrey stood unsteadily, knowing that further pursuit of the archer was hopeless. Instead, he went to see whether he had harmed the driver of the cart. It lay on its side, one wheel bent, and the other lying in pieces next to it. The mule was trotting up the path, already some distance away. Sitting among the wreckage was the parish priest, rubbing his wrist and surveying the remains of his cart in shock.

"Oh, Lord!" muttered Geoffrey, torn between mounting a hunt for the archer and helping Father Adrian. "Are you hurt?"

Adrian shook his head and allowed Geoffrey to assist him to his feet. "But unfortunately, the same cannot be said for my cart. I doubt even the best blacksmith could repair that."

"I am sorry," said Geoffrey, genuinely contrite. "I will buy you another one."

"Will you, now?" asked Adrian, the hint of a smile playing about his eyes. "And what with? I hear you brought no booty home from the Holy Land, unlike your young men-at-arms."

"I have some books that I could sell," said Geoffrey defensively.

The priest shook his head, and laughed. "Never sell a book, Sir Geoffrey. They are not so easy to come by that they can be dispensed with so casually."

"I have an Arabian dagger, then," said Geoffrey. "Should your taste extend to murder weapons."

Adrian shuddered. "It does not. But never mind the cart—I was lucky it survived the winter, and I will not be needing it now that I hear Goodrich is to pass to the Earl of Shrewsbury. I doubt *he* will be requiring my services as parish priest."

"He has a priest of his own," said Geoffrey. "He acts as his scribe. Let me see your hand. Is it broken, do you think?"

"No," said Adrian, flexing it. "Although it might well have been, given the speed at which you hurled yourself from the woods. What were you doing? What if I had been an old woman or a small child, instead of a young and resilient priest?"

"I am sorry," said Geoffrey, a second time. "The man I was chasing fired an arrow at me. As you can imagine, I was keen to catch him and ask him why."

"An arrow?" echoed Adrian. He rubbed at the bristles on his chin. "Bows and arrows are not common around here, because we are in the King's forest. It will not have been one of Goodrich's villagers. Perhaps it was someone from Lann Martin, doing some illegal hunting."

"Caerdig told me that none of his villagers hunt," said Geoffrey, thinking about Aumary's death. "Do you know different?"

Adrian shook his head. "Not for certain, but it has been a long winter and food is scarce. It would not surprise me to know that some people transgress the King's laws and hunt for hares and fowl. I suppose it is even possible that Caerdig might not know about it."

"He cannot be a good leader," said Geoffrey, "if he does not know that his people break the law."

"He does well enough," said Adrian. He took a deep breath. "Help me move this wreckage off the path, or it will cause another mishap."

"Shall I fetch back your mule?" asked Geoffrey, watching the animal amble round a corner and disappear from view.

"It knows its way home," said Adrian. "But I am concerned about this archer. I hope this nasty incident will not herald the return of outlaws to the area. It is possible that rumours have already spread that Godric has died and that the Earl of Shrewsbury is to inherit, and the villains of the area are massing to take advantage of the chaos that is inevitable when one master takes over from another."

Geoffrey suspected that the archer's attempt to kill him had nothing to do with mere outlaws, and was more likely to be connected to one of the murderous occupants of the castle, but he did not want to discuss it with the priest.

He searched his memory yet again for some recognition of the face he had glimpsed so briefly, but the features remained shadowy and blurred. He was fairly certain it was not one of his brothers, since they all had good reason to want him alive. Was it one of the Earl's retinue—Malger, perhaps, or Drogo? Could it have been someone employed by his brothers—their truce was only a recent agreement, and perhaps news had not yet reached their hired assassins? He looked down the path after the mule, and rubbed his chin thoughtfully.

"What were you doing in the woods anyway?" asked Adrian. "It is almost dark."

Geoffrey saw no reason not to tell him. "I was looking for Rohese. She went into hiding the night the Earl favoured Goodrich with his presence, and has not been seen since."

"Poor child!" said Adrian, horrified. "I heard the Earl intended to have her, but that she could not be found. Do you think she might be in these woods? How could she have escaped from the castle?"

Geoffrey shrugged. "Perhaps she did not, but no one has seen her in it."

"Poor child," said Adrian again. "Can I help you look? It is growing dark, but there is light enough to see by yet."

"I do not think she is here," said Geoffrey. Not alive, anyway, he added to himself. "I will look in the castle again."

"You are kind to be so concerned," said Adrian. "Enide told me you had a good heart. No one else at the castle seems concerned for their father's whore."

"Chambermaid," corrected Geoffrey. He caught Adrian's eye and they smiled at each other.

"I was coming to the castle anyway," said Adrian. "I have had word that Godric is finally laid out in the chapel, and I wanted to say a mass for him."

Geoffrey was sure that Godric's black soul was in need of all the masses it could get, so he led Adrian along the path to the front of the castle, and hammered on the gates to be let in. The guards did not even break their conversation—something to do with pig breeding—to acknowledge them. Geoffrey was certain that their futures would be bleak indeed if they did not look more lively when the Earl came into power.

The castle chapel contained no Godric, and Geoffrey assumed that Walter had still not moved him out of his bedchamber. He wondered whether Godric's poor corpse would even manage to arrive at its own funeral, given the stately progress of the body to its grave so far. Meanwhile, the hall was deserted, and so Geoffrey led Adrian up the stairs to Godric's room.

Godric looked considerably more decent than he had that morning. The bedcovers had been straightened, and the body laid neatly on top of them. It was clean, too, and wrapped in Mabel's grey sheet. Coins were placed across the eyes to keep them closed—although Geoffrey wondered if they would be there the following morning if no vigil were kept—and two candles had been lit, one at the head and the other at the feet.

Meanwhile, Geoffrey still had not examined the documents that he had retrieved from Enide's old hiding place. He sat on a low bench in the garderobe passage, and pulled them from inside his shirt, listening with half an ear to the dull mutter of Adrian's prayers coming from the bedchamber. Since the passage was dark, he lit a candle.

Geoffrey looked at what lay in his hands. There were two documents, folded together and held in place by a small metal pin, and the leather pouch. He unfastened the pin, and inspected the parchments first. One was an itinerary of a journey Godric had taken around Normandy from January to April 1063 with the Conqueror. Geoffrey was bemused until he realised that Stephen had been born in the November of 1063. Here then was the alleged proof that Stephen was no son of Godric's, since Godric had been absent at the time that Stephen had been conceived. The second document stated that Godric had been married to Herleve of Bayeux in the spring of 1059, with a note scrawled across the bottom to say that one Walter Mappestone, a babe in arms, had been among the wedding guests.

Geoffrey had seen the spidery writing of these parchments be-fore—when he had received letters from Godric to ask for money and to inform him about Enide's death. It was a distinctive hand, with peculiarly formed vowels, and Geoffrey had no doubt what-soever that it belonged to his father's scribe. Geoffrey knew that Norbert had not been in Godric's service before Geoffrey had left. And that meant that the documents Geoffrey held had been written a good many years after the events in question, and could not possibly be genuine. In a nutshell, Norbert had forged them.

Further, it showed him that Enide had not destroyed these so-called incriminating documents as Godric had claimed. Geoffrey wondered what could have possessed her to keep them. Surely *she* had not been planning to stake a claim on Godric's inheritance and try to use them as evidence against her older brothers? Geoffrey could not imagine that any such plot had passed her mind. She had never written of it in her letters to him, and he felt sure she would have mentioned something of such significance.

He refolded the parchments and turned his attention to the pouch. Inside were more letters. Geoffrey looked closer. They were not so much letters as notes—short, concise missives that aimed to provide information rather than entertain. He held one close to the candle and read.

"Midnight on the fifth day of June 1100. Expect five."

Nonplussed, he read another.

"Midnight on the twenty-fifth night of July 1100. Everything is almost in readiness. Only details regarding horses left to manage."

And another.

"The first day of August at Brockenhurst. The evil is about to end."

He gazed at it blankly. Had Enide gone to Brockenhurst on the first of August for this meeting? he wondered. It would have been shortly before her death.

He scratched his head and pondered. These documents were not written in Norbert's spiky scrawl, but they were not in Enide's writing either. This was a confident roundhand that made use of an archaic form of the letter *T*. Were these messages written for Godric, who was not adverse to dabbling in subterfuge and secrecy from time to time? Or were they for one of the others—Stephen perhaps, who of the three brothers was easily the most cunning and devious? Or was Enide involved in something else? Geoffrey thought about the claim that she was being poisoned, before someone had come along early one morning and whipped her head from her shoulders. Had she died for these fragments of parchment and their sketchy, indecipherable scraps of information?

He leapt to his feet in alarm as he became aware that Father Adrian was standing over him.

"I have finished my prayers, Sir Geoffrey," said the priest, regarding Geoffrey curiously. "I called out to you, but you did not answer me."

"Sorry," said Geoffrey, stuffing the parchments back into the pouch. "I was reading some letters of Enide's."

"Enide?" asked Father Adrian, startled. "I do not think so!"

"What do you mean?" asked Geoffrey, wondering how the priest imagined *he* would know whether Enide had kept letters hidden away in a secret place, and resentful of his presumption.

"Enide never wrote letters," said Adrian. "She could not."

"What are you talking about?" demanded Geoffrey, bewildered. "She could read."

"She could read," agreed Adrian. "But she could not write. She had an accident—probably not long after you went to Normandy—and it left her right hand virtually paralysed. She could manage simple tasks with it, but never something like writing."

CHAPTER TEN

Geoffrey did not believe Father Adrian's claim that Enide had lost the use of her writing hand for an instant. He pushed past the priest to go back into Godric's bedchamber, annoyed that he had allowed himself to be caught reading what might be vital clues to the mystery. Adrian followed him.

"Many things must have changed since you left all those years ago," said the priest. "I suppose Enide's accident happened so long ago, and her family grew so used to her injury, that they came not to notice it any more. The same would have been true of me, but I tried to persuade her to learn to write with her other hand. It became something of a contest of wills." He smiled, perhaps more fondly than was appropriate for a priest reminiscing about one of his parishioners.

"You must be mistaken," said Geoffrey. "She wrote to me often after I left. And she mentioned no accident."

"She was proud," said Adrian, shrugging. "She did not like anyone to know that the accident had deprived her of the ability to perform certain functions—she could no longer sew, for example. And she certainly could not write."

"But I had letters from her several times a year," insisted Geoffrey. "You must be thinking of someone else."

"Do I seem like some doddering old fool who cannot tell the difference between women?" demanded Adrian, finally nettled into sharpness. "If you had letters from her, then she paid for someone else to write them—because, I assure you, she could not. Ask any of your family. Ask Francis the physician."

"What happened to her, then?" asked Geoffrey, still far from convinced.

Adrian shook his head. "The accident occurred many years before I came here. She told me that she had been picking plums in the churchyard and had fallen. She landed awkwardly, breaking the bones in her arm, so that her hand muscles no longer worked. She usually had it wrapped in a scarf or tucked inside her gown, but she showed it to me once, and it was withered into a claw, like this."

He hooked his fingers and splayed them out to show Geoffrey what he meant. He saw the knight's consternation, and patted him on the shoulder.

"It happened many years ago, and she said it gave her no pain. She probably did not mention it to you because she was sensitive about it, and she was fond of you. She would not have wanted you to consider of her maimed."

"I would never have thought such a thing," said Geoffrey, stung. "I thought we were friends."

"Then perhaps she did not tell you at the time because she did not want to worry you, or because she thought it would heal. And then, by the time she came to accept that her arm would be crippled permanently, it was too late. And why should she confide in you, anyway? You were absent for twenty years."

"But we often talked of my coming back in our letters," protested Geoffrey. "Especially early on, when we were still young."

"But you never came, did you?" said Adrian. He softened. "Look, I am sorry to have upset you. It is the second time I have spoken out of turn about her, it seems. I took you unawares about the nature of her death, too."

"I do not seem to know much about her life either," said Geoffrey, not without rancour. "Is there anything else about her that I should know? Was her face green? Did she play with the fairies at night? She was a woman, I take it, and not a man in disguise?"

"Sir Geoffrey!" admonished Adrian, shocked. "Not so bitter!" He smiled suddenly, almost wistfully. "Her face was pale and delicate, like a blossom. She did not dance with the fairies, although she danced with an elegance and energy I have never seen equalled. And I can assure you that she was most certainly a woman!''

"You seem very sure of that," said Geoffrey, his eyebrows raised.

"Just because I have sworn a vow of celibacy does not mean that I can no longer tell the difference between a man and a woman," said Adrian, his smile fading.

"She wrote to me . . ." Geoffrey hesitated. "Her letters mentioned that she had a lover. At first, I thought it was Caerdig, who later asked to marry her. But now I think it was you."

"Please!" exclaimed Adrian, turning away. "Think about what you say! I am a priest!"

"So?" asked Geoffrey. "Tell me the truth, Adrian!"

The priest refused to meet his eyes, and Geoffrey understood exactly why Enide had not mentioned the name of her lover in her letters. She could hardly tell her brother that she had fallen in love with the parish priest, who had sworn a vow of chastity.

"You loved her dearly, I see," Geoffrey said softly, watching the priest's inner struggle. "But someone killed her, Adrian! Tell me what you know and together, perhaps, we might catch her murderer."

"No!" said Adrian with sudden force. "That is *not* what she would have wanted—I have already told you that. You will only put yourself in danger if you persist with this, and it will do no good anyway, given the amount of time that has passed. One of the last things she said to me was that I should let her die peacefully and unavenged."

"So, she told you where she was to be buried, and she instructed you that no one was to avenge her death?" said Geoffrey, his stomach churning at the notion that his sister had so despaired of her hopeless situation that she had made ghoulish arrangements for her funeral and mourning. "She knew she was going to die, and you did nothing to save her?"

Tears glittered in Adrian's eyes, but he did not seem angered by Geoffrey's accusation. "She knew she was in some danger," he said in a low voice. "The morning of her death, as I have told you, she was anxious and restless, but she would not tell me why. If only she had confided in me, I might have been able to keep her safe."

"Probably not," said Geoffrey, using a more gentle tone as the priest turned away to hide his grief. "If she were anxious enough to be talking about her death to you, then she was probably in a greater danger than you would have been able to protect her from."

"Do you think so?" asked Adrian uncertainly, still with his back to Geoffrey. "But what was it? What could she have done or said that had landed her in such dire peril?"

"I hoped you might be able to tell me," said Geoffrey, thinking about the letters tucked down the inside of his shirt. "Did she meet anyone unusual, or leave the castle for any period of time?"

"She visited Monmouth last June," said Adrian. He wiped his eyes on his wide sleeve, and faced Geoffrey. "She said she wanted to purchase new rugs for Godric's chamber, but when she returned, she had forgotten to buy them."

"So, she went for some other reason, then," said Geoffrey. "Did she know anyone in Monmouth?"

"Possibly she did," said Adrian. "She was an intelligent woman, and people sought her out for advice. She may have met someone— at the Rosse market, for example—who lived in Monmouth. She told me that King Henry was at Monmouth when she visited— although he was not King then, of course. His brother Rufus was."

"Do you think she went to meet King Henry?" asked Geoffrey, startled.

"I would not imagine so," said Adrian, with a short, nervous laugh. "She had never met him before, and women do not simply arrive at the court and introduce themselves."

Unless they had something specific to tell, thought Geoffrey, wondering anew about the pieces of parchment in his surcoat. But he was allowing his imagination to run away with him. How could Enide have anything to say that would interest a prince? And how could she possibly have come by such information anyway, tucked away in Goodrich Castle all her life?

He looked at Adrian, who had slumped on the chest at the bottom of the bed, his hands dangling between his knees. Adrian had been kind to him when he was trying to overcome the unpleasant after-effects of his poisoning and, although Geoffrey knew better than to put too much faith in first impressions, the priest seemed to have been genuinely fond of Enide. Geoffrey decided to take a risk and show Adrian the scraps of parchment. The knight had little to lose, since his own investigations were taking him nowhere, but he might gain considerably if Adrian could throw some light on what the mysterious messages might mean. And if Adrian turned out to be not quite the simple priest that he claimed, then Geoffrey had only a few more days in Goodrich in which to be cautious. He, unlike Enide, was unlikely to allow himself to be caught unawares and have his head chopped off.

"Have you seen these before?" he asked, taking the scraps from his shirt and handing them to Adrian.

The priest rifled through them without much interest. "No. Why? Did they belong to Godric?"

"I do not know," said Geoffrey. "But I think Enide may have hidden them away for safe-keeping."

Adrian took the candle from Geoffrey, and inspected them again. "Times and dates," he mused. "Wait!" Geoffrey sat next to him, and looked at the parchment that had caught the priest's attention. "This one! 'Midnight on the fifth day of June 1100. Expect five.' That was the night before Enide left for Monmouth."

"How can you be sure?" asked Geoffrey. "It was a long time ago."

"Because the sixth of June was the Feast of Corpus Christi. It is one of the most important religious festivals in our Christian calendar," he added when Geoffrey looked a little blank. "Did the knights on God's holy Crusade not mark such an important occasion?"

"We may have done," said Geoffrey vaguely. Despite the acclaimed sanctity of their mission, religious celebrations were a long way from the minds of most Crusaders. There were monks and other holy men in the company, but they tended to keep their distance from the rabble of knights and soldiers who formed the bulk of their number. Meanwhile, Geoffrey's attention had been taken more by battles and fighting the more dangerous enemies of the desert—hunger, thirst, and disease—than with observing religious festivals.

"But what does the Feast of Corpus Christi have to do with Enide?" he asked.

"On the morning that our celebrations were to begin, Enide announced that she was leaving for Monmouth immediately."

"Just like that?" asked Geoffrey.

"Just like that," said Adrian. "It takes a good deal of work to organise these festivities, and it would have been pleasant to have had Enide's help and support. It is one of the most important days of the year for me, and I was hurt that she considered buying rugs for Godric more urgent."

"But she bought no rugs, you said," said Geoffrey.

"And that fact made her actions sufficiently odd to stick in my mind," said Adrian. "I am certain I am correct in my memory about the date."

"So, we are to assume that Enide met five people at midnight on the fifth day of June and left the following morning to go to Monmouth, abandoning her obligations to the village celebrations," said Geoffrey. "What could she have been doing?"

"The sixth day of June was two months before King William Rufus was killed," said Adrian.

Geoffrey gazed at him in disbelief. "What are you suggesting? That Enide killed him? A fine, loyal lover you make for her! Accusing her of regicide!"

Wordlessly Adrian held up another of the scraps of parchment. Geoffrey took it. " 'The first day of August 1100 at Brockenhurst. The evil is about to end,' " he read. "So?"

"Brockenhurst was Rufus's hunting lodge in the New Forest," said Adrian. "He was killed near it on the second of August."

Geoffrey looked down at the scrap of parchment again, but then stood abruptly. "This is ludicrous," he said impatiently. "I do not know why I am here listening to you. There are more important things I have to be doing. I need to find Rohese."

"Enide left Goodrich for a second time during the third week of July," said Adrian. "He held up the third scrap. I cannot be as certain of the dates this time, but this one reads 'Midnight on the twenty-fifth night of July 1100. Everything is almost in readiness. Only details regarding horses left to manage.' I think she attended this meeting before leaving for another—at Brockenhurst in the New Forest on the first day of August."

"Enide never went to the New Forest," cried Geoffrey, appalled by what the priest was implying. "What is wrong with you? I thought you cared for her!"

"So I do," said Adrian.

He sighed heavily and inspected the backs of his hands. When Geoffrey took a step towards the door to leave in disgust, Adrian began to speak again.

"She told me she was going to check your manor at Rwirdin when she left Goodrich in July, and that she would be there for a month or so. It so happened that I found myself in the area at about that time. No, that is not true. I deliberately sought out business nearby so that I could visit her there. A month seemed such a long time to be away from her."

"Well?" asked Geoffrey uneasily. "What happened?"

"She was not there," said Adrian. "And the steward said that he had not seen her that summer, and had been sent no word that she was coming. When Enide rode out of Goodrich Castle that morning in July, she never had any intention of visiting Rwirdin."

"This is all gross speculation," said Geoffrey, pacing up and down. "Perhaps she had another lover—Caerdig, perhaps—with whom she wanted to spend time."

Adrian flinched. "That is what Godric said when I told him that Enide was not at Rwirdin," he said. "I was worried about her, you see. I was afraid she had been attacked on the roads, and harmed. But, in the middle of August, she came home."

"Did you ask her where she had been?"

"I did," said Adrian. "And it proved to be something of an unpleasant confrontation, actually. I told her I had been to Rwirdin to see her, and had found she was not there. She informed me that I was mistaken. When I insisted I was not, she told me I had either visited the wrong manor or that I was drunk."

"Do you drink?" asked Geoffrey, recalling other priests he had met who were seldom sober.

"I do not!" said Adrian indignantly. "I take only watered ale, and nothing stronger. Not only was I sober, but I have been to Rwirdin before, and know it well enough to be certain that I had visited the correct manor. I recognised the steward, anyway. But Enide would not admit that she had lied. She grew angry. She was not a woman normally given to rage, but, as I said, she was anxious and tense the few weeks before her death. She refused to admit that she had been anywhere but Rwirdin."

"But that is no reason to suppose it was Brockenhurst, where Rufus was killed," said Geoffrey.

Adrian played restlessly with the cord that was tied about his waist. "When someone you love lies to you and will not confide, you do not overlook it, you try to discover why."

"Tell me about it," said Geoffrey dryly, thinking of Enide's palsied hand.

"It was so with Enide," said Adrian. "I thought of little else. I tried to see a pattern in the dates that she was away, and I paid careful attention to whom she met and to whom she spoke."

"And?" asked Geoffrey. "What did your spying tell you?"

"Nothing at all," said Adrian, ignoring the jibe. "I thought she was just being careful not to let me see anything unusual. But these notes suggest that I should have been watching her at midnight, not during the daytime. I was a fool to think I could have bested her in such a matter."

"It would have been difficult to leave the castle at midnight," said Geoffrey, still not certain that his sister would have been making mysterious assignations with people in the dark. "The guards would not have let her out—or if they had, news that she had gone for some secret assignation in the small hours would have been all over the village by morning."

But Mabel had entered and left the castle unobserved, he thought, by using the secret passageway that came out by the river. And Enide had insisted that Godric use *her* room for his romps with his whore—perhaps not, as everyone had assumed, because she was keen for him to use Rohese rather than Mabel, but because she had wanted Godric's room so she could use the tunnel. Mabel had been Godric's whore for many years, and it made no sense that Enide had suddenly developed scruples about the fact that her father had a mistress in the village, rather than one more discreetly lodged inside the castle.

And the other business—Adrian's wild assumptions regarding a link between Enide and the killing of William Rufus? Geoffrey did not believe a word of it.

"Have you mentioned your suspicions to others?" he asked.

Adrian regarded him steadily. "I discussed some of it with Fran-

cis the physician after Enide became ill from the poison. Francis
believes that her poisoning and death were at the hands of one of
your brothers, who wanted her dead for their own reasons."

"Then I suggest we keep your theory about Rufus to ourselves
until we have more information," said Geoffrey. "If we go round
proclaiming that Enide shot Rufus with this withered hand you say
she had, we will probably be incarcerated as madmen."

"I did not say she shot him!" said Adrian quietly. "Quite the
reverse. I imagine she would try to prevent it."

"Well, whatever we think is irrelevant, because we have nothing
to back it up," said Geoffrey. He stuffed the parchments back inside
his shirt. "And these tell us very little, despite your association of
dates and times with the last months of Enide's life. They might have
had nothing to do with Enide. She might have hidden them away
to protect the identity of someone else."

But why had she hidden them at all, he wondered, when it
would have been so very much safer to have burned them?

The next evening, while his family discussed their plans to reclaim
Goodrich from the grasping fingers of the Earl of Shrewsbury, Geoffrey sat in Godric's room alone.

That day, Godric's body had at last been moved to the chapel,
and Geoffrey had asked that the bed be removed from the chamber
on the grounds that it made him sneeze. No one seemed particularly
surprised by the request, and no one had immediately offered to
burn it to rid themselves of incriminating evidence. Indeed, Walter
had even asked if he might have it for his own room, and had only
been dissuaded by Bertrada's firm conviction that she would never
rest easy in a bed on which a man had been murdered. The others
showed scant interest, and did not so much as glance up as two
servants hauled it across the hall to take it to a storeroom in the inner
ward. Geoffrey saw it safely installed in a shed, and sent Julian to ask
the physician to come and inspect it.

Then he had spent a fruitless afternoon riding out to a few of
the surrounding villages and hamlets that were scattered in glades
through the dense green of the forest, looking for Rohese. No one

admitted to seeing her, and all the hiding holes and haunts he remembered from his childhood—a cave near the river, the bole of a rotten oak, an outcrop of rocks near Coppet Hill—were abandoned, and no frightened runaway loitered there. Reluctantly, Geoffrey returned to the castle and headed for Godric's chamber.

Without the gigantic bed, the room felt empty. Geoffrey threw open the window shutters and sat on the chest for a few moments, looking around the dismal room that had been Godric's whole world for the past few weeks. Unable to put off the grim business of the tunnel any longer, he went to the garderobe passage, his heart already beginning to thump. He pulled at the shelves until the door slid open, and reached inside for the torch and kindling Mabel had pointed out, careful not to look into the tunnel's gaping maw. Recalling Mabel's warning that he would not fit down it wearing his armour, he removed his surcoat, but decided that if he could not squeeze through wearing his mail tunic, then he would not be going at all. Holding the torch aloft, he turned to face the black tunnel.

His nerve was already failing. The flame from the torch shook and wavered on the walls, and the slit of darkness looked about as appealing as a snake-pit. Perhaps Rohese had not escaped down it at all, he thought; and if she had, she would scarcely still be in it days later. He almost convinced himself that he did not have to go, but then there was the matter of Enide. This sinister corridor might hold the secret to her murder, and Geoffrey knew that if he did not explore it, he would spend, the rest of his life despising himself for his cowardice.

Taking a firm grip on the torch, Geoffrey took his first few steps down the passageway. Mabel had been right in that it was a tight fit. Geoffrey was too tall for it, and had to bend his head to prevent it from bumping against the roof. There was barely enough room for him to walk, even turned slightly sideways. His sword scraped along the wall, and was the only sound except for his unsteady breathing.

Cautiously, he edged along the passageway until he came to a steep flight of stairs. The torch was not bright enough to light what lay at the bottom, and it seemed to Geoffrey that the steps disappeared into a pit of nothingness. The air in the tunnel was still and damp, and Geoffrey began to imagine that it was also thin and stale. He started to cough, and only prevented himself from turning and racing back the way he had come by taking several deep breaths, closing his eyes tightly, and resting his head against the cold stone wall. In control of himself once more, he forced himself to take a step down, and then another. His leather-soled boots skidded in some slime on the third step, and he took the next few faster than he intended, coming to a small landing. Beyond, more stairs sloped away into the darkness.

Godric's bedchamber was on the keep's top floor, and Geoffrey tried to estimate how far he had descended as he walked. Below Godric's room was the hall, and below the hall were basements— large, dank rooms filled with bags of flour and barrels of water to be used should the castle ever come under siege. Geoffrey had the feeling that he had descended a good way past the storerooms before he reached the bottom of the stairs.

He was surprised that Godric had managed to have the stairs inserted without anyone knowing. Walter, Joan, and Stephen were all old enough to recall the great keep being built, and Geoffrey was curious that none of them had stumbled upon Godric's secret while playing around on the walls. But a closer inspection revealed that the stairs had been added later, and comprised roughly hewn blocks inserted into a vertical slit that ran parallel to the garderobe shaft, Despite his unease, Geoffrey smiled at Godric's cunning. His secret stairs had clearly been disguised during construction as a shaft that, to all intents and purposes, appeared like a sewage outlet running down the inside of the wall to drop into the moat. Of course, the slit descended a lot farther than the moat, and delved into the rock beneath the foundations.

At last, Geoffrey reached the bottom of the stairs, his legs aching from tension. He paused to wipe the sweat from his eyes and looked around. The tunnel changed abruptly from a neatly made passage with straight walls to an unevenly hewn cave, sloping downwards in what Geoffrey assumed to be the direction of the river. The rock underfoot became slick, and the walls glistened with moisture.

The tunnel walls and roof were of sandstone, a soft rock that Geoffrey knew from personal experience was prone to collapses. It had been a sandstone tunnel in which Geoffrey had been trapped in France. Here and there, small piles of dust and stones indicated where parts of the roof had fallen, and Geoffrey felt the strength drain from his limbs as he contemplated the possibility of a cave-in. He had written to Enide about his unnatural horror of dark, confined places, but could only assume that if she had made the same journey, then it was most certainly not a fear that she had shared.

As he scrambled over an especially large pile of rocks, the walls of the tunnel came close together as they snaked between two large boulders. Geoffrey squeezed between them, but the space was narrower than he thought, and he became wedged. With a show of strength made great by blind terror, Geoffrey ripped free of the confines of the walls, and shot forwards onto his hands and knees.

In front of him was a stout door. Geoffrey heaved a sigh of relief, aware that he had reached the end of the tunnel, and that he would soon be out. Warily, he listened at the door for a few moments, before taking the handle and hauling it open.

"Malger!" he exclaimed in astonishment.

Sir Malger of Caen, the Earl of Shrewsbury's chief henchman, looked up from where he knelt next to a prostrate figure on the ground. Seeing Geoffrey, he leapt to his feet, hauling his sword from his belt, and assumed a fighting stance. Grateful that he had not abandoned his chain-mail completely, Geoffrey drew his own sword, and met Malger's lunge with an ear-splitting clash of metal, dropping the flaming torch as he used both hands to parry the blow.

He sprung backwards as Malger lunged a second time, kicking out so that the other man lost his balance and stumbled against the wall. Before he had a chance to take advantage of Malger's vulnerability, a moving shadow seen out of the corner of his eye warned that there was someone behind him. Ducking instinctively, he span round as Drogo's sword whistled through the air above his head. While Drogo recovered from his wild swing, Geoffrey jabbed his own sword forwards, and succeeded in slicing through the chain-mail on Drogo's arm. Drogo let out a howl of pain and rage, and came at Geoffrey, wielding his sword around his head, and striking sparks as it grazed the ceiling.

Meanwhile, Malger had regained his balance, and was advancing. Geoffrey darted forwards when Drogo's sword was high in the air, and drove the knight hard up against the wall, before grabbing his arm and swinging him round to collide with the advancing Malger. Both men stumbled, but not before Drogo had seized a handful of Geoffrey's tunic to haul him down with them.

Aware that Malger was already drawing his dagger, Geoffrey scrabbled his way clear of the thrashing melee of arms and legs, pausing only to bite a hand that made a snatch at his throat. Drogo grasped his leg, and brought him crashing to the ground, while Malger was on his feet and was coming forwards at a crouch, dagger at the ready. Geoffrey's well-aimed swipe with his own sword sent it skittering from his hand, and drew a cry of pain from Malger. Drogo hurled himself forwards, pinning Geoffrey's legs under his heavy body, leaving the knight all but helpless as Malger advanced yet again.

But Geoffrey had faced worst odds in the Holy Land, and was determined that he was not going to be summarily dispatched by the henchmen of the Earl of Shrewsbury. He twisted violently, so that Drogo's grip loosened, and he was able to strike at Malger with his sword. Malger ducked backwards and Geoffrey brought the heavy hilt down square upon Drogo's helmeted head. The resounding clang made Geoffrey's arm ache, and Drogo went limp. Malger backed off farther as Geoffrey struggled out from under Drogo's inert body. Then Malger's arm flicked upwards, and Geoffrey was enveloped in a cloud of swirling dust.

Geoffrey flapped it out of his face, but it was in his eyes, blinding him, and catching at the back of his throat. He began to cough, straining to look with his smarting eyes to where Malger might be. A shadow moved to his left, and Geoffrey whipped round, painfully aware that he could barely see, and struck out wildly with his sword. There was a grunt, and then a thrown stone struck him hard on the chin. Reeling, he lunged again, stabbing with his dagger in one hand and his sword in the other.

"Leave him," shouted Malger as Drogo, thick skull quickly recovering from the stunning blow to the head, moved forwards again. Geoffrey leapt towards the voice, but his eyes were now stinging so much that he could not open them at all. Footsteps of someone running echoed briefly. Then there was the sound of a heavy door slamming, and all was silent.

Geoffrey groped his way to the wall, and slid into a sitting position, his eyes closed tightly and streaming. His instinct was to rub them, to rid them of the dust, but he knew from experience of desert storms that rubbing was likely to embed small particles in them, and make them worse. He sat blinking in the darkness, feeling tears course down his face, and hoping they were washing the dust away. He poked at his chin, where the rock had struck him, aware that, if it had been just a little higher, he might have lost some teeth. Geoffrey, unlike most men who had spent a lifetime fighting, was still in possession of a complete set of strong, white teeth, and he fully intended to keep it that way.

Eventually, the burning in his eyes lessened, and Geoffrey was able to open them and look around. Not that it did him any good, for Malger and Drogo had taken the torch with them, and Geoffrey had dropped his own when he was first attacked. It was pitch-black. As the realisation dawned on him that he was trapped in an underground cave in a darkness that was total, Geoffrey felt a familiar sensation of panic rising up inside him. His breath began to come in shallow gasps, and he felt as though he were suffocating.

He leaned back and clenched his hands tightly, forcing himself to take deep, long breaths, and trying to clear his mind of everything but his breathing, a technique to subdue his fear he had learned from a woman he met in the Holy Land. Gradually, the tightness in his chest eased, and the sense that he was being crushed by the weight of rock above faded. Once he had his breathing under control, he let himself relax, resting his hands on his knees, and leaning his head against the stone wall behind him.

It was not so bad, he told himself. The very worst that could happen was that he would have to climb back up the stairs again in the dark. But then the tunnel's narrowness would work to his advantage, because he could brace a hand on either side so he would not fall. Carefully, he clambered to his feet, thinking that he would feel around to see if he could find the torch he had dropped.

Still holding his sword, he began to prod about on the floor. His shuffling feet bumped against something soft, and he bent to put out a hand to feel it. Something flailed out and struck him, sending him sprawling before he realised what had happened. With a sickening clarity, he recalled that Malger had been kneeling over someone who lay prostrate on the ground. Even with Malger and Drogo gone, Geoffrey was still not alone.

Geoffrey sat in the blackness of the cavern, his ears ringing from the blow that had knocked him from his feet. He felt dizzy too, although whether that was from the punch or the disorienting effects of the darkness, he could not say.

"Who is there?" he called, knowing it was a stupid question, but short on other ideas.

"Get away!"

"Rohese?" he called, relieved as he recognised her voice.

"Leave me alone!"

"Rohese, it is Geoffrey. There is a torch on the floor. Help me find it, and then I will take you out of here. There is nothing to fear. Malger and Drogo have gone."

He was aware of someone moving around behind him, and he turned, looking about him blindly. Then all was silent.

"Rohese, listen to me. Julian is worried about you. Help me find the torch, and I will take you to her."

There was still no reply. Geoffrey thought he could probably wheedle and comfort all night long, but Rohese would not be easily convinced. He restarted a tentative search of the floor, keeping a careful ear out for any more tell-tale noises that might precede an attack. Eventually, after several collisions with the uneven walls of the cave, Geoffrey found the torch. He sat with it between his knees and struck a flint into the kindling he had brought.

The cave flared into light, and Geoffrey saw the terrified eyes of Rohese regarding him from the other side of it. He smiled reassuringly.

"See?" he said. "It is only me. Come. Julian will be pleased to see you."

He stood, and walked towards her, holding out his hand. She appeared to be frozen with fear, until the moment when he leaned down to help her to her feet. Then she shied away from him, and darted away to the other side of the cave. Geoffrey did not want to spend all night chasing Rohese across an underground cavern, and felt his patience wearing thin.

"Rohese," he said firmly, "you are quite safe now. The Earl has gone, and Julian is worried about you. You cannot stay here, so come with me."

"Please!" she whispered. "Do not kill me. I promise I will not tell!"

"Tell what?" he said, without thinking.

"I promise I will not tell that you killed him," she whispered.

"Killed who?" he asked, puzzled. "I have killed no one. Well, not in England, at least."

"Of course!" she said, nodding furiously. "I will tell them that you did not do it."

"Damn!" said Geoffrey as realisation of what she was talking about dawned on him. "I was hoping you might be able to help me, but now it appears you cannot."

"I can!" she cried. "I will! Only please do not kill me."

Geoffrey rubbed the bridge of his nose. "You think I am responsible for my father's murder. I can assure you, Rohese, I am not."

Rohese looked at him in confusion. "But who else could it have been?"

"Walter?" suggested Geoffrey. "Or someone who came into the room after I was asleep."

"Walter left," said Rohese. "It was not him."

"Did anyone else come in?" asked Geoffrey.

"I do not know," sobbed Rohese. "I fell asleep—it was warm inside those mattresses. But I heard you talking to Sir Godric before he died."

"When exactly?" asked Geoffrey.

Rohese gazed at him in mute terror. He perched on a rocky ledge, well away from her so she would not feel threatened, and spoke gently.

"Think, Rohese. I am hardly likely to murder my own father while you hid under the mattress, am I? And if I were, I would have killed you there and then. After I fell asleep, I spoke to no one until I was awoken the following morning with a bucket of cold water.

But tell me what you saw or heard, and we might be able to work out who did murder Godric."

"Joan came out of the garderobe after you slept—"

"Joan?" asked Geoffrey, startled. "But she was not in Godric's chamber."

"She was," insisted Rohese. "She must have come out of this passage."

"Yes," said Geoffrey, his thoughts whirling. "So she might."

So, Joan knew of the presence of the secret tunnel, too. Had Enide told her? Had Godric? Or had she discovered it by some other means? Geoffrey supposed that Joan was unlikely to be indulging in anything overtly sinister the night that Godric died with the Earl in the chamber below, and so she had probably been checking the passage to ensure Rohese had not hidden there—in which case, Rohese was lucky Joan had not caught Geoffrey hiding her between the mattresses.

And that, Geoffrey realised suddenly, was what Godric had meant when he had warned Geoffrey against letting Joan discover that he had played a role in hiding Rohese away. Godric must have known that Joan was in the garderobe passage searching for Rohese, because he would have seen her enter it and not come out again. Geoffrey rubbed his itching eyes. Godric might have warned Geoffrey and Rohese that Joan was nearby and likely to catch them. But, Geoffrey supposed, if Joan had emerged and caught him red-handed, then Godric would have had a highly entertaining scene to watch— yet another argument between two of his children. The wicked old man was probably hoping Joan would catch Geoffrey hiding poor Rohese.

"What happened after Joan came out of the garderobe passage?" he asked, starting to pace back and forth restlessly.

"She pushed the chest back from where you had put it near the door, and left. Then there was an almighty competition between you and Walter to see who could snore the loudest—"

"I do not snore!" said Geoffrey indignantly.

But he might have done, he thought, since he had been heavily drugged. And Walter was drunk: he had slept through Geoffrey moving the chest towards the door and Joan pushing it back again, and nothing had roused him until dawn the following day.

"Then he left, and—"

"Who left?" asked Geoffrey.

"Walter," said Rohese, as though it were obvious. "And then you and Sir Godric had this argument before . . ."

She trailed off. Geoffrey regarded her blankly. "None of this makes sense. Tell me again. After Walter and I were asleep, Joan came out of the garderobe passage, presumably having come through the hidden door, where she had been searching for you in the tunnel. She moved the chest from where I had put it against the door, to where it usually stood at the bottom of the bed. She then left. Correct?"

Rohese nodded, her eyes still wary, and fearful.

"Then Walter also left. How long after Joan had gone was this?"

Rohese swallowed. "I do not know. I fell asleep. But I think it was quite some time, because the fire had almost burned out. Walter was gone when I woke, but you still slept."

"Good," said Geoffrey. "Then what?"

"Then I grew uncomfortable under the mattresses. I thought I might never walk again if I did not stretch my legs. I climbed out, and began to walk around the room. Then I saw the door at the end of the garderobe passage. Joan must not have closed it properly when she left. I know now that you need to slam it hard to make it stay shut, and Joan obviously could not slam it if she wanted to sneak out of Sir Godric's chamber without waking you up. I think she *thought* she had closed it properly, but it came open later by mistake."

"Good," said Geoffrey again, appreciating her logic. "Did you know what this tunnel was, or where it went?"

Rohese nodded. "Enide mentioned it once. Although she would not say so, I think she liked to use Sir Godric's chamber from time to time so that she could slip out and see her lover."

"So you hid in this passage?"

"Not immediately. There was no need at first. The Earl seemed to have given up his search, and I thought I could just stay in Sir Godric's room until the next day."

"So what happened next?"

"I took a torch, and went to look at the passage—more for something to do than anything else. I had peeped under the window shutters, you see, and it was only just beginning to grow light outside. I did not want to go back to sleep, but it was too dark to do anything in Sir Godric's chamber."

"Then what?"

"As I was exploring, I heard voices. I thought it was you talking to Sir Godric. He was shouting with anger, and I was afraid he might wake the Earl and cause him to come to the chamber, where I would be discovered. It was then that I went back and closed the door."

"And what was my father saying?"

"I do not know," said Rohese. "I did not listen very carefully. Sir Godric is always angry about something or another, and it is usually something silly or boring. And once I was in the tunnel, I could not really hear anyway."

"But it was a man's voice that you heard, talking with him?" asked Geoffrey, thinking that he could at least eliminate Joan as a suspect for the murder—which would be a relief, for he suspected that out of all of them she might prove the most formidable in the end.

Rohese frowned. "It may have been a woman. Joan, Hedwise, and Bertrada often go to Sir Godric during the night. There would have been nothing odd in them being there."

"There is when my father claimed someone was poisoning him," said Geoffrey. "Why did they ever need to come anyway? I thought you were his . . . chambermaid," he said, selecting the term Julian had used.

"Not for the last few weeks," said Rohese. "Before he became ill, he would come to my chamber—Enide's chamber, I should say—and spend the night there. I hate that room of his, and Enide said I did not have to sleep there if I did not want to."

"And you heard nothing at all of this conversation between this person and my father?" said Geoffrey. "Not a single word?"

"Well, I might have heard a few," said Rohese vaguely. "But I did not really understand what they were talking about. I only listened so that I could hear when they had gone, and I would be able to come out again."

"Yes?" asked Geoffrey, his hopes rising. "What did you hear?"

"I cannot be certain. I think I heard Sir Godric say 'Tirel.' "

"Tirel?" asked Geoffrey. "You mean Walter Tirel?"

"Yes!" said Rohese, giving a faint smile. "Walter Tirel. That was it. Who is he?"

"The man who shot King William Rufus in the New Forest," said Geoffrey. His thoughts reeled. Was Adrian right after all? First, they found that the dates on Enide's hidden parchments corresponded to possible events connected with the murder of Rufus, and now the name of the murderer was mentioned in Godric's chamber by the person who seemed to have killed Godric himself.

Rohese sniffed. "Well, I do not know about things like that," she said. "But later, I think I heard someone say 'Norbert.' "

"Norbert?" asked Geoffrey. "Godric's scribe?"

"I do not know," said Rohese again. "You keep asking me questions, and I do not know the answers. I do not know whether they meant Norbert the scribe or another Norbert."

"Do you know another Norbert?"

She considered. "No. I suppose they must have meant Norbert the scribe, then."

"Is that all?" asked Geoffrey when she was silent. "You heard nothing more?"

"After a few moments, Sir Godric gave a great groan, and started muttering and moaning. I thought he must have made himself ill, perhaps with that vile wine he drinks. Eventually, when I was certain he was alone, I crept out, to see if I could help him, but there he was, lying in the bed and all covered in blood."

"And he was dead?"

"No," said Rohese. "He was not dead. He was groaning and crying and making fearful noises, and cursing and swearing. . . ."

Geoffrey could well imagine how the ill-tempered Godric would take his impending death. "Did he say anything to you?"

"Oh, yes," said Rohese. "He cursed you all—although he called you Godfrey, so you need not worry too much. He told me that I should go to the tunnel in the garderobe and stay there until I was sure it was safe to come out—he said they would kill me for certain if they knew I had been there. I am still not sure it is safe, so I am still here."

"Did he say who had killed him?" asked Geoffrey, knowing the question was useless because Rohese, apparently, had thought it was him.

As he had predicted, she shook her head. "He just said that there were dangerous men in the castle, and that I should never reveal to anyone that I had been listening in the garderobe passage the night he died."

Geoffrey sighed. Godric, with his desire to protect his whore, and by not mentioning the names of the dangerous men to her, had closed an avenue of investigation.

"I stayed with him until he died, and then I left."

"Did you look at the wound that killed him?"

"No," said Rohese, surprised by the question. "It was in his stomach, though."

So, Geoffrey thought, Godric had been stabbed in the stomach with his own dagger and had died. But who had come to his chamber later, after he was dead and after Rohese had left, and stabbed him a second time, on this occasion with Geoffrey's Arabian dagger and in his chest?

Certain things were clear though. Someone had planned his father's death with some care. Geoffrey stared at Rohese without really seeing her, trying to make some sense of the mass of information he had gathered. Someone had ensured that Walter and Geoffrey were drugged or drunk while Godric had been murdered, and that Geoffrey was still asleep the following morning to be discovered in a horribly compromising position with Godric's corpse.

Geoffrey rubbed one eye that was still sore from the dust. Rohese had said that Walter left the room before Godric was murdered. Walter had denied moving the chest to get out, and this was true, because, according to Rohese, Joan had moved it already. Walter claimed he rose early, and that Godric had still been alive. Rohese's evidence indicated that he was telling the truth.

However, while Rohese had explored the tunnel, someone had entered Godric's room and argued with him, after which Godric had been stabbed. The killer had then tipped the wine out of the window and followed it with the murder weapon. Rohese had emerged, and found Godric dying. Once he was dead, she had fled back to the tunnel, after which the killer, or yet another person, had entered Godric's chamber and stabbed the corpse a second time with Geoffrey's weapon. Was this to make Geoffrey appear guilty of the crime, or to make absolutely certain the old tyrant was dead? Godric had pretended to be dead the morning after Geoffrey had arrived, so that his youngest son would catch the others in the act of looting his corpse. With wily old Godric, it would certainly have paid to be certain.

He rubbed his eye harder. All he could deduce was that someone already inside the castle had murdered Godric, and that the culprit had not left via the tunnel *after* the crime because Rohese would certainly not be alive to tell the tale. And just because Walter had left the chamber before Godric was killed did not mean that he had not returned later to argue with and slay the old man.

Geoffrey thumped the rocky wall in frustration. He had a witness who had been awake and in the same chamber the night his father had been murdered, and yet she was able to tell him virtually nothing—even whether the voice of the killer was male or female.

"Did anyone else use the tunnel after you did?" he asked, certain that they had not because Rohese was still alive, but wanting to be thorough.

Rohese shook her head. "No one at all. I have been here all alone. Except for her."

"Her?" queried Geoffrey. He turned to where Rohese pointed, and promptly dropped the torch in shock, plunging all into darkness once again.

CHAPTER ELEVEN

G eoffrey's hands fumbled and shook, and he found himself unable to relight the torch. Rohese eased him out of the way.

"Let me do it," she said. "I am not afraid."

"I am not afraid, either," snapped Geoffrey. "Just shocked, that
is all."

"I was afraid at first," said Rohese, as if he had not spoken. "But
not any more. She cannot harm anyone, the poor creature."

Once again, the cave sprang into light. Geoffrey snatched the
torch from Rohese, and went to inspect the thing in the alcove.

It was, without doubt, the severed head of a woman. Geoffrey
fought to keep the torch steady, but he found he could not. He
swallowed hard, and looked at the leathery skin that stretched across
the skull like a mask and the gauzy hair that cascaded around it, and
searched for some sign that he was gazing into the face of Enide.

He raised a shaking hand to his mouth, and promptly turned
away. Adrian had told him that Enide's head had never been recovered: Geoffrey now knew that the reason was because someone had
hidden it in Godric's tunnel. Had Godric known it was here? Or
had it been put in its niche after Godric had been confined to his
bedchamber because poison was eating away at his innards?

He rubbed harder at his eye. Joan's role in Goodrich's sordid
affairs was beginning to look very suspicious: she knew about the
tunnel—and therefore also about Enide's head—and Rohese had

not been able to tell whether a man or a woman had argued with Godric before killing him. Also, severing a head from the shoulders with a sword was something a knight might do—a man such as her husband, Sir Olivier. And finally, it was Malger and Drogo, friends of Olivier, whom Geoffrey had fought in the tunnel. How else could the Earl's henchmen have found out about the tunnel, other than through Joan?

Geoffrey looked around the chamber properly for the first time. It was roughly rectangular, with a door at each end, both of which stood open. One was the door through which Geoffrey had entered the cavern, while beyond the second was another tunnel, leading, Geoffrey assumed, to the woods, since Drogo and Malger had fled down it. A heap of rags on a low ledge in a corner had apparently been serving as Rohese's bed, and there was a shelf along one wall. In the middle, displayed with some pride, was Geoffrey's heavy silver chalice—the one that had been stolen from his saddlebags as he had rescued Barlow from the river.

Bewildered, he picked it up. It was without question the one Tancred had given him—there was a dent in the rim where Tancred had used it to brain the man from whom he had stolen it. Geoffrey stood on tiptoe to see if the shelf held anything else, and reached up to retrieve his Hebrew and Arabic scrolls that had been stolen at the same time. Someone had ripped them in half, perhaps in anger at not being able to decipher them. Saddened, he placed them carefully inside his surcoat, grabbed the cup carelessly by its stem, and turned to Rohese.

"You must be hungry," he said. "Come on. Let's go."

"There was bread and water here," said Rohese, pointing. "And cheese and some wine."

"Really?" asked Geoffrey. He bent to inspect Rohese's bed. He had been wrong when he had assumed it comprised rags: it was actually several warm blankets. Next to them stood a jug and the remains of a loaf of bread. Someone else, apparently, had intended to stay a while in the underground chamber.

"These were here when you arrived?" he asked. "You did not bring them here yourself?"

"Of course not," said Rohese. "I did not know the tunnel existed until the other night. These things were just here."

"And have you seen anyone else at all since you arrived?"

"I already told you, no," she said.

"Did you not consider it curious that someone thought to provide bread and water, when no one knew you were coming to stay?"

"I do not imagine they were put here for me," said Rohese, looking at him as though he were stupid. "But I have been wondering when someone else might come. I have been ready either to flee up the tunnel to Godric's chamber or down to the river as soon as I heard someone coming."

"But you were not fleeing when Malger and Drogo were here," Geoffrey pointed out. "They had caught you."

Rohese shuddered. "I ran out of water and had to start drinking the wine instead. It must have made me sleep heavier than I intended. And I was tired. I have not really relaxed much down here."

Geoffrey could imagine why. Personally, he would rather have taken his chances sleeping in the woods than being locked in the oppressive chamber with only a severed head for company. Rohese, however, seemed quite sanguine over her ordeal. She continued.

"The bread was quite fresh when I arrived, so someone must have put it here very recently."

"Was it Drogo and Malger who brought the supplies, do you think?" asked Geoffrey, more to himself than to her. "Do you think they might have stayed here from time to time?"

"No," said Rohese, frowning in thought. "They did not know where they were going when they came in—it was as if they were exploring the tunnel for the first time. By the time I heard them it was too late to run, so I hid under the blankets hoping that they would miss me, and I might escape while they investigated the stairs. But they started prodding at me with their swords. Then you came."

"But how did they know it was here?" asked Geoffrey. "It is supposed to be a secret."

Rohese shrugged. "I do not know. And I would not rub your eye like that if I were you. It is already quite red."

Geoffrey looked around the chamber once more, hunting for a piece of cloth. Finally, he settled for a strip from one of the bed covers, which he hacked off with his sword. Gritting his teeth against a curious gamut of emotions, which included disgust, sorrow, and tenderness, he took the head from its alcove and wrapped it carefully in the blanket.

"Come on, Rohese," he said. "I have had enough of this place."

She hesitated.

"You cannot stay here forever," he said gently. "And Julian is fretting. She thinks the Earl of Shrewsbury has done away with you."

Reluctantly, Rohese glanced around her sanctuary before following him to the door.

"Which is the quickest way out?" he asked. "Up the stairs or towards the river?"

"To the river," she replied. "But we cannot go that way. The Earl's knights might be waiting."

"I hope they are," muttered Geoffrey. "Nothing would give me greater pleasure than another encounter with those two. I have some questions I would like to ask them."

"You would fight them again?" asked Rohese fearfully. "But they might kill you this time!"

"And I might kill them," said Geoffrey. "Will you take these?"

He handed Rohese the ominous bundle he carried under his arm and the chalice. He would need both hands free if he were to fight Malger and Drogo a second time. He drew his dagger, picked up his sword, and was ready. Clutching the bundle and cup, Rohese followed warily.

To Geoffrey's profound relief, the tunnel leading to the woods was only a short distance, and then they were out in the fresh air. He motioned for Rohese to remain where she was, while he crept around in the darkness, looking for signs that Malger and Drogo were lying in ambush. He imagined that they would not be expecting him to leave the underground cavern via the woods, but that he would return to the bedchamber so he would not be outside the safety of the castle walls. Therefore he did not really anticipate that they would be waiting, but only a fool would not be cautious.

When he was certain that the Earl's henchmen were not lurking nearby, he turned his attention to the hole that marked the tunnel's entrance. Mabel had been right when she said that no one would find it unless they knew where to look. It was buried deep in a hawthorn thicket, and emerged near the riverside path. Taking Rohese by the hand, partly to ensure that she did not lag behind, and partly because she was frightened and it seemed to calm her, Geoffrey strode towards the village. Rohese was soon out of breath from trying to match his rapid pace, but valiantly trotted along beside him.

"What will you do now?" she gasped. "Will you look for the Earl's men and kill them? Or will you look for the man who murdered your father?"

"How do you know it was a man who murdered him?" asked Geoffrey. "You said you could not tell whether the voice belonged to a man or a woman."

"I suppose I did," said Rohese. "But Godric said the person who killed him was one of you. That is all he kept saying. I cannot imagine Joan knifing a man in the stomach, so it must have been Walter, Stephen, or Henry. They are all mean and vicious. Poor Julianna has had to pretend to be a boy to escape their foul attentions, and none of them will pay for the houses to be mended in the village and they are falling about our ears."

"Can you remember Godric's exact words?" asked Geoffrey, trying to force himself to be patient with her rambling. He glanced down to ensure that she still held the grisly bundle. "What precisely did he say when he lay dying?"

"I have already told you," she said. "And he certainly did not say who had rammed the dagger into his bowels—or I would not have assumed it was you, would I?"

"Right," said Geoffrey, forcing himself not to snap. "But tell me again *exactly* what he said. There may be something of importance that you might have overlooked."

She shook her head firmly. "You will be angry if I tell you his precise words."

"I will not be angry," said Geoffrey, thinking that he very well might be if she continued to prove so irritating with her tantalising fragments of information.

"Sir Godric said that his whelps had killed him at last," she said, glancing at him nervously. "He kept calling his children things like his 'brood,' and his 'litter.' He really was not very polite."

"I would not be either, if one of them had killed me. Did he mention anyone by name?"

"Yes," said Rohese, after some serious thought. "He mentioned

Walter, Stephen, Henry, Hedwise, Bertrada, Joan, Olivier, and Enide. Oh, and you, of course, but he called you Godfrey. He cursed each one of you in turn."

"But he did not indicate which one might have killed him?" asked Geoffrey, exasperated.

"I have already told you, no," said Rohese, with a long-suffering sigh. "He just said his brood had killed him—as though you had all come and done it together. Then he cursed you all, and Norbert the scribe, too. He was just starting on Francis the physician when he died."

That, Geoffrey realised with disappointment, told him nothing more than that Godric was railing against virtually everyone who had come into contact with him over the past few months. And one thing was clear: his family was unlikely to co-operate over his killing. Their hatreds ran deep enough that it would be only a matter of time before one of them betrayed another in a fit of pique, or because it might give him an advantage over the others. Even though they were united in battling with the Earl of Shrewsbury over Godric's will, Geoffrey was certain it would not be long before the uneasy truce would be broken.

"But what will you do now?" he asked Rohese, dragging his thoughts away from his kinsmen. "Do you want to return to the castle? Or shall I escort you somewhere else?"

"Will you be at the castle?"

"No," said Geoffrey. "Not for a while, at least. I want to talk to Helbye."

"I do not want to be there if you are not," said Rohese, fearful again. She jumped as an animal rustled among the leaves at the side of the path and Geoffrey raised his sword.

"Then you can stay with Sergeant Helbye tonight," said Geoffrey. "He will not let anything happen to you."

"Can I not stay with you?" she said. "I would feel safer. You have rescued me twice now—once from the Earl and once from Malger and Drogo." She hesitated. "Now that Sir Godric has gone, I could come to you. . . ."

"Thank you, but I will not be here long," said Geoffrey quickly.

He was certain he was old enough to be her father, and wondered what Enide could have been thinking of, to thrust a child into the clutches of a man like Godric. But at least Joan had shown some sense over Julian, or Geoffrey realised that he might have been leading two whores to safety, not one.

"But what shall I do?" whispered Rohese. "Sir Godric is dead. Enide is dead. Joan will not have me back after I defied her over the Earl. And I have no trade, other than as a chambermaid. I will not serve that stingy Walter, nor that crafty Stephen."

"We will see tomorrow. Perhaps there is something you could do at Rwirdin," said Geoffrey wearily. They had reached the village, and the church was a dark mass at the side of the road. "Do you mind waiting for me for a moment? There is something I need to do."

She glanced around nervously. "Will you be long?"

"I hope not," said Geoffrey. "I want Father Adrian to take . . . I need him to bury it properly, where it belongs."

Wordlessly, she handed him the bundle containing the head and the chalice, and followed him through the churchyard to Father Adrian's house. A candle burned within, and Geoffrey thought he could hear voices. It was late, but Geoffrey supposed priests might be called upon at any time of the day or night for spiritual guidance or various other parish emergencies. He knocked softly, hearing the voices suddenly stilled.

"Yes?" called Adrian after a moment. "Who is there?"

"Geoffrey Mappestone from the castle. Will you come out? I need to see you about something."

There was a short pause, and Adrian opened the door. He looked strained and tired, but stood aside for Geoffrey to enter his house. Rohese closed the door behind them and watched.

Geoffrey put his bundle on the table and stood back. "I have found it," he said, gesturing for Adrian to unwrap the blanket.

Curiously, Adrian peeled back the covers to reveal the sad object within. He caught his breath in a strangled cry and backed away.

"I am sorry," said Geoffrey softly. "I did not know how else to tell you. Will you bury it with her body?"

"With whose body?" asked Adrian shakily.

"With Enide's body, of course," said Geoffrey, regarding him askance.

"Hardly!" said Adrian, raising a shaking hand to rub his chin. "Unless you do not care with whom she shares a grave. That is not Enide's head."

"What?" exclaimed Geoffrey, startled. "But this must be her!"

"It is not Enide!" said Rohese, as startled as was the priest. "You never told me you thought that, Sir Geoffrey, or I would have told you that you were wrong."

"Well, how many corpses are there at Goodrich missing their heads?" cried Geoffrey, looking from one to the other in confusion.

"I am beginning to wonder the same thing," said Adrian sombrely, regarding Geoffrey with troubled eyes. "But I can assure you that this not Enide's."

"How can you be sure?" asked Geoffrey. "Look again. You must be mistaken."

"I am not mistaken," said Adrian. He indicated a figure standing in the shadows holding something carefully in both hands. "Because this man has just brought me Enide's head."

Mark Ingram stepped forward importantly and set his bundle on the table next to the one that Geoffrey had brought. With a flourish like something a juggler might have employed, he plucked away the cloth that covered it, and revealed the severed head that lay beneath, setting it upright on the stump that had been its neck when it tipped to one side. Geoffrey sank down onto a bench, and regarded the face about which he had wondered for so long.

Enide had possessed thick brown hair, darker than Geoffrey's, and the teeth that were bared in a disconcerting grimace were white and strong. But the skin was discoloured and rotten, and Geoffrey could not tell whether she had been beautiful in life or not.

"She looks like you," said Ingram to Geoffrey, glancing from one to the other.

Adrian silenced him with a glare, while Rohese ran from the house with her hands over her eyes.

"Is it really her?" asked Geoffrey, tearing his eyes from his sister's face to look at the priest. "Is this really Enide?"

"It is Enide," said Adrian unsteadily. He came to sit next to Geoffrey on the bench, and they stared at the head together. "I would know her anywhere."

"But Enide died at the end of last summer," objected Geoffrey. "It seems to me that this poor woman has not been dead three weeks!"

"You are wrong, Geoffrey," said Adrian. "This is Enide without question. And she did die last summer. I saw her body, remember?"

"Ask the physician," said Geoffrey, his thoughts spinning. He had encountered many dead during his life as a soldier and, although no expert, was certainly able to tell whether a person had been dead three weeks or four months. "This is not the head of a person dead since September."

Adrian looked away. "Please cover her," he whispered.

When Ingram did not move, Geoffrey snatched the cloth from him, and draped it over the head. Geoffrey saw that the priest was deathly white, and his eyes were hollow with shock. It had been a shock for Geoffrey too—for he had not imagined that he would set eyes on the face of a sister so long in her grave—but he had not known her as Adrian had, and his grief was not so ragged and raw.

"And how do you happen to possess my sister's head so suddenly, Master Ingram?" Geoffrey asked, thinking that a few days ago, he could never have imagined uttering such a sentence.

Ingram's eyes glittered. "That is information which will not come free. That silver chalice you seem to have found again will make an acceptable payment."

Geoffrey was across the room and had the young soldier by the throat almost before he had finished speaking.

"I think I misheard you, Ingram," he whispered menacingly, holding the soldier up against the wall by his neck so that his feet barely touched the ground.

"Geoffrey, please!" said Adrian, coming to pull at his arm. "I want no violence in my house. It stands on hallowed ground."

"Not far to go for a burial, then," said Geoffrey, not relinquishing his vice-like grip on Ingram. "Now, where did you get it?"

"I found it!" squeaked Ingram, the malicious glint in his eyes replaced by fear. "Please! I cannot breathe! Let me go!"

"Let him down, Geoffrey," said Adrian, tugging harder. "I do

not want more filthy murders committed, and I will not stand by
and watch one happening under my very nose."

"Where did you find it?" demanded Geoffrey, ignoring him and
giving Ingram a shake.

"In the churchyard," gasped Ingram. He lashed out in a feeble
attempt to escape, but Geoffrey leaned his weight against the struggling soldier to pin down the flailing arms. Ingram shrieked.

Geoffrey felt his dagger hauled from his belt and shoved at his
side. He turned to the priest in surprise.

"Enough!" said Adrian, firmly. "There will be no more violence! Let him go, Geoffrey."

The priest held the knife awkwardly, demonstrating that he had
little experience with weapons. Geoffrey turned his attention back
to Ingram. "Where in the churchyard did you find it?"

He gasped suddenly as the dagger dug into him, and Ingram
went sliding to the floor. Geoffrey gaped at the priest in astonishment.

"I said enough!" shouted Adrian angrily. "I want no more violence!"

"Not so much as to prevent you from stabbing me," said Geoffrey, holding his side. "God's teeth, man! That hurt!"

"You were going to strangle him," raged Adrian. "In my
house—on consecrated ground!"

"Whereas you have just knifed me," retorted Geoffrey. "On
consecrated ground! You do not know me very well, priest! I would
not have strangled that snivelling little dog, although God knows he
deserves it."

"Your eyes are red with the blood lust of killing!" snapped
Adrian, defensively.

"They are red because there is sand in them," shouted Geoffrey.

"Tell me, Mark," said Adrian, pushing Geoffrey away and
kneeling next to Ingram, who half sat, half lay against the wall, gasping and clutching his throat. "Where did you find it?"

"Go to hell!" Ingram croaked hoarsely. "I will never tell you
now! Even if you were to give me that chalice."

"Please, Mark," said Adrian. "Look, here is the chalice. Take
it. But tell Sir Geoffrey what he would like to know."

Ingram scrambled to his feet, and snatched the silver cup from

Adrian's hand. Then he spat, straight into the priest's face, and darted through the door, taking the chalice with him.

"Oh," said Adrian, looking at the dagger he still held, and wiping his face with his sleeve.

" 'Oh,' indeed," said Geoffrey, sinking down on the bench, his hand still to his side. "Now what do you suggest? Shall we chase after him and offer him the church silver if he will answer our so-politely-put questions?"

"I was doing what I thought was right," said Adrian defensively. He flung Geoffrey's dagger away from him in sudden disgust, while the knight twisted awkwardly to see if Adrian's nasty jab had damaged his chain-mail. "I thought he might tell us where he had found her if we treated him with kindness, rather than roughness."

"Then clearly you do not know *him* very well, either," said Geoffrey. "Ingram is absolutely capable of digging up a grave in order to make a profit. He has been ferreting around in the village and asking questions of all sorts of people about Enide, my father's poisoning, and the death of that drunken servant—Torva. I wondered why. Now it is clear he was bent on extortion."

"No!" protested Adrian. "His father is my verger, and Mark Ingram himself has been on God's holy Crusade. He would not do something so despicable."

"Really?" said Geoffrey. "So you think his demand for my chalice in return for information was so that he could make a donation to the poor, do you?"

"It is possible," said Adrian. "You are too quick to see the evil in people."

"And you are too quick to see good that is not there," snapped Geoffrey. He rubbed his sore side and sighed. "Arguing will get us nowhere. Are you sure that second head belonged to Enide?"

"For God's sake, yes!" cried Adrian. "How many more times must I tell you? It is my Enide!"

"All right," said Geoffrey, unnerved by the priest's sudden display of emotion. He stood. "I must take Rohese to Helbye. Then I need to talk to the physician to ask what he discovered about the bed. And then we will bury Enide and whoever that other poor woman was."

The priest nodded, fighting to bring himself under control.

Geoffrey left him and collected Rohese from where she sat crying softly under a tree. Miserably, she trailed after him along the muddy lane to where Helbye's house stood. Geoffrey knocked at the door and waited.

Suddenly, the door was wrenched open and Helbye shot out, wielding his sword. Geoffrey, not anticipating that he would be attacked by someone he considered a friend, was completely unprepared to parry the hacking sword as it swept toward him. He saw the glittering blade begin to descend, and knew that he would not be able to move quickly enough to avoid it.

Rohese's shrill scream ripped through the air, making Helbye falter just long enough to allow Geoffrey to dodge out of the way of the wickedly slicing blade, although it passed so close that he felt the breeze of it on his cheek. He had hauled his own sword from his belt to meet the next blow before his brain had even started to question why his sergeant should be trying to chop him in half.

"Will!" he yelled. "What are you doing, man?"

"Sir Geoffrey!" gasped Helbye in startled horror. He gazed from the knight to the sword in his own hand. "My God! I almost killed you!"

"So I noticed," said Geoffrey, putting his weapon away. "What has happened to lead you to give friendly visitors this sort of welcome?"

Helbye looked both ways along the lane, and then hauled Geoffrey and Rohese inside, slamming the door behind them.

"Something dreadful is going on in this place," he said in a whisper.

Geoffrey did not need to be told that the village and its castle were not all a pleasantly prosperous settlement should be. He looked around the house's single room. Helbye's wife sat on the floor near the hearth, while in front of her lay the prostrate form of Francis the physician. Despite her most valiant efforts, Francis was bleeding to death from a wound in his side. Geoffrey looked from the dying man to Helbye in confusion.

"Ingram did it," said Helbye tiredly. "God knows why. I heard

a scuffle outside, and went to see what was going on. I found Master
Francis clutching his side, and saw Ingram racing away up the lane
as though the very hounds of hell were on his heels."

"They may well be, soon," said Geoffrey, doubting that the
spiteful young soldier would be able to lie and bluff his way out of
this mess: even the heroes of the Crusades could not be permitted
to swagger around the countryside and kill whosoever they pleased.

Geoffrey knelt next to Francis and addressed Helbye. "Has he
said anything?"

At the sound of his voice, Francis opened his eyes and gave a
ghastly smile.

"You brought a devil home from the Holy Land, Geoffrey Mappestone. What changed the lad? He was never so vile when he was
a boy."

"Was he not?" asked Geoffrey, unconvinced. "He has been
pretty unpleasant ever since I have known him. But why has he
done this to you? What could you have said to lead him to murder?"

"Nothing," breathed Francis, closing his eyes. "He came towards me smiling and then, without the slightest provocation, he
plunged his dagger into me. And do not try to tell me that I will
live. I am a physician—I know a fatal wound when I see one."

"He just stabbed you? With no explanation?" Geoffrey was nonplussed. The physician's shabby robe and dirty clothes clearly indicated that he was not wealthy, and therefore would not be worth
robbing. And Geoffrey found it difficult to believe that someone
would kill an old man for no reason at all, even the aggressive and
cowardly Ingram.

"I was looking for you anyway," whispered Francis. "I did as
you asked—I went to the castle and inspected the mattress. But there
was nothing amiss with it. You were wrong: there are no poisons
hidden in any part of the bed that I could find."

"Are you sure?" asked Geoffrey, disappointed. He had been
convinced that his deduction had been correct.

"One can never be sure with poisons," said Francis, a touch of
his characteristic smugness back in his voice. "But I am reasonably
certain that the mattress is innocent of Godric's death. It must be
something else. The rugs, perhaps."

"Well, it does not matter," said Geoffrey, "so you should not tax yourself about it now. Rest."

"Rest for what?" asked Francis. "So that I can spend longer dying?"

"Will you fetch Father Adrian?" said Geoffrey to Helbye.

"Later," said Francis as the sergeant rose. I have a while left to me yet."

"You need to make your confession," said Helbye. "You do not want to die unshriven."

"Claptrap!" said the physician. "If I die sorry for my sins, then God will not care whether I have been absolved or not. You must have seen hundreds die unshriven on the field of battle, Will Helbye. Do you think God will not care for them because they did not confess?"

Helbye, very much a man who believed anything the Church told him, pursed his lips and did not deign to reply to such heresy.

"I will ride to Walecford for a physician," he said stiffly.

"No! That man is a leech and a charlatan," said Francis. "I want no physicians near me as I die."

"Now you know how the rest of us feel," muttered Helbye.

"Can we give you anything?" asked Geoffrey. "What about that potion you were making the day I first met you—the one that binds wounds? Can I fetch that?"

"Thank you, no," said Francis with a shudder. "I have learned that the shock of having that applied tends to kill a patient in moments."

His fingers fluttered over one of his pouches and Geoffrey helped him to open it.

"It is poppy powder for the pain," the physician said weakly, drawing out a small packet. "Enide told me that you can read. Follow the instructions on the outside and make it up for me."

Geoffrey unwrapped the package, and set about measuring the correct amount of liquid for the powder. He was on the verge of scattering it into a bowl of water when his attention was caught by the handwriting—a firm roundhand with a curiously archaic *T*. He had seen that writing before—on the parchments he had found hidden in Enide's room. He stared at it, his thoughts whirling, until a sharp poke from Helbye's wife brought him to his senses.

"Did you write these?" he asked Francis. "These instructions?"

"I did," said Francis feebly. "Why? Can you not read them? That is a shame, because the pain has dimmed my eyes, and I cannot see them myself. But never mind, just add the whole packet. It matters not whether I die from the wound or from the medicine. Hurry up, boy! I suffer."

"I can read it very well," said Geoffrey, dumping the powder in the bowl and stirring it with his dagger. "Just as I have read other notes and messages written by you of late."

"What are you talking about?" demanded Helbye's wife. "Give that to me. He will be dead by the time you finish messing around with it."

She snatched the bowl from Geoffrey, and helped the physician sip it until it had all been consumed. The lines of agony on Francis's face eased, and his breathing became less laboured.

" 'Midnight on the fifth day of June,' " said Geoffrey, when Francis opened his eyes again. " 'The first day of August at Brockenhurst.' "

Helbye gave him an odd look, but knew better than to ask questions. His wife, however, did not, and pushed Geoffrey away from the physician roughly.

"Leave him be," she said. "Make yourself useful and go to fetch Father Adrian."

"No," said Francis, as Geoffrey prepared to leave. "Stay with me for a while longer. I can see you have questions to ask, and I am of a mind to answer and make a clean breast of matters before I die."

"You should do that with Father Adrian," said Helbye's wife critically. "Confessing to these two will not save you from the fires of Hell."

"Neither will Father Adrian," said Francis. "For my sins are great indeed, and I have something I need to ask of Sir Geoffrey."

"You do?" asked Geoffrey uneasily.

"Only you are left now, young Geoffrey: Godric is murdered, Enide is murdered, Pernel is murdered. All have gone."

"Who is Pernel?" asked Geoffrey. "The other woman who lost her head—the one I found in the tunnel?"

Francis looked blankly at him. "I do not understand what you are talking about. But Pernel was your brother Stephen's wife. You never met her, but I know Norbert wrote to you in the Holy Land to tell you that she had died last year. She was with us."

"With you?" asked Geoffrey, bewildered. "What do you mean?" He glanced up as Helbye's wife made a circular motion near her temple with her hand to suggest that the old man might be delirious.

"Pernel was a part of our plan to save England from the vile clutches of that unnatural man," said the priest. "As were Godric, Enide, and I."

"Oh, no!" said Geoffrey in horror, as he realised what the old man was saying. "Do not tell me that Father Adrian was right, and that you were all a part of the plot to shoot King William Rufus in the New Forest last year—that you committed regicide!"

Francis gave a red-toothed smile. "We were certainly part of *a* plot. But that evil beast was slain by the hand of God long before we could put *our* plan into action."

"The courtier called Tirel shot Rufus," said Helbye, looking from Francis to Geoffrey in confusion. "And it was an accident. What are you two talking about?"

"I can only assume that there were others who felt like us," said Francis, ignoring the sergeant. "And that they decided Rufus could not continue with his acts of debauchery and vice. Tirel killed him before we could take the action that we had planned."

"Which was what?" asked Geoffrey coldly. He was not sure that there was a great difference between actually committing the crime, and planning a murder that failed only because someone else got there first.

"Rufus was due to spend time hunting in the New Forest later this year, and we intended to kill him there. But Tirel—damn him to Hell—killed him first and far too soon."

"Too soon for what?" asked Geoffrey. "Too soon for Rufus certainly."

"Before everything was in place," said the physician. "People were not ready, and by the time we found out what had happened, it was too late for us to act."

"But Enide did go to the New Forest," said Geoffrey slowly. "According to one of the notes you wrote—and assuming that

Adrian's memory regarding the dates is accurate—it seems that she was somewhere nearby when Tirel shot Rufus."

"She arrived after he died," said the physician. "The roads were bad and her horse went lame. She did not reach Brockenhurst until three days after Rufus died, and by then Henry was King."

Geoffrey was uncertain. "It seems odd that she should just happen to decide to make a visit to the New Forest, and that around the same time Tirel should just happen accidentally to shoot Rufus."

"She went to assess Brockenhurst," said the physician. "She went to learn the lay of the land, and to observe how that foul beast who called himself King managed his hunting days, so that we could adapt our plan accordingly. But as I said, she arrived too late. Rufus was already dead."

"But how could you even consider such a dangerous venture?" cried Geoffrey, aghast. "It might have plunged the country into civil war, not to mention what might have happened had you been caught. Who would stand to gain from the cold-blooded murder of Rufus?"

"The whole country stood to gain," mumbled Francis. "England needed to be rid of his oppressive laws and his evil suppression of the holy Church. And then, when Rufus was dead, we intended that the Duke of Normandy should come to take the throne. The Duke has been on God's Crusade, so how could He fail to smile upon England's fortunes with such a man wearing the crown?"

"Crusaders are no angels," said Geoffrey. "And the will of God was the last thing on their minds as they looted, pillaged, and murdered their way to Jerusalem. But this is all beside the point. What were you thinking of? England was stable under Rufus. His laws might not have suited some people, but they were adequate."

"He was a pervert!" snapped Francis. "He engaged in unnatural acts with his courtiers. Why do you think he never married? Why do you think he never presented England with an heir or acknowledged illegitimate children?"

"I imagine because he thought he would have time for such things later," said Geoffrey. "He was only around forty. There was time enough to marry and provide an heir."

"And we knew he would not have relinquished his hold on

Normandy when the Duke returned from the Crusade," said Francis, as if Geoffrey had not spoken. "Rufus would have kept from the Duke what was rightfully his—just as this present usurper is doing."

Geoffrey started back in alarm. "Do not tell me that you are planning to kill King Henry, too?"

The physician said nothing. Geoffrey and Helbye exchanged a look of dismay.

"King Henry is due to go to Monmouth soon," said Helbye in a soft voice. "The constable told me so when we were at Chepstow. Perhaps these plotters mean to strike then, when King Henry goes hunting in the Forest of Dene. King Henry loves to hunt every bit as much as Rufus did."

Geoffrey took a deep breath and addressed Francis, who was becoming drowsy from the poppy powder. "But you will not kill a second king. You have just said all the plotters are dead. Godric, Enide, Pernel, and you."

The physician smiled again. "I am dying, and I know that to kill is a terrible sin. But I am willing to risk the fires of eternal damnation by asking you to carry on our work."

Geoffrey gazed at him in astonishment. "I do hope you are not asking me to kill King Henry for you!" he said, feeling that the request was so outrageous that it was almost laughable.

"He is rambling," said Helbye in a whisper. "See how his eyes are unfocused? He does not know what he is saying."

"I am not rambling," said Francis irritably. "I love my country, and I would serve it any way I can, even as I die. I was glad when Rufus was killed, but I would die happier knowing that the rightful King—the Duke of Normandy—will wear the crown. He is a good and virtuous man, not like this grasping Henry. Please, join us."

"I will not," said Geoffrey firmly. "And I will do all in my power to prevent another death."

Francis sighed. "No matter, then. I am sure the others will manage without you."

"Others?" asked Geoffrey in horror. "What others? You said they were all dead."

"I did not," said Francis in a breathless whisper. "I said that

Enide, Godric, Pernel, and I were dead. But there are others who think that the usurper King Henry should be ousted to allow the Duke to accede."

"But this is a dreadful idea!" cried Geoffrey. "It must be stopped! The Earl of Shrewsbury waits in the wings like a vulture at a kill. If Henry is murdered and the Duke seizes the crown of England, the Earl will gain control of the country for certain. The last person you want ruling your precious England is the Earl of Shrewsbury."

"The Duke would not permit Shrewsbury so much power," said Francis weakly. "And anyway, Shrewsbury has his own estates to run in Normandy. He will not bother with England."

"He is massing his strength in this area so that he will be ready to aid the Duke when he attacks England to seize the throne from Henry," said Geoffrey. "Shrewsbury admitted as much himself. He claimed that the Duke would appoint him as regent."

Francis shook his head. "The Duke would not leave England once he had taken the throne, and the country will be ruled by a just and noble leader who will make good laws."

"But the Duke did not make good laws to rule Normandy before he pawned it so he could go Crusading," objected Geoffrey. Loyal though he might be to the Duke, he was not blind to the fact that the weak and vacillating Robert of Normandy left a lot to be desired as far as leadership went.

But Geoffrey could see that his arguments were lost on the physician, whose eyes gleamed with the light of fanaticism. He studied the old man. He looked benign, grandfatherly almost, and yet had embarked upon a plot that would not only leave the King dead but that might plunge the country he professed to love into a state of anarchy.

"Is that why Ingram killed you?" he asked. "Because you are involved in a plot to kill King Henry?"

Francis's eyes closed. "You are a fool, despite what Enide said about you. How could a boy like that know of our plans? We kept our group deliberately small, so that there would be less chance that someone would betray us."

"So the group comprised my father, Enide, Stephen's wife, and you," said Geoffrey. "And who else? Father Adrian?"

Francis's mouth opened in astonishment, and he gave a wheeze that Geoffrey thought was meant to be a laugh. "Adrian? Just because he was Enide's lover does not mean that he shared our plans! The man is a weakling."

Geoffrey's still-aching side belied Adrian's reputed aversion to violence. "Who, then? Olivier? He is a kinsman of the Earl of Shrewsbury and would have a good deal to gain."

"He is an even greater weakling than the priest!" said Francis, with the ghost of a smile. "If you will not join us, you will get nothing more from me."

"So that is why my father was being poisoned," said Geoffrey, understanding slowly. "Because someone was trying to prevent him from killing every king foolish enough to take the English crown. And Enide was poisoned for the same reason."

"Enide was certainly slain because of her involvement," said Francis. "You see, Pernel was delighted to be a part of the plan that would rid England of Rufus. She was too open with her feelings on the matter, and someone at the castle betrayed her."

"Stephen's wife was murdered, too?" asked Geoffrey, confused.

"But Lady Pernel died of a falling sickness," said Helbye's wife, shaking her head to Geoffrey to indicate that the physician was speaking nonsense. "I was there. She emerged from the church and fell down dead. Half the village saw it happen."

"It seems to me that Father Adrian's masses are dangerous events," said Geoffrey. "Enide, too, died after attending one of his services."

"There are poisons that can make a person's death appear to be a falling sickness," said Francis. "Perhaps Adrian fed it to her in the Host. He acted most oddly after Enide's death too—the man was blindly in love with her, and yet his grief was short and shallow."

Geoffrey stared at him. He thought about what he had been told about Enide's death. She had emerged from the church and Adrian had found her body shortly afterwards. Adrian had no one to corroborate his story, but no one had thought to disbelieve him. So, had Adrian killed her? But why? Was Adrian not a priest at all but an agent for one of the kings who Enide had plotted to kill? Since King Henry seemed to know that Goodrich was a hotbed of insurrection, it might make sense to place such an agent in it. But Henry

had only been King for a few months, and Adrian had been at Goodrich for years. Geoffrey sighed. It made no sense.

"Godric was poisoned for his role in our plot," Francis continued. "What other reason would there be to kill him?"

"His lands," said Geoffrey. "Or because Goodrich Castle is
stuffed full of his avaricious offspring who are desperate to lay their
hands on his money."

"You might be right," said Francis, swallowing with difficulty.
"Although I would not have credited any of that brood with choosing such a subtle poison that I have never been able to trace it."

"It was in his room, I am sure," said Geoffrey, thinking back to
what he had reasoned as he sat with Godric's body. "It was not in
the food or the drink. It was not in the mattress."

But it was certainly in the chamber, because Geoffrey had been
ill each time he had slept in it. Geoffrey was a man who generally
enjoyed robust good health, and was seldom ill. But he had felt
unwell several times since arriving at Goodrich—mostly in the castle,
although he had almost thrown up in Francis's outhouse when he
had visited the physician to ask about Godric's alleged poisoning.
Something clicked in Geoffrey's mind, but Francis had slipped into
a semi-conscious doze, and was no longer in a condition to engage
in analytical conversation.

Geoffrey rubbed his eyes. "What a mess," he said to Helbye.
"Is there anyone in this godforsaken place who is not a murderer,
or who would not like to be? Enide, this Pernel, and my father were
aiming to kill Rufus; my father and the physician, cheated of killing
Rufus, then set their sights on the death of King Henry. Meanwhile,
someone was slowly poisoning my father; two others stabbed him
during the night with different knives; there are at least two severed
heads circulating; and someone has tried to poison me, and has shot
at me twice in the woods. I tell you, Will, the Holy Land is nothing
compared to this!"

Helbye raised his shoulders in a shrug. "It looks as though we
should plan a visit to Monmouth soon, Sir Geoffrey," he said stoically.

Early the following morning, long before the sun was up, Geoffrey waited impatiently by the river for Helbye. His horse snorted and pawed at the ground, its breath billowing out in great clouds of white, while his dog snuffled about in the grass. Mist rose from the silent river as it meandered glassily southwards, and the forest was silent and still.

Geoffrey had passed what remained of the night in Helbye's house, spending most of it talking, for the elderly soldier was as reliable a friend as Geoffrey had in Goodrich. Helbye had listened in silence, not in the least bit unsettled by the devious plots that had been hatched in the castle. The sergeant had heard him sympathetically, and had said little, but the simple act of talking had allowed Geoffrey to clarify in his mind at least some twists and turns of the plot.

Geoffrey tensed as he heard a sound from the woods, and drew his sword in anticipation of a hostile encounter.

"Father Adrian!" he exclaimed, as the priest walked towards him. "Have you buried Enide yet?"

The priest shook his head. "I will do that when we return."

"Return from where?" asked Geoffrey. "Where are you going?"

"With you," said Adrian. "To Monmouth."

"Not a chance," said Geoffrey. "You would be too slow. And anyway, you might stab me again. Go back to your church and bury your dead."

The priest looked down the river. "The head you brought to my house last night belonged to a woman who lived in the village, and who died in childbirth some months ago. I cannot imagine how you came to be in possession of it."

"More to the point," said Geoffrey, "how did *she* come to lose it?"

The priest was silent.

"Go and bury them, Father," said Geoffrey, reluctant to talk to the priest, whose role in the plotting and subterfuge he had uncovered was still far from clear. "You should not leave heads sitting on your kitchen table—someone might find them, and then you would have some explaining to do."

"I put them in the charnel house," said Adrian. "I will bury them later, but today, I am coming with you."

"No," said Geoffrey. "You will not be able to keep up with us on foot, and anyway there might be some of that violence that you find so abhorrent."

"I do not understand all this evil," said Adrian softly. "Francis the physician has just informed me that he and the woman I loved more than life itself have been plotting murders together."

"Go home," said Geoffrey. "Francis will be needing you to give him last rites."

"He is dead," said Adrian. "It was when I heard his final confession that I knew I had to come with you. Perhaps I can save her yet. I can speak in her defence to King Henry."

"Save who?" asked Geoffrey, removing his helmet and rubbing at his hair underneath. He wondered what could be keeping Helbye.

"Save Enide," said Adrian.

"You would do better burying her decently," said Geoffrey. "It is too late for anything else."

"She is alive," said Adrian.

"But you identified her head only last night," pointed out Geoffrey, wondering if grief had robbed the priest of a few wits. "She cannot be alive without it."

"I lied about that," said Adrian, refusing to meet Geoffrey's eyes. "It was not hers."

"For God's sake!" cried Geoffrey in exasperation. "What is going on? You say you saw her body. Then you say you saw her head. Are you now saying that you saw neither?"

"It was not her body outside the chapel," said Adrian. He looked down at his sandalled feet. "I lied to protect Enide, and only I know that it was not *her* body in the grave that bears her name."

Geoffrey gazed at him, the full implications of Adrian's claim striking home for the first time. "Enide is alive?" he asked in a whisper. "My favourite sister is alive?"

Adrian nodded, more miserably than he should for a bearer of such glad tidings.

"But I saw her grave," Geoffrey persisted. "And others saw her dead—Henry and Walter."

Adrian still said nothing.

"How could she do this?" asked Geoffrey, bewildered. "How could she let those who love her believe she was dead?"

He recalled his grief when he had received the note bearing the news, and the emptiness he had felt when he knew the last and only pleasant tie with his family had been severed. He swallowed hard, and regarded Adrian doubtfully. No wonder Francis had noticed that Adrian's grief for Enide had been brief and shallow. It was doubtless difficult to grieve for someone who was still alive.

"You used that other woman!" he said, the sudden loudness of his voice making his horse start. "Walter and Henry did not see Enide at all: they saw the body of the poor woman who had died in childbirth the day before—who you told me was in the parish coffin waiting to be buried that day! You said you had left the church later than everyone else on the day that Enide was killed, because you had stayed to say a mass for this woman."

Adrian nodded miserably.

"And you sliced the head from this woman's shoulders so that no one would be able to identify her," said Geoffrey. "Why? How could you do such a thing—you who claim to dislike violence? I am not surprised you felt obliged to pray for her after everyone else had gone!"

"I did it for Enide!" protested Adrian. "She came to me in great fear and said that one of her brothers or her sister was going to kill her. The poor lady had already been poisoned—like Godric—and so I had no reason to disbelieve her. She was so frightened that I decided I would do anything to help her. We agreed that we would use the body of the woman who lay in my church to make everyone believe Enide was dead—so that she would be safe."

"But chopping the head from a corpse!" said Geoffrey in disgust. "The Crusaders could learn a good deal from you!"

"Actually, the decapitation was not part of the arrangement," said Adrian shakily. "The plan was that I should bury a shroud filled with earth in the other woman's grave, and then say that I had found Enide's body in the churchyard. I was immediately to seal 'Enide's' corpse in a coffin—to stop your family from looking at it. My shock was as great as anyone's when Henry—against my protestations—dragged the lid from the coffin to look inside. Enide told me later that she knew he, or one of the others, would not be prevented from looking, and so she had hacked off the head to hide the fact that the corpse was not hers."

"And what of Enide's hand?" asked Geoffrey coldly. "The one that you told me was withered from her childhood accident? Did they not look at that for identification? Or was that a lie too?"

"That was the truth," said Adrian. "I suppose they were so shocked to see the body headless, that they did not think of such things. Anyway, the corpse was tightly wound in its shroud, and it would have been some effort to undo it."

"This is horrible!" said Geoffrey, gazing at the priest in distaste. "No wonder you were surprised when I showed you what I had found in the room at the end of the tunnel. It was the head of that poor woman whose body you so callously used for your own devices, was it not?"

Adrian nodded miserably. "I searched the churchyard for that head so that I could bury it decently," he said. "But Enide refused to tell me what she had done with it.

Geoffrey took a deep breath. The priest seemed genuinely contrite, but how far could Geoffrey trust him? He had already admitted to weaving a fabric of lies around the events leading to Enide's death, so how did Geoffrey know he had decided to be truthful at last? Francis had suggested that Adrian might have killed both Pernel and Enide at his masses, but now the priest was claiming that Enide still lived and Geoffrey no longer knew what to believe.

He took a deep breath, oddly relieved that the grisly head he had bundled in the blanket had not been Enide's after all. And the other skull? Geoffrey himself had already suggested that Ingram would not have been loath to dig up a grave to acquire himself a head that he could use to force Geoffrey to pay for information. And that, thought the knight with sudden realisation, was exactly what Ingram had done.

"Mabel, the buttery-steward at the castle, told me that she was leaving Goodrich because her sister's grave had been desecrated," he said to Adrian. "She assumed that the Earl of Shrewsbury had done it, because he has such a dreadful reputation. Walter said it was dogs. But we know different, do we not, Father Adrian?"

"The head Ingram brought does look as if it belongs to Mabel's sister," admitted Adrian sombrely. "The poor woman died of an ague about three weeks ago."

"And that is why you allowed Ingram to escape when I asked him where it had come from," said Geoffrey. "You did not want me to press him to reveal where he unearthed this poor head—because you intended me to believe it was Enide's. Or did *you* charge him to dig it up, unaware that I was bringing you a similar gift?"

"No!" cried Adrian, horrified. "Ingram has been fascinated by this whole business from the start. He has been ferreting about and asking questions of just about everybody. He managed to drag out from your father's food-taster that Enide had been seen leaving my house after she was supposed to have been dead. Ingram has been obsessed with Enide's death—just like you."

So that was why the food-taster was so reluctant to speak to anyone, Geoffrey thought. He knew he had stumbled upon a plot that would have been very dangerous to investigate further—and that seemed to involve murdered corpses wandering through the village.

"But Ingram's unwholesome interest in my affairs still explains nothing," said Geoffrey coldly.

Adrian sighed. "Ingram presented me with his . . . find, and asked if it could be Enide. I told him it could, because I wanted him to cease his questioning before someone did it for him. He would not be the first around here to be silenced for his curiosity: I do not think that Godric's first food-taster drowned in the castle moat by accident."

Geoffrey was sure he was right.

"Then Ingram told me that he planned to make you pay dearly for the information he had gathered," said Adrian. "He claims that you sometimes prevented him from looting in the Holy Land, and that he came back poorer than he should have done."

Geoffrey had forbidden his men to loot on certain occasions—especially when the victims were already on the brink of starvation or he felt that they had suffered enough at the grasping hands of the Crusader army. But he had not realised that his few attempts to instil a sense of compassion and decency in his troops would have such far-reaching consequences.

"Did Ingram tell you what kind of information he had amassed from his enquiries?" he asked.

"No, and I knew he did not have the real truth," said Adrian. "I was afraid he would make things up that would mislead you, and that would put you in danger when you went to investigate them."

"So you prevented me from forcing him to admit that he had excavated Mabel's sister's grave to get a head," said Geoffrey. "You did not want me to guess that Enide might still be alive—which I would have done had Ingram told the truth, because there were two severed heads in your kitchen, and yet neither was hers. You would have been exposed as the liar you are, and Enide's secret would have been out."

"I was only thinking of you," said Adrian tiredly. "Believe what you will, but I have been scurrying around trying to make amends for others" evil deeds for weeks now. Of course I wanted to protect Enide, but I did not—do not—want to see you harmed in all this mess. I thought if I could keep the truth from you for a few more days, you would leave anyway."

"Francis told us that there were others who intended to kill King Henry," said Geoffrey, thoughtfully. "If Enide is still alive, as you claim, then I think she may well be planning to visit King Henry to demonstrate first-hand her penchant for regicide."

"You are quite wrong," said Adrian forcefully. "I spoke with her after you left my house last night. She set off several hours ago to become a nun at Glowecestre Abbey."

"Enide has already left?" cried Geoffrey aghast.

Adrian nodded. "She often said she was considering taking the veil."

"The only veil Enide will be considering is the one that will cover King Henry's corpse!" cried Geoffrey. "How could you believe her after all this lying?"

"You are talking about your sister," said Adrian coldly. "She cares deeply for you."

"So she might have done, once," said Geoffrey. "But a long time has passed, and it seems we are both different people. I thought I knew her from her letters, but you yourself have told me she could not write. I have been living under a false impression of Enide for twenty years. The child I left behind would not have murdered kings, or chopped off the heads of corpses! I neither know nor understand the woman she has become."

"Then do what you will, but remember that she always said she liked you better than the others."

"That is probably because I was not here to argue with. But enough of this; here is Helbye. And Barlow with him," he added in surprise, seeing the two soldiers picking their way along the path on sturdy mounts. "Go home, Adrian. You have done more than enough harm already."

"I must try to put an end to all this," said Adrian, grasping the reins of Geoffrey's horse. "I will come with you, and explain to the King what has been happening."

"You would be a fool to try," said Geoffrey. "Do you think he will pat your head and allow you to leave after you admit that you knew of the plot to kill his brother?"

"But I do not believe that Enide was trying to kill Rufus," objected Adrian. "She went to Brockenhurst to *warn* him. And she has no intention of harming King Henry. You are wrong!"

"I am not," said Geoffrey wearily. "And you know it. Francis the physician must have told you what he told me—that his little gang planned to kill Rufus, and now want to kill King Henry."

"No!" cried Adrian desperately. "Enide would never harm anyone."

Geoffrey regarded him sombrely. "Really? I think she has already taken someone's life."

He hesitated. It was not pleasant to see his cherished memories of his younger sister so brutally shattered, but Enide, it seemed, had been more treacherous and cunning than the rest of the Mappestones put together. Or was he misinterpreting what he had learned, to draw grotesquely inaccurate conclusions?

Adrian was gazing at him. "Who do you think Enide has killed?"

"She told you that she was in fear of her life from one of the family, so you helped her steal and desecrate the corpse of a woman who had considerately timed her death to coincide with Enide's need for a body."

The blood drained from Adrian's face. "I see what you are thinking, but you are wrong! That woman passed away in childbirth."

"And was Enide present when this woman died?" asked Geoffrey. "Did she help the midwife?"

"Well, yes, she did, actually" said Adrian. "But Enide did do kind things from time to time."

"I am sure she did," said Geoffrey bitterly.

"It did not seem such a terrible crime to use the body of one already taken to God to save the life of another," said Adrian weakly.

"That does not sound like your own logic, Father," said Geoffrey. "I imagine that is how Enide argued her case. But let us continue. Anyone who has had any dealings with my brother Henry will know that he would not stand by and accept the word of a priest that his sister was dead. He would want to see for himself. Enide knew this perfectly well, and deprived the corpse of its head, secreting it away in a niche in Godric's secret tunnel—it would not do for it to be found, because then everyone would suspect that Enide was not dead at all. After all, how many decapitated corpses are there around here?"

He and Adrian exchanged a glance that suggested there were rather more than most people imagined. Adrian opened his mouth to speak, but Geoffrey hurried on.

"So Enide was then free to do whatever she pleased. Even her fellow conspirators—my father and Francis—did not know she was still alive, and she allowed her family to grieve without the slightest regret. Now she tells you she is going to Glowecestre to take the veil, and you believe her?"

"Yes, I do," said Adrian sincerely. "She said that she wants to atone for desecrating the corpse."

"And then there was Stephen's wife, Pernel," said Geoffrey. "Pernel was indiscreet about the plan to kill Rufus, and so she was killed. I wonder who arranged that."

"But Pernel died of a falling sickness," said Adrian, startled. "It happened just after mass. Pernel was not a good woman—she was unfaithful to her husband and she was greedy and scheming—and everyone assumed she had died because God had punished her for setting foot in His church."

"Do you believe that?" asked Geoffrey sceptically. "If so, it does not offer much hope for the rest of us miserable sinners."

Adrian shook his head, then nodded, then made a gesture of exasperation. "I do not know! I do not understand anything about this business. But if Enide really did embark on all this subterfuge— and I say *if*—then her reasons would have been purely honourable."

"Reasons for murder are seldom honourable," said Geoffrey.

Without waiting for the priest's reply, he steered his destrier around and headed for the path that led to Monmouth, some six miles distant, with his sergeant and man-at-arms close behind him. He glanced round briefly, jamming his conical helmet on his head. The priest stood dejectedly in the middle of the path, looking like a man who had been through a battle.

'Barlow insisted on coming," said Sergeant Helbye, once the track had widened sufficiently to allow him to draw abreast of Geoffrey. "He heard that Ingram has murdered the physician, and I think he wants to prove to you that it had nothing to do with him."

"I know that," said Geoffrey. "It was Ingram who was asking all the questions about my family and complaining that I had prevented him from looting, not Barlow."

"Why were you shouting at the priest?" asked Helbye. "Father Adrian is a gentle man and is greatly loved by the villagers."

"He is a gentle man who has been party to murder, the desecration of corpses, treachery, and lies and deceit beyond your wildest imaginings," said Geoffrey wearily, sorry that a man like Adrian should fall victim to Goodrich's creeping evil. "I should take a torch and burn this whole place to the ground, and rid the world of it! That poor Earl of Shrewsbury does not know what he is letting himself in for!"

"I am sure he will manage," said Helbye. "But what ails you? Is it your family again?"

"I should say," said Geoffrey bitterly. "I have just learned from Father Adrian that Enide is alive and well. And I suspect that having failed to slay one king for the simple reason that someone got there before her, she has her murderous sights set on another."

"Enide?" asked Helbye, giving the matter some serious thought. "Yes, I suppose I could see her doing all that."

"What?" exclaimed Geoffrey, startled "You believe my accusations so readily?"

"Oh, yes," said Helbye, as if it were obvious. "You left here a long time ago, while Enide stayed to grow up with your older brothers and sister. So, is it really surprising that she lost the gentleness you remember? By the time she was twenty, she was just as bad as the rest of them for plotting and fighting. She was not downright evil or anything like that, but just like the others—greedy, bitter, and ill-humoured. I always wondered why you singled her out for such affection. Begging your pardon, sir."

"But she wrote such beautiful things," said Geoffrey sadly. "She told me about the wildflowers at springtime, and about poetry she had read or ballads she had heard sung. And Father Adrian said she was kind and gentle."

"You cannot trust letters, lad," said Helbye sagely. "If you believe her to be some kind of saint on the basis of some silly scrawls on parchment, then you need your wits seeing to. But there is a lot about this that I do not understand. The physician said Enide is going to kill King Henry, but Father Adrian, who is a good and honest man, believes you are wrong."

"The good and honest Father Adrian still knows more than he is saying," said Geoffrey. "Either that, or he is one of the most gullible men in the kingdom."

"So what exactly is happening?" asked Helbye. "Are we off to save the King?"

"I suppose so," said Geoffrey. "Enide and some others apparently developed a plot to kill Rufus in the New Forest, but someone beat them to it—they intended Rufus to have died this coming summer, when the Duke of Normandy would be ready to take the throne. But Tirel's shot caught them before they were fully ready, and King Henry seized the crown instead. Now Enide plans to rid England of King Henry, too, to provide the Duke with another chance."

"But Rufus's death was an accident," protested Helbye. "Tirel claims he did not mean to kill him."

"Actually, Tirel is now claiming that he did not fire the arrow at all," said Geoffrey. "But whether he did or not is irrelevant, because it seems plans were afoot to kill Rufus anyway. The wrong successor took advantage of the empty throne, and now a second murder is required."

"Who, other than Enide, is involved in all this?" asked Helbye, accepting the twists and turns of the plot far more stoically than Geoffrey had done.

"According to the physician, the cabal comprised himself, Enide, Stephen's wife, and my father. There were also others, but he declined to mention more names. I suppose Stephen might be one of the plotters, since his wife was involved."

"So, what about this poisoning business?" asked Helbye. "Do you think that was done by someone loyal to the King to prevent the plot from hatching?"

"Godric and Enide thought so," said Geoffrey. "But their alleged poisonings have nothing to do with anything—no one poisoned Godric and no one poisoned Enide."

"How so?" asked Helbye, bewildered. "Sir Godric was dying from the toxins in his body."

"I did not say that he was not being poisoned," said Geoffrey. "I said that no one was responsible. Well, not directly, anyway. Father became ill when he handed the running of the manor to Walter and Stephen. In order to pass the time, he took up painting, using pigments that were made by the physician, who enjoyed playing with different compounds. It was the paint that poisoned father. It made Enide ill too, when she slept in his chamber so that she could take advantage of the secret tunnel for her clandestine meetings."

"Paint?" queried Helbye. "How? Surely they did not drink it?"

"No, but it must create poisonous miasmas. I felt unwell each time I slept in my father's chamber. At first, I assumed that I had caught an ague from falling in the river. Later, I thought it was the after-effects of the ergot. But really, it was the paint. Francis told me that he used lead powder in the darkest pigments; perhaps that was responsible. Then I experienced the same nausea in Francis's laboratory where he was making the stuff, as I did in father's room."

That, and the idea of Hedwise's fish sauce being added to it, he recalled with distaste.

Helbye rubbed his chin thoughtfully. "For a physician, Master Francis was not a healthy man. My wife tells me that it was something of a joke in the village—who wants to go to a medical man who is always ill himself? Anyway, I wonder whether he could have made himself sick with these paints of his, too.''

"He did," said Geoffrey, as something else clicked in his mind. "He offered me a physic that day because he felt unwell himself and was about to brew something to alleviate the symptoms. And my dog knew—he ran away from Francis's garden, and even abandoned a stolen ham so that he would not have to stay. He must have smelt the stuff. How could I have been so blind, with these facts staring me in the face all along?''

"It is hardly blindingly obvious, lad," said Helbye consolingly.

"But it *is* obvious, Will! The poison could not have been food or drink, because both had been tested by Francis, and either Torva or Ine. Therefore, it had to be something to do with the room itself. It was not the mattress, and there is very little else in the room except the rugs and the chest. There are not that many rugs and it is a large chamber anyway, while Rohese and Mabel both spent some time in the chest without ill-effects. But there are plenty of paintings. Father used every available patch of wall for his art. And he always insisted that the windows remained closed, thus concentrating the fumes.''

"And Enide and Sir Godric both became ill around the time that Sir Godric gave up his manor to Walter and Stephen, so he assumed he was being poisoned because they wanted him out of the way once he had started to delegate his powers," said Helbye, nodding.

"Quite. He saw that the onset of his illness corresponded with the time he began to relinquish his authority, and drew the conclusion that there was a direct link. The link was actually indirect: the more ill he became, the more responsibilities he needed to delegate to his sons; and the less time he spent running his estate, the more time he spent painting.''

"And the more painting he did, the more sick he became," finished Helbye. "I see.''

They rode in silence for a while, until Helbye spoke again.

"Actually, I do not see. You told me that Sir Godric painted other chambers, too. Joan was never ill, and neither was Rohese, and everyone in the village knows that their chamber was painted, because Joan was so angry about it.''

"I think that was because only the dark colours contained whatever it was that made father and Enide ill," said Geoffrey. "Father painted the other chambers in pale greens and yellows, saving the blacks and browns for his own chamber. Rohese never slept in father's room, because she did not like the paintings—luckily for her, or she might have been dying, too. When Enide insisted that Father make use of her chamber—ostensibly because she was being kind to Rohese, but really so she could use the tunnel—she saved Rohese from being poisoned, but fell victim to it herself."

"But someone still stabbed Sir Godric, lad," said Helbye. "Twice, you tell me. And someone put ergot in your wine and broth, and later hid the evidence. And someone went to some trouble to see that you would be found asleep in the chamber where Godric was murdered. Was that Enide, too?"

Geoffrey sighed. "I cannot see how," he said. "I suppose she might have come up the tunnel while I lay drugged, but I do not see how she could have arranged for me to be drugged in the first place."

"I expect Stephen did it," said Helbye. "It was Stephen who gave you the wine, and Stephen who took your dog so it would not bark and wake you when Enide sneaked in to kill Godric."

It made sense to Geoffrey. Francis had said that Stephen's wife was involved in the plot to kill Rufus, and Geoffrey could well imagine that his sly second brother might prepare the way for someone else to kill Godric and ensure that Geoffrey was blamed for it.

"That paint caused Walter to lose Goodrich, you know," mused Helbye. "If Godric had not been so certain he was being poisoned, he would not have informed King Henry and the Earl of Shrewsbury about it. And Shrewsbury would never have come up with his faked wills."

"The wills were not the only things that were faked," said Geoffrey. "The documents proclaiming that Walter was illegitimate and that Stephen was no son of Godric's were written by Norbert, who was not in Godric's service at those times. With Walter and Stephen out of the picture, and me away on Crusade, Enide would only have had Henry and Joan ahead of her to succeed to Goodrich."

"Your brother Henry is unpopular in these parts," said Helbye.

"Especially after the murder of Ynys of Lann Martin. He would not live long if *he* were lord of Goodrich with his violent ways. That only leaves Joan."

Geoffrey was silent, trying to come to terms with the waves of conflicting emotions that flowed and ebbed through his mind. He had been at Goodrich less than nine full days, during which time he had learned that his favourite sister had been horribly murdered, and then that she was alive and well and happily desecrating corpses; that she was behind a thwarted plot to kill King William Rufus, but planned to try again with King Henry; that no one in the castle or village had the slightest qualms about procuring bodies to suit their needs; and that the real killer of his father, undoubtedly the same person who had intended that Geoffrey should hang for the crime, was still very much at large.

He rubbed his eyes, trying to formulate a plan of action. He would try to speak to the King in Monmouth and warn him of what might be afoot. And then he would leave England forever, and his squabbling family could kill each other or fight as they would. His father was an evil, scheming liar, who had planned to kill a king. Someone else could avenge his murder. And someone else could deal with the treacherous Enide too, because Geoffrey did not want to meet her.

CHAPTER TWELVE

Early morning in the Forest of Dene was a miserable affair, and the sky remained a dull, leaden grey long after the sun was up. It was cold, too, and Geoffrey grew more and more chilled as he, Helbye, and Barlow rode along the path to Monmouth. Then it began to rain. It was not a downpour, but it was persistent, and of the kind that Geoffrey knew would be likely to continue all day. On either side of the increasingly sticky track stood the forest itself, a vast expanse of trees and heath that stretched right across to the mighty River Severn.

Geoffrey spoke little, ignoring the complaints of Barlow as they grew wetter, thinking about the web of intrigue that his family had spun. It had been bad enough to learn that one of his brothers or Joan had wanted him hanged for his father's murder, and it had not been pleasant to suspect that Sir Aumary's fate had been intended for him, but these were nothing when Geoffrey considered the actions of his youngest sister.

He drove bitter thoughts from his mind as the path crested a hill and the little hamlet of Genoreu came into view. It was an unprepossessing place, squashed into a dip between two hills, and comprised a rickety wooden church and several shabby hovels. The path degenerated almost immediately into a morass of thick, black mud through which Geoffrey's destrier was loath to walk. Geoffrey steered it to one side, easing it through the long grass and weeds that grew at the path edge.

Behind him, Barlow began to moan even louder, and Geoffrey wondered what he had done to deserve men-at-arms like Ingram and Barlow. One detested him sufficiently to rob graves in order to extract money from him, while the other was always too cold, too hot, thirsty, hungry, or tired. He forced uncharitable thoughts about Barlow from his mind: the lad was no longer obliged to follow any orders of Geoffrey's, but he had volunteered to come along with him nevertheless.

Genoreu was deserted except for a straggly chicken that did not long survive the dog's ready jaws. Geoffrey was uneasy at the silence, and drew his sword. Helbye watched him.

"You *have* been away a long time, lad," he said. "It is Wednesday."

"So?" asked Geoffrey, standing in his stirrups to gain a better view of the track that wound ahead.

"Market day," said Helbye. "It is the only way that the people who live in this place can make enough money for bread. They catch fish—and perhaps a few hares or birds, although they will not be sold openly, given that hunting is illegal in the King's forest—and they gather sticks to sell at the market. With luck, they will earn enough to buy flour for bread for the next week."

"Oh, yes, of course," said Geoffrey, relaxing. He replaced his sword, and urged his horse past the village towards the next hill crest. The dog, with tell-tale feathers around its mouth, trotted next to him, but then stopped dead with an ominous growl. Geoffrey knew the dog was as likely to growl at a large cat as a potentially hostile army, but he slowed his pace nonetheless. Helbye and Barlow followed suit as another small band of riders rode over the crest of a hill.

"Geoffrey!" exclaimed Stephen in surprise, reining in next to his brother.

"I knew it!" yelled Henry furiously. "Geoffrey is off to the King to stake his claim while he thought we were all otherwise engaged. His fine plan was just a ploy to get us out of the way."

"If I did want to see the King without your knowledge, I would hardly choose to travel the road that you would use on your way back," said Geoffrey. "Do you take me for a fool?"

Henry was about to reply in the affirmative when Stephen intervened.

"What is wrong, Geoffrey? Where are you going? Has the Earl arrived early?"

Geoffrey shook his head, wondering how best to answer. He did not think that Stephen or Henry would take kindly to the knowledge that Geoffrey was on his way to warn the King that their sister Enide had designs on the regal life—especially given that she was supposed to be dead, and even more particularly because Henry had hanged her supposed murderers himself.

And of course, Geoffrey had his suspicions that Stephen might well know all about the plot to kill the King anyway. On the spur of the moment, however, he could think of no lie that they would believe. He decided a little honesty might not go amiss—first, it would allow him to gauge Stephen's reaction, and second, Henry was unlikely to believe anything Geoffrey told him anyway, so there was no point in spinning elaborate yarns.

"I believe there may be a plot afoot to kill the King," he said. "I am going to warn him."

"The King is not at Monmouth," said Stephen, frowning slightly. "He left at dawn to hunt."

Geoffrey gazed at him in horror. Was history about to repeat itself? Was there another Tirel standing in the trees, ready to loose an arrow as a king hunted in the forest?

"Then I must try to find him," said Geoffrey. "Do you have any idea where he might be?"

"I might," said Henry with satisfaction. "But I will not tell you. And this is a big forest—who knows what might happen to you as you wander through it."

"You tried that once before, and you were unsuccessful," said Geoffrey, thinking of Aumary, killed with an arrow and all but forgotten by Geoffrey in the turmoil of life at the castle. "What makes you think your luck would be better today?"

"Tried what?" demanded Henry. "If I had tried anything, you would not be sitting there so proud and fine on your splendid horse!"

"The King went Lann Martin way," said Stephen, glaring at Henry for his belligerence to the man who might yet cheat the greedy Earl of Shrewsbury of the inheritance they all wanted. "But I would not go there, if I were you. Caerdig will not take kindly to uninvited Mappestones on his land."

"And of course, you do not want me dead before you have used me to file your claim against Shrewsbury," said Geoffrey dryly.

"That is right! We do not!" exclaimed Henry, oblivious to the irony in Geoffrey's comment. "I forgot. But Lann Martin is where the King has gone. It is said that a great white stag has been seen there, and the King means to have it before he leaves the area."

"Let's hope that is all he leaves with," murmured Geoffrey, urging his destrier back the way he had come. "And not an arrow in his heart like his brother Rufus."

"What are you muttering about?" called Henry after him, spurring his own mount to follow. "You have taken to muttering since you got back. You never used to mutter."

"Do not antagonise him, Henry," shouted Stephen, keen not to be left behind. "If we win our claim, and it is ruled that Geoffrey owns Goodrich, you will not be able to negotiate for a share if you have driven him to dislike you."

Dislike! thought Geoffrey, amused despite his growing concerns that he was already too late to help the King.

"You will not win any claim if anything happens to the King," he shouted over his shoulder as he rode. "Because then there will be no one to stop the relentless advance of Shrewsbury, and by the time the Duke of Normandy sails from France to take the vacant throne, the Earl will have taken a good deal more than Goodrich."

"You are right," said Stephen, breathing hard as he tried to keep up. "But on what evidence do you base your claim? How do you know that someone means the King harm?"

"Francis the physician is dead, and he told me of a plot," replied Geoffrey vaguely, not wanting to reveal too much to Stephen.

"Geoffrey, stop!" shouted Henry, as Geoffrey spurred his horse to a faster pace still. "We cannot go to Lann Martin—Caerdig would kill us for certain. It is all very well for you wearing all that armour, but what about us?"

"You do not have to come," replied Geoffrey, blinking as mud kicked up by Helbye's horse in front of him splattered into his face. "Go back to Goodrich and wait for me there."

"But what if you do not return?" cried Henry. "Then our last chance to claim Goodrich will be gone."

"I am touched by your fraternal concern," yelled Geoffrey. "But with all due respect, Goodrich can go to the Devil!"

"It *will* go to the Devil if you do not come back," said Stephen quietly. "And that Devil is the Earl of Shrewsbury! Return to Goodrich if you like, Henry. I am riding with Geoffrey. Caerdig would never dare attack a knight like him, anyway."

Geoffrey wished Caerdig had known that before his ambush nine days earlier. He slowed his horse as they approached an especially muddy stretch of land, and Stephen was able to trot next to him.

"The King was furious when he heard what the Earl had done to get Goodrich. We told him your theories about the forged wills, and he is going to back our claim. But he said only the will citing Godfrey as heir stands any chance of succeeding, because it was made recently, but apparently we will need to provide incontrovertible proof that Godfrey was an affectionate name used for you by our father."

"That might be difficult," said Geoffrey, not particularly interested in fighting for something that his brothers intended to wrest from him at the first opportunity anyway. "Father is dead; the physician is dead; Norbert has disappeared; and Father Adrian is a less than reliable witness."

"Adrian is a well-respected man," said Stephen. "He might be persuaded to come to our assistance in this matter."

"You mean Adrian might be persuaded to lie for you?" asked Geoffrey dryly.

"Unfortunately not," said Stephen with real regret. "Adrian is a man of scruples, more is the pity. Perhaps one of our neighbours might help us out—no one is going to want the Earl of Shrewsbury living next door. We could offer some of our sheep as an incentive."

"Why am I even listening to you?" wondered Geoffrey aloud. "The King is about to be murdered as he hunts, and all you can do is think about which one of your neighbours you can bribe to lie in court. Believe me, Stephen, Shrewsbury will offer any witnesses you can find a good deal more than a few sheep. He might even agree not to murder them."

"You are right," said Stephen. "We need something better than livestock."

He dropped back, deep in thought, as Geoffrey urged his horse forward again. The knight glanced behind at him. Stephen and Henry had three of the guards from the castle with them, all mounted and well armed, although Geoffrey had seen nothing to suggest that they were competent. And Geoffrey had Helbye and Barlow. He imagined that they should have no problem with Caerdig, should he make an appearance. Geoffrey had bested him once before with three fewer men than were with him this time—although, of course, none of them had been the slippery Stephen, the hateful Henry, or the incompetent gatehouse guards.

He reached a fork in the road and slowed. To the right lay the long route back to Goodrich; to the left lay Caerdig's lands.

"Go right," called Helbye. "Lann Martin is right."

Geoffrey gazed at him askance, and wondered whether the sergeant genuinely did not know, or whether he was merely attempting to prevent Geoffrey from riding into what promised to be a dangerous situation.

Ignoring the sergeant's protestations, he urged his horse down the left-hand track. It was steep and muddy, and liberally scattered with rocks, so that Geoffrey was forced to slow his speed, or risk ruining his horse. The path meandered through some boggy forest, and then went straight as an arrow across a patch of heathland, swathed in a gloomy pall of mist.

"The King is a fool to come hunting in this," mumbled Barlow, wiping away the rain that dripped from his long hair into his eyes. "He should be indoors, wenching next to a roaring fire."

"Quiet, Barlow," said Geoffrey sharply. They were drawing near to Lann Martin itself, and Geoffrey had no intention of walking into a second ambush. "Listen!"

He reined in his horse and sat still, closing his eyes to hear the sounds of the forest. A gentle wind whispered through the bare branches, and raindrops splattered down onto the litter of dead leaves below. A bird sang a few piercing notes and then was silent, and Stephen's horse pawed at the ground. And then he heard it. In the distance, came the faraway voices of men shouting. He opened his eyes and looked at the others, wondering if they had heard it, too.

Were they shouts of alarm, claiming that the King had been shot and lay dying in some scrubby glade? Or were they simply the sound of the beaters driving the forest animals to where the King and his entourage waited with their bows and arrows?

He unfastened his shield from its bindings, and slipped it over his arm. Drawing his sword, and checking that he would easily be able to reach his dagger, he rode towards the noise.

"My God, Geoffrey!" breathed Stephen, watching his precautions with unease. "There is no one here. The place is deserted. I expect all the villagers of Lann Martin are out acting as beaters for the King. He pays handsomely, I am told."

Geoffrey said nothing, but jabbed his heels into his destrier to urge it to move faster. When Stephen began to say something to Henry, Geoffrey silenced him irritably. At the far end of the clearing, the path disappeared again between two dense walls of trees. Geoffrey eased his way along it, listening intently, and watching for even the slightest movement in the trees ahead that might warn him of an ambush. Gradually, the sounds of shouting grew louder.

Geoffrey's fears were somewhat allayed. It was not the clamour of alarm that was echoing through the woods, but the meaningless yells of the beaters, walking in a long line with their tufter hounds, and making as much noise as possible to drive the beasts of the forest towards the waiting hunters.

The shouting grew louder still, and Geoffrey tensed as a flicker out of the corner of his eye showed where a small deer had darted, frightened by the increasing clamour. He slowed his destrier, angrily quelling the impatient whispers of his brothers behind him with an urgent gesture of his hand. Rufus had been slain by a stray arrow during exactly the same circumstances, and Geoffrey had no intention of falling that way, too. And there was also the possibility that the king-killer was there, lurking somewhere in the trees to await the right moment. He might well loose an arrow at Geoffrey and his companions if he thought they might interfere with his purpose.

The path cut to the left, and then to the right, emerging into another clearing. The noise of the beaters was very close now, and Geoffrey was aware that the glade in front of him might well hold archers in the King's party, waiting for animals to be driven past. There was a flurry of movement, and a hare appeared, heading for a sandy bank on the opposite side. With a yelp of delight, Geoffrey's dog was after it, snaking through the grass in a blur of black and white. Then Geoffrey heard a snap, and saw an arrow arch high in the air.

At the same time, a man with a bow stood from where he had been kneeling behind a bush on top of the bank, and fired another arrow, which sped upwards to cross the first.

"No!" yelled Stephen, thrusting Geoffrey out of the way to gallop forwards.

As the arrows reached their zeniths, two stags burst from the forest at the far end of the clearing, pursued by Caerdig, who was wielding a stick in the air and screaming in Welsh. More arrows flew as the stags tore towards Geoffrey. Henry's horse, panicked by the terrified beasts bearing down on it, whinnied in panic: it could not escape the way it had come, because that route was blocked by Helbye and Barlow, so it charged from the shelter of the bushes and bolted at right angles to the stags, with Henry clinging to it for dear life.

More archers appeared from nowhere, and arrows hissed through the air, aimed at anything that moved. Geoffrey spotted the stocky figure of the King standing near the bank where the hare had run. Simultaneously, Geoffrey saw a dark shadow on the opposite side of the clearing nock an arrow in a bow and point it directly towards the monarch.

With a piercing battle cry learned from the Saracens, Geoffrey exploded out of the forest and bore down on the indistinct figure of the archer. He felt as if his horse were moving in slow motion. He watched the archer falter as he saw Geoffrey thundering towards him, but then saw him straighten with resolve, and fix the King once again in his sights. Geoffrey spurred forwards desperately yelling to the King to duck, although he knew the King would neither hear nor have time to act.

The arrow was loosed. Geoffrey did not look to see where it fell, but continued to bear down on the archer. The figure in black nocked a second arrow to his bow, and aimed again, this time at

Geoffrey. Instinctively, Geoffrey raised his shield, and heard the arrow thud into it, splitting the wood, so that the point emerged on the other side, a hair's-breadth from his arm. Geoffrey hurled the damaged shield from him and leapt from his saddle as the figure abandoned his bow and began to race away. Geoffrey landed badly and stumbled, losing vital moments.

He smashed through the forest, heavy footed and encumbered by his chain-mail and surcoat. The figure ahead of him clambered over a fallen branch, and zigzagged through the trees. Who was it? Geoffrey strained to recognise the figure that dashed this way and that, but his movements were unfamiliar. Was it Enide? Had she acquired the skill of archery through the years as she had changed from his much-loved sister into a Mappestone? But her hand was withered, so how could she hold a bow? Or was that story simply another lie told to mislead him?

Geoffrey thrust all thoughts from his mind other than the running down of his quarry. He was losing the man. Geoffrey was simply too slow in his armour, and Norman knights were not designed to chase assassins through the forest on foot. He fell heavily, and rolled down a bank until he crashed up against the trunk of a tree that stopped him dead. Gasping for breath, he righted himself and staggered on, seeing the figure dart through the trees ahead.

Then the archer tripped, too, legs ensnared in a mass of bindweed that grew across a shallow depression in the ground. He struggled frantically, kicking against the fibrous plants, and trying to regain his footing. Geoffrey was almost on him. The archer thrashed his way free of the last few tendrils and scrabbled to his feet. Geoffrey hurled himself full length, and succeeded in gaining a handhold on the man's ankle. The man kicked with his other foot, trying to dislodge Geoffrey's grip, but Geoffrey held on grimly. The force of the kick made the archer lose his balance, giving Geoffrey time to grab the hem of his cloak. Although the archer was lighter and faster, he was no match for Geoffrey once he had been caught. Pinning the man beneath him, Geoffrey wrenched the hood from the bowman's face.

"Norbert!" he exclaimed in astonishment.

But there was no time for analysis. Norbert seized on Geoffrey's momentary surprise to land a hefty blow with a piece of wood that his groping fingers had encountered on the ground. Stunned and dizzy, Geoffrey felt the clerk sliding out from his grasp, and fought against the lights that danced in front of his eyes to lay hold of him again. He struggled to his knees, and grabbed the clerk a second time. Norbert struck out with his branch, but this time Geoffrey blocked the blow with an upraised arm. And then Norbert collapsed on top of Geoffrey in a spurt of hot blood.

Startled, Geoffrey gazed at him. From Norbert's chest protruded the shaft of an arrow. Abandoning the dead clerk, Geoffrey looked around him wildly. How could he hide? He had been grappling with Norbert and so had no idea from which direction the arrow had been fired. He flinched instinctively as another thumped into a tree a few inches from his head, and he dropped full-length into the weeds. He knew now!

Wriggling forwards on his stomach in a way most Norman knights would never consider, he reached the trunk of a thick oak tree, and edged around the back of it. Raising himself to a crouch, he drew his dagger and listened.

There was nothing, except distant, excited shouts from the clearing. Was the King dead? wondered Geoffrey. Had Norbert succeeded in his mission? He risked peering out from the tree to look around. Norbert's body lay where it had fallen, but otherwise, there was no movement.

A sharp crack from behind him made him spin round, but there was nothing to see. He looked back to Norbert. Even from a distance, Geoffrey could see that the arrow that had killed the clerk was smooth and straight—it was an archer's arrow, not something that a villager might own with which to shoot hares or birds. And it was almost exactly the same as the one that had slain Aumary, fired with a good-quality bow that had the power to drive it through chain-mail. Had it been otherwise, Geoffrey would have risked bursting from his hiding place and running, trusting that his armour would protect him. But he knew chain-mail would be useless against the kind of weapon that his assailant held.

Another sharp crack sounded, this time to his right. Geoffrey frowned. Was someone throwing stones to mislead him and coax him from his hiding place, or did Norbert have more than one assistant hidden in the forest? But Norbert's accomplices would not have killed Norbert, reasoned Geoffrey; they were supposed to be on the same side. So who had?

Geoffrey winced as an arrow hit the trunk of the tree so close that it all but grazed his ear. He leapt to his feet, and started to run in the opposite direction, only to find himself hard up against the sword of Sir Drogo, the Earl of Shrewsbury's sullen henchman. Geoffrey backed away, but to his left was Sir Malger, armed with a fine bow and a good quantity of pale, straight arrows. And to his right was a woman, stepping out from behind another tree and smiling enigmatically.

"Geoffrey," she said, coming towards him. "So we will meet after all! I did not think I would have the pleasure."

Geoffrey did not need to be told the name of the woman who smiled at him so beguilingly in the forest clearing. He would have recognised her even if she had appeared in the Holy City with a troop of jugglers, for she looked very much like Geoffrey himself. With sudden clarity, he recalled the face of the child who had said a tearful farewell to him twenty years before—a face that had grown shadowy and indistinct through time, but now blazed in his mind as clearly as if it had been yesterday.

Enide was a good deal taller now—almost as tall as Geoffrey, in fact—but her hair was the same, and when she turned, he saw that it fell in a thick, glossy plait down her back in the same peculiar style she had adopted when she had been young. Her face had maintained the slight pinkness of fine health, and her cheeks were as downy and soft as they ever were. Her eyes, too, were the same pleasant green as were Geoffrey's, and held the twinkle of mischief that he remembered so well.

"Will you not greet me, Geoff?" she cried, the smile dissolving to hurt.

Geoffrey's heart wrenched, recalling that same sudden fading of laughter from years before, when Stephen had said something cruel or Henry had used his superior strength to take something from her. He swallowed, but said nothing.

"Geoffrey!" she said. "Do you not know who I am? It is me!

Enide! I had to feign my death so that one of our brothers would not kill me because they believed I was poisoning our dear father."

"Any one of them would have been delighted if you had poisoned our dear father," said Geoffrey harshly. "But first, no one poisoned him. And second, someone most certainly stabbed him. Was that you?"

"It most certainly was not," she said indignantly. "What have people been saying? To what lies have you been listening?"

"Father Adrian has been saying nothing but good," said Geoffrey evasively.

"Adrian!" she said with an indulgent smile. "Poor, dear Adrian. He always believes anything I tell him. But what is this about Godric? He *was* being poisoned, you know—the physician said so."

"He was poisoning himself," said Geoffrey. "With his paints."

"The paint?" echoed Enide. She laughed suddenly. "Oh, Geoff! Trust you to work that out! You always were quick minded. So, Godric lay in his vile chamber, slowly being killed by the fumes from his revolting paintings? And that explains why, before he became too ill to move, I was sick when I slept in his room. Godric spent his last days wailing and whining that someone was killing him, and all the time it was suicide!"

"Enough of this," said Malger, stepping forward and nocking an arrow in his bow. Geoffrey noted that the knight's chain-mail was carelessly maintained, revealing gaps and missing links that Geoffrey himself would have been ashamed of. His lack of attention to the details that might save his life indicated that he had been so sure of their success that he considered them unimportant. Geoffrey wondered whether he would be able to exploit such over-confidence to his own advantage. "Norbert missed the King, and I could not see well enough to get off a good shot. The King lives and so we should not tarry here and wait for him to accuse us of treason."

"There will be another chance to kill him," said Enide, unperturbed. "The King loves to hunt."

"Fine. But I do not want him hunting us," said Malger firmly. "The Earl will hardly be able to speak out for us if we are caught, and doubtless your brother here has spread the news all over the county that we would rather have the Duke of Normandy as King than the usurper Henry."

"Geoff would not do that," said Enide. "How could he? He has not had sufficient time to work all this out."

"Maybe so, but I do not care to take the risk," said Malger, raising the bow.

Geoffrey braced himself, but Enide strode over to Malger and put her hand on the arrow, forcing him to lower it. Her hand, Geoffrey noted, was rigid, like a claw.

"Malger! This is a brother I have not seen for twenty years." She turned to Geoffrey, and her eyes were hard as flint. "I would have appreciated your help in keeping Goodrich from the likes of Walter, Stephen, and Henry, but I have achieved my objective perfectly well without you anyway."

"You forged documents," said Geoffrey, remembering the parchments he had found in her secret hiding place.

"Well, I did not do it myself," she said bitterly, holding the claw-like hand close to his face. "Norbert's documents—despite his dreadful writing and worse spelling—served to rid us of Walter and Stephen. Godric loathed them both, and was only too happy to go along with what he knew were lies—Godric never went campaigning with the Conqueror in 1063; and our mother certainly would not have wasted her time in breeding before she was married."

"So, both Walter and Stephen are Godric's legal heirs?" asked Geoffrey.

"Yes, but Norbert's forged documents will 'prove' them otherwise. And the next in line to inherit Goodrich is Joan. Now, Joan is wed to Olivier, and Olivier is a relative of the Earl of Shrewsbury, who does not want Olivier to have Goodrich because he is a weakling. That leaves Henry, who is so hated by his neighbours that no one would have done more than heave a sigh of relief when he was found with a knife in his back. After all, it was Henry who murdered the popular Ynys of Lann Martin."

"So that was you, was it?" asked Geoffrey heavily. "You killed poor Ynys, and made certain that the suspicion fell on Henry."

"Quite. But, of course, nothing could ever be proven against Henry," said Enide, "because Henry did not really do it. He did, however, have a very convenient argument with Ynys in front of the entire village—over sheep, would you believe? Words were exchanged, and that night Drogo ensured that Henry's threats were carried out. Ynys was wandering alone in the forest, no doubt pondering how to heal the ever-widening rift between Lann Martin and Goodrich, and Drogo dispatched him."

"Ynys did not deserve to be used to further your vile plot," said Geoffrey, sickened. Ynys had been a kind and gentle man whom Geoffrey had respected. "And neither does Henry."

"Henry's innocence or guilt is irrelevant," said Enide. "The point is that his neighbours have become more wary of him than ever, a feeling that is intensified, of course, by his own charming personality. His hot denials of Ynys's murder, and his refusal to answer any questions about it because he was so affronted by the charge, meant that he dug his own grave in that respect."

"Goodrich is almost ours," said Malger, looking at Enide with a leer that suggested their allegiance was more than a business relationship.

"Ours?" asked Geoffrey.

"Malger has been my lover for many years," explained Enide to Geoffrey. "We will make Goodrich more powerful than ever, and then unite it with the Earl's lands to the north."

"What about Father Adrian?" said Geoffrey, wondering just how many lovers his sister had stashed away. Was one of them the great Earl himself?

"Adrian was always on hand," said Enide, oblivious or uncaring of Malger's jealous glower. "And he loves me so much that he will do anything for me—even provide me with a corpse, although he would not decapitate it for me. I had to do that myself."

Geoffrey swallowed hard, not liking the image of his sister sawing the head from a body.

"And then we had news that you had survived the Crusade, and might even pay us a visit—twenty years too late for me to care, but a visit nevertheless. We tried to prevent you from arriving at all. But I thought my Crusader brother would be the more richly dressed knight of the pair who wandered into the ambush at Lann Martin. I told Malger as much, and he concentrated his efforts on the wrong man. I should not have been so easily misled—you always were scruffy and uninterested in appearances. I should have known that the taller, more practically attired knight was you."

"So Aumary was killed because you thought he was me?" asked Geoffrey.

"Yes and no," said Malger, eager to join in and show off his own cleverness. "It would have been an excellent opportunity to get rid of you—and Caerdig's pathetic little ambush provided a perfect cover. But whether we shot you, or Aumary, or both, it would have worked to our advantage."

"How?" asked Geoffrey, puzzled.

"Because of these arrows," said Malger, raising his bow again. "They were made by the same fletcher who made the arrow that killed King William Rufus. And King Henry would recognise them anywhere. You did what we could not: you took one of them right into Chepstow Castle and presented it to the King himself. And you can be assured he recognised it for what it was."

Geoffrey recalled the King's reaction to the arrow. He had studied it long and hard, but had refused to touch it. Eventually, he had ordered Geoffrey to throw it in the fire.

"So it was a warning to the King that an attempt would be made on his life?" asked Geoffrey. "But why bother with that if you planned to kill him anyway?"

"It was part warning and part message," said Enide. "It was a warning that the King's life could be taken as easily as had his brother's; and it was a message that Rufus's death was by no means the accident that everyone seems to have accepted."

"You mean that Rufus really was murdered that day, even though your own plot failed?" asked Geoffrey. "That is no great revelation. Tirel is claiming that he did not fire the arrow."

"Hmm," said Enide, eyeing him critically. "Perhaps you are not so quick-witted after all. Of course Rufus was killed deliberately, but it was not by Tirel. Kings do not die in silly accidents like that! Do you think Tirel would have loosed his arrow had he thought that the King was anywhere near where it might have landed?"

Geoffrey was silent. So, Enide and Malger had used him to deliver their message to the King. It explained why the King had pretended that the recipe for horse liniment was so important, too. He did not want to tell Geoffrey that the real message lay in the corpse of Aumary, slain by a distinctive arrow; so he had snatched the scrap of parchment the constable had found and made a show that it was something vital. Since few men in Henry's court could read, Henry had assumed—erroneously—that Geoffrey was also illiterate. Geoffrey was fortunate that the King had realised that he was innocent of all this treachery, or he might well now be languishing in the dungeons of Chepstow Castle. Or not languishing anywhere at all.

"And you robbed me later," he said. "You stole my scrolls."

"And that lovely chalice, yes," she replied. "Although I was not there, personally. Fortunately, you left Ingram with your horses while you went dashing off to jump in the river after that other lout. Malger was all for slaying the whole lot of you, but Ingram virtually unbuckled your saddle for him, so keen was he to save himself from Malger's sword. In the event, it was simpler to have Ingram hand us your 'treasure' and leave peacefully."

"Ingram told me he was attacked by thirty outlaws," said Geoffrey. "And all along it was merely two of the Earl of Shrewsbury's hirelings?"

Drogo growled at the back of his throat, and Malger's arrow came up. Enide pushed it down irritably. Remarkably, Malger made no move to disobey her, despite the sounds of the King's party coming closer. Had Geoffrey been Malger, he would have ignored Enide, fired his arrow, and been away.

"I had expected your saddlebags to be loaded with plunder," she said to Geoffrey, moving so that she stood in Malger's line of fire. "Malger was most disappointed when he found only books."

"I will bear that in mind next time," said Geoffrey. "But why did he take the scrolls?"

"We knew you had been to see the King, and Malger thought they might be important messages. He cannot read, so did not know what they were. But I could see that they were just some worthless decorated manuscripts, probably in Arabic or Hebrew. Am I correct?"

Geoffrey nodded. "I was going to translate them."

"Too late for that," said Malger, raising his bow and stepping round Enide for a clear shot.

"Really, Malger," said Enide reproachfully. "At least grant me a few moments with my favourite brother before you kill him."

"Why did you shoot Norbert?" asked Geoffrey quickly, hoping

to prolong the discussion long enough to allow the King's men to find them. "I thought he was on your side."

"He was," said Enide. "But we will need to travel quickly now he has failed to kill the King, and Norbert, although an excellent shot, is not a good rider. He would be caught in no time at all—and then he would reveal our identities to the first person who asked, to save his own miserable neck. He has not been himself since his marriage to Helbye's wife was dissolved."

Geoffrey knew from personal experience that Norbert was not a fast mover. He had almost caught the scribe once before—when Norbert had loosed an arrow at Geoffrey as he had looked for Rohese in the woods near the river. The glimpse of the scribe's face as he had glanced back after Geoffrey had collided with Adrian's cart had not been sufficient to identify him, but the archer had worn the same dark clothes and had run with the same distinctive gait as Norbert. Geoffrey was surprised that he had not associated Norbert's penchant for bows—which Geoffrey had discovered when he had followed him into his outhouse in the castle bailey one night—with the mysterious archer before.

"Who else was involved in this plot?" he asked. "I now know about Malger, Drogo, Norbert, Stephen's wife, the physician, Father, and Adrian."

"Not Adrian," said Enide. "I could never trust him with business like this. It was bad enough persuading him to help me feign my death. I had to cry all night to achieve that. But you are right about the others."

"And you killed Pernel?"

"Malger did. He is good at that sort of thing. He should have gone on Crusade; he would have been a hero."

Malger blushed modestly.

"Pernel was a silly, empty-headed woman," said Enide. "She was so proud to be part of a plot to kill Rufus that she wanted to tell everyone about it. She was, quite simply, too dangerous for us. Malger had some concoction that he fed to her in a sweetmeat during mass—serve her right for eating in church—and it brought on the 'falling sickness' that the whole village witnessed."

"I do not understand why you are doing this," said Geoffrey. "You can scarcely rule Goodrich if you are thought to be dead."

"I do not have to stay dead," said Enide. "The Earl of Shrewsbury will sort it all out. We will have Goodrich yet."

"You trust the Earl to pay you for all this?" asked Geoffrey
doubtfully.

Drogo stiffened angrily at the insult to his liege lord, wielding
his sword dangerously. Enide raised her hand imperiously, and the
heavy knight stayed his hand.

"Why not?" she asked. "He is no more and no less honest than
the next man."

Geoffrey suspected that the Earl was a good deal less honest than
the next man, assuming of course that the next man was not a Mappestone or King Henry.

"And who else is involved in this plot, if not Adrian?"

"There is one other person—"

"Enough!" snapped Drogo, striding forwards. "Listen—they are
searching for us. Kill him, and let us be gone."

"Who is the other?" asked Geoffrey, ignoring Drogo.

"If you cannot guess, you will never know," said Enide lightly,
as though she were playing a game of fireside riddles with him.

"Enide!" warned Malger. "Time is short. We must kill him and
be away."

"I am sorry, Geoff," said Enide, with what seemed to be genuine
regret. "I would love to let you live—for old times sake—but you
know all about us, and that will not do at all. All right, Malger. Do
what you will."

Malger brought up his bow and pointed the arrow at Geoffrey, while
Drogo stood next to him, his sword in his hand as he glanced around
uneasily. Enide gave Geoffrey a sad, parting smile, and then turned
away. Malger's eyes followed her, admiring the way her hips moved
under her close-cut gown. While his attention strayed, Geoffrey
hurled himself forwards, crashing into the tall knight, and sending
him sprawling. Arrows scattered everywhere, and Geoffrey heard
the bow snap under their weight. Malger struggled to draw his dagger, while Drogo advanced on them both with his sword. Geoffrey
pummelled Malger's startled face with his mailed fists, and then

rolled, hauling Malger's body on top of his as Drogo began to stab indiscriminately with his sword.

Enide screamed, and Geoffrey saw her throw herself at Drogo to make him desist, lest he harm Malger. Malger, finding himself unexpectedly uppermost, scrabbled to clasp his fingers around Geoffrey's neck, and then gasped in shock as Drogo scored a hit with his sword.

"Drogo!" screamed Enide. "Kill Geoffrey, not Malger! Be careful for Malger!"

Geoffrey jammed the heel of his hand under Malger's nose, and heaved him to one side, struggling free of his grasping hands. Drogo hurled Enide away from him, and took his sword in both hands, preparing to dispatch Geoffrey with a single swipe.

"Kill him now!" screamed Enide, as Geoffrey began to back away.

Geoffrey had dropped his own sword when he had leapt from his horse to chase Norbert, and his shield was lying in the clearing with Norbert's arrow embedded in it. Drogo, like Geoffrey, was a trained knight, and Geoffrey knew his chances of winning a fight while he was unarmed were small, especially with Enide hurling stones to keep him off balance, and Malger struggling to his feet behind her. But Drogo was slow and brutal, and Malger was brash and over-confident; Geoffrey, unlike either, was used to fighting with his wits as well as his weapons.

He dodged behind the oak tree, hearing its bark splinter as Drogo's sword smashed into it, then whipped round to thump the knight as hard as he could in the small of his back as he strained to pull his blade from the tree. Drogo dropped to his knees with a cry of pain, and Geoffrey turned his attention to Malger, who was trying to haul his sword from his belt. It had become tangled in the fight, and Malger could not free it. Geoffrey drew his dagger and sprang forwards, raising one hand to protect himself from the hail of stones and sticks cast by Enide.

"Help!" yelled Malger in a most unknightly way as Geoffrey advanced.

"Stop!" shrieked Enide. "Leave him alone, Geoffrey! Damn you!"

An especially large stone struck Geoffrey's helmet, knocking it from his head. He staggered backwards as Malger's sword came free. With a sigh of relief, he faced Geoffrey, holding the weapon in two hands. Unlike Drogo, he did not swing wildly, but waited, ready to see whether Geoffrey would move to the left or to the right.

Geoffrey did neither. He flung his dagger at Malger, using the instant when the knight ducked out of the way to launch himself into him. Both fell to the ground, and they were back to fighting with their bare hands. Malger, too, lost his bassinet, then Enide came in close, flailing at them with a rotten branch. When the branch began to disintegrate without having added any perceptible advantage to Malger, she abandoned it, and went back to pelting Geoffrey with her stones. Meanwhile, Drogo had begun to recover. He reeled across to them, and hauled Geoffrey away from Malger, wrapping one arm around his neck. Malger scrambled to his feet, but then stumbled dizzily as his bare head came into the direct path of one of Enide's stones. He fell backwards and lay still.

Although slow, Drogo was strong, and Geoffrey found he could not struggle free of the brawny arm that gripped his neck. And he was beginning to tire, so that the more he fought and squirmed, the less chance there was of him escaping. Enide, meanwhile, was bending over the inert form of Malger. Then she stood and, throwing back her head, uttered a long, low keening sound that made Geoffrey's blood run cold. Even Drogo was affected, for the arm that held Geoffrey slackened slightly. When the echoes from the eerie sound had faded, Enide turned to Geoffrey.

"You have killed him," she whispered. "He is dead. There is an arrow in his back."

Looking at Malger, Geoffrey saw it was true. The knight had fallen onto one of his own arrows, which had wedged itself point-up on a rotting piece of wood, and had slipped through a gap in his poorly maintained chain-mail. Malger, thus, had died in very much the same way as had his victim Aumary—with an arrow in his back.

"Quickly!" urged Drogo, tearing his eyes away from Malger's body. "Get that dagger and make an end to him while I hold him still. We might yet escape."

"You killed my Malger," Enide whispered, turning eyes filled with hurt on her brother.

"You did, actually," Geoffrey gasped, struggling to breathe

against the increased pressure of Drogo's arm. "You threw the stone that stunned him and made him fall, not me."

His voice seemed to bring her out of her dazed shock. Her eyes snapped into alertness, and she pulled herself together. Quickly, she bent to retrieve the knife, and moved towards Geoffrey with an expression of purpose that left him in no doubt that this time there would be no escape. The knife blade glittered dully in her hand, and Geoffrey looked away from it into her face. She was concentrating on the task in hand; her eyes were searching for the best place to stab him and nothing else. She chose her spot and began to push. Geoffrey closed his eyes, waiting for the searing pain that would end his life.

Suddenly, there was a high-pitched squeal of terror, and Geoffrey opened his eyes to see something large, brown, and hairy hurtling towards them. Drogo released Geoffrey with a muttered obscenity and shoved him forwards, directly into the path of the enraged wild boar.

For a moment, Geoffrey was aware of nothing but the sound of the boar's screaming and flashes of yellow-white as its tusks flailed at him. Then one of them struck home, slashing through the chain-mail on his forearm, and he came to his senses. He staggered to his feet, kicking out at the furious animal as it attacked. He groped for his dagger, but it was not there, and he could not recall where he had lost it. The animal crashed into his legs, knocking him from his feet.

He covered his head with his arms, feeling its pointed feet gouging into him. Despite his predicament, Geoffrey could not help but see the ironic side. He had survived attacks by two fully armed knights and an insane sister, only to fall under the tusks of a pig! He felt the animal's hot breath on his cheek, and then he realised he was not alone.

Something black and white was at the corner of his vision, worrying at the boar and snapping at its legs. More enraged than ever, the animal shifted its attention from Geoffrey and turned on the dog, standing stock-still for an instant in readiness for a charge. The dog eyed it uncertainly, realising too late that it had attacked something larger and stronger than itself. It braced itself to bolt. And then an arrow thudded into the boar, and the dog ambled forwards to sniff at it nonchalantly. Geoffrey struggled away from the dying animal, and looked for Enide and Drogo. A short distance away, two branches swayed gently, as though someone had recently passed between them, but the forest was otherwise as still and silent as the grave.

King Henry stood over Geoffrey, graciously accepting the accolades of his fellow huntsmen for his excellent shot. Geoffrey sat on the ground trying to make sense out of what had happened.

"My brother the Duke of Normandy did not train you very well if he taught you to fight boar with your bare hands, Geoffrey Mappestone," said the King when his courtiers had finally finished with their praises.

"I seem to have lost my dagger," said Geoffrey, dazed and climbing slowly to his feet.

"My point is proven," said the King, turning to his retinue in amusement. "Most of us would hunt the boar with a bow or, if we were feeling exceptionally vigorous, a lance. None of us would consider taking one on with a dagger. Or even a sword!"

His entourage laughed politely. Well, not all of them, Geoffrey noticed. The Earl of Shrewsbury was not smiling.

"So we are even," said the King. "I shot the boar that was mauling you, and you thwarted the archer who tried to kill me. His body is there, I see. I suppose you do not know his name, do you?"

"Norbert," said Geoffrey. "He was my father's scribe, but became embroiled in a plot to kill first your brother Rufus and now you."

The King's eyes narrowed. "Plot?"

Geoffrey took a deep breath to try to control the tremble of exhaustion in his voice. "Last year, a small group of fanatics planned to kill Rufus because they considered him an inappropriate ruler. The murder was to take place in the New Forest, it was to be a hunting accident, and it was to occur this coming summer when the Duke of Normandy would be well placed to take advantage of the vacant throne. But Rufus died of a hunting accident quite by chance before these people had the opportunity to put their plan into action."

Geoffrey paused, aware that he had not only the King's complete attention but that of his entire retinue.

"Pray continue," said the King, his expression unreadable.

"Rufus's death did not achieve what these plotters intended, however. He died too soon for the Duke of Normandy to take advantage of the situation, and they found themselves not with the Duke as King, but with you. Rather than abandon a plan that had promised to be so rewarding, they simply put it into action again, the only difference being that this time, you were to be the victim."

"I see," said the King. His eyes were dark, and Geoffrey was not sure whether the King believed a word he had said. "And who are these plotters?"

"I am not sure of all of them, my lord," said Geoffrey. "But Norbert was one, Malger who lies dead over there, another—"

"Malger of Caen?" asked the King, taking a few steps to examine the body Geoffrey had indicated. He looked from it to the Earl of Shrewsbury. "He was in your service, Shrewsbury. Am I correct?"

"I do not think so, my lord," said the Earl, striding forward and poking at Malger with his foot. "He does not seem familiar."

"Really?" asked Geoffrey, his astonishment at the Earl's blatant falsehood making him incautious. "Malger was under the impression that he was one of your most valued henchmen."

"Then that was probably just wishful thinking on his part," said the Earl, bringing his cold, reptilian eyes to bear on Geoffrey. "I do not know this man. But you have only recently returned to the country after an absence of many years, so it is not surprising that you cannot recall whom you saw where."

Geoffrey saw that, short of calling the Earl a liar, he was not going to win this argument. He wondered who the King's retinue was more likely to believe—an impoverished Crusader knight, or the great Earl of Shrewsbury.

"The other plotters include . . ." He paused, uncertain how to proceed. Would it be prudent to claim that one of them was another knight in the service of the Earl of Shrewsbury, while the others included his sister and father?

"These alleged plotters," said the King, as Geoffrey hesitated. "Are they alive or dead?"

"Mostly dead," replied Geoffrey, disconcerted by the King's abrupt loss of interest in the plotters" identities. "Only two remain alive that I know."

"My chief huntsman will track them down and kill them," said the King.

He snapped his fingers, and a burly man in forest greens slipped out of the ranks and disappeared into the trees, several similarly clad men on his heels.

"Of course," the King continued, "if they cannot find this pair, I shall expect you to ferret them out and dispatch them yourself. And then we will say no more about this business. You have done well, Sir Geoffrey. Now, I understand you have recently lost your father?"

Geoffrey nodded uncertainly, at a loss at how to react to the King's sudden changes of subject.

"My condolences. He was a loyal man, and you have followed in his footsteps. I always reward loyalty."

Here he paused, and beamed around at his retinue, allowing his eyes to remain a little longer on the Earl of Shrewsbury than the others.

"I would like to assure you that I will apply to my Archbishop to ask him to honour the marriage made in faith by your father and mother. This means that Goodrich will stay in your family, because all Godric's offspring will be legitimate once more. I am sure Shrewsbury will not object to my rewarding you for saving my life?"

The Earl gave the King an elegant bow. "Loyalty should always be repaid, my liege."

He fixed his beady eyes on Geoffrey, leaving the knight in no doubt that the manor of Goodrich was certainly not what he had in mind.

The King smiled and moved away, pausing to inspect Norbert's body once more, and to work out where his would-be murderers had stood. His courtiers followed, keen to miss nothing of the excitement.

"Really, Geoffrey," said the Earl, reproachfully. "What have I done to make you hate me so? I was looking forward to adding

Goodrich to my estates, and now you have deprived me of it."

"Not intentionally," said Geoffrey. "And I have good cause to hate you, as well you know. You took my sister, and allowed her to be drawn into this foolish plot to kill King Henry."

"Actually, I did nothing of the kind," said the Earl. "It was Enide who came to me with the plot. I told her to wait. The time is not yet ripe—the Duke needs to be properly warned, or he will miss his opportunity once again; and I am not yet as powerful as I would like, to assure our success. There is little point risking all in an invasion to place the Duke on the throne if we cannot be certain of victory. I urged her to do nothing, but she defied me."

"But you denied that Malger was in your service—"

"A game, Geoffrey. The King knows as well as I do that Malger was one of my most trusted knights. I denied it and he did not contradict me. The King also knows perfectly well who is responsible for the attempt on his life. Why do you think he did not press you for the names of these plotters? It is because he already knows who they are. In fact, he has known for some time: I told him myself, you see."

"You?" cried Geoffrey, bewildered. "But why?"

"Because I knew it would fail when Enide refused to wait. I did not want to be associated with a doomed plot, so I told the King about it. Thus, I gain credit for my loyalty to him, but yet I am still in a position to reap the benefits from any attempt on the King's life should Enide have succeeded. Do not look so shocked, my fine knight! This is called politics. If you do not like the stakes, do not play the game."

"Would that I had not," said Geoffrey bitterly. "I hate this sort of thing."

"Most knights do," agreed the Earl. "They prefer straightforward slaughter. But I expected more of you, Geoffrey. I thought you were a cut above the rest of the rabble."

"Who else is involved, other than Enide and Malger?" asked Geoffrey, rubbing his head with a shaking hand. "And Drogo. Whom I suppose you also do not know."

"Good. You are learning," said the Earl appreciatively. "Aside from those three and that pathetic little clerk, there was a physician and the wife of one of your brothers—Petrella?"

"Pernel?"

"Pernel, yes. Your father was involved with the plot to kill Rufus, but he declined to have anything to do with the murder of King Henry. And your sister will tell you that there is another plotter, but I do not know whether that is true or not."

Neither did Geoffrey, and his mind reeled with the possibilities—Walter, Bertrada, Stephen, Joan, Olivier, Henry, or Hedwise? Or was it someone he had not yet encountered—someone from the village, perhaps?

"Of course," continued the Earl smoothly, "you still have to discover which one of your family stabbed your father on his sickbed—assuming that you are still interested in investigating plain old murder after you have just averted a regicide. But perhaps the culprit was Enide, slipping up that tunnel she told Malger about. She hid there when she was supposed to be dead, you see."

But Geoffrey knew that was impossible—Rohese would have seen her. The Earl continued with his reasoning, a smug gloating in his voice that suggested he relished the fact that Geoffrey still had a long way to go before he solved the riddle of Godric's death.

"But then again, Godric's death might have nothing to do with this plan to kill the King, and your siblings or their spouses might be responsible. Perhaps one of them believed that he or she stood a better chance of gaining Goodrich with Godric dead than with Godric alive. After all, the old man did delight in producing forged documents to prove one or other of them was ineligible to succeed him."

"Does the King really want me to hunt Enide down and dispatch her, as he asked?" said Geoffrey, watching the monarch stoop over Malger's body.

"Yes, I think so," said the Earl, after a moment of thought. "I would like you to spare Drogo, though. He is my cousin and I am fond of him. I am sure I will be able to dissuade him from other regicidal attempts, if you send him back to me."

"I will see what I can do," said Geoffrey flatly. "But I do not understand why the King does not send his own agents after Enide, to ensure the job is done properly—assuming that his chief huntsman has no luck."

"Oh, that is simple," said the Earl, "although I have already told you the answer once. The King was not overly surprised when I told him about the plot Enide and her followers had hatched to kill him. The reason, of course, was that he already knew of the one they hatched to kill Rufus. The King would not want Enide yelling details of that to all and sundry as she is dragged to the execution block—his hold on his crown is not so secure that he can risk the scandal of being accused of Rufus's murder."

"So, you are saying that King Henry was prepared to stand by and see his brother assassinated?" asked Geoffrey, although he had already surmised as much. "So that he could take the crown for himself?"

"Why not?" asked the Earl. "Your brothers would do the same for you. You see, the execution of Rufus would have done King Henry no good at all if it had been left until later this year. By then, the Duke of Normandy would have rallied enough support to take the crown himself. So, Rufus was killed last year instead."

Geoffrey suddenly understood exactly why King Henry had changed the subject so abruptly when Geoffrey had been telling him about the plot: he had not wanted Geoffrey to become more explicit in front of his retinue, any more than he had wanted Enide making public statements.

Geoffrey thought about the pale-shafted arrow that had killed Aumary—a message from Enide to the King to tell him that she knew of his role in the death of Rufus. A similar pale-shafted arrow was embedded in Malger, and the King had seen it. His abrupt change of subject had prevented Geoffrey from revealing all he had learned or surmised about the plot. Did that now mean that Geoffrey should expect a dagger in his back one dark night, so he would never complete his story?

"So King Henry was complicit in his brother's murder last summer, so that he might be King of England," he summarised.

"Not so loud, Geoffrey. Just because something is common knowledge does not mean that you should bellow it from the rooftops. But here comes one of your brothers. Draw your dagger to protect yourself: he looks unhinged to me."

"I have just seen Enide risen from the grave!" blubbered Henry, his face white. "And Stephen has been shot and mortally wounded!"

CHAPTER THIRTEEN

"S o, it is over," said Helbye in satisfaction, watching as the last of the King's men rode away from the forest clearing. "The attempt on the King's life has failed; Goodrich belongs to the Mappestones again; Malger and Enide are dead; Drogo will flee back to hide under the Earl's skirts; and Stephen will not live to see the sun set tonight."

"Do not be so sure all is finished," muttered Geoffrey, kneeling in the grass with the dying Stephen. Henry crouched opposite, rubbing Stephen's bloodless hand in a rough—and belated—attempt at affection. "The King's huntsman said he thought he injured Enide, not that he killed her."

"He killed her sure enough," said Henry, looking across at him. "The fellow is the chief huntsman, for God's sake. He would not hold that position unless he were an excellent shot. He might not have killed her outright, but it will not be long before she is dead."

"We will see," said Geoffrey, unconvinced. "The hounds found no trace of her."

"The place is boggy," said Henry, exasperated. "The scents are confused, and the dogs did not really know what they were supposed to be sniffing for. But I can assure you, Enide's corpse will appear sooner or later. And then we can put it back underground, where it belongs."

"I saved that fine dog of yours," said Stephen breathlessly, squinting up at Geoffrey. "He ran almost directly into the line of that arrow, but I managed to save him."

Geoffrey looked to where the dog lay, unconcerned, a short distance away, happily chewing at something it had nuzzled out of Stephen's pocket.

"I hope you are not telling me that someone tried to shoot the dog and that you put yourself into the arrow's path," he said nervously. The greedy, selfish black-and-white dog certainly had done nothing in its miserable life to deserve that kind of sacrifice.

"Not quite," said Henry, when Stephen could not summon the strength to reply. "I saw what happened. You know how it is with hunting—there are only a few moments between the time when you see a movement that heralds the appearance of your prey, and the time when it will disappear from your range. You shoot instinctively."

"I know," said Geoffrey, guessing that he had probably been on a good many more hunts than Henry. And Henry's horse had bolted, too, suggesting that he had little or no experience of controlling it in such situations. "But what did Stephen do?"

Henry paused, and looked down at his dying brother with a mixture of pity and resignation. "Your dog darted out from the trees and someone fired. Intent on grabbing it to save it from entering anyone else's line of fire, Stephen rushed after it and was felled by the King's arrow. He did not deliberately put himself between the dog and the quarrel, but the outcome was the same."

"The King shot Stephen?" said Geoffrey, appalled. "But he did not say so. He—"

"Well, he would not, would he?" snapped Henry. "The King would hardly admit to killing one of his own subjects. It was probably an accident anyway."

"Was it an accident?" Geoffrey asked Stephen.

Stephen swallowed. "Who knows? I only wanted to save the dog."

"Did Enide really try to kill the King?" asked Henry of Geoffrey in a horrified whisper. "After she was dead, too! I always knew there was something sinister about her. Even in her grave she cannot help spreading wickedness."

"And you avenged her death by hanging two poachers in the forest," said Geoffrey coolly. "What have you to say about that?"

"They had her veil," said Henry defensively. "And I told them that I would cut them into little pieces if they did not tell me the truth. They confessed to killing her, so I hanged them."

"They told you what you wanted to hear," said Geoffrey wearily. "I might confess to murder if there was someone like you threatening to tear me from limb to limb."

"But they had her veil!" insisted Henry.

"And how did they tell you they came by it?" asked Geoffrey. "Did they claim it had been given to them by a beautiful woman, who had told them she no longer had need of it because she was going to become a nun."

"How did you know that?" asked Henry, astonished.

"Because Enide is nothing if not thorough," said Geoffrey with a sigh. "With the death of two men found in possession of her veil, the business of her alleged murder was at an end. No one would think any more about it—which was what Father Adrian said she had intended. She wanted to disappear as completely as possible, and she did not want discussions of her unsolved murder to keep her memory fresh in people's minds."

"Are you accusing me of slaying innocent men?" demanded Henry.

"Since you saw Enide alive yourself a few moments ago, what do you think?" said Geoffrey, eyeing his brother askance. Henry had always been slow, but increasing age had made him much worse. "They made a false confession to you because you terrified them into it."

"Oh!" said Henry. "What have I done?"

"What indeed?" asked Geoffrey. "Next time you kill someone, you might want to pay a little more attention to detail. Such as whether you have the right victim. And now, since you killed their menfolk, you are responsible to ensure that their families do not starve—assuming that they have not done so already. You should bring them to Goodrich, and find some employment for them."

"I will do that," said Henry fervently. "I will. Lord save us. What a mess! That Enide! What has she done to us?" He rose to his feet again. "I will kill her for this!"

"You told me the King's chief hunter has already had that honour," said Geoffrey.

"Would that he had not!" shouted Henry. "I would sooner slay her myself. The treacherous, murdering, lying, evil—"

"Initially, the conspirators were Enide, Godric, Norbert, the physician, Malger, Drogo, and your wife," said Geoffrey to Stephen, ignoring Henry's futile rage. "Pernel was killed because she was too gleeful about the plot, and Enide was afraid she might betray them all with her indiscretion."

"I always suspected Enide had something to do with poor Pernel's death," said Stephen weakly. "And I threatened to kill her for it. But someone got there before me—or at least I thought they had."

Geoffrey nodded. That made sense. Enide had decided to disappear after she had become ill from the paints in Godric's room and had erroneously deduced that someone was trying to kill her. Since Stephen had threatened to do exactly that, to avenge his wife's death, Enide had probably assumed he was already trying, and so she had inveigled Adrian into faking her death so that she would be free to act without Stephen dogging her every step.

"That business with Pernel is long since done and forgotten," said Henry soothingly. "Do not dwell on the matter now."

"She is not forgotten by me," said Stephen, so softly he was difficult to hear. "She was my wife."

"But she cuckolded you," said Henry harshly. "She slept with any knight who visited the castle, and she was greedy, cruel, and selfish."

"She must have fitted in well at Goodrich, then," murmured Geoffrey, although not loud enough for Stephen to hear.

Stephen's eyes welled tears. "Perhaps she was not all a wife should have been," he said in a whisper. "But I still loved her. She was so beautiful!"

Geoffrey rubbed his chin and looked down at his brother. Stephen's short hair was wet from sweat, and his eyes were black and sunken. Geoffrey took a deep breath, and pressed on. There was not much time left.

"Last spring, when father first believed he was being poisoned, he hired a food taster called Torva to find out who was the culprit.

Torva began to investigate, and uncovered not the plan to kill Father but the one to kill Rufus. Pernel was apparently fanatical about it, and was so pleased to be part of the plot that she probably told Torva."

"Rufus was a hateful man," whispered Stephen. "He was unnatural and deserved to die. Pernel was a good woman and his behaviour offended her Christian virtues."

Geoffrey had heard that argument before, and was not convinced that offending Christian virtues was an entirely acceptable motive for murder. After the Crusade, he was no longer certain what Christian virtues entailed—other than an excuse to loot, murder, burn, rape, and pillage in other people's countries.

"So Torva learned about Pernel's desire to kill Rufus, and what happened next, Stephen? Did he try to blackmail you after she had died?"

"Worse," breathed Stephen. "He tried to blackmail Enide. Foolish man! I saw Enide leave the castle shortly after Torva went to indulge in his nightly binge at the tavern. Torva never came back alive, and the following morning, Enide was back in her chamber as though nothing had happened."

"Stop this, Geoffrey," protested Henry. "Now is no time for such revelations—Stephen needs a priest, not a meaningless conversation about things that happened a long time ago."

"Then fetch Father Adrian," said Geoffrey. "You can be to Goodrich and back in an hour."

"It might be too late by then," said Henry. "And anyway, this is Caerdig's land. I am not riding alone through it with him skulking in the woods."

"Take Helbye," said Geoffrey. "He will protect you."

Henry glowered at him and declined his offer, so Geoffrey sent Barlow for Father Adrian.

"I will not live to see a priest," said Stephen weakly. "I will make my confession to you, my brothers. Then you can avenge my death, and make an end of her."

"There has been enough avenging already," said Geoffrey. And he had no wish to know Stephen's sins. "This family makes the Earl of Shrewsbury seem like a saint."

"It is not us, it is *her*," said Stephen. "She was always causing us to fight. When we were at peace with each other, she would needle us into arguments, pretending to find some document that proved someone's illegitimacy, or saying that she had overheard one of us making secret pacts with Godric."

"That is true," agreed Henry. "My wife, Hedwise, was always saying we would fight less if Enide were not here."

"She was not here when I returned a few days ago, but you were still fighting," Geoffrey remarked.

"That was different," said Henry. "By then, she had sowed so many seeds of discontent, that we would have had enough to quarrel about had Godric lived to be a hundred."

"Listen, Stephen," Geoffrey said. "Shrewsbury told King Henry about the plot to kill him, because he did not think it would succeed and he wanted to be on the winning side. By then, Godric was dying and Pernel had been killed by Malger. Now Norbert is dead, also killed by Malger; Malger is dead, killed by Enide; Drogo has not the sense to keep himself alive without Malger; Enide is said to have been shot by the chief huntsman; and the physician was killed by Ingram."

"The physician?" asked Henry. "Francis? Killed by Ingram?"

"I expect one of the King's agents paid Ingram to do it," said Geoffrey. "The boy is stupid and greedy enough to accept such a commission for pay. And finally, you, Stephen, very conveniently happened to ride in front of the King's bow."

"The King would never shoot a man deliberately," proclaimed Henry hotly. "He is honest and just. I have already told you—when you are on a hunt and you see something move, you just fire at it while you have the chance. The beaters are always getting shot by mistake."

"No wonder the King pays them good money," said Geoffrey. "But whether it was an accident or not, every one of the King's would-be killers is now dead. Were you one of those, Stephen?"

"What proof do you have for these accusations?" demanded Henry, rising abruptly and standing over Geoffrey with clenched fists. "You come prancing back from the Holy Land, without so much as a silver goblet to show for it and accuse your own family of committing terrible crimes!"

Geoffrey was silent. He had very little to support his guess that

Stephen was the last of the conspirators, although Stephen had denied nothing. Was Enide telling him the truth when she had said there was one other? Or was she simply trying to confuse him?

"Well?" asked Geoffrey of his dying brother. "Am I right? Did you conspire to kill the King?"

Stephen closed his eyes, and gave an almost imperceptible shake of his head. "Because Pernel was so deeply involved in the plot to kill Rufus, others have assumed that I shared her passion. I did not. I never plotted to kill Rufus, and I most certainly did not conspire to kill King Henry. In fact, I tried hard to dissuade Pernel from getting involved at all. She would not listen. I did not even know that Enide was still alive until the night Godric died. I met her then."

"You were locked out of the castle," said Geoffrey, thinking fast. "Malger had replaced our guards on the gates with his own, because he thought ours were inadequate. By the time you returned from seeing the dog that was about to pup, the guards would not let you in again. So, you used the secret tunnel to gain entry instead."

"What tunnel?" demanded Henry.

Stephen nodded. "I met Enide in the chamber at the bottom of the stairs. I cannot tell you which of us suffered the greater shock! She told me of her plan to kill King Henry. I tried to dissuade her, as I had Pernel, but she was beyond reason."

Then that must have been while Rohese was still sleeping under Godric's mattresses, Geoffrey thought, or they would all have bumped into each other. "And she let you leave unscathed?" he asked. "That does not sound like Enide."

"She let me go because I offered to inform Godric of what was afoot," said Stephen. "She could not: she was supposed to be dead. Godric and I argued about it—or rather, he yelled at me about it. I wondered then how you could sleep through it, but assumed you simply wanted to listen without becoming involved. I had no idea you were drugged. I am guilty of concealing Enide's resurrection from you all; I am guilty of concealing the fact that I suspected Enide of killing Torva; I am guilty of not forcing Pernel to give up her foolish notions of regicide. But I have not killed, and I have not plotted to murder any kings."

His eyes closed in exhaustion. Geoffrey rubbed his temples,

sighed, and tipped his head back, looking at the low, grey-bellied clouds that scudded above him.

"I told you it would be too late to fetch Father Adrian," said Henry in a low voice.

Stephen was dead.

It was a sombre procession that wound its way along the path that led from Lann Martin to Goodrich bearing the body of Stephen across Geoffrey's destrier. The path was grassy and overgrown from lack of use. Geoffrey remembered that it had been well trodden when he was a boy, and was angry that Enide's plotting and intrigue had spread not only to devastate her own family but had even touched the innocent villagers of Lann Martin, too. The route to the market town of Walecford through the Goodrich estate had been a convenient and useful short-cut from Lann Martin in former, happier days.

"Caerdig?" Geoffrey yelled to the silent trees.

Henry regarded him askance. "Caerdig is not here. And less of this unseemly shouting. We are bearing the corpse of our brother here. Have you no respect for the dead?"

To one side of them, the trees parted and Caerdig stepped out, followed by several of his villagers. All carried the sticks and staves that they had been using to beat the game through the forest for the King and his hunting party.

"God's blood, Geoffrey!" muttered Henry, snatching his sword from his saddle. "What did you call him for? Now we will all be slain!"

"Put your sword away," said Geoffrey, not taking his eyes from Caerdig. "You have nothing to fear. We have been trailed ever since we left the forest clearing, and if Caerdig had wanted us killed, we would be dead already."

"And we might kill you yet," said Daffydd, the man who wore the strange cap, as he fingered a sword with a broken tip.

"Hush, Daffydd," said Caerdig. "This might be our chance for peace."

"Peace?" thundered Henry. "Peace? Why should I make peace with you?"

"Less of this unseemly shouting," said Geoffrey to Henry. "Have you no respect for the dead?"

"We need peace because too much evil has been perpetrated here already," said Caerdig. "And who among us would not like to walk these paths without expecting a knife between the shoulder-blades at every step? It is time this nonsense ended."

"Why now?" demanded Henry. "Do you think the Mappe-stones are weak because Stephen is dead?" He spat in derision.

"I tried for peace before, if you recall," said Caerdig. "I offered to marry Joan or Enide, so that our estates would live in harmony."

"But you have stolen my inheritance!" snarled Henry. "Lann Martin is mine, left to me by my mother."

"It was not hers to leave," said Caerdig firmly. "It belonged to Ynys, and Ynys wanted me to succeed him."

"You are not Ynys's legitimate heir," shouted Henry, furious. "And so the estate should have passed back to us."

"And that is why you killed Ynys!" yelled Caerdig back. "You struck a coward's blow in the dark, so that you could inherit! Well, Lann Martin stands on Welsh soil, and by Welsh law, it belongs to me, as his named successor."

"I did not kill Ynys—"

"Enide arranged for Drogo to kill Ynys," said Geoffrey quietly. Despite his low voice, the other two turned and regarded him with disbelief.

"Henry's belligerence is all the proof I need of *his* guilt," said Caerdig. "I was prepared to let Ynys's slaying go unavenged—he would not have wanted it to have caused continued bloodshed—but I will not do so if Henry is not man enough even to admit to his crime."

"Enide arranged Ynys's death," persisted Geoffrey. "She wanted Henry accused of the murder, so that no one would raise questions when Henry was stabbed in the back one dark night. And then, doubtless, it would have been your turn, Caerdig—you would have been the prime suspect for Henry's murder, and either hanged or slain by an act of revenge by some unidentified member of the Mappestone household. Then Enide would have had not only Goodrich but Lann Martin, too."

"My God!" breathed Caerdig. "And this was the woman I offered to take as my wife?"

"Enide fooled many people," said Geoffrey. "But the real issue is will you agree to a truce? If you two continue to fight, Enide will have won a small victory, and I am loath to see her win any at all. The people on both estates are suffering—you should stop wasting funds on this silly squabble and put them into the welfare of the people you need to make your lands profitable."

Henry pursed his lips and folded his arms across his barrel chest. Caerdig scratched his chin thoughtfully.

"We can try, I suppose," said Henry eventually. "I have never liked Lann Martin much anyway. It is full of Welshmen. And anyway I have Goodrich now. Take Lann Martin, Caerdig. It is yours."

Caerdig gave him a look of dislike. "Then we will start our peace by allowing you to pass unmolested through our lands. And as an act of faith, we will not follow you to ensure you leave. Go home, and bury your dead."

Geoffrey supposed it was as good a start as he was likely to accomplish. Henry took the reins of his horse and led the small procession on. Geoffrey lingered as the others left, and caught Caerdig's arm as he made to stride away.

"I saw who drove the boar forward when Enide was about to kill me," he said.

"It did not go quite according to plan," said Caerdig ruefully. "I was almost too late for a start, and I did not intend for the wretched thing to attack you. A deer would have been a better animal to use, but time was short and the boar was the only beast available to me." He grinned suddenly. "You should have seen Enide run when she saw it coming!"

Geoffrey could well imagine. There was little as dangerous or aggressive in an English forest as a furious wild boar. His arm still ached from where the animal's tusks had raked him, and he knew the repairs to his chain-mail would be expensive.

Caerdig reached out and punched Geoffrey lightly on the shoulder. "We are even now, you and I. You spared my life when we tried to ambush you, and I prevented that witch from driving her dagger through your ribs. Do you think Henry will honour my right to Lann Martin now?"

"I do not know," said Geoffrey. "He is as likely to break a promise as to make one."

Caerdig grimaced. "Well, there will always be a hearth for you in Lann Martin if Goodrich becomes too hostile. Do not forget that, Geoffrey. You may need a haven from time to time. Enide and Stephen may be dead, but there are still Walter, Joan, and the dreadful Henry to contend with."

He called to his men to follow him and walked away, leaving Geoffrey to make his way home alone with Stephen's body. By the time the sturdy bulk of Goodrich Castle came into view, Geoffrey felt drained. He was cold and wet from the rain; his body was stiff and bruised from his fight with Drogo and Malger; and his chain-mail was damaged in several places. He felt he barely had the energy to reach the castle.

Geoffrey trudged through the mud, leading his destrier by the reins with Stephen's body still flopping across the back of it. Henry had met Father Adrian by the ford, and the two of them were waiting for him, watching in silence while Geoffrey waded through the icy water. Adrian said nothing when he saw Stephen's body, but his face was grey and his hands shook as he opened his Psalter to begin reciting prayers for the dead.

When they reached the castle, the gates stood wide open and the guards were nowhere to be seen. Geoffrey felt a surge of anger at their negligence, until he looked inside the barbican gatehouse and saw the two bodies that lay inside. Abandoning his horse to Julian, he ran up the steps into the inner ward. It was deserted.

Geoffrey bounded up the stairs to the keep and shot into the hall, Henry and Adrian not far behind him. Bertrada sat at the far end of the chamber, near the hearth, cradling Walter on her knees. Next to her was Joan, holding a bowl of water and gently wiping Walter's face. Olivier stood by his wife's side, resting his hand on her shoulder and muttering what sounded to be comforting words, while Hedwise knelt in front of the fire to stoke it up.

"Oh no!" groaned Geoffrey, sagging against the door frame.

Henry elbowed him out of the way. "God's blood!" he exclaimed. "Who has done this? Was it Caerdig, do you think, while we were otherwise engaged?"

"Of course it was not Caerdig," snapped Geoffrey, rubbing a hand across his face and continuing to stare. "How could he? He was in the forest all morning helping the King to slaughter deer."

"Who then?" demanded Henry. "Old Sir Roger from Kernebrigges way? He has not liked Walter since we cheated him over those rams."

"Enide," said Geoffrey in a whisper. "Who do you think?"

"But Enide is dead!" cried Henry. "She was shot by the King's chief huntsman!"

"Apparently not," said Geoffrey.

He walked down the hall and came to stand over his eldest brother. Walter's eyes were closed, and his balding pate was a curious purple colour and strangely flattened. Geoffrey knew he had been beyond any ministrations that Bertrada and Joan could offer him from the moment he had been struck. The blow, although it had caused virtually no bleeding, had smashed the skull and crushed the brain beneath.

Joan looked up at Geoffrey. "Olivier says Enide came and attacked Walter," she said, bending and wiping the dead man's face again.

"Olivier has been at the wine," said Bertrada, her voice harsh with shock. "Enide has been in her grave these last four months."

"Enide has been everywhere but her grave," said Geoffrey. "She has been living in a room at the end of the passage that ran from Godric's chamber to the woods outside."

"In that filthy tunnel?" queried Joan. "She would have been better in her grave!"

So, Joan knew about the passage, thought Geoffrey. And in that case, so probably did Olivier. Were they the killers of Godric? Or was that Stephen, who confessed to using the tunnel when he found himself locked out of the castle the night that Godric was killed?

"Enide is dead," said Bertrada flatly. "I saw her corpse. Father Adrian said there could be no mistake, despite the fact that they had stolen her head. The priest is a good man with no reason to lie."

Adrian closed his eyes in despair and guilt. "It was not Enide's body," he said in an agonised whisper. "She was afraid that one of you would kill her, as she believed one of you had been poisoning Godric, and she asked me to help her feign her death. The body you saw was not hers."

"But why would she want to harm Walter in particular?" asked Joan, wiping again. "He has never done her ill."

"None except to be Godric's oldest son," said Olivier. "Perhaps she intends to kill you all one by one, and then reappear to claim Goodrich."

"Do not be ridiculous, Olivier!" snapped Bertrada. "How could she hope to wrest Goodrich from the Earl of Shrewsbury? It is he who owns Goodrich now."

"So, what happened?" asked Geoffrey quickly, before they could start one of their arguments.

"I was coming from the stables a short while ago," said Olivier, "when I saw someone entering the hall. It was Enide. At first, I thought someone must have been poisoning *me,* and that I was dreaming, but it was Enide sure enough. By the time I had reached the hall from the stables, she was standing over Walter's body with that skillet in her hand."

He pointed to a large, heavy cooking pan that had been used for toasting chestnuts over the fire when Geoffrey had last seen it.

"Did she say anything?" he asked.

"I asked her what she had done." He pursed his lips. "A foolish question, I suppose, given the circumstances. She told me she killed Walter because he had slain Godric."

"What?" cried Bertrada. "Walter did not kill Godric! Geoffrey is the most likely one of us to have done that. It is *he* who should be lying here, not my Walter!"

Had Walter killed Godric, Geoffrey wondered. Why not? Godric had died the night after he presented his children with a will proclaiming Godfrey as sole inheritor—before the Earl of Shrewsbury had come up with his own ideas on the matter. Perhaps Walter had thought that by killing Godric he might invalidate the will somehow, and that his own claim by primogeniture—the first-born—would be upheld.

"Did Enide say anything else?" Geoffrey asked of Olivier.

"She told me that if I let her leave unmolested she would not harm me. So I did."

"You let her go?" exploded Henry in disbelief. "Good God, man! You are a knight and she is a woman! Why did you not prevent her from leaving, and keep her here to answer for her crimes? Call yourself a warrior?"

"Leave him alone!" snarled Joan. "What action Olivier chose to take is none of your affair. He did not know when he let her out that Walter lay fatally injured."

"Well, it is obvious that Walter did not faint with the delight of seeing her," said Hedwise, taking part in the conversation for the first time.

"Where did Enide go?" asked Geoffrey. "Did she go to Godric's room?"

"No," said Olivier, puzzled by his suggestion. "She ran out of the hall and down through the inner ward to the barbican. Then I saw Sir Drogo emerging from the gatehouse. He had horses at the ready and they left."

"We will never catch them now," said Henry, disappointed. "They could be anywhere!"

"I do not think they will get far," said Geoffrey. "Where could they go?"

"Well, they will not stay around here," said Henry. "It is far too dangerous. But what of Walter, Joan? Shall I ride for a physician? There is a good one in Walecford."

"It is too late," said Geoffrey. "Walter is already dead."

Bertrada bit back a sob.

"No," said Joan. "He is just stunned. He will awaken given time."

"He will not," said Geoffrey gently. "The blow probably killed him instantly. He needs Father Adrian, not a physician."

"But there is no blood!" protested Joan. "And the wound is only slight."

"His head is flattened," said Father Adrian, peering closer. "He is dead, Joan. Let him go."

Geoffrey leaned down and helped Bertrada to her feet, while

Olivier solicitously helped Joan, fussing about her and smoothing wrinkles from her gown.

"Is it true?" Joan asked of the small knight. "Is Walter really dead?"

Olivier nodded, and put a comforting arm around her shoulders. "You did all you could for him. Come away now. You, too, Bertrada. We should let the priest see to him.

Bertrada allowed herself to be assisted to a chair near the fire, while Adrian knelt and began intoning prayers for the dead.

"Now what?" asked Henry in an undertone to Geoffrey. "It seems that Enide is intent on wiping out everyone connected with Goodrich. Who will be next, I wonder. You or me?"

That night, Geoffrey sat in Godric's chamber, staring into the flames that licked at the damp logs. The window shutters stood wide open so that the poisonous fumes from Godric's paintings might be dissipated, and the wind that gusted in chilled the room and made the flames dance and roar.

Geoffrey rubbed at the bridge of his nose, and glanced at the hour candle that stood in a protected corner of the room. He sighed, and then stood to pace for a while to prevent himself from falling asleep. It was well past midnight, and still she had not come. Perhaps Henry was right after all. When Geoffrey had stated his intention to wait for Enide to come through the secret tunnel, Henry had sneered in derision, maintaining that Enide was no fool, and would be well on her way to the coast to avoid being hanged for treason by the King. Olivier had agreed, while Joan had seemed too confused to think anything.

Hedwise had wept bitterly when she had learned of Stephen's death, and Geoffrey asked himself whether their relationship had been all it should. Joan and Olivier had retired to their chamber, and Geoffrey had heard them talking in low voices behind the door he was certain had been barred.

Bertrada had seen her husband laid out in the chapel next to his father and brother, and announced that she would be leaving Goodrich as soon as Walter was buried. Geoffrey had studied her sharp, hard features in the flickering light from the sconce. Her mouth was drawn in a bitter, bloodless line, and her eyes were cold and calculating. Was she fleeing the scene of her crime, he wondered, now that Enide had ensured that Walter would never inherit Goodrich? Was it Bertrada who had stabbed Godric, so that Walter could have the estates and the uncertainty would be over? Seeing him staring at her, she gave a mirthless smile, and offered him mulled wine that he refused.

He had taken nothing to eat and drink that evening, a precaution he felt justified in taking when even the dog declined to eat the various titbits offered by the others. Stephen was dead, and so would not be bringing Geoffrey wine doctored with ergot to drink, but there was still Henry, Olivier, Joan, Hedwise, and Bertrada who might harbour murderous intentions towards him.

Sitting alone in Godric's chamber, Geoffrey began to think that Henry was right to have scoffed at his belief that Enide would come that night. It would be a rash thing to do—she would be a fool not to guess that the household would be on the alert for her, and Enide was certainly no fool. Adrian had offered to wait with him, but Geoffrey had no intention of being stabbed at a vital moment by a lovelorn priest, and had asked Olivier to see Adrian away from the castle altogether.

The hour candle burned lower still. Geoffrey opened the door to the spiral stairs and listened. The castle was still, but not silent. Joan and Olivier still muttered in their room, and somewhere, someone snored at a volume loud enough to wake the dead. Geoffrey closed the door again, and went to the window, leaning out to take deep breaths of cold, crisp air. Joan and Olivier seemed to be finding a good deal to discuss. Were they talking about how they had murdered Godric, and how they might still turn his death to their advantage? And Henry and Hedwise—now the likely heirs to Goodrich Castle—were they sitting somewhere plotting and mixing their ergot and poppy powders?

He rubbed his eyes and looked at the candle. It was probably around two or three in the morning. The inhabitants of Goodrich had not been much interested in knowing the time, and all the hour candles that Geoffrey had managed to find were old and cheap. Geoffrey was not at all certain whether the wicks would burn at the correct rate. He turned back to the window again, looking at the pale glint of the river in the moonlight, and the dark mass of the tree-shrouded hills beyond. He entertained the notion that he might be better going to find a safe bed with Helbye than pacing in the castle all night.

Yet Geoffrey was convinced that Enide would come. Henry was right in that she would certainly flee—to Normandy probably, where the Duke would welcome her at the recommendation of his friend and ally the Earl of Shrewsbury—but he could not see her leaving unfinished business. Henry was still alive and stood to inherit Goodrich and, according to her reasoning, Geoffrey had slain her lover of many years" standing. She would not leave without having her revenge.

But as the darkness faded to pale grey, Geoffrey realised he had been wrong. He slumped against the wall and stared at the white embers of the dead fire. Enide must have decided to leave revenge until later. He hauled off his surcoat, and then tugged at the buckles on his hauberk with cold fingers. Divested of his armour, he went to a bowl of water on the chest and splashed some of it over his face, wincing at the chill. As he dried his face on his shirt-sleeve, he heard a faint tap on the door.

"Yes?" he called, striding across the room to where his sword lay under his pile of chain-mail. He relaxed when he saw it was only Hedwise carrying a tray. She balanced it on her knee, and turned to close the door, so that their voices would not disturb others who still slept.

"She did not come?" she asked unnecessarily, glancing around the empty room.

Geoffrey shook his head. "I was wrong and Henry was right. She will be well on her way to the coast by now. Then she will board a ship for France, and will not return until the Earl of Shrewsbury has determined that England is ripe for an invasion by the Duke of Normandy."

"You look tired," said Hedwise, sympathetic to his frustration. "Come and sit down. I have brought you some of my broth. I will build up the fire, and then you should rest. Your father and brothers will not be buried until mid-morning, and you should try to snatch some sleep before then."

She set her tray on the table, and pulled out a stool for Geoffrey to sit on. He flopped down and rested his head in his hands.

"I was certain she would come tonight," he said. "But it seems I am seldom right when it comes to Enide. She is not the person I once knew."

"I really could not say," said Hedwise. "I have known her only as she is now. Your hands are frozen. Here, drink some of this broth."

She pushed a steaming bowl into Geoffrey's hands, and stood behind him. A strong smell of fish rose into his face, and his stomach rebelled.

"What is it, ergot flavour?" he asked, somewhat discourteously, given that she had just been kind to him.

"Well, yes, actually," said Hedwise, as, simultaneously, Geoffrey felt the sharp prick of a dagger through his shirt. "And you have a choice: drink the soup, or have me run you through. Which will it be?"

"It was you?" asked Geoffrey, startled. He started to turn, but Hedwise dug the dagger into him in a way that made him certain she was in earnest. "You poisoned me last time?"

"I put ergot in the broth, but I miscalculated and you survived. I suppose you did not finish it. There were only so many times that I could urge you to drink without arousing your suspicion. Afterwards, I guessed it would only be a matter of time before you worked out that the ergot was in my broth, not Stephen's wine—"

"So you came back later, and added ergot to the wine, too— which is why the physician found ergot and poppy powder in both."

"Correct," said Hedwise.

"But why?" asked Geoffrey. "I was not a danger to Henry and his inheritance. Even if the will naming Godfrey as his heir had been approved in court, I would not have taken Goodrich."

"So *you* say," said Hedwise. "But as it happened, it was Walter I was after—your death was just part of my plan to get *him* out of the way. Walter had had a good deal to drink, and is a heavy sleeper anyway. My notion was for you and Godric to be found dead, and Walter blamed. But you survived, and that ridiculous Henry started claiming that *you* were responsible for Godric's death! It was so ludicrous that I almost laughed. I tried several times to dissuade him and shift the blame to Walter, but you heard how he would have none of it."

Geoffrey was angry with himself. He had assumed that because the ergot had not killed him and because his dagger had been used to stab Godric, the would-be poisoner had wanted him accused of the murder. That the whole elaborate situation had been devised to place Walter in a dreadfully compromising position had not crossed his mind.

"But why Walter? What has he done to deserve all this?"

"He was simply the first on my list. Getting rid of you was a bonus, but not really an important one because you are younger than Henry and so do not present a threat. Stephen was to be next."

"I take it that Henry is unaware of all the pains you are taking to secure his inheritance?"

She laughed. "Do not ask stupid questions! Of course he does not know what I am doing—he has neither the brains nor the capacity for the discretion that is necessary for a successful outcome. But I do not have all day. Drink the broth or I will stab you. I recommend the broth, because it will kill you without too much discomfort. I cannot say the same for the knife, since I have not done it before. It might take more than one attempt."

Geoffrey took a tentative sip at the broth, pretending to take more than he had. He grimaced at the strong flavour and the way the poison burned his mouth—even from the tiny amount he had taken.

"What is wrong?" asked Hedwise. "Do you not like it?"

"Not especially," said Geoffrey. "It is too hot."

He set the bowl on the table and Hedwise gave him a poke with the dagger.

"Broth is meant to be drunk hot. Pick it up."

Geoffrey lifted it. "But you did not kill Father, did you? You might have intended to, but you did not actually do it."

He could hear her breathing behind him. "No. He was already dead when I came for him. He often calls out in the night, and so would have thought nothing odd about me bringing him fish soup around dawn. But, as you seem to know, he was already dead. Now I realise that Enide must have killed him."

"She did not," said Geoffrey. "In fact, she was one of the very few for whom Father's murder would have been impossible. Rohese heard him alive and arguing with Stephen, and then stayed with him until he died. At father's insistence, Rohese fled to the tunnel after he was dead. No one used it after that, so while Enide might well have come up it to kill him, she could not have left that way. And any other way would have been difficult, since everyone but Stephen thought she was dead. It would have caused a stir to say the least."

"Well, who did kill him then?" asked Hedwise. "Do you know?"

"Actually, no one killed him," said Geoffrey. "I think he killed himself."

There was a pause, and then Hedwise laughed. "I know what you are trying to do. You think you can distract me by spinning wild tales. Drink the broth, Geoffrey, or it will be cold. Then it will not be nice at all." The dagger pricked again, adding venom to her words.

Geoffrey pretended to take another sip from the dish, almost gagging as the smell of fish long past its best wafted into his face. He had no intention of drinking the stuff, and Hedwise was right: Geoffrey intended to talk to her and tell her what he had reasoned until an opportunity arose that would allow him to overpower her.

"Stephen met Enide, and he learned from her that she planned to kill King Henry in Monmouth. Stephen then told Father, who was appalled and started to shout his objections to the plot. Rohese heard him carrying on, but I did not because I was drugged. Walter had already left by then. Father knew that he would be implicated in the plot, guilty or not, and rather than risk the shame and inevitable punishment that such an accusation would bring in the last few days of his life, he decided to take his own life, so that his reputation could never be so besmirched."

"He killed himself to avoid a scandal?" asked Hedwise in disbelief.

"More or less. The King had overlooked Father's part in the plot to kill Rufus, but he would not overlook one to kill himself. Father had been given his chance, and so could not expect to evade justice a second time. He decided to kill himself, so that no one could accuse him of anything. I have seen men kill themselves with daggers before. The way he died was very typical of a self-inflicted stroke."

"But you have no evidence! This is all supposition."

"Not all," said Geoffrey. "Father was killed with the dagger that William the Conqueror gave him—I found it bloodstained in the moat a couple of days ago. You had all been hunting around for it when you thought he was dead—just after I arrived—and he told me he had hidden it where no one would find it. It was clear that none of you knew where it was—and therefore none of you could have killed him with it. He retrieved it from wherever it was secreted, and stabbed himself."

"But he would go to Hell for suicide," said Hedwise, unconvinced.

"I do not think he saw it as suicide," said Geoffrey. "Rohese said he blamed us for killing him—he believed that his children had murdered him because he saw us as responsible for putting him in the situation where he was forced to take his own life. Anyway, he always maintained that as long as he confessed his sins before he died, he would go more or less straight to the pearly gates. Shrewsbury's fat priest had heard his confession that very night, and had given him last rites. What better a time?"

She was silent. Geoffrey swirled the contents of the bowl around absently.

"And then you came in," he continued. "You found that I was still alive, but that Father was dead. You took my dagger and plunged it into his chest in the hope that one of us—Walter or me—would be accused of his murder. You tipped the wine out of the window to make it appear as though I had been drinking heavily, and then you threw his precious dagger after it."

"Very good," said Hedwise. "But enough of all this speculation. Drink the damn broth!"

Geoffrey half lowered the broth, and then with a sudden, abrupt movement, he hurled it over his head directly into her face. She gagged and choked and staggered backwards. At the same time, he heard a sound from the garderobe passage.

He leapt towards his armour and snatched up his sword, just as Enide emerged into the chamber. She smiled when she saw the sword and stepped aside. Drogo entered, carrying a bow with an arrow already nocked and his right hand ready to draw back the bowstring and fire.

"Good God, Geoffrey. What have you done to Hedwise?" said Enide, suddenly aware of the gagging figure crawling on hands and knees on the floor.

"She has just tried her nasty fish soup," said Geoffrey. "Would you like some?"

CHAPTER FOURTEEN

Geoffrey stood in Godric's chamber and looked at his sister Enide, shifting from foot to foot and assessing his chances of div-
ing at Drogo before the older knight had the opportunity to loose
the arrow that was pointing unwaveringly at him.

"I hoped you would be here," said Enide, moving to one side
to give Drogo space to operate. "You killed Malger, a man who has
been more dear to me than any other. I mean to make you pay."

On the floor, Hedwise gurgled pitifully, scrabbling at her throat
with her fingers as she struggled to breathe. For the poison to have
had such a dramatic effect in such a short space of time implied that
she had added a powerful dose to her vile fish broth—she had wanted
no mistakes this time. Enide followed his gaze and gave an unexpected chuckle.

"Stephen told me that someone had poisoned you. It was Hedwise, was it? I congratulate her. I did not think she possessed the
intelligence or the courage."

"Stephen is dead," said Geoffrey, realising too late that he should
have maintained his silence.

"Did you kill him?" she asked, intrigued. "Poor Stephen! He
connived and lied and plotted, and prided himself on the miscon-
ception that he was the most devious of us all."

"I see you hold that honour," said Geoffrey.

"He was spineless, too," she continued as though he had not

spoken. "Pernel was different. She had the courage to follow her convictions. Stephen had no strength at all."

"I do not blame him," said Geoffrey. "It was Pernel's courage that led her to plotting to kill a king, and brought about her murder by her co-conspirators."

"Stephen was not happy about that," said Enide. "But she had to go."

"Why not kill him too? Why did you risk letting him live, if you are so cautious?"

"He knew nothing of consequence," said Enide with contempt. "Godric wanted to bring him into our plan to slay Rufus, but we all argued against that, even Pernel."

"Then Stephen was not your 'one other'?" asked Geoffrey, surprised to feel relieved that the one brother he had almost started to like had not been involved.

"Do not be ridiculous, Geoff!" said Enide. "I have just told you several good reasons why he was not to be trusted. Walter was the last of us. Could you not even work that out?"

"Walter?" echoed Geoffrey in astonishment. He forced himself to concentrate. "Walter did not support King Henry, and he was loyal to the Duke of Normandy. But he was so open about it."

"So?" asked Enide. "Why should he not be? He felt very strongly that the Duke of Normandy would make a better king than his duplicitous younger brother. But, like Pernel, Walter was becoming unstable. I brained him with the skillet to ensure that he did not panic after our lack of success yesterday afternoon and tell everyone what we had attempted to do. And now I have come for you and the deplorable Henry."

"I do not understand why you are doing this," said Geoffrey, bewildered by the intensity of her hatred. "What caused you to plot to kill kings?"

"I grew tired of plotting to kill brothers," said Enide. "Oh, Geoffrey, do you really not understand? It was so tedious here. The only fun to be had was setting our brothers at each others" throats, but even that became so easy it was not worthwhile."

"But Father Adrian told me that you went to see King Henry in June—before he was king—in Monmouth. Adrian believes you told him about the plot to kill Rufus."

"And so I did," said Enide. "He thanked me most courteously, and informed me that he would tell his brother to be on his guard. Then he dismissed me from his presence. And as if that were not bad enough, he claimed the throne after Rufus's death before the poor Duke of Normandy could do a thing to stop him."

Geoffrey laughed, despite the gravity of the situation. "I see. So you told King Henry of the plot to kill Rufus, so that he could be ready to support the Duke of Normandy, but all you really did was to warn him to be alert to the opportunity of grabbing the crown for himself. You could not have done him a greater favour. He should have given Goodrich to you!"

"I will have Goodrich yet," said Enide coldly. "When you are dead and Henry is dead, it will be mine. The Earl will never allow Joan and Olivier to hold it—Olivier is too feeble."

"But you will have no Malger at your side," said Geoffrey, playing with fire. "Which other lover will you take to help you run it? Drogo? Adrian?"

Geoffrey had expected her to hurl herself at him in fury—had hoped she would, so that he might turn the situation to his advantage somehow—but he had underestimated her capacity for self-control. · She smiled icily and refused to be drawn.

"Charming though it has been chatting with you again, I am a busy woman, and have a good deal to do before I leave." She turned to Drogo. "Do get it right this time."

Drogo was in the process of drawing back the bowstring, when there was an almighty crash and the door burst open. Drogo jumped in alarm, and Geoffrey used his momentary confusion to grab his surcoat from where it lay on the floor, and fling it towards the startled knight. It entangled itself on the arrow, and Drogo swore as he tried to shake it away. Geoffrey leapt at Drogo, but a mailed fist shot out in a punch that set Geoffrey's senses reeling. He fell backwards, scrabbling to keep his grip on Drogo as the older man fumbled for his dagger.

As Henry darted into the room with his own bow, Enide leapt towards the garderobe passage.

"Shoot!" yelled Geoffrey as Drogo's knife came out of its sheath and missed his cheek by the breadth of a hair.

Geoffrey seized Drogo's wrist and tried to push it away, while his other hand fought to prevent Drogo from striking his eyes with splayed fingers. At first, Geoffrey thought he could force Drogo to drop the dagger, but Drogo was far stronger than he looked, and Geoffrey felt the dagger being forced relentlessly towards him, coming closer and closer to his throat. He tried to struggle away, kicking at Drogo's legs, but although the older knight grunted and swayed slightly, his chain-mail prevented Geoffrey's blows from doing real harm.

Geoffrey squirmed away as the cold tip of the dagger grazed against his skin, but Drogo thrust Geoffrey up against the wall so hard that it drove the breath from his body. The dagger dipped towards him again, and Geoffrey knew that he did not have the strength to stop it. He tried to shout to Henry for help, but no sound came.

And then Drogo crumpled suddenly, the dagger clattering harmlessly from his nerveless fingers. Joan stood over him, holding the same skillet that had been used to brain Walter.

"That will teach him not to tangle with the Mappestones," she muttered. She turned on Henry. "Foolish boy! What were you thinking of? Why did you not shoot? Could you not see that this oaf was about to slit Geoffrey's throat?"

"I could not fire," stammered Henry, his face white.

"And why did you bring a bow?" snapped Joan. "Surely, even you should have been able to see that a sword would have been the weapon of choice for fighting in a small room."

"It was what came most readily to hand," mumbled Henry. "And anyway, my sword is with the blacksmith for sharpening—we cannot be too careful now that Caerdig of Lann Martin thinks he has a truce with us."

"But you did not even fire your bow," pressed Joan.

"I could not," said Henry in a low voice. "It was too close."

"What was too close?" demanded Joan, the skillet still clutched in one meaty hand.

Henry hung his head. "I could not be certain I would get the right one," he mumbled.

And which one would that be? wondered Geoffrey, looking down at the crumpled form of Drogo, and feeling his neck to see if the dagger had nicked him. Henry gave a gasp of horror as his eyes fell on the still-gagging figure of Hedwise lying on the floor.

"My God! What have you done to Hedwise?"

"She swallowed some of her ergot soup," said Geoffrey. "But I do not think she has taken enough to kill her. But while we have been chattering here, Enide has escaped!"

He darted towards the garderobe passage, but Enide was long gone and the door was closed. He rushed towards it, hauling on the handle, but it had been locked from the inside. He thumped it in frustration with his balled fists.

"Kick it open," instructed Joan, following him in. "The bolt on the other side is not very strong."

Geoffrey had already surmised Joan knew about the secret tunnel, but he was impressed that she had observed the size of the bolt. He stood back and aimed a hefty kick at the door, which shuddered and groaned but showed no signs of opening.

"Again!" ordered Joan.

Geoffrey obliged, and saw it budge slightly. He kicked it a third time, and it went crashing back against the wall, the sound reverberating all over the castle.

"Henry?" said Joan imperiously. "Come with me. Not unarmed, man! Bring your bow! And arrows might help, too," she added facetiously as Henry made to come without them. "Olivier, bind Hedwise and Drogo, and ensure they do not escape. Geoffrey, take your sword and follow me."

"Down there?" asked Geoffrey in horror.

"Of course down there!" said Joan, looking at him askance. "That is where Enide went, after all. Look lively, Geoffrey! We have a murderer to catch."

"I could go the other way," temporised Geoffrey. "I could block the exit at the far end."

He expected her to argue, but she gave him a soft and somewhat unexpected smile. "You will be too late by the time you run round the river path. She will have gone. Stay here if you would rather, and guard this pair of ruffians. Olivier! Come with me."

Geoffrey could not, in all conscience, allow Enide to escape because he had entrusted her capture to the likes of Olivier and Henry. Joan, he imagined, would probably do better, but she possessed no real weapons. Filling his mind with images of Stephen,

Godric, and Walter, all dead, directly or indirectly, because of Enide, he snatched the torch from Joan and marched into the black slit of the tunnel.

Geoffrey had not taken more than a few steps before the torch started to splutter, and he faltered. Was the air too old and stale in the passage to allow the thing to burn properly, or was it just a poorly made torch? The thought had barely formed in his mind, before whatever imperfection had been in the flare had righted itself, and it burned bright and steady again. Geoffrey forced himself to walk on.

It was not a long journey, he told himself, and the tunnel was dry for the most part. There was plenty of air, too. But he had not gone far before he felt his mouth go dry, and the familiar tightening around his chest began. He hesitated, despite his resolve to catch Enide.

"Geoffrey," called Joan from behind him, giving him a firm but gentle push in the back to make him start moving again. "Did Hedwise kill our father with poisonous fish soup?"

"No," called Geoffrey wearily, picking his way down the dark, slick steps. "He killed himself because Enide was preparing to murder another king. King Henry is cleverer than Rufus, and Father knew she was unlikely to succeed."

"Rubbish!" came Henry's voice from above him. "Enide would have succeeded very well if you had not intervened. Norbert had a good clear shot, and would most certainly have killed the King had you not distracted him."

"Maybe," said Geoffrey. "But Father did not want himself associated with it, and he knew he would be because the plotters were basically identical to the ones that hatched the first regicide—the one that never happened because someone else thought of it first."

"And since I suspect that King Henry knows more than he is telling about his brother's timely demise we had better not ask who," said Joan. "So, all those accusations and counter-accusations about Godric's murder were for nothing—no one killed him, no one poisoned him or Enide?"

"Right," said Geoffrey.

"Well, at least the Earl of Shrewsbury did not get away with foisting his false will on us," she said, after a moment. "Olivier managed to get his fat priest drunk and indiscreet, and he learned that the Earl really *did* forge the document that claims Godric left Goodrich to him. But it does not matter now—Goodrich is ours once more."

"I cannot imagine that the Earl will accept defeat lightly," said Geoffrey. "He will be back to try again."

"I do not think so," said Joan confidently. "He is no fool. He knows he has been beaten over Goodrich, and he will not risk the King's anger to continue his war of attrition with the Mappestones. He might come for us if the Duke of Normandy ever claims the crown of England, but that will not be for many years yet—if ever."

They had reached the large chamber at the bottom of the stairs. Geoffrey entered it cautiously, holding the torch above his head and his sword at the ready. The room was deserted, and appeared exactly as it had done the last time he had been there.

Joan shuddered. "What a foul place. And this is where Enide lived for four months?"

"Not all of the time," said Geoffrey. "I imagine she stayed with Adrian on occasions, or Malger. She has not been here since Father's murder or Rohese would have noticed."

"I had no idea this room existed," said Joan, running her fingers along the shelves curiously.

"But you knew of the tunnel," said Geoffrey. It was not a question.

"Oh, yes. I was in my teens when the keep was being built, and since girls are not permitted the freedom of boys to go gallivanting around the countryside, I watched the castle's progress with some interest. I guessed what the shaft was for, and I did my own exploring, and discovered the tunnel and where it went. Godric thought it was his secret, and I did not tell him that I knew about it."

"He might have had you executed as a threat to his security," said Geoffrey, smiling, but not entirely sure that it was too remote a possibility.

Joan grinned. "He might well have done. I explored the passage as far as the door to this room, looking for Rohese the night Godric died, but it was barred from the inside. I have never actually been in here."

So that cleared up another loose end, thought Geoffrey. Joan had not been able to enter the room at the end of the tunnel because it had been barred at that point. Rohese, however, had found it open, and so Stephen must have unbarred it when he had gone from the woods up to Godric's chamber. He had slipped through Godric's room while Walter, Geoffrey, and Rohese had been sleeping, and returned later to argue with Godric after Walter had left.

Joan continued to explain. "When I got back to Godric's room, you and Walter were preparing to go back to sleep. I hid in the garderobe passage until you dozed, so you would not know where I had come from. I had to move the chest from the door, back to the end of the bed. I wondered why you slept through the noise I made: Walter was drunk, but you were not. I did not know then that you had been drugged."

"Why did you move the chest?" asked Geoffrey.

Joan regarded him with a sideways tilt of her head. "Because I wanted to leave, bird-brain! I could not get out with the chest blocking the door, could I? Anyway, I did not realise why you had put it there in the first place. I thought Walter had placed it there by mistake in his drunken stupor."

"Hunting Rohese down to sleep with the Earl seems a little callous," said Geoffrey. "She is only a child and surely too young to be thrust into the clutches of a man like him, even for only a night."

"Nonsense," said Joan. "She had been with the Earl every night since he forced his presence on us at Rwirdin—except for the last one, when he chose a girl from the village. Rohese was unreasonably jealous, and refused her favours to show him her displeasure."

"She slept with him voluntarily?"

"Of course she did," said Joan, surprised by the question. "Do you think I would let her go to him if she were not willing? It is something about which I happen to feel very strongly. I am in the process of preventing Julianna from falling victim to a similar fate, but Olivier mentioned that he had told you about that. I was a little concerned, actually, thinking that a Holy Land knight was hardly someone to be trusted to protect a young virgin. But you have proved that my fears were unfounded: not only have you not forced your attentions on her but you have been kind to her and Rohese."

So Rohese had not been strictly truthful with Geoffrey when he had been so gallant in saving her from what had seemed to be a fate worse than death. He wondered what other lies or misleading statements she had made to him.

"Did you stand in for Rohese when she could not be found?" asked Geoffrey, and immediately regretted his impertinence. If she had, it was none of his business.

Joan glared at him in outrage. "I most certainly did not! What do you take me for? Have I changed that much since we last met?"

Geoffrey thought that she had changed very little. She was still aggressive, sharp-tongued, critical, and intolerant, but she was also somewhat prudish and not especially attractive. She certainly was not the kind of woman to leap into bed with any passing earl—or be the kind of woman any passing earl would want there. Geoffrey was embarrassed that he had asked such a question.

"Olivier stayed with the Earl that night," said Joan stiffly.

Geoffrey was more embarrassed than ever. Joan saw his reaction and sighed in exasperation.

"Geoffrey, what is the matter with you? Has your stay in the Holy Land deranged your mind? Olivier played dice until the Earl was ready to sleep, and then played the rebec. Olivier is a very skilled musician and the Earl finds his playing soothing."

"Ah," said Geoffrey, not knowing what else to say.

Still offended, she looked around the room. "Someone has made this hole quite comfortable."

"Do not stand around chattering," called Henry, who had gone on ahead and was at the door that opened into the woods. "This door is locked and I cannot open it."

Geoffrey's blood ran cold. "We are trapped?"

Joan watched him. "We are not," she said firmly. "Enide has just blocked the door, that is all. Give it a push with your shoulder, Henry."

Henry did as he was told, but the door was stuck fast. Geoffrey inspected it, and then gave it a solid kick at waist level. It moved a little.

"A stone is blocking it," said Henry, elbowing him out of the way. "Move. I can open it now."

Geoffrey stood back and watched as Henry heaved and shoved at the door, accompanying his efforts with an impressive litany of curses and blasphemies. Geoffrey offered to help, but there was only enough room for one, and Henry was clearly intent on doing it himself.

"Making up for not firing your arrow at Drogo to save Geoff, are you?" asked Joan waspishly.

Henry glared, leaning his back against the door and shoving with all his might. "I could not be sure that I would not hit Geoffrey," he grunted. "Then you would have been all over me for murder."

"That would not usually stop you," said Geoffrey.

"Well, things are different now," muttered Henry. "I am lord of Goodrich; I can afford to be gracious."

If not committing murder was Henry's notion of being gracious, Geoffrey decided yet again that the sooner he was away from Goodrich, the better. He backed away from the door to give Henry more room.

"It will not budge," said Henry. "You try."

Geoffrey leaned his weight on the door, and pushed as hard as he could. It remained fast.

"This is useless," said Henry, watching. "I need a lever." Before Geoffrey could stop him, he had grabbed the torch and darted back up the stairs, leaving Joan and Geoffrey alone in the darkness.

The pitch-blackness in the cavern pressed down on Geoffrey. Somewhere, he heard a light patter as some sand fell from the roof. The soft stone through which the tunnel had been excavated was completely inappropriate for such a structure, and Geoffrey felt part of the wall crumble even as his outstretched hand brushed against it. And then there was a hiss and a crackle as yet another trickle of earth and pebbles dropped from the ceiling. He found he could not breathe deeply enough to draw air into his lungs, and he started to cough.

He began to walk blindly towards the stairs, hoping to catch up with Henry, but he had not gone far before his foot caught on the uneven floor and he went sprawling forwards onto his knees.

"Geoff? Where are you?" came Joan's voice. He felt her hand on his shoulder. "Do not try to chase after Henry. He will not be long."

"We are trapped in the dark," said Geoffrey tightly. "And the dust is choking me."

"There is no dust," said Joan reasonably. "And we are not trapped. We will be out soon, and we can always go back up the stairs to Godric's chamber, anyway."

Geoffrey swallowed, and tried to bring his panic under control. "I know."

"I understand your dislike of enclosed spaces," said Joan sympathetically. "You wrote about it in your letters."

"My letters to Enide," said Geoffrey, still coughing. "Or rather my letters to some scribe, who was doubtless enjoying himself thoroughly at my expense. Still, at least I know it was not Norbert. That man could not pen a decent letter to save his life."

"Actually, they were letters to me," said Joan in the darkness. "You addressed them to Enide, but she lost interest in writing to you within a year of you leaving—especially after her accident. Dictating a letter takes a long time, and she was too active and too impatient to sit so long at one task. She usually left them lying around in our room, and I took them to Olivier to read."

"So my letters were to Olivier?" asked Geoffrey, horrified. "Wonderful!"

"It was wonderful for me," said Joan quietly. "It gave me an excuse to see him, and we enjoyed the business of composing letters to you together. He wanted me to tell you that it was us and not Enide when we first started to write to you, but I was afraid that if I did, you might not write again, and then I would have lost two things I had come to care about—my reason for spending so much time with Olivier, and writing to you."

"No wonder Olivier knew that I had been transferred to Tancred's service, but my brothers did not," said Geoffrey, recalling his surprise when the small knight had mentioned it when they had first met.

Joan nodded. "He has followed the career of a fellow knight with great interest."

"And it was not Enide who was considering becoming a nun," Geoffrey went on, remembering another subject in the letters. "It was you. And it was not me you were telling—it was Olivier, so that he would make up his mind and marry you."

Joan sighed softly. "It did not work—I think that ploy was too subtle for him. But I felt that I came to know you much better after you had left than I had when you were here. And then, when Enide died—or we thought she did—it was too late to be honest. We had to stop writing, even though we longed to continue."

"But it was all based on deceit!" objected Geoffrey. "You are right—I might not have written back to you had I known what you had done."

He was startled to hear a soft intake of breath that sounded like a sob. He reached out in the dark, but she moved away from his hand. He scratched around for something to say to break the uncomfortable silence that followed.

"I wrote to you for twenty years. Did you love Olivier all that time?"

Her voice was unsteady when she spoke. "I fell in love the first time I saw him, but you see how he is. He would never have gathered the courage to ask me to be his wife. In the end, when I was almost resigned to remaining a maiden all my life, Walter took your manor at Rwirdin so that the Earl of Shrewsbury would become interested enough to force him into action."

"So, first you steal my letters intended for Enide, and then you steal my manor," said Geoffrey, unimpressed. "All to secure Olivier for yourself."

"It was worth it," said Joan, sounding defiant. "I might have lost you now, but I gained Olivier in the process. He might not look much, but he is the most gentle, charming man I have ever met, and quite unlike all the other pigs that call themselves knights—including you. You can keep your paltry manor! I do not need it now. I have what I really want."

Geoffrey recalled the tender words about the lover he had assumed was Enide's. So, it was Joan's, and the astonishing object of her affections was the cowardly Olivier, a man so feeble that he had taken years and years to secure his wife. Geoffrey recanted that thought almost immediately: Joan was a formidable woman, and perhaps Olivier had done well in eluding her amorous clutches for so long.

Geoffrey recalled how he had so cleverly deduced that the lover in the letters was Adrian, the parish priest, written of with such loving care by Enide. But that had been no more than a lucky guess, inspired by Adrian's clear infatuation with Enide when he spoke of her. Geoffrey's assumption that Enide had declined to mention his name because Adrian was parish priest could not have been more wrong: all Joan's words of affection and devotion had not been to Geoffrey at all but to Olivier.

A few particles of sand dropped from the ceiling and landed near him, making him jump violently. He felt sweat breaking out on his forehead and the small of his back. He started to cough again when dust swirled into his face. Then Joan moved next to him, slapping him vigorously on the back.

"Easy now," she said, gruff in her attempt at comfort. "Move this way a little, away from the dust. You have no cause to fear this cave, Geoff. It has been here for nigh on thirty years, and has not collapsed yet. Henry will not be long."

The air was clearer where Joan had pulled him, and Geoffrey took a deep breath and leaned back against one of the walls. To his horror, he felt part of it crumble.

"Think of something else," said Joan, crouching near him and taking one of his hands in hers. "There are many things about this mystery that I do not understand. For example, this tunnel was very busy the night Godric died. I am confused about the order of events. Will you clarify that for me?"

Geoffrey understood that she was attempting to distract him from his escalating terror of the cavern, and that she was trying to be kind. He did not feel in the least like listing a catalogue of his relatives' deeds that fateful night, but the logical part of his mind told him it was probably better to occupy himself with something other than fevered imaginings about cave-ins.

He took another deep breath and began. "You were all concerned over Father's new will, and Hedwise determined that Henry was not to be cheated out of his inheritance. She decided that if he could not obtain it by legitimate means, she would try alternative methods. As the Earl slumbered happily to the dulcet tones of Olivier's rebec, Hedwise prepared some of her infamous fish soup. . . ." He paused, the mere thought of it making his stomach churn.

"I do not like it much either," said Joan. "You know she uses the giblets, blood, and heads of fish to produce that very strong flavour?"

Geoffrey thought he was going to be sick. "I hate fish."

"Olivier loves it," said Joan fondly. "But we digress. Hedwise prepared her broth . . ."

"And flavoured it with enough ergot and poppy powder to kill. She gave me a bowl before we slept. Walter was blind drunk. Her intention was to return early the next morning, feed more of the poisoned soup to Father, and have Walter blamed for both murders."

"But you do not like fish," predicted Joan. "And so you did not finish the soup."

The cave leapt into light as Henry returned, bearing a stout bar. Joan released Geoffrey's hand and moved away quickly, almost guiltily, as though one Mappestone showing affection for another was something to be ashamed of.

"This should do it," said Henry. "Did I hear you talking about Hedwise's fish soup? Delicious stuff! It is the one thing about her I will miss if she is imprisoned for attempted murder."

"I did not finish the soup," said Geoffrey. "Although the little I drank was enough to render me insensible for the rest of the night. I saw and heard nothing until Henry did the honours with his bucket of water the following morning."

Henry chuckled, and paused in his labour to wink at Geoffrey. "That was a satisfying moment, I can tell you—one of the very few in the history of our relationship, I might add."

"Do be quiet, Henry," snapped Joan. "We are not on a pleasant excursion here. We are dealing with a murderer who is escaping as you waste valuable time with trivialities."

Henry winked at Geoffrey again, and started to heave and push at the lever. Geoffrey resumed his tale.

"While Walter snored in his drunken slumber and I was drugged, you emerged from the tunnel where you had been searching for Rohese. You moved the chest that I had placed to block the door, assuming that Walter had put it there for some obscure purpose rather than my precaution against hostile intruders. Meanwhile, Rohese was hidden between Father's mattresses—"

"So that is where she was," said Joan, nodding appreciation. "How clever of her." She gave Geoffrey a sideways glance. "Or, more likely, how clever of you."

"Be quiet, Joan," said Henry. "We are not on a pleasant excursion here. A murderer escapes while you waste time with trivialities."

"While *you* waste time!" said Joan, angered by his irritating manner. "It is not I who cannot open the door so that we might give chase. Lord! What was that?"

A heavy thump sounded against the door.

"Enide," said Geoffrey, grimly. "She is still blocking the door with stones. Hurry, Henry! The longer we take to open it, the more difficult it will become."

"You mean she is on the other side of the door now?" asked Henry, amazed. "She has not fled?"

"No," said Geoffrey, exasperated at his brother's slowness. "She is continuing to block the door. Give me the lever if you cannot move it."

"I can do it," said Henry, pushing Geoffrey away. "Carry on with this tale of yours. It will make me angry, and I am stronger when I am angry."

Geoffrey exchanged a long-suffering glance with Joan, and continued his story.

"As Father, Rohese, Walter, and I slept, Stephen emerged from the tunnel. He had been to see a dog in the village, and Malger's guards would not let him back in again. He used the tunnel instead. In this very room, he met Enide—each giving the other the fright of their lives if Stephen is to be believed—and Enide told him of the plot to kill King Henry. She wanted his help, which he declined to give her, and so she settled for him taking a message to Father."

"So Stephen opened the door that had been locked from the inside when I had been looking for Rohese," said Joan thoughtfully. "And I was just an arm's reach from Enide."

"Yes," said Geoffrey. "If you rattled the door, you probably startled her, and Stephen also using the tunnel must have convinced her that she could stay here no longer. She doubtless went to seek sanctuary with Malger. Stephen did not want to disturb Father in the middle of the night, so he decided to wait until dawn. Shortly before he arrived, Walter woke and went to find some breakfast, and Rohese woke and began exploring the tunnel for something to do."

"She is a nosy girl," said Joan, nodding. "I told her it would lead her into trouble. Julianna is the same."

"When Stephen came to speak to Father, Rohese was in the tunnel, Walter had left, and I was drugged. I imagine he tried to wake me to tell me to leave, but obviously was unsuccessful. When Stephen told him about the plot, Father was horrified. Rohese heard him yelling. She also heard him mention Tirel, the man who really shot Rufus—or so the Court claims—and Norbert the scribe, who was the marksman who was to kill King Henry. Stephen left, and Father, seeing that he would be unable to prevent the plan being put into action, stabbed himself. Rohese came when she heard him groaning. She said he blamed us for his death."

"But you said he killed himself," said Henry. "Make up your mind!"

"He means metaphorically, Henry," said Joan impatiently. "He blamed Stephen for bringing him the news, and Enide and Walter for plotting, I suppose. We three had nothing to do with it."

"Father told Rohese to hide in the tunnel until it was safe to come out. This she did, and was here days later when I found her. After Rohese had fled, Hedwise arrived, armed with some of her poisoned fish soup for Father. She was appalled to find her plan had gone so badly wrong: Father was already dead, Walter had recovered from his drunkenness and had left, and I was still alive. She decided that she still might gain something from it, if she acted quickly. She pulled Father's knife from his stomach and tossed it out of the window. Then she emptied the pitcher of wine after it, and stabbed him in the chest with my Arabian dagger."

"I see," said Joan. "By making it look as though *you* had downed the wine and stabbed Godric, she could eliminate you as a potential rival for the estates."

"Yes—although she was disappointed not to have eliminated Walter instead. Later, she returned and added ergot to the bottle of wine Stephen gave me, so that I would not be able to tell whether she or Stephen had poisoned me. Later still, she decided that was too risky, and so she cleaned the broth bowl and put a new bottle of wine in place of the poisoned one, forgetting to break the seal."

"Lord spare us," gasped Henry, grinning in satisfaction as the door moved slightly. "It is all highly complex!"

"Not really," said Geoffrey. "Just several people operating independently and with their own axes to grind."

There was a hiss, and a few pebbles dropped from the ceiling onto Geoffrey's head. He shoved Henry out of the way and snatched the lever from him. Henry might claim that anger made him strong, but Geoffrey's terror of being caught inside a collapsing cave made him stronger still. The door budged slightly, and he heaved even harder, feeling the blood pound in his head with the effort. He was dimly aware of Henry and Joan urging him on, but he needed no encouragement from them to effect an escape from the cave. The door moved again, and then he was able to insert the lever into a better position.

With a groan of protesting wood, the door inched open sufficiently for Geoffrey to squeeze partway through. His inclination was to bolt out as quickly as possible when he saw the grey light of early morning seeping in, but he forced himself to emerge cautiously, sword in hand. Enide had been piling stones against the door and was likely to be nearby.

He was not mistaken. As he emerged, he detected something moving out of the corner of his eye. Enide stood there with a jagged rock held above her head. With a shriek of triumph, she brought it down with all her might, aiming for Geoffrey's unprotected skull.

Geoffrey had been anticipating an attack from Enide, and so was ready to duck sideways as the rock came plunging downward. The stone grazed down the arm that was raised instinctively to protect his head, and then dropped harmlessly to the ground. With a howl of frustration, Enide was away.

Geoffrey wriggled the rest of the way through the gap, his shirt snagging and catching, so that Henry was forced to push him hard from the inside. The others, being smaller, had no such difficulties and were able to slip through with relative ease.

"You should have let me go first," said Henry accusingly. "I would have been able to grab her."

"You would have been dead," said Joan. "You would not have emerged with the caution that Geoffrey exercised, and Enide would have brained you."

Enide had stacked a sizeable pile of rocks, some of them quite large, against the door. Geoffrey was impressed at her physical strength, especially given her useless right hand, and was not surprised that the exit had been difficult to open. He took several deep breaths of air, and felt the unsteadiness in his limbs begin to recede.

"There!" Joan grabbed his arm and pointed. In the pale light of dawn, a tall, slender figure could be seen, weaving its way through the trees. Enide had made a mistake: she should have left Goodrich under cover of the night, for had it been dark they would never have spotted her. Perhaps she was not infallible after all.

Geoffrey darted after her, hearing the others following him, Joan graceful but slow, and Henry like a great panting ox. There was no chain-mail to weigh Geoffrey down this time, and he made good progress. The pale figure ahead of him saw him gaining on her and increased her speed. She was almost at the river.

The rain of the last few days had caused the river to swell, and it was now a great brown snake that tore at its banks in a mass of whirlpools and waves. Branches and bits of vegetation were dragged along it, turning and twisting in the crazy currents. Enide swerved to the right, and began running along one side of it, away from the village. Geoffrey followed, and saw she was aiming for a man on the path who was holding the reins of two horses. Geoffrey recognised him, even at a distance.

"Ingram!" he yelled, thundering down the trackway.

The young soldier balked at the sound of Geoffrey's voice. Enide snatched the reins from his hands and prepared to mount. Then there was a singing sound, and the horse crumpled.

"Damn it all!" shouted Henry, lowering his bow. "I missed her!"

He tried again, but the missile went wide, falling harmlessly in a bed of nettles. Observing his appalling skills, Geoffrey was suddenly very grateful that Henry had declined to shoot Drogo when they had been struggling in Godric's chamber.

Enide grabbed the reins of the second horse, impatiently gesturing for Ingram to help her mount.

"But what about me?" Geoffrey heard him protest. "What do I ride?"

"Help me up!" Enide screamed. "Stupid boy! Help me!"

Ingram hesitated and Geoffrey saw the flash of a blade.

"Ingram!" he yelled again. "Get away from her!"

His warning came too late. Ingram fell to the ground and the horse, alarmed by all the shouting, began to buck and prance.

"The Devil take you, Geoffrey!" Enide screeched, abandoning the animal, and turning to continue to race along the river path.

But someone else was on the path, too: Father Adrian had seen everything. Enide tried to dodge round him, but he dived full length and pulled her to the ground. She fought, kicked, and screamed, and Adrian only just managed to hold her until Henry was able to reach him to help.

Meanwhile, Geoffrey crouched next to Ingram, inspecting the wound that Enide had inflicted.

"I need a priest," the soldier gasped. "Get me one, fast! I am dying!"

Geoffrey called for Adrian, who left the spitting Enide for Joan and Henry to hold. The priest knelt next to Ingram and began to recite the prayers for the dying. Geoffrey wondered how many more times he would hear Adrian's requiem before he was able to escape from Goodrich. As he listened, he saw something protruding from Ingram's hauberk.

"My chalice," he said, reaching out to take the handsome silver cup that Tancred had given him.

Adrian caught his hand. "Would you rob a dying man?" he asked reproachfully.

Geoffrey was about to point out that he was a knight, and that most knights had gone on a Crusade to do exactly that, when Ingram pulled it from his hauberk himself. He thrust it at Adrian.

"This is for your church if you will say masses for me. I confess to killing Francis the physician. Absolve me, quick, before it is too late!"

"This is not yours to give, Mark," said Adrian. "Anyway, I do not need to be paid for the masses I will say for your soul. But I cannot absolve you unless you repent. Are you sorry for murdering Francis?"

"Yes, but *she* told me to do it," Ingram said breathlessly, glancing to where Enide still struggled in the arms of Henry and Joan. "I did it for her, and his blood is on *her* hands, not mine. She dragged me into all this, even though she is my mother!"

"Who is your mother?" demanded Geoffrey. Realisation dawned suddenly. "Enide? You claim that *Enide* is your mother?"

"She is; she told me," said Ingram. "And it makes sense that I am the son of nobility—I have always known I was different from the rest. She said Goodrich was rightfully mine, and that she would help me get it as soon as you lot were out of the way."

"You *are* different," said Geoffrey coldly. "I have never met such a worthless, snivelling snake as you. And I can assure you that you are certainly not related to me!"

"Geoffrey!" snapped Adrian. "Either be quiet or leave. Continue with your confession, Mark."

"She told me the truth about my ancestry when I got back from the Holy Land. I gave her all my treasure, so that she could help me take Goodrich. She needed the funds, you see, to hire lawyers and to petition the King."

"I knew you were gullible," said Geoffrey in disgust. "But I did not think you were insane! What were you thinking of? How could you part with all your treasure, just like that? What about your family?"

"*She* is my family," said Ingram fiercely.

"You are distressing the boy," said Adrian, standing and glaring at Geoffrey. "I must ask you to leave."

"Willingly, Father," said Geoffrey. "Get up, Ingram. You are not dying. Your wound is only superficial. If you had ever fought a battle in the Holy Land, instead of skulking in some dark cellar until it was time to come and join in the looting, you would know this very well. Fortunately for you, the chalice deflected the knife, and your mother's blow was not a fatal one."

Astonished, Ingram sat up, poking at himself doubtfully. "I will not die?"

"Not yet," said Geoffrey. "Although you have the physician's murder to answer for."

"Give me the cup," said Ingram, making a grab for it. "I will need it to hire lawyers."

Geoffrey caught his wrist. "You gave it to Father Adrian for his church, and that is where it will stay. If you steal it, I will hunt you down and chop your hands off."

Ingram paled.

"You are a fool," said Geoffrey, wearily. "And that is your best defence. How could you believe that Enide is your mother? Plead insanity to the judges, Ingram—tell them that you believed that a Norman lady gave birth to you when she was only eight years old, and yet managed to keep the secret so that only she knew; tell them that you gave her all your wealth in order to become lord of the manor at Goodrich; and tell them that you had a tiny scratch on your arm and you made a confession to the priest because you believed you were dying."

From where she was being held in Henry's tight embrace, Enide laughed bitterly. "Greed, my dear brother. People will believe all manner of insanities for wealth and property."

"Enide!" said Father Adrian, turning shocked eyes on her. "What evil have you done now? You used me, you used Ingram, and you have killed. Confess now, before the Devil comes to claim you."

Enide sobered suddenly and went limp in Henry's arms. "You are right," she said softly. "I will make my confession. You can let me go, Henry. I will not try to escape."

"No, Henry!" yelled Geoffrey, as Henry released her.

Freed from his grip, Enide spun round, and kicked Henry hard in the shins. As he staggered, she shoved him hard, so that he fell backwards into Joan, who was advancing purposefully. Both went tumbling to the ground. Henry bellowed in pain and fury, while Joan spat some ripe curses. And then Enide was off again, tearing along the river path with almost impossible speed.

"After her!" shouted Joan, although Geoffrey was already running. "Father Adrian, stay with Ingram. And do not let him escape, or you will have even more on your conscience."

Clever Joan, thought Geoffrey as he ran. Adrian was already

wracked with guilt over his unwitting role in Enide's plotting—
Joan's statement would ensure that Ingram would not escape him.

Enide managed a remarkable pace, although Geoffrey knew she
would be unable to sustain it for long. She disappeared around a
corner and, afraid that he would lose her in the forest if he could
not see her, Geoffrey ran faster. He tore blindly round the bend,
expecting to see her running ahead of him on the path. His mind
registered that she was not there at exactly the same time that the
branch swung towards his ankles and he lost his balance, stumbling
to his knees. He saw her dagger glint, and heard Joan scream behind
him. As Enide brought the dagger down, aiming for his unprotected
neck, Geoffrey took a hold of her legs, and pulled her off balance.
Then they were both rolling down the bank and into the brown,
churning water.

For a moment, all Geoffrey could do was to struggle wildly,
trying to claw free of the choking water and of Enide who clung to
him. Then he felt the soft bottom of the river-bed under his feet,
and he fought to stand upright.

"Take my hand!" yelled Henry, sliding down the bank towards
him.

Geoffrey reached out, but then Enide was on him, dagger flash-
ing as, even in the dire peril of being swept down the river, she tried
to stab him. He lost his footing, and they were both away, gasping
and struggling as the current caught them and dragged them farther
from the banks. Geoffrey wanted to shout to stop her, but his mouth
was full of water, and he knew she would not listen anyway. Enide
was doomed, and she intended to take Geoffrey with her.

She lashed out wildly with the dagger, stabbing at him when he
tried to push her away. Her frenzy was more than he could combat,
and he felt himself losing ground. He tried to hold the arm that
brandished the knife, but his own hands were cold and clumsy, and
he did not possess her demonic strength. He kicked away from her,
and saw her disappear from his sight. Thinking that she must have
been swept away, he turned, and tried to strike out for the bank.

He had made some headway when he felt his legs grabbed from
underneath, and then his world was nothing other than the roar of
water and filthy brown bubbles. He kicked loose, but felt Enide's
one good hand clawing at his stomach, gaining a hold on his belt.

He wondered whether she had risen from the dead after all, for whereas Geoffrey was growing weaker and was struggling for breath, Enide did not seem to need any.

She ducked him under a second him, putting her arm around his neck like a vise. He bit her as hard as he could, and felt himself released momentarily. Then a floating branch caught him on the side of his head, and he felt his senses darkening. He began to feel as though he no longer cared: the intense, numbing cold of the water passed and the burning sensation in his lungs began to recede.

Then she had him again, fastening her good arm around his chest, and dragging him through the water. But at least he could breathe. He looked up at the sky above, and wondered distantly whether it was blue or just dark grey. Then his feet were touching the river-bed, and he was aware the current no longer dragged and tore at him—and he realised that the arms around his chest were supportive rather than bent on his destruction.

Strong hands reached out to haul him and Joan from the water, both coughing and gasping.

"I almost lost you both!" cried Henry, horror in his voice. "The current was so strong!"

Geoffrey saw what they had done. Joan had tied a rope around her waist and had gone into the water to catch him as he drifted past. Henry had hauled them both out again. Geoffrey could not have imagined such trusting co-operation occurring a week before, when the most important thing in their lives was the inheritance of Goodrich.

He sat up, still gasping for breath.

"Geoffrey! Are you all right? She was trying to drown you!" yelled Henry, pounding his younger brother vigorously on the back.

"I had noticed," said Geoffrey, raising an arm to fend him off. "But you saved my life."

"I do not know why," Henry muttered. "I suppose I did not want that witch to deprive me of doing something I have been longing to do for years."

"Thank you anyway, both of you," said Geoffrey, scanning the water for Enide. It was brown and flat, and there was no sign of her.

"She is dead," said Joan softly. "She was swept past me when I was reaching for you. Her eyes were open, but she was dead."

"Are you sure?" asked Geoffrey doubtfully.

"Of course!" said Henry. "No one could survive that. You would not have lasted much longer yourself. Look at that current! I wager you it will only get stronger as you go downstream."

"So, I leave Goodrich as I arrived," said Geoffrey, wiping the water from his eyes. "Soaking wet after a dip in the river."

"You are leaving, then?" asked Joan.

"Yes," said Geoffrey. "Today or tomorrow."

"Tomorrow, then," said Henry decisively. "Or even the next day. Give yourself time to dry out."

"And will you visit us in another twenty years?" asked Joan, looking away down the river.

"Perhaps before," said Geoffrey. "And I will write regularly."

Joan smiled at him suddenly, and he smiled back. Henry looked from one to the other mystified, and then helped haul both of them to their feet.

"She has gone," he said in satisfaction, making his way back up the bank. "Things will be different from now on. Goodrich is mine, as it should be, and there will be no brothers and no Enide and Hedwise to poison our lives. Bertrada will leave soon, but Joan and Olivier can stay on and help look after my estates. It is just that it has worked out this way, and the only good that will disappear with the evil is that wonderful fish soup."

Joan and Geoffrey exchanged a knowing glance and stood side by side a moment longer, looking down the river where Enide had disappeared. Just as he was about to follow Henry, Geoffrey caught the faintest glimpse of white some way down the opposite bank. He peered at it, but there was nothing to see. He decided that he must have been mistaken, and that his imagination had run away with him. Then he glanced at Joan, and saw her staring at the same spot.

"Did you? . . ." he began.

"I cannot be sure," she replied hesitantly. She shook her head. "No. There was nothing there. I must have imagined it."

They exchanged a look in which the uncertainty of both was reflected, before following Henry up the slippery bank to head back to Goodrich Castle.

HiSTORiCAL ΠOTE

In September 1087, William the Conqueror died, leaving three sons to fight over his kingdom. The eldest was Robert, who was to inherit the Dukedom of Normandy; the second was William Rufus, who hastened to the French coast so that he could be in England to seize the English throne; and the youngest was Henry, to whom the Conqueror bequeathed a quantity of silver, but no land. Another son had been killed in a hunting accident some years before.

Rufus had much of the strength of character that made his father such a powerful king. His thirteen-year reign was reasonably successful and, as time passed, his grip on the crown became ever more secure. Some historians have suggested that Rufus dabbled in the black arts and that the fact that he never married indicates that he was a homosexual. There is no incontrovertible evidence for either claim, and the accounts that were written immediately after Rufus's death were penned by monks, who had good reason to blacken his name: Rufus's dealings with the Church were violent and unscrupulous, leading many churchmen to disclaim him as an agent of the Devil. Whether he was "hated by almost all his people and abhorrent to God," as attested by the *Anglo-Saxon Chronicle,* is still a matter for debate among historians.

Relations with Rufus's elder brother, Robert, Duke of Normandy, were never easy, since the Duke did not take kindly to his younger sibling claiming the larger part of their father's dominions. But in 1096, the Duke heard Pope Urban's call for a great Crusade to set the Holy Land free from the Infidels who ruled it. Rashly, the Duke pawned Normandy to Rufus to raise funds for the adventure. A document was also signed by Rufus and the Duke to the effect that if either were to die childless, each would succeed to his brother's estates.

For three years or so, Rufus ruled both England and Normandy, while Henry, still landless, frittered away his time at court. Then news came that the Crusade was over, and that Jerusalem had been wrested from the control of the Saracens and was in Christian hands. The Duke began his return to Normandy. The journey took some time, since the Duke, never one to decline enjoyment, was persuaded to remain for several months as the honoured guest of the rich and powerful Geoffrey of Conversano. The Duke married Geoffrey's daughter, and the dowry she brought him was ample to pay off the mortgage and reclaim Normandy from Rufus. Circumstances were looking bleak indeed for Prince Henry: one brother was firmly entrenched as King of England, while the other was returning to reclaim Normandy, complete with a wife who would doubtless provide him with an heir. The birth of a son to the Duke would take Henry yet one step further from his dreams of lands and power.

On 2 August 1100, while staying at his manor of Brockenhurst, Rufus decided to go hunting. It is difficult to distinguish between legend and truth about the events on the day that Rufus died, but accounts say that Rufus was ill, and the hunting expedition that was due to leave in the morning was postponed until the afternoon. Several noblemen were in the company of the King's little party, including Prince Henry; Sir Walter Tirel, the Count of Poix; and Earl Gilbert and his brother, Richard, of the large and powerful house of Clare.

As was the custom, the party split to hunt, and Rufus and Tirel found themselves together. One account maintains that a fletcher made a gift of fine arrows to Rufus before the hunt, and Rufus generously presented half of them to Tirel, reputedly a good shot. As evening drew in, the beaters began to herd the deer towards the forest glade in which Rufus and Tirel waited. What happened next will never be known for certain. The story goes that as the frightened stags were driven into the clearing, Rufus fired and missed; Tirel's arrow was said (by the chronicler Oderic Vitalis in 1135) to have "shaved the hair on the animal's back, sped on and wounded the King standing beyond." Rufus pitched forwards and drove the arrow farther into his chest. Tirel promptly fled the scene of the crime and headed for France. Years later, he swore an oath to the saintly Abbot Suger of Paris that it was not his arrow that had killed Rufus, and even that he was not in the same part of the forest.

Prince Henry immediately rode for Winchester, where the royal treasury was held, reaching it that evening. He demanded the keys to the treasury, and, within three days, he had been crowned King of England. Rufus's body was taken to Winchester the day after his death, where he was buried. In 1107, the tower of Winchester Cathedral collapsed, and some sources suggest it was because such an evil man lay in a sacred place. The chronicler William of Malmsbury, however, notes that the structure of the tower was inherently unstable long before Rufus was buried under it.

Meanwhile, there is no evidence that Walter Tirel ever gained from his alleged part in the killing: he received no manors and no favours from the new King. The powerful Clare family, however, went from strength to strength. Earl Gilbert's brother, Richard, was one of the first to gain from Henry's largesse, and he was made Abbot of the wealthy monastery of Ely before Christmas that year. It should also be noted that Tirel's wife was Alice Clare, and that some historians consider the possibility that Tirel may have been a scapegoat in the hands of his powerful relations.

It is impossible to say whether Rufus's death was a tragic accident or the result of a carefully executed plan. However, the one person clearly to gain from Rufus's sudden death was Prince Henry. Henry acted quickly and without hesitation, and was crowned before many people in England even knew that Rufus was dead. And there was also the Duke, riding back to reclaim Normandy. Had Rufus died in October, it would have been too late for Henry to benefit: the Duke would have taken the throne based on the document in which Rufus had named him heir in the event of his death. In the words of the eminent historian Christopher Brooke: "It is impossible to avoid altogether the suspicion that Rufus's death was the result of a conspiracy in which his younger brother and successor was involved. . . . If Rufus's death in August 1100 was an accident, Henry I was an exceptionally lucky man."

Goodrich Castle stands on a rocky spur overlooking the River Wye in the county of Hereford and Worcester. Historical documents of around 1100 mention a castle on the site—called Godric's castle—

that was apparently built by a man called Godric Mappestone. Godric was mentioned in Domesday Book as the holder of a manor called Hulle (Howl) in Walecford (now Walford). It seems that this Godric Mappestone built a fortress to guard the ancient ford across the River Wye. By 1144, however, the Mappestones had lost Goodrich, and it passed into the hands of the Lord of Monmouth, and then the Crown.

Goodrich Castle can still be visited today, and is in the care of English Heritage. It is a spectacular sight, with great buttressed towers standing over a rock-cut moat. No traces of Godric's buildings remain, although it is likely that the outline of the later fortress followed the lines and boundaries established by him. Most buildings date from the twelfth, thirteenth, and fourteenth centuries, although the most impressive is the mighty Norman keep, three storeys high and pierced with small round-headed windows.

Meanwhile, one of the most powerful lords along the Welsh borders in the early twelfth century was Robert de Bellême. He was lord of several large stretches of countryside in Normandy, where he ruled tyrannically until he inherited lands from his brother in England in 1098. These included the earldom of Shrewsbury, the lordship of Montgomery, and a number of smaller estates. In 1101, the Duke of Normandy staged an invasion to grab the throne from King Henry, and the Earl of Shrewsbury was one of his most powerful supporters.

The invasion was unsuccessful, but King Henry was not a man to allow such matters to go unavenged. By 1102, Henry's spies had amassed so much evidence proving Shrewsbury's treachery, that he was summoned to the king's court to answer for his crimes. Knowing that he would be found guilty, Shrewsbury prepared for battle. The King himself took to the field, and Shrewsbury was finally captured and banished, losing all his English estates. Shrewsbury returned to Normandy, where he vented his spleen on his hapless subjects, committing atrocities that appalled even hardened medieval barons.

Henry was still not satisfied, and set out to wrest Normandy from his brother. After a series of battles, Duke Robert was captured and condemned to spend the rest of his life in an English prison. He died twenty-eight years later in Cardiff Castle at the age of eighty. The slippery Shrewsbury escaped, but fell into Henry's hands in

1112. He, too, was imprisoned, but no one knows when he died. Records show that he was still incarcerated at Wareham in 1130.

Even by medieval standards, Shrewsbury was a monstrous figure. Perhaps the best description of him is given by the Oxford historian A. L. Poole: "The most powerful and the most dangerous of the Norman baronage, he was also the most repellent in character. In a society of ruffianly, bloodthirsty men, Robert de Bellême stands out as particularly atrocious; an evil, treacherous man with an insatiable ambition and a love of cruelty for cruelty's sake; a medieval sadist, whose ingenious barbarities were proverbial among the people of that time."